The Shavian Playground

FINKELSTEIN
MEMORIAL LIBRARY
SPRING VALLEY, N. Y.

The Shavian Playground

*An Exploration of the Art
of George Bernard Shaw*

MARGERY M. MORGAN

Methuen & Co Ltd
11 New Fetter Lane London EC4

84-31514

First published in 1972 by Methuen & Co Ltd
11 New Fetter Lane London EC4
First published as a University Paperback 1974
© 1972 Margery M. Morgan
Bernard Shaw previously unpublished texts © 1972 by
The Trustees of the British Museum, Governors and
Guardians of the National Gallery of Ireland and
The Royal Academy of Dramatic Art

Printed in Great Britain by
Butler & Tanner Ltd, Frome and London

ISBN 0 416 82500 1

This paperback edition is sold subject to the condition
that it shall not, by way of trade or otherwise, be lent, resold,
hired out, or otherwise circulated without the publisher's prior
consent in any form of binding or cover other than that in which
it is published and without a similar condition including this
condition being imposed on the subsequent purchaser.

Distributed in the USA by
HARPER & ROW PUBLISHERS, INC.
BARNES & NOBLE IMPORT DIVISION

For Siriol

'Linguistic usage . . . is wont to designate as "play" everything which is neither subjectively nor objectively contingent, and yet imposes no kind of constraint either from within or from without.

. . . In a word: by entering into association with ideas all reality loses its earnestness because it then becomes *of small account*; and by coinciding with feeling necessity divests itself of its earnestness because it then becomes *of light weight*.

. . . how can we speak of *mere* play, when we know that it is precisely play and play *alone* which of all man's states and conditions is the one which makes him whole and unfolds both sides of his nature at once? What you, according to your idea of the matter, call *limitation*, I, according to mine – which I have justified by proof – call *expansion*.'

Schiller, *Aesthetic Education*,
Letter XV, trans. Wilkinson and
Willoughby

'The well-fed Englishman, though he lives and dies a schoolboy, cannot play. He cannot even play cricket or football: he has to work at them . . . To him playing means playing the fool.'

G. B. Shaw, Preface to
Three Plays for Puritans

Contents

List of Illustrations

Acknowledgements

Chapter 5 of this book substantially reproduces the Introduction to *You Never Can Tell*, Gateway Library (Sydney, Melbourne, Brisbane: Hicks Smith, 1967). A variant form of Chapter 8 has appeared in R. Zimbardo (ed.), *Twentieth Century Interpretations of Major Barbara*, Spectrum Books (Englewood Cliffs, N.J.: Prentice-Hall, 1970). Chapter 11 and the section on *The Apple Cart* in Chapter 17 incorporate material published respectively in *Modern Drama*, Vol. IV (1962), and *The Shavian*, Vol. II, No. 6 (1962), this last under the title of 'Two Varieties of Political Drama'. Chapter 13 is a revised and extended version of an article originally published in *Essays and Studies*, New Series, Vol. XIII (1960), and reprinted in R. J. Kaufmann (ed.), *G. B. Shaw*, Twentieth Century Views (Englewood Cliffs, N.J.: Prentice-Hall, 1965).

Unless another version is specified, the text of Shaw's plays, prefaces, novels and shorter pieces is quoted from the Standard Edition of *The Works of Bernard Shaw* (London: Constable, 1931–50) and Shaw letters of the early period from Dan H. Laurence (ed.), *Bernard Shaw: Collected Letters, 1874–1897* (London: Max Reinhardt, 1965), volume I of an immense project. Permission to quote published writings by Shaw has been granted by the Society of Authors for the Bernard Shaw Estate. For access to unpublished material, including Rehearsal Copies of plays, I am indebted to the staff of the Department of Manuscripts in the British Museum, the Keeper of the Enthoven Theatre Collection in the Victoria and Albert Museum, and the Librarian of the British Drama League.

Acknowledgements are due to the Beacon Press, Boston, and Sphere Books, London, for permission to quote from *Eros and Civilization*, and to Allen and Unwin, London, and Russell and Russell, New York, for permission to quote from *The Birth of Tragedy*.

My gratitude to individuals is very inadequately suggested by the occasional reference in the notes. I should also like to thank Professor H. F. Brooks of Birkbeck College and my colleague Mr Peter Naish for reading and criticizing certain chapters in manuscript. Special mention is due here to Mrs Maureen Mann, for assistance in compiling the index, and to Mrs Elizabeth Moore for much unofficial help in the preparation of the typescript.

I am grateful to the Council of Monash University for granting me the period of study leave which made the final compilation of my work possible.

The author and publishers wish to thank the following for permission to reproduce the illustrations that appear in this book:

Castle Studio for no. 4
Musée Condé and Bibliothèque Nationale, Paris, for no. 1
Cyril Cusack for no. 5(b)
Enthoven Theatre Collection, Victoria and Albert Museum, for no. 13
Harvard Theatre Collection for nos. 10 and 15
Raymond Mander and Joe Mitchenson Theatre Collection for nos. 12, 20(a), 21 and 22
Mansell Collection and Alinari, Florence, for no. 16
Lewis Morley Studios for no. 9
Franciszek Myszkowski for no. 18(a)
New York Public Library for no. 11
Phaidon Press for no. 8
Radio Times Hulton Picture Library for no. 19
Houston Rogers for no. 20(b)
Routledge and Kegan Paul, Columbia University Press and Professor Glynne Wickham for no. 14
State Historical Society of Wisconsin for no. 6
Tate Gallery Publications for no. 7
John Vickers Studio for no. 5(a)
Victoria and Albert Museum for nos. 2 and 3
Yale University School of Drama for no. 17.

Introduction

Man is an animal that laughs; he also possesses faculties of speech and reason more highly developed than in other animals. The observation is older than Aristotle. The curiousness of the combination it recognizes forms the basis of the drama of G. B. Shaw, himself supremely endowed with all three powers: laughter, speech and reason.

The element of truth in the twentieth-century view of Shaw as a late Victorian sage needs to be supplemented by recognition that there was no place in the official Victorian canon for his greatest and most characteristically 'Shavian' virtue: gaiety of mind. Matthew Arnold had repressed his share of that quality. Oscar Wilde's insinuations against earnestness were partly disabled by their author's reputation for cynicism and his ultimate fate. Twentieth-century criticism has been slow to appreciate the seriousness of humour, although Freud considered jokes worthy of deep attention and acknowledged the value of humour as a weapon against neurosis,[1] and Nietzsche had rejected a god of gravity for one who could dance.[2] It has been justly remarked that a true assessment of Shaw cannot be made without an understanding of comedy – as the twin rather than the degenerate poor relation of tragedy. For the dramatist who wrote, 'The lot of the man who sees life truly and thinks about it romantically is Despair' (Preface to *Three Plays for Puritans*), the difference between tragedy and comedy is a matter of perspective and deliberate attitude; and humour is a response to distress, cleansing the personality of morbid emotions and intimate confusions which otherwise inhibit positive action and limit the possibilities of change.

Victorian popular culture preserved the crudest and most vigorous forms of comedy in its theatre: in farce, the swiftest paced of dramatic

[1] Many of the examples of 'jokiness', including the literary example of Heine, discussed by Freud in *Jokes and Their Relation to the Unconscious*, trans. James Strachey (London: Routledge, 1960), are interestingly comparable with Shaw.

[2] See the quotation from *Thus Spake Zarathustra* included in the discussion of *You Never Can Tell*, p. 90 below.

styles, which defies reason and has no need of speech; and in burlesque, which always preserves a relation to some vision and set of values outside the comic mode. Eric Bentley has asserted,[1] and Martin Meisel has amply demonstrated,[2] the importance of connecting Shaw's art with this popular tradition. But insistence on his technique of borrowing the conventions of his day, and proceeding to invert or distort them, has involved a neglect of the compulsive quality in Shaw's procedure. A happy inability to treat either his material or his medium with consistent seriousness made him one of the most idiosyncratic of Victorian novelists before ever he wrote for the theatre; Granville Barker drily called him 'a merry fellow' for laughing through his mother's funeral; such jokiness as traditionally afflicts medical and theological students was evident in the remark, 'No flowers, no congratulations,' made on the occasion of his wife's death.[3] Burlesque was a fashion of the day, but it was also expressive of Shaw's personal response to some kinds of experience.

The comedian's cast of mind is sometimes embodied in a character who functions to preserve the comic balance in a play that might easily have overbalanced into another category. Even Lickcheese, in *Widowers' Houses*, operates as such a control more than as a source of incidental comic relief. Frank Gardner, Burgess, Apollodorus, Charles Lomax, the Dauphin are other figures serving the same general purpose, though the style of comedy they embody varies from one to another. There is a tragic idea to be abstracted from *The Doctor's Dilemma*, but the play is a 'tragedy' only in a sense unique to Shaw whose impulse was to guy the form – as Dubedat does. The Epilogue to *Saint Joan* constitutes a decisive rejection of the finality of tragedy. Even Shavian melodrama, as in *Captain Brassbound's Conversion* or *Heartbreak House*, is more properly to be termed farcical melodrama (like Stevenson and Henley's *Macaire*). *The Shewing-up of Blanco Posnet* is Shaw's straightest exercise in the convention, and even here the sense of make-believe and the sceptical

---

[1] 'Critics who see Shaw's relationship to the ordinary Victorian theatre, or even to Gilbert and Wilde, are likely to avoid the errors of those who see only his relation to the Higher Theatre movement under whose auspices his plays first appeared.' (Eric Bentley, *Bernard Shaw*, revised and amended edition (Norfolk, Conn.: New Directions, 1957; 2nd ed. London: Methuen, 1967), pp. 174–5.) Cf. the well-known passage from the Preface to *Three Plays for Puritans*: 'my stories are the old stories; my characters are the familiar harlequin and columbine, clown and pantaloon . . . ; my stage tricks and suspenses and thrills and jests are the ones in vogue when I was a boy, by which time my grandfather was tired of them.'

[2] Martin Meisel, *Shaw and the Nineteenth-Century Theater* (Princeton: Princeton University Press, and London: Oxford University Press, 1963).

[3] See (e.g.) St John Ervine, *Bernard Shaw: His Life, Work and Friends* (London: Constable, 1956), p. 453.

coolness of distance are sufficient to dissipate the true tone of melodrama.

As an imitator of Ibsen, Strindberg, Chekhov or Shakespeare, Shaw produced work that impresses us much more by its differences from his models, radical differences of tone and quality, than by the detectable similarities. Did he believe that he was carrying out William Archer's plan when he began to write *Widowers' Houses*, then to be entitled *Rhinegold*? How like what is usually known as Pre-Raphaelite art is Shaw's 'Pre-Raphaelite play', *Candida*? It is not only when his point of departure is a commonplace, or even shoddy, domestic drama, or social problem play, or romantic historical play, that the result is a travesty of the source. Whatever he borrowed was transformed in an imagination so extravagantly individual that it takes a strict dialectical framework to hold its anarchic energies. He joked about the extraordinariness of his perfectly 'normal' eyesight; its mental equivalent is just such a natural gift as El Greco's astigmatism, rendering what he sees surprisingly different from the way most of us customarily see it. Whether he was as aware of the difference as we are is not always clear. The problem of determining where the dividing line falls between conscious contrivance and unconscious effect continually nags at the student of Shaw's plays and will be one of the preoccupations of this book. Like all reformers, he had to fight his chosen enemies within himself as well as in society, and the battle proceeds on other levels besides the rational. Under the extreme pressures of puritan tradition in morals and manners, humour may be both personally liberating and socially subversive in a gradual and insidious fashion.

There is nothing ambiguous about Shaw's addiction to knockabout scenes of crude physical violence: from Blanche Sartorius's attack on her maid right through to the Interlude in *The Apple Cart*, *The Millionairess* and *Good King Charles's Golden Days*, the element of physical aggression challenges any account of the plays as intellectual drama, in the usual tepid sense which disdains such violence on stage as undramatic and in effect interprets man as mind. These scenes farcically underline the equal aggressiveness in the verbal assaults and conflicts the plays contain. There may be an underlying connection to be traced with Rugby-inspired notions of muscular Christianity. Certainly there is an inheritance from eighteenth-century rumbustiousness and its relation to the idea of natural man, such as George Meredith also derived from Fielding.

The relation between jest and earnest is not constant throughout the plays, and to define its nature in each instance is one of the main tasks of the critical interpreter; not, of course, to explain the jokes away. Shaw employs a considerable range of comic forms, and the degree of subtlety in

his comedy varies greatly. There is an element of truth in the caricaturist's
view of him as a clown with a trick of standing on his head to catch the
crowd's attention. No term has been bandied about more freely in discussion of his work than 'paradox', usually with this clownish image in
mind. Used precisely to indicate a strategy of bringing to light the
neglected aspects of accepted truths, to reveal the relativity of all truth,
or to induce a widening of the horizons of our thinking, it is indeed
acceptable as a central term of Shaw criticism. In so far as it is loosely used
of exhibitionist shock-tactics, perpetrated by a fundamentally irresponsible
intellectual, I have chosen to avoid it at least until the case is proven
one way or the other. A questioning of the value and function of reason
in relation to the rest of the personality is one continuing concern of
Shaw's drama anyway.

Certainly there is intellectual control in his plays, most obvious when
he moves away from plots of strong narrative interest to the dramatic
equivalent of philosophical debate. This can be seen as an aspect of his
discarding of the artistic conventions of realism in a move towards greater
abstraction. But he also seems to have felt restricted from the first by
tight, 'organic' plots inasmuch as they excluded any play of fantasy or
comic improvisation. His experimentation with fragmented, wilder-
seeming forms, approximating in some degree to the extravaganza, can
be traced back at least as far as *Caesar and Cleopatra*. Alternatively, and
in line with symbolist practice, he sought a fluidity of development in
emulation of music.[1] In this respect, the handling of dialogue in *Candida*
anticipates the much more fully 'musical' structuring of *Misalliance* and
Heartbreak House. The more completely he was able to convert the
dramatic medium to his own ends the more likely is the real unity and
coherence, which all art must have, to be pervasive; but the conceptual
principle from which the play has sprung may then be hidden deep and
takes patience to tease out.

Only in one instance, in *Fanny's First Play*, does Shaw actually employ
a critical frame-play around an inset as Fielding, his admired predecessor,
sometimes did. But general practice of burlesque can be related to
Fielding's practice of the 'journalism of the theatre', the staged topical
commentary or satire written in the margins of literary drama, bringing
that more self-contained art closer to the daily concerns of the audience.[2]

[1] See Charles Loyd Holt, Doct. Diss. (Wayne State University, 1963); 'Music
and the Young Shaw', *The Shavian*, Vol. III (1966), pp. 9–13; ' "Candida" and
the Music of Ideas', *Shaw Review*, Vol. IX (1966), pp. 2–14.
· [2] *Pasquin* and *The Historical Register for the Year 1736* are the most obvious
examples from Fielding, though all his plays can be considered in these terms.
Shaw expressed his consciousness of following in the steps of Fielding in the
Preface to *Plays Unpleasant*, where he calls him 'the greatest practising dramatist,

As puritan and as politician, Shaw was opposed to any autonomous, enclosed world of art, without social responsibility and cut off from public affairs. Even the blatantly stagey quality of his drama is anti-illusionist, a reminder that even a national theatre, where such a play as *John Bull's Other Island* might be part of an actual election campaign, is still a playhouse licensed for the enactment of fantasies.

It is significant that Shaw never wrote a naturalistic play which remained in that style throughout its length, though he sympathized with the principles of naturalism. Another political dramatist, Bertolt Brecht, who learnt much from Shaw, explained his own avoidance of naturalistic technique when he observed: 'That "assimilation of art to science" which gave naturalism its social influence undoubtedly hamstrung some major artistic capacities, notably the imagination, the sense of play and the element of pure poetry. Its artistic aspects were clearly harmed by its instructive side.'[1] One of the aims of the present book is to explore the relationship between Shaw's art and his politics, to discover the extent to which his art is political and the sense in which it is political. He was well known outside the theatre as a dedicated socialist, an active public speaker and pamphleteer for the cause. But the wares inside can seem oddly at variance with the sign over the shop: Shaw's first socialist hero is a mountebank who conducts his operations under cover of an antic disposition and the absurd false name of Smilash; Candida devastates her Christian Socialist husband with the revelation that his oratory is an effective form of sexual display; Jack Tanner's socialist challenge to old-fashioned liberalism is brushed aside as peripheral to an apparently apolitical theme, in *Man and Superman*. It is all drama of ideas in a superficial sense: epigrams fly thick like missiles through the air; theories are expounded which testify to the range of Shaw's reading and the eclectic habits of his mind. His description of himself as a crow that has followed many ploughs[2] sounds as little like the cry of a man who has found some absolute value as it is a claim to originality. Some of the late plays, notably *On the Rocks* and *Geneva*, are centrally concerned with political themes of some topical urgency. But to suppose that the dramatist acted as the delegate of the socialist, even here, is too naïve.

Imaginative thinking, thinking through the medium of art, is a different activity from scientific reasoning or the mode of argument followed by a political orator, educator or polemicist. The two types of

---

with the single exception of Shakespear, produced by England between the Middle Ages and the nineteenth century'.

[1] *Brecht on Theatre*, trans. and notes by John Willett (London: Methuen, 1964), p. 132.

[2] Preface to *Three Plays for Puritans*.

activity seem to have been complementary to each other in Shaw's life: the one didactic and directive, the other turning inward with a self-searching regard as much as outward in communication with others. Shaw's methods of self-publicity gave a lead to commentators which has continued to draw attention away from his work towards his public personality (including the 'private' personality he chose to display). The present study is an attempt to let his art speak for itself with a minimum of interpolation. Accepting that the understanding of the artist, reached through imaginative processes, is richer and deeper than the man is often able to reach in other contexts, I have generally refrained from interpreting the plays in the light of what Shaw said, or wrote, or is thought to have believed, on other occasions. The total structure of the individual work defines the ideas it contains. In the complex metaphor which any Shaw play is, what Comte, or Lamarck, or Samuel Butler, Schopenhauer, or Nietzsche may have supplied becomes part of the imagery. To extract such elements of 'thought' and substitute them, literally interpreted, for the play's aesthetic statement has been common practice in Shaw commentary, the body of which has not been distinguished for rigour of method or imaginative grasp.

Alongside this tendency, I have found it necessary to challenge the supposition that Shaw's plots, whether adapted or invented, do not count; that these and other elements of his art that give pleasure to audiences and readers of no highly intellectual pretensions were offered merely as sugar-coating to the valuable mental stuff of the plays. At the very least they served their author as a genial, temporary environment for thought. To identify certain recurrent features of plot, recurrent situations or character-types, as stock items in contemporary or earlier theatre is not enough in itself. Shaw's selection of these fictive elements from a much larger range of possibilities is likely to correspond to certain persistent preoccupations; and their dramatic functioning may be more interesting than their origins. I have given them their due of attention as bridges for communication with audiences whose human nature is open to conversion by pleasurable emotion as by no unaided theory, but also as consciously or unconsciously expressive of forces at work in the intimate personality of the artist. I have settled on the idea of the mask as a meeting-point of theatrical tradition with the private symbolism employed in a search for identity. The idiosyncratic treatment of conventional plots I see as developing, in the course of Shaw's career, in directions similarly both more personal and more universal: from some variety of intrigue-plot towards allegory, or fable, or myth, approaching the patterns of ancient drama even as form becomes more plastic to the current of the author's thought and feeling on his chosen theme. To understand Shaw involves appreciating the relation of his drama to Aristophanes, to Molière, to Mozart, but also not neglecting the significance for his art of his friendship with Gilbert Murray and his championship of Wagner, both associated with the nineteenth-century cult of Dionysus: the discovery of the unconscious in individual man and in human communities.

A considerable proportion of Shaw's dramatic *œuvre* is still little known. Certain of the plays are well established in the general theatrical repertoire. Others, particularly the plays following *Saint Joan*, have rarely if ever been revived since their original production. The availability of texts in popular cheap editions has contributed to general familiarity, or tired over-familiarity, with some plays, while others are forgotten. The inferiority of the less familiar (and the over-familiar) is often assumed, and perhaps wrongly assumed. *Misalliance* is an example of a play from what is often regarded as Shaw's peak period, which made little mark theatrically when it was first performed because of circumstances that had little to do with the play's quality.[1] The natural caution of directors and entrepreneurs meant that it had to wait before a small number of productions in different parts of the world established its theatrical merits. But it is not one of Shaw's easy plays for amateurs, and it has not been made widely available in paperback form. Uninterpreted in stage terms, it has puzzled readers and been given little critical attention. *You Never Can Tell* has been much better known and widely enjoyed, but Shaw's own deprecating description of it as a pot-boiler, when it seemed acceptable to a theatre that had rejected his earlier work, seems to have discouraged the serious critical treatment it deserves. A few recent scholars, in particular Martin Meisel, have drawn attention back to the late plays by making higher claims for them than have been heard before. In one instance – *Too True to be Good* – subsequent production has vindicated the claim. But the unspoken assumption that Shaw, after *Saint Joan*, was too old to write good plays has to be defeated by such close scrutiny of the others as they have never yet had. His art changed direction many times. Difference in kind from an established favourite need not mean failure. And it is time it became impossible to base critical dismissal on ignorance of a play's nature and meaningful coherence.

By discussion of individual plays one by one, or in small related groups, I hope to encourage theatrical attention to neglected works as well as the understanding of readers that Shaw's plays are artistic unities. The coverage of this book, long as it is, is not encyclopedic: some minor plays, or plays about which I had little to say that had not been said better

[1] On the conditions of the first repertory production, see P. P. Howe, *The Repertory Theatre* (London: Martin Secker, 1910), pp. 151–64, and C. B. Purdom, *Harley Granville Barker* (London: Rockliff, 1955), pp. 99–107.

already, are not discussed, or are only mentioned in passing. On the whole, the order of treatment is chronological. The table of contents indicates the exceptional instances where I have grouped plays according to category and thus drawn one or more out of its place in the sequence of composition. And because my interest is chiefly in imaginative constructs, I have chosen to begin with a look at those first substantial works of the Shavian magination, the novels.

1

The Novels

Bernard Shaw had already put novel writing behind him when he undertook to provide J. T. Grein's Independent Theatre with a play that eventually saw the light as *Widowers' Houses* in 1892. His years as a journalist critic, first of art, then of music, and finally as drama critic to *The Saturday Review*, followed after the fifth novel, *An Unsocial Socialist*. This novel first and then three of the others were published during this interim period of the eighties. As substantial evidence that Shaw was all along drawn to some form of imaginative communication they must count to any student of his plays, though insufficiently stringent revision and failure to recognize the need for strong thematic unity within the loose organization of the novel form have left most of them unsatisfactory in themselves. They contain some illuminating anticipations of the plays that seem worth touching upon.[1]

Signs of an interest in the theatre give warning of the shift to dramatic form that lay ahead, when the impact of Ibsen made it clear that drama might be a viable alternative to the novel for a young writer who wished to be in the mainstream of the arts of his day. Robert Smith, the young clerk who is the hero of *Immaturity* (1879), when newly arrived in London, finds his way to the Alhambra, then a home of *opéra bouffe*, and sees the last act of *Le Voyage dans la lune* and one of the ballets for which the theatre was celebrated. Except for falling in love with the prima ballerina, Smith was more appreciative of the first half of the programme: 'He was moderately pleased by the gorgeous dresses and

---

[1] The novels have been the subject of a full-length study which has appeared since this chapter was written: R. F. Dietrich, *Portrait of the Artist as a Young Superman* (Gainesville: University of Florida Press, 1969). Alick West, *A Good Man Fallen Among Fabians* (London: Lawrence and Wishart, 1950) devoted the first two chapters to perceptive commentary on the novels. See also Stanley Weintraub, 'The Embryo Playwright in Bernard Shaw's Early Novels', *Texas Studies in Language and Literature*, Vol. I (1949), pp. 327–55, reprinted in *The California Shavian*, Vol. IV (1963).

scenery; yawned at the long processions; and laughed at the horseplay; for he loved the humor of harlequinade.' The description of the evening is quite vivid, heightened through Smith's consciousness of the less than fully respectable character of the theatre and the counter-attraction to the stage offered by the drinking bars.

The Irrational Knot opens behind the scenes at a charity concert. Two of the amateur performers later go on to the Bijou, nearer in character to a music hall than the Alhambra. Here they are entertained by a burlesque, starring Lalage Virtue, who in private life is Susanna Conolly and sister to one of the visiting pair, though the other does not know this. The fastidiousness of Robert Smith's tempered enjoyment appears in a less flattering version as the self-conscious and priggish disdain Conolly shows, by contrast with the infatuated enthusiasm of his companion, Marmaduke Lind. Certainly there is an inverted form of family pride at work, but Conolly's critical attitude is also in keeping with the reserved, impassive manner he chooses to cultivate in general. The comic spirit is too alert in Shavian drama to leave intact characters who much resemble Conolly in this; but there is here an indication of how the author's own enthusiasm for popular art and his guard upon it not only made him insistent on high critical standards, but contributed to the blend of learning and intellectual seriousness with unsophisticated high spirits that is characteristic of the plays. A touch of cultural snobbery and more than a touch of puritanism came between Shaw and the straight-forward practice of the popular arts that appealed to his vitality. The contemporary popularity of burlesque offered a way out; the fooling could be rooted in classical models that had been studied seriously.

This ambiguous attitude to the theatre has coloured the treatment of Susanna throughout the novel. She is admired as an independent woman who earns her own living, is free to decide rationally against marriage and chooses to live in self-respecting openness with her lover. In these ways she is an early example of the Shavian 'original moralist'; but her story is more conventionally conceived, and the integrity of the character breaks under its pressures. It may be that an underlying conviction of the dangerousness of an actress's life persisted in the mind which could not be quite at ease in the Alhambra or the Bijou and looked towards a 'higher drama' in which the taste for theatre could be indulged with a good conscience. At any rate, Susanna is brought to the appropriate bad end for such a black sheep in the Victorian fold: her strength of character and her professional talent go down before alcoholism, which leads to her death in a drunken fit, against the back-ground of a dingy boarding-house in New York. It is patent that alcohol-ism, in a conventional enough way, symbolizes the perils inherent in economic independence and sexual freedom. So subconscious, convention-derived doubts eventually defeat conscious opinions.

One of the main characters in *Love Among the Artists* is an actress. Madge Brailsford escapes from her respectable middle-class home to go on the stage. She takes lessons in elocution from a musician of genius (Shaw's emphasis on professional discipline and hard work as saving graces is again illuminating) and serves her acting apprenticeship in a provincial stock company. Her ordeals include having to play Shakespeare with an eminent visiting tragedian (a character based on Barry Sullivan). Martin Meisel has observed that Shaw's knowledge of the Theatre Royal, Dublin, was sufficient to give him the material for the whole episode.[1] Its interest is, indeed, largely documentary in nature. There is little trace of unresolved conflict here. Madge Brailsford's ambitions are culturally superior to Lalage Virtue's, as her family is better class; and she herself, as a woman, acquires an ethic beyond the domestic and romantic ideals of conventional women who live entirely on the level of personal relations. Shaw remarks 'the first dim stirring in her of a sense that her relation as an actress to the people was above all her other relations.' And the whole book is concerned with a society in which artists are accepted as respectable people, as decorous and dignified and moral as any other group.

Cashel Byron's mother, who loses sight of her son casually and welcomes him back with floods of sentiment, has achieved the status Madge Brailsford dreams of reaching. She is a famous actress who, when studying the role of Constance in *King John* for a leading actor-manager's production, can meet the blue-stocking heiress, Lydia Carew, as an equal and be invited to lunch with perfect propriety. The knighthood of Irving and all it signified of respect for theatrical eminence, and the attractions of the stage for the children of the aristocracy and the clergy in the late nineteenth century, are reflected in the situation.

Writing his novels in the English tradition, Shaw was naturally concerned to imagine men in their social relations; and attitudes to the theatre reflected in his books link up with a more general concern with the social position and social recognition of the artist. In the Preface to *Immaturity* he admits his ignorance of the realities of society in his novel-writing days. The genre demanded a social panorama, and what he did not know he was driven to imagine on the basis of what he had read, mostly in the form of fiction. Still it is curious how he shifts the milieu of his first novel: Book I, entitled 'Islington', may owe something to Dickens as well as to first-hand observation, in its presentation of the medley of characters in a boarding-house, including an

[1] Martin Meisel, *Shaw and the Nineteenth-Century Theater*, p. 17.

eighteen-year-old clerk, a young dressmaker, a slatternly maid, a broken-down drunkard of a 'gentleman', and an evangelist who falls in love with the dressmaker; in Book II, 'Esthetics', these characters are rather surprisingly drawn into a more aristocratic society, where Lady Geraldine Porter and others of her class mingle with rising and respectable artists. The principal setting is now a wealthy country house: 'Mr Halket Grosvenor, of Perspective, Richmond, was a munificent patron and hospitable entertainer of artists of all denominations,' the Book begins. The country house of the Earl of Carbury is among the chief settings against which *The Irrational Knot* unfolds its story; a society rather like that at Perspective, if less plutocratic, is located at Windsor in *Love Among the Artists*; Lydia Carew of *Cashel Byron's Profession* and Sir Charles and Lady Brandon of *An Unsocial Socialist* represent a world of rich landowners who have no need to be other than idle and cultured, or followers of the traditional country pursuits of the gentry. We may well be surprised to find the future socialist writing so generally of such classes. In the last of the novels, the socialism of Trefusis (who might, like the later Tanner, have well described himself as M.I.R.C. 'Member of the Idle Rich Class') admittedly serves to challenge the values and security of the other characters. There is no such evident challenge in *Cashel Byron's Profession:* at the end of the novel Cashel is left to enjoy his rank as a gentleman and his title to a hereditary country estate, together with his share in the fabulous fortune of his wife, and there is no suggestion that either he or Lydia should have a bad conscience in the matter.

This is more than a simple matter of writing to suit the taste for fashionable novels. Though it does not emerge with full objective clarity, something close to a social ideal does show through the element of poor boy's daydream: an ideal of an area where the hosts have money, the manners are good and the morals sound, and to which the entrée is on grounds of personal distinction. In *Cashel Byron's Profession*, the most consistent and clear of the novels in thematic intention, the ultimate prize Cashel wins, Lydia Carew herself, a great prize indeed, verges on symbolism of traditional European civilization in all its abundance and variety.

The novelists mentioned as literary models in the Preface to *Immaturity*, Scott and Dickens, are in fact less obvious begetters of *The Irrational Knot*, *An Unsocial Socialist* and even *Cashel Byron's Profession* than are Jane Austen and Thackeray, the ironists. Certainly the strong-minded women characters, Harriet Smith of *Immaturity*, Agatha Wylie of *An Unsocial Socialist*, or Lydia Carew of *Cashel Byron's Profession*, are in this line of descent. In the relations between Agatha Wylie and her school-fellows a resemblance to Becky Sharp and the Amelia's of convention can be traced; there is more than a little of Becky in Susanna Conolly, too: the adventuress whose boldness and decisiveness and frankness of egotism compel admiration, however much they are censured. Shaw's application of the term 'original moralist', to such characters is less ambiguous than Thackeray's method of challenging the truth and even the attractiveness of the ideal Victorian heroine and exalting vitality in a woman, perhaps even because it might lead to unscrupulous violation of social codes. The link is worth stressing, if only because it can illuminate the perplexing quality of some of the plays that came later. In particular, Candida may reveal her generic similarity to Rachel Castlewood, in which likeness of situation – the youth adoringly in love with a woman old enough to be his mother – is less significant than the blurred division between conscious and unconscious attitudes, between deliberate irony and ambivalence on the part of the author, or the impossibility of clearly distinguishing between social caution and personal inhibition as determinants of the peculiarly muffled quality of the criticism. (Of course, it is a distinctively Victorian mode of irony, familiar in Tennyson too.[1])

The difficulty of assuming openly the stance of satirical moralist that came so readily to the eighteenth century is reflected in the grotesqueness of the satiric mechanism employed in *An Unsocial Socialist*, where the hero appears in double guise: as Trefusis, a wealthy man and dedicated socialist, and under the alias of Smilash, a labourer, which he adopts in fantastic pursuit of his political ends, dubiously connected with his sexual ends. For Trefusis is both Hamlet to a clownish *alter ego* and the first of Shaw's Don Juan figures, concerned to assert his power over women, to seduce them intellectually as he proselytizes for his political cause. His emotional detachment is rationally justified on the grounds that men and women are important in proportion to their potential usefulness to socialism. His unconventional manner misleads Gertrude into believing that he is in love with her and wishes to marry her. His confession of motive is hardly more convincing to the reader than to her:

> . . . we Socialists need to study the romantic side of our movement to interest women in it. If you want to make a cause grow, instruct every woman you meet in it. She is or will one day be a wife . . .
> I used to flirt with women; now I lecture them . . .

---

[1] I have in mind particularly the ambiguities and uncertainties that are almost inseparable from the dramatic monologue convention (in 'Maud' and 'Locksley Hall' as in Browning's poetry), though something comparable, never achieving the freedom of ironic distancing, may be perceived in Tennyson's addiction to paradox and the strategies of ambiguity best known in 'Tears, Idle Tears'.

But Gertrude's instinct tells her that the lecturing is still not totally
unrelated to the flirting; both convey a possibly self-defensive contempt
for the woman that is openly expressed in a letter from Trefusis to the
author, a Thackerayan device, which forms the epilogue to the book:

> . . . the novel readers and writers of our own century – most of them half-
> educated women, rebelliously slavish, superstitious, sentimental, full of the
> intense egotism fostered by their struggle for personal liberty, and, outside
> their families, with absolutely no social sentiment except love . . .

The splitting of the character is comparable to Brecht's reduplication
of the central figure in *The Good Woman of Setzuan* as Shen Te and Shui
Ta. The lesson conveyed there, that good has to adopt the methods of
evil in the world as it is, that virtue cannot survive except in alliance
with calculation, hardness and deceit, may have some relevance to the
Shavian context. Trefusis's socialism is presented as inseparable from
elements of knavery and folly. The fact that *An Unsocial Socialist*, like
Man and Superman later, associates the mask of Don Juan with the
wealthy socialist may express an ambiguous attitude to money. How much
of Trefusis's mountebank quality is feigned, how much is simply exaggerated in a self-caricaturing disguise, is no easier to determine than the
precise division between the mind of the character and that of his author.
Certainly a peculiarly self-conscious view of human identity as a matter
of pose and attitude lies behind the adoption of the masking device:
such a self-consciousness as troubles Sergius Saranoff, tormented by
the discrepancy between his ideal self and the 'lower' self of his everyday actions. As a writer of comedy, Shaw tests his motives and convictions
by embodying them externally, as objective hypotheses, the truth or
falseness of which is not to be known except in the acting out. Had
he been able fully and clearly to explain the subterranean connection
between political attitudes and attitudes to women, it is probable that
he would have been less obsessed with it through so much of his career
as a dramatist. He never goes so far as to approve of Don Juan; the
type remains a social as well as a sexual delinquent in his work. The
furthest he goes towards making a hero of him is done by proxy in John
Tanner's dream of Juan as enemy of the prevailing false God and, in
effect, as prophet of a truer religion.

Trefusis's conduct with women receives a gloss from a passage in
Shaw's Preface to his *Letters to Ellen Terry*:

> Possibly a little allowance should be made . . . for the very objectionable
> tradition of eighteenth century gallantry into which I, as an Irishman, was
> born . . . as, like all reactionaries, I was steeped in the tendency against
> which I was reacting, it was part of my conventional manners to concede
> a pedestal to every woman as such; and . . . I did not pause to consider

whether this attitude would have earned the approval of Ibsen or Strindberg.[1]

This was not the only way in which his Irish background made the
English eighteenth century more comprehensible to him than the
nineteenth. The very choice of names in his novels suggests a familiarity
with the world of Jane Austen: Harriet, Marian, Elinor, Lydia, Bingley
(Byron), the Brandons. Elinor and Marian, cousins and friends, living
like sisters in the same house, are strongly contrasted in temperament and
represent the opposite poles of sense and sensibility, as do their prototypes
in Jane Austen. It is between these poles that the action of *The Irrational
Knot* is traced. Occasional details in all the novels recall Jane Austen
directly: Sholto Douglas, at the concert with which *The Irrational Knot*
opens, conducts himself much like Darcy at the Ball; Cyril Scott's
proposal to Harriet Russell, in *Immaturity*, is a fresh and original
version of the set-piece familiar in Mr Collins's proposal to Elizabeth
Bennett; Lydia Carew of Wiltstoken Park takes Alice Goff from the village
to be her companion and protégée much as Emma takes Harriet Smith.
More significantly, Lydia is described in Chapter I of *Cashel Byron's
Profession* with an irony recognizable as a broader version of Jane
Austen's method:

> This Miss Carew was a remarkable person. She had inherited the Castle
> and park from her aunt, who had considered her niece's large fortune in
> railways and mines incomplete without land. So many other legacies had
> Lydia received . . . that she was now, in her twenty-fifth year, the indepen-
> ent possessor of an annual income equal to the year's earnings of five hundred
> workmen . . . In addition to the advantage of being a single woman with
> unusually large means, she enjoyed a reputation for vast learning and
> exquisite culture . . .

The conception of aristocracy in terms of a landed gentry, which is
marked in the Shavian novels, fits Ireland in the nineteenth century;
the theme of reason *versus* passion is aptly set within an eighteenth-
century tradition of manners and values late persisting there. As well
as a familiar cultural tradition, the Austen novels offered Shaw a precedent for writing extensively in dialogue to give vividness to incidents
and, particularly, to carry a didactic burden (as when Owen Jack talks
to Madge Brailsford, or Lydia to her cousin Lucian, or Trefusis to
Gertrude), perhaps satisfying a dramatic tendency of his imagination
anterior to art. The liveliness and substantial importance of the women
characters in his books coincides with the social phenomenon of the New
Woman; but on the whole it is as individuals, not representatives of a

[1] Christopher St John (ed.), *Ellen Terry and Bernard Shaw: A Correspondence*
(London: Reinhardt and Evans, 1949), pp. xi–xii.

social type, that these characters are impressive: responsible persons, as Jane Austen saw them, not objects of others' regard.

The Irrational Knot is marred by inconsistency in the drawing of its heroine, Marian Lind, which matches (though contrastingly) the double standard applied in the same book to Susanna Conolly. Marian is first presented as a victim of her environment, especially of the false tradition of the lady cultivated in an idle society. Apart from this severe limitation, she is a true heroine, as good and virtuous as the tradition could produce to justify itself. She is amiable, sincere, with an instinct of fairness towards others, never wilfully harsh or cruel, but unintellectual, essentially uncultured, more ignorant than she knows, a little sentimental. But Shaw seems not to have made up his mind how much of a fool she is, and his zeal as prosecuting counsel repeatedly robs her of her moral victories and forces her through what is virtually the same lesson again and again. Her failure to take any interest in Conolly's explanation of the operations of electricity and the nature of his invention is poor preparation for the practical efficiency she later shows during her morning lessons in Jasper's workshop; then, after he has married her to Conolly, Shaw seems to forget that she has ever learnt to put a machine together and shows her up once more as quite incapable. There is a similar fluctuation between description of her general growth towards mature wisdom and responsibility and reiteration of a static contrast between Marian and Conolly; when the two are together, she almost invariably seems more of a fool than when apart from him. The cynical Elinor testifies to her cousin's quality: 'I have known her to pity people who deserved to be strangled; but I never knew her to be attracted by any unworthy person except myself; and even I have my good points.' The clear-eyed view of her marriage that she herself gives to Elinor makes it difficult to believe, as we are told, that she was unable to talk sensibly to her husband on the subject, especially as Conolly is no Torwald Helmer, but a man who wants a real wife, not a doll. If Shaw's artistic conscience had been more strenuously at work before he let the book be published, the compulsive antagonism to the 'womanly woman' might have been disciplined to greater fairness and objectivity. Like his hero, he can let tenderness come through when the sufferer's claims are abandoned: an unsentimental, yet genuine sense of the pains, difficulties and dangers of being human, and the inexorable burdens involved, is conveyed in the last chapter of the book. There is no buoyancy in the mood. Conolly puts to Marian the alternatives before her – 'You are free to choose' – and then indicates just how much all individual freedom is worth:

> One or two conditions more or less to comply with, that is all: nature and society still have you hard and fast: the main rules of the game are inviolable.

It is in the light of such a conviction – 'The main rules of the game are inviolable' – that the dramatist gives his moment of pity to Gloria, in *You Never Can Tell*, to Julia in *The Philanderer*, even just a little to Ann Whitefield. *The Irrational Knot* betrays the writer's part, alongside society and nature, in fettering his characters to their fate.

Conolly, active, efficient, forward-looking, well informed, unerring in his natural tastes and confident in his personal morality, is certainly an embodiment of characteristics the author admired. Shaw's realization that his hero was too good to be tolerable is recorded in Elinor McQuinch's attack on him, after Marian has left him:

> Good God, man, what woman do you think *could* wish to live with you! I suppose Marian wanted a human being to live with, and not a calculating machine . . . you are a stone full of brains . . .

The reflection with which Conolly ends this book, 'It is impossible to be too wise, dearest,' is incontrovertible; it is not at all the same statement, however, as Susanna has made, a little sourly, about her brother: 'he is always blameless.' The portrait is not saved by recognition of what was wrong, and dissatisfaction with it spills over into *Love Among the Artists*, where Conolly appears as a minor character to advise Mary Sutherland against false idealism:

> Did you ever live with a person whose temper was imperturbable . . . ? One who, whatever he might be to himself, was to you so void of the petty jealousies, irritabilities, and superstitions of ordinary men, that, as far as you understood his view of life, you could calculate upon his correct be- haviour beforehand in every crisis with as much certainty as upon the striking of a clock . . . you want a man that is not Passion's slave. I hope you may never get him; for I assure you you will not like him. He would make an excellent God, but a most unpleasant man, and an unbearable husband . . .

Instead of correcting a technical fault, by introducing greater realism and more subtlety of detail into the characterization, Shaw chose to impugn from the outside the self-indulgence that had led him to offer a prig as a hero. The external approach of setting attitude against attitude, rather than working within the first to modify it and humanize it, is less suitable for the realistic novel form than for the stage.[1]

Insufficiency of passion is deliberately exposed as a defect in Lydia Carew, who otherwise serves as the intelligent consciousness through which the truths that come to light in *Cashel Byron's Profession* are mediated. Whereas Conolly's dignity is kept in safe isolation from comic irreverence, the figure of Lydia is an essential element in the

---

[1] *The Devil's Disciple* is a good example of the use of this method. See below, p. 240, in my discussion of Shaw's history plays.

smiling absurdity of this novel. She is part of an elaborate, large-scale joke. Shaw's Preface to the book discusses it as though it were no more than an attempt to strip prize-fighting of false glamour and reveal it for the profitable brutality it is. But the zestful, *Boy's Own* quality of much of the writing matches the attractiveness of the hero, to which Lydia is as susceptible as the reader. Perfectly developed physically, so that she identifies him at first glimpse with the Hermes of Praxiteles, Cashel is natural Adam unfallen, unsophisticated, virtually untouched by experience. Sophisticated modern society has no place for him; it leaves him no other way of making his living than by the exploitation of his bodily strength and skill in a sport that is politely disapproved, when it is not forbidden by law; and it excludes him from respectable company, outside the lower classes, on the grounds of his profession, despite the genius he shows. His moral being seems rudimentary, and the ethic it has evolved comes in terms of the only 'science' he possesses. It takes Lydia, or the reader, to recognize the wider applicability of the truths Cashel speaks, and she is only able to do so because ignorance of how he makes his living allows her to remain open-minded:

> 'I am a professor of science,' said Cashel in a low voice, looking down at his left fist, which he was balancing in the air before him, and stealthily hitting his bent knee as if it was another person's face.
> 'Physical or moral science?' persisted Lydia.
> 'Physical science,' said Cashel. 'But theres more moral science in it than people think.'
> 'Yes,' said Lydia seriously. '. . . I can appreciate the truth of that. Perhaps all the science that is not at bottom physical science, is only formal nescience . . .'

Unconsciously, she demonstrates the truth of what she is saying in her ridiculously stilted speech. Yet the attention she gives to Cashel's words is entirely warranted. For Cashel is not merely the embodiment of natural physical life, he is the straightest and clearest thinker on social and political issues that the book contains; Lydia has only to follow and reflect on what he says. Part of the joke is that she justifies their marriage on the theory that Cashel's warm spontaneity will repair her own want of impulse and his physicality will correct her overbred, scholarly nature, when in fact the union is not a misalliance because his intelligence is as good as hers; it is an alliance of truth and wisdom, but still nature employs its irony at the expense of human logic:

> For as they grew up, and the heredity scheme began to develop results, the boys disappointed her by turning out almost pure Carew, without the slightest athletic aptitude, whilst the girls were impetuously Byronic . . .

1 Jean Fouquet, 'The Martyrdom of St Apollonia'. A medieval theatrical performance
(see p. 86).

2 Ottavio from the Italian Comedy (see p. 103).

3 Il Dottore (see p. 92).

THE NOVELS   19

The joke is not complete until its seriousness is perceived. The title of
the novel indicates that Shaw was here making his first trial of a formula
he used later in *Mrs Warren's Profession* and in *Major Barbara* (which
he once thought of calling *Andrew Undershaft's Profession*): taking a
profession which society officially repudiates as a metaphor for the way
in which that larger society is really conducted, under all the hypocrisies.
Lydia enquires of her cousin Lucian about Cashel and is answered: 'He
is simply what his name indicates. He is a man who fights for prizes';
to which she retorts: 'So does the captain of a man-of-war.' The definition
is general enough to be applicable to any competitive society, too general
for real satiric bite except as it reflects on the gratuitous moral distinction,
the form of snobbery, which operates against the man who does frankly
in the simplest way what others conceal. (For one theme that unites this
book with the other novels and sets it apart from those two plays is the place
society accords to the man of outstanding talent.) One episode, at least,
makes the application with more point: the African king, in whose
primitive eyes the greatness of Cashel appears indisputable, had been
taken to visit Woolwich Arsenal, 'the destructive resources of which were
expected silently to warn him against taking the Christian religion too
literally'. This anticipates the argument of *Major Barbara*. Cashel's
physical strength is a simpler form of the same brute force as sustains
British imperial power. Cashel, as well as his adoptive mother, is ready
to defend his profession, as Undershaft declares himself 'Unashamed'.
To Lydia he pleads that his 'science' counts for more than his muscle:
'I know what a man is going to do before he rightly knows himself. The
power this gave me, civilized me.' This is certainly an indication of the
superiority of moral power over merely physical; but it is, necessarily,
balanced by Cashel's lengthy exposition, at Mrs Hoskyns's party, on the
theme of 'executive power'. He has picked up the phrase from a disserta-
tion on art just given by a German professor invited for the purpose, but
he demonstrates it with palpable practicality:

> . . . he made a light step forward, and placed his open palm gently against
> the breast of Lucian, who, as if the piston-rod of a steam-engine had touched
> him, instantly reeled back and dropped into the chair.

The 'perpetual fighting metaphor', as Lydia calls it, is not just a metaphor
after all; Cashel has no doubt of the aggressive attitude life demands and
that it is a full trial of every kind of strength that is in a man:

> . . . What is life but a fight? The curs forfeit or get beaten; the rogues sell
> the fight and lose the confidence of their backers; the game ones, and the
> clever ones, win the stakes, and have to hand over the lion's share of them
> to the moneyed loafers that have stood the expenses . . .

B

His prize is Lydia, and the shadow of an allegory in their marriage anticipates the union of moral purpose and physical power, of virtue and wealth,
towards which *Major Barbara* drives. But, in comparison with the
insistent and multiple-layered ironies of the play, the novel, with its
fable clear in, but not dominating, the narrative, is as innocent as its
hero.

The simplicity of its organization and the consistency of its unexag-
gerated, but unmistakable, comic tone are major factors in the success of
Cashel Byron's Profession. The other novels attempt too much on the
basis of insufficient 'science' and collapse in shapelessness and incon-
clusiveness. But these years of writing in the much looser genre undoubtedly helped to save Shaw's plays from dominance by the tight
construction of the *pièce bien faite* and encouraged the experimental
flexibility that is a mark of his theatre. As for his art of comedy, the novels
had given him scope to work out the variety it was capable of embracing:
realism and fantasy, satiric harshness, the physical humours of farce, the
sweet-tempered mood, when delicacy of feeling is released in laughter.
In all the novels there are passages of brilliance that far exceed the quality
of the whole. A majority of these bring out the childishness and, with it,
the liveliness of the characters. The proposal episode from the first novel,
Immaturity, is a good example with which to close this brief survey.

The scene is Perspective, where Harriet's aunt, Mrs Summers, is
housekeeper. Mrs Summers's chief anxiety is that her niece may spoil
her prospects by appearing inferior to Cyril Scott, the artist, whose
purpose in calling is an open secret between them. But Harriet, the
dressmaker, is determined that Scott shall ask her to marry him with his
eyes wide open to her position. So her opening remarks are about her
'shop' and its trade and the quality of customers (including Lady Pentry's
maid) at whose service she is. Perfectly at ease – the only one of the three
who is – she flaunts her social disadvantages, referring to her early life
and memories of running to her father in the bar of a public house, in a
way that demonstrates present assurance in her personal qualities. When
Scott adds to a deprecatory comment by Mrs Summers, 'Anything that
concerns Miss Russell, interests me', Harriet responds with a curtsey,
'and sat in silence, at her ease, and unreasonably happy'. Visitors to the
house draw Mrs Summers away, and Harriet with characteristic directness
turns to listen seriously to what Scott has to say. He begins at once with
a proposal 'in form'. When his words, 'though I am conscious of expressing
myself very lamely', give her the chance, she scatters his pretence of
dignity with deflating pertness: 'On the contrary, Mr Scott, you are
making quite a speech.' It finishes any convention that she is his inferior;
they are now quite out of the polite world. His volatile temper roused, he

throws all his arts of persuasion to the winds in apparent forgetfulness of loving her and wanting her, and simply grumbles:

> Even if you had the common amiability to listen to me, you would not have the heart to appreciate what I mean. As well talk to the wall as to a woman.

Harriet's suspiciously over-soft answers are fuel to his wrath: 'there is an end even to my patience,' he declares on a minimum of provocation; but he is sensitive and intelligent enough for her prompt 'Yes' to drive him to silent reflection. This is a human being, not a farcical ogre, such moments remind the reader. But before long, as Harriet does not give her acceptance readily, he is beside himself with distress and exposing his folly more and more. How much egotism goes to the making of passionate love is clearly revealed:

> You might, for once, think of something besides yourself. It is always the same with women. They profess to be devotion and self-sacrifice incarnate. In reality they are utterly selfish.

This is not the lover but the husband speaking, and Harriet's unruffled calm supplies some justification for his fretting and fuming, ill judged and futile as it is. She attempts to leave him to calm down, but he is before her – and the scene moves into a new phase of absurdity:

> Harriet looked at him. He returned the look in a manner which shewed that he had no intention of moving from the door. He was nervous and muscular, but small. To her strength, activity, and indifference to the superiority of his sex in combat, many a hardy urchin at Little Kinross could have testified; and Scott . . . little knew that her last thought . . . had been a regret that she could not with dignity obey her impulse to give him a shaking and throw him away from the door . . .

Mentally and emotionally, they are now right in the world of farce. 'You could have gone out through the window,' Scott soon retorts, in answer to her protests; and indeed she could. For it is not reason that governs Harriet, either. She can see all that is against this marriage (and all that is against all marriages):

> . . . when you forget your design and fall into your natural manner, you try my patience almost more than I can endure for an hour. Do you think I could endure it for a lifetime?

Yet she is in love and 'unreasonably happy' and she gives her consent. Shaw now mars the balance of his account by dwelling over long on the mutual discomfort of the physical gestures of lovers, but ends his chapter more subtly:

> 'I wish you would go now' she said.
> 'Why?'

'Because I have taken a great step today; and until I am alone and quite at rest, I shall feel as if I were carrying a burden. Dont you understand?'

The artist did now understand. 'I am a wretched animal' he said; 'but I understand. Artists understand love better than marriage; but I am capable of learning. From you.'

Harriet smiled quite radiantly.

The constantly shifting mood and tone of the whole chapter have produced an effect such as music can produce. Even at the close, it is not simple love-melody: Harriet's smile has implications of amusement as well as joy; and Scott's self-knowledge as an artist remains a dubious quantity.

Shaw is anti-romantic, no doubt, but he is well aware of the exhilarating pleasure of combat as one of the joys of life – and of love:

She had not been in love with the cowboy, whose head she had subsequently knocked against the gate; and she was in love with the artist. Nevertheless her fingers had tingled . . .

2

Socialist Drama

The story of the writing of Bernard Shaw's first play has been told many times, and its genesis considered and debated more than the quality of the finished work, in isolation, would justify. How much he had still to learn about the art of drama in 1892, when he undertook to supply a play for J. T. Grein's recently established Independent Theatre, has been amply demonstrated by Charles Shattuck in his comparison of the text published in 1893 with the revised version Shaw issued in 1898.[1] The revision still left the play a very patchy affair, showing signs of having been composed in fragments that do not fit very well together or fall into any satisfactory dramatic rhythm; the characterization is generally rough and ready; the mechanical plot-structure creaks; the scheme remains too bare, without the richness of interest that marks Shaw's imaginative development of later plays; and, even after the excision of puerile quips in 1898, too many of the clever lines are momentarily amusing without contributing to the exposition of a central theme. A perfunctoriness of treatment is evident in the arbitrary, isolated character of certain passages that do not forward the action – notably the scene of Blanche with her maid, which remains crude and violently interjected even in its rewritten form. Here, apparently, is something Shaw very much wanted to assert; whether or not it might prove farcically amusing, as part of a predominantly naturalistic play it is calculated to outrage audiences.

The mixture of styles has to be regarded as a technical fault: the transformation of the agent, Lickcheese (an early rehearsal for the transformation of Doolittle in *Pygmalion*), is a strong, if conventional, theatrical stroke, but it is unsupported by any freedom of fantasy in the rest of the action; the conversion of the hero, Harry Trench, is not a theatrical stroke at all, but the main dramatic event, and the failure to show motives at work in the process of change leaves it imaginatively unrealized and not at all seriously affecting. By the time he came to write the part

[1] Charles H. Shattuck, 'Bernard Shaw's Bad Quarto', *Journal of English and Germanic Philology*, Vol. LIV (1955), pp. 651–63.

of Vivie Warren, Shaw knew what he should have done with Harry
Trench, and the difference can be measured in terms of imaginative
commitment to the character and loving attention to detail in the play.

Widowers' Houses is not very like the well-made play it took as its
starting-point, in its generic form or in the particular example of Augier's
Ceinture dorée, supposed to be the basis of the scenario with which Shaw
had been supplied by William Archer in the first, collaborative stage of
work on the drama.[1] Shaw's impulse to reject the type seems stronger
already than his reliance on its formulae, but what he might reject it *for*
still awaited discovery. The character of Trench's friend, Cokane, is an
instance of how encumbering a formula could remain: the playwright
made two distinct attempts, in 1892 and 1898, to turn a mere theatrical
functionary, the confidant of the hero, into a useful and interesting
figure. The elderly, waspish apostle of social 'tact' and hypocrisy of the
revised version has little in common with the original Cokane, a young,
married man-about-town, except an incredibility corresponding to the
contempt with which he has been drawn. The same name is kept, a
label for an illusionist. And the apparently superfluous character was
bequeathed to later plays: Praed, in *Mrs Warren's Profession*, and
Roebuck Ramsden, in *Man and Superman*, are less obviously descended
from the confidant; they are characters on the sidelines, well intentioned,
professedly liberal – and impotent, figures of major importance in the
Shavian analysis of society.

The real originality of *Widowers' Houses* lies in the dramatic tension
it pursues – and sometimes achieves – between socialist logic and private
emotion. While the firmness and clarity with which the play diagnoses
social ills are attributable to Shaw's self-education in Marxism, following
his reading of Dickens and his discipleship to Henry George, its force is
supplied by the passionate mysogyny more overt in some of his early
unpublished work (e.g. *The Cassone*, or even in the drawing of Mary in
his juvenile *Passion Play*).[2] For Blanche is a misogynist's portrait of a
woman: a spoilt termagant, sexually attractive (hence enslaving), basically the enemy of men (whom she scorns and devours), with no moral
sense or any but the most narrowly selfish interests. And the anti-romantic
nature of his heroine consorts with Shaw's final choice of title for the play:
the domestic situation of the widower's daughter is significantly related to

[1] See Archer's account in the Independent Theatre Edition of *Widowers'
Houses* (1893), taken from *The World* (14 Dec. 1892), and Shaw's Preface to
Plays Unpleasant; also Eden Greville, 'Bernard Shaw and His Plays', *Munsey's
Magazine*, Vol. XXIV (1906), pp. 765–6, quoted in Anna I. Miller, *The Independent Theatre in Europe* (New York: Blom, 1931; reissued 1966), pp. 172–4.
[2] The texts are in the British Museum. See references in relation to *Candida*,
p. 73 below.

the theme of slum-landlordism. The most frequented ground of the later plays is staked out here in the clash of domestic values and public values, in the relation of political and economic questions to the woman's world of home and family life.

The good humour, which is the charm of the later heroines, Candida and Ann Whitefield, and baffles attempts to define the dramatist's attitude to them in any simple terms, is conspicuously lacking from Blanche's make-up. The playwright himself scorns tact here. This is an 'unpleasant' play and works by a process of disenchantment. This peculiarity of its approach distinguishes it from its Dickensian analogue in *Little Dorrit*,[1] as from Shaw's own later domestic plays. For the different impression made by the two daughters is what chiefly conceals the likeness between Shaw's group of landlord, agent, landlord's daughter (and her young man) and Dickens's presentation of Casby, Panks and Flora. Like Casby, Shaw's Sartorius is a widower with an indulged daughter, his only child. The name, Blanche, signifies the innocence of ignorance which Dickens treats ironically in so many aspects of *Little Dorrit*. Sartorius is less cherubic than Casby, but equally respectable in the public eye and benevolent in his private aspect. Like Panks, Shaw's Lickcheese has to collect the slum rents and fulfils the role of scapegoat whereby the public and official 'innocence' of the landlord is preserved. In naming Sartorius (as in the transformation of Lickcheese), Shaw was certainly drawing on the Swift–Carlyle tradition of metaphor which represents social institutions and manners as clothes that may be changed,[2] and it is not unlikely that he remembered the incident of Panks's exposure of his master by literally stripping him of his disguise, the respectable hat and snowy locks. Both rent-collectors rebel against their cruel service and undergo a form of conversion; but, whereas Panks becomes a good-hearted dupe of another kind, still enmeshed in the system, Lickcheese emerges as a personification of Henry George's view of the

[1] Shaw's allusions to *Little Dorrit* are so frequent and commendatory (as in the Introduction to the collected *Prefaces*, where he includes Dickens's novel in a list that otherwise consists of the Gospels, *Utopia*, *Tom Jones*, Aristophanes, Euripides and the 'Socratian [*sic*] dialogues of Plato'), that the hypothesis of direct imitation may fairly be made. Dickens's hero, Arthur Clennam, is a more complex and psychologically interesting character than Harry Trench, but both are innocents who undergo enlightenment as to the nature of the society they live in. Unlike Arthur, Harry does not escape relatively uncorrupted.

[2] The point is made in an interesting discussion of Sartorius and his successors by Stanley Marquis Holberg, 'The Economic Rogue in the Plays of Bernard Shaw', *University of Buffalo Studies*, Vol. XXI (1953), pp. 34–119. For a general account of the relation of Shaw's work to Carlyle's, see J. B. Kaye, *Bernard Shaw and the Nineteenth-Century Tradition* (Norman, Oklahoma: University of Oklahoma Press, 1958).

origin of capital – in the middleman who is neither owner of property nor labourer, but able to persuade the landowner of the value of his service.

The coldness of Blanche, as opposed to the good-hearted eccentricity of Flora, whose foolish affections have been victimized in the past as a matter of business, is the condition of a further differentiation of Sartorius from Casby. Through the coldly dignified public manner and the sentimental devotion to his daughter, with a hint of deep attachment to his mother's memory, Shaw has achieved the impression of Sartorius as a very shy man, frightened of people and ineffectual in personal relationships. Not Sartorius but Blanche is the dominant personality in this pair, and hers is the more complete ruthlessness; in effect, Shaw has detached from the father the force of evil to which he has succumbed and identified it with the female figure. Though Trench fills the role of innocent at the beginning of the play, by the end it is the innocence of Sartorius that is exposed:

> SARTORIUS (revolted). Do you think, Lickcheese, that my daughter is to be made part of a money bargain between you and these gentlemen?

Trench sulkily echoes this as a matter of convention:

> I wont have the relations between Miss Sartorius and myself made part of a bargain.

But there is no innocence left in Trench after he chooses to accommodate himself to the evil system revealed to him in Act II; moral lethargy and stupidity have proved dominant in him and inform his words here. The final truth remains hidden from Sartorius because a more generous and sympathetic emotion blinds him, a limited altruism: his affection for the daughter who is about to turn, under the audience's gaze, into the naked appetite of egotism. Lickcheese is to be stage-manager of this final scene in which Blanche appropriates Harry; and Lickcheese's retort to Sartorius, like his earlier 'Here we are, all friends round St Paul's', implies recognition of a society like enough to that of *The Merchant of Venice:*

> Oh come, Sartorius! dont talk as if you was the only father in the world. I have a daughter too; and my feelins in that matter is just as fine as yours. I propose nothing but what is for Miss Blanche's advantage and Dr Trench's.

Spiritually, Blanche is the daughter of the Jew, triumphant in her alliance with the Gentile that her father's money will endow. Shaw has separated off the cynicism of *The Merchant* from the romantic element, with its shadow of a more ideal condition. Only a travesty of any such ideal is admitted to *Widowers' Houses;* as Lickcheese puts it:

> Why not have a bit of romance in business when it costs nothing?

It is romance gone very sour, by the end of the play. The effect is satirical, working through revulsion.

The view of society that the play unfolds is of a conspiracy between the aristocracy of 'birth' and the self-made middle class against the poorest section of the community. (Such remains the alignment, more elaborately embellished, in *Major Barbara*.) Sartorius's wealth is extracted as rent from the labour of the class he thus contrives to keep poor and helpless. The wealth is shared with an idle upper class in return for the patents of respectability – admission to 'society' – that class is able to bestow. Cokane's mechanically reiterated insistence on 'tact' gravitates naturally towards the blackmail Lickcheese turns to; such parasites flourish where the appearance of virtue can lull moral consciences into apathy. The conventional docility of mankind readily acquiesces in the apophthegm: whatever is generally accepted must be right. Revolution, or even evolution, is prevented and the social order kept static by inducing an easy determinism in the minds of any idealists who consider themselves detached enough to want reform. Lickcheese and Harry, for all the difference of character and circumstances that divides them, are both brought to heel by the realization that they are already part of the system and the fear that they cannot possibly survive outside it. The aim of the conspirators is to persuade all potential re- formers of the inevitability of the prevailing system and the helplessness of individuals to change a condition of society that all right-minded men deplore. This is Sartorius's line with the initially rebellious Trench:

> If, when you say you are just as bad as I am, you mean that you are just as powerless to alter the state of society, then you are unfortunately quite right.

> . . . your feelings do you credit: I assure you I feel exactly as you do, myself. Every man who has a heart must wish that a better state of things was practicable. But unhappily it is not.

The abrogation of moral responsibility turns such sentiments into a luxurious self-indulgence which corrupts the mind that entertains it. The parody of romance which Shaw's play offers is a satirical attack on the tendency to such self-flattering sentiments on the part of his audience. Stung to a sufficient alertness, it is left to them to draw the responsible conclusion that the dramatist has refrained from drawing: that Sartorius's euphemistic dismissal of evil can and should be turned on its head – not 'just as bad . . . mean[s] . . . just as powerless to alter the state of society', but 'just as powerless . . . mean[s] . . . just as bad'.

The relative inadequacy of *Widowers' Houses* to its theme is thrown into relief by a comparison with Brecht's mature treatment of what is

basically the same issue in *Mother Courage*. The view of human life
Brecht's play offers is tragic – until the possibility of using Marxism
as a weapon against tragedy is admitted; it is as essentially religious a
solution (gambling on the power of faith to change the world) as was the
admission of Christian redemptive doctrine into the bleakly determinist
tradition behind medieval tragedy. Courage acquires the stature of a
tragic figure: humanity endlessly suffering under the rod of an implacable
fate, chained to the ceaselessly turning wheels of a process that is the
condition of her existence. Shaw has not begun to identify the hypocrite's
deliberately contrived picture of capitalist society with a profoundly
tragic world-view, only answerable by the defiant human will guided by
intelligence, pitting itself against the frame of things entire and any
concept of deity that sanctions such an order. Yet, even in this first
play, he was feeling his way along personal lines to the conclusion that
there can be no effective revolution that does not pull down the gods
too.

It is ironic that Cokane's silliness voiced to Harry in Act I is proved by
the play's action to be a truth with teeth:

> You dont know the importance of these things; apparently idle ceremonial
> trifles, really the springs and wheels of a great aristocratic system.

The mechanistic image has full value. The name of Lady Roxdale, an
off-stage presence, is reverently invoked by Cokane, Sartorius, Lickcheese,
in recognition of the ultimate power of the aristocracy. On stage, it is
rather differently represented by Blanche. 'I see I have made a real lady
of you, Blanche' is the recognition Sartorius comes to. And again:
'Well, my child, I suppose it is natural for you to feel that way, after
your bringing up. It is the ladylike view of the matter.' It anticipates
Mrs Warren's judgement on what she has done for Vivie.

The error of both the Shavian parents is also the error of Mother
Courage: putting private affection, the care of their own, before public
responsibility (Mother Courage loses all her children, despite her efforts
to save them; the dumb Catherine, with a more universal maternal
impulse – and with little else to live for – saves the children of the
threatened town). Sartorius, whose early motivation is implied in the way
he speaks of his mother –

> . . . do you know, Blanche, that my mother was a very poor woman, and
> that her poverty was not her fault?

> . . . What would you be now but for what your grandmother did for me
> when she stood at her wash-tub for thirteen hours a day and thought herself
> rich when she made fifteen shillings a week?

– is guilty of having preferred to raise his daughter out of his mother's class to standing with that class against its exploiters, and his punishment is to have his daughter despise the people he comes from and feels with. (*In* the play, the shift of allegiance from the weaker to the more powerful is caricatured in the conversion of Lickcheese to a rich man.) Mrs Warren's alliance with the 'capitalist bully' was a misuse of her energy that enabled her to turn her daughter into a 'lady' who not only denies any bond with her mother, but, for all her idealism, ends up defeated in a more refined version of the same conspiracy against the class her mother rose from.

Shaw does more than point the moral. The first venture of his drama into myth comes in the revelation of Blanche, not just as a product of the system, but as an incarnation of the primitive passion at work, in all these instances, against social good. Blanche, raging with physical violence against her maid, may be accepted as an object-lesson on the folly of 'spoiling' a child with over-indulgence; and the spoilt child makes an ironic contrast with the hungry children 'crying for bread', known to Lickcheese and ruthlessly sacrificed for Blanche's sake. It is significant that the immediate victim remains devoted to her: an anticipation, this, of the way that Harry, the victim of her later, different rage, succumbs to her; and a hint at the foolishness of society's victims in their passive, brain-washed submitting to the violation done them. In performance, this passage and her final scene with Harry inevitably stand out as requiring special handling by the actress; Shaw demanded no new naturalism here, but old ham: the virtuoso depiction of passion. It is astonishingly out of key with the rest, and may shock us into seeing the social thesis of the play as itself a rationalization of the danger of private emotion, paternal love or sexual passion.

Or we may recognize in the final scene a manifestation of the *dea ex machina*. The passion of *possession* transfiguring the woman, the maternal passion of the female animal with its young, reaches a climax in the savage force of Blanche's final words to Harry.

> (. . . *She flings her arms round him, and crushes him in an ecstatic embrace as she adds, with furious tenderness*) How dare you touch anything belonging to me?

The likeness of the incident to the ending of *Man and Superman* cannot fail to be recognized. But the Life Force incarnate in mother-woman is hardly endorsed with approval at the end of *Widowers' Houses*. This victory of the domestic over the social is morally and emotionally revolting.

A predilection for myth, or a wish to establish the general validity and relevance of his fable by conforming it to a mythic pattern, is indicated in a letter to William Archer, surviving from an early stage in the evolution of this play: '. . . provided you allow for the inevitable postponement of the glimpse of the underworld to the second act caused by your own insistence on my beginning on the Rhine.' (Shaw, *Collected Letters*, I, p. 388.) Perhaps it was Archer who insisted on adherence to the order of scenes in Wagner's *Rhinegold* (after which the projected play was originally to have been named). Yet Shaw was to remain curiously faithful to this source of ideas and images right through his career as dramatist. If the private experience of family life remains one constant boundary of his political and social drama, the opposite boundary is commonly supplied by myths, or fantastic hypotheses, which are emotionally satisfying to him. Though the Preface to *Plays Pleasant* rejects the founding of social institutions on the basis of 'ideals suggested to our imaginations by our half-satisfied passions', the most potent images of Shavian drama have been generated in just this way – and the list can start with Blanche and Lickcheese. The latter has the impervious, immortal fixity of Loki himself, the shifty, supernatural rogue Wagner elaborated from Germanic legend. His glee matches the challenging and baffling ironies, often layer upon layer, which Shaw's art of comedy presents.

The Philanderer, the second of the Unpleasant Plays, has received scant critical attention. This may be connected with the difficulty of approaching it satisfactorily as a thesis play about a contemporary social evil, like slum-landlordism, or prostitution. Those specific evils are, of course, paradigms of the larger, ultimate concerns of *Widowers' Houses* and *Mrs Warren's Profession*. But Shaw employs a different strategy in *The Philanderer*, and with considerably greater cunning than he had shown in the first of the plays.

True, it has a topical-symbolic setting, in the Ibsen Club, appropriate for an examination of the 'advanced' views and attitudes of the nineties. Political and economic questions have been put aside, but the social institution of marriage enters into the discussion and also supplies a pretext for the plot. How marginal Shaw's concern now was with the institutional aspect, or the laws governing marriage, can be gauged from the way the stock arguments of the time against marriage are reeled off, for what they are worth, by Charteris to Julia:

> You regarded marriage as a degrading bargain, by which a woman sells herself to a man for the social status of a wife and the right to be supported and pensioned in old age out of his income. Thats the advanced view: our view. Besides, if you had married me, I might have turned out a drunkard,

a criminal, an imbecile, a horror to you; and you couldnt have released yourself. Too big a risk, you see. Thats the rational view: our view.

Belfort Bax was to be given his due in *Getting Married*; meanwhile Shaw was more concerned with what the Ibsen Club version of his criticisms takes pains to disregard and exclude: human emotion. The rages of Blanche Sartorius, differently approached, had provided the subject for the new play. Julia Craven, the woman of passion, is hounded down by the author and his deputies to the end of *The Philanderer*, which leaves her looking more of a victim than a villainess. No attempt is made to diagnose the social origins of Julia's emotions: neurotic, hysterical, characteristically violent, they challenge the intelligence and the compassion of an audience rather as the spectacle of Hedda Gabler's frustrated and destructive vitality does. Implied in the individual figure is the sickness of a society; but the public aspect of its disease is not admitted to the picture.

The play supplies a name for the disease, and the title is farcically disputed between doctor and patient:

> PARAMORE (*despairingly*). The worst of news! Terrible news! Fatal news! My disease –
> CRAVEN (*quickly*). Do you mean m y disease?
> PARAMORE (*fiercely*). I mean m y disease: Paramore's disease: the disease I discovered: the work of my life! . . .

This is an echo of an earlier passage:

> SYLVIA. . . . when we learned that poor papa had Paramore's disease.
> CHARTERIS. Paramore's disease! Why, whats the matter with Paramore?
> SYLVIA. Oh, not a disease that he suffers from, but one that he discovered.

Facile as the jest is, it neatly exposes the dramatist's ironic awareness of what he himself was doing: divorcing critical intelligence from feeling; claiming an impossible objectivity in his denunciation of folly and vice. As 'The worst of news' to Dr Paramore is that his discovery was false and the disease does not exist, a reading of the play which sees its satire as turning back on itself would seem to be sanctioned by the author.

The Philanderer certainly offers a rationale of his peculiar temperament and mentality, but it cannot be dismissed simply as a private drama, or in terms of exhibitionism or special pleading. Assuming the validity, however limited, of any individual, idiosyncratic view, Shaw's procedure is to use it deliberately as a weapon against error in conventional generalizations and as a tool of philosophic enquiry. The dramatic clash of individual intelligence pitted against conventional thinking, stale, confused and mechanical, the clash of Charteris, the dramatist's comedy *persona*, with the fathers, Cuthbertson and Craven, provides a series of predictably easy triumphs for a clever clown at the expense of his stupid foils. The hypocrisy, ignorance and self-delusion that swell support for the common view are exposed and routed. The true tension and conflict in the play lie elsewhere, however, and arise from the author's recognition that there is a negative and potentially dangerous side to the exercise of reason and its control of emotion. His aggressive method, calculated to provoke and alert his audience, works no simple conversion to his expressed view; it ensures an ambivalent reaction to himself and his principal characters. And the effectiveness of the play turns on this ambivalence: on the backwash of compassion for the victims of rational detachment and indignation against their treatment, set up in the process of enquiry and enlightenment.

The subjective. bias of the satirical dramatist (and his juvenalian quality) is itself satirically mirrored in the play in the character of Dr Paramore, whose practice of vivisection in the interests of medical science is congenial to the meanness and coldness of his constitution. Whether the social result of his experiments justifies the means is open to question. He is certainly indicted for greater concern for his theory than for his patients – and indicted through the mouth of Charteris, whose superior expansiveness and buoyancy of spirit make him Jekyll to the other's Hyde:

> CHARTERIS. . . . The Nonconformist conscience is bad enough; but the scientific conscience is the very devil . . . I have no conscience in that sense at all: I loathe it as I loathe all the snares of idealism; but I have some common humanity and common sense . . . Now it's a perfectly damnable thing for you to hope that your liver theory is true, because it amounts to hoping that Craven will die an agonizing death.

Charteris entertains us with his wit and engages us with the frank appeal from his amorality and natural selfishness to ours, usually schooled and suppressed in the interests of social convention. Laughing with him brings release to our own potentially subversive vitality. (Brecht recognized the importance of the rogue character to the revolutionist, the responsible use of natural irresponsibility, in his own dramatic practice and as he observed it in Shaw's.) It is the response of good-fellowship which theatrical self-projection can bring to the writer at odds with society: not sympathy, which implies the recognition of a pathetic, or even tragic, element – 'I dont think you like to be loved too much,' says Grace to Charteris – but amused liking, in which detachment and respect are balanced. It is a good feeling, and a welcome one in life; Shaw is right about that, and our assent, however unconsciously given, is essential to true judgement of the situation and the alternatives that the play lays before us.

The farcical action can be seen as a conflict between male and female selfishness; or, from Charteris's point of view, as his self-defensive manoeuvring against emotional blackmail. Julia's pursuit of him is visibly, if often covertly, conducted on the stage. His claim to the moral position, with right on his side, simply balances hers; and his aggressiveness is not greater. She suffers and he does not, except as he has to guard his sensibility always against the assaults of her suffering. From Julia's point of view, Charteris is no better than Paramore:

It is you who are the vivisector: a far crueller, more wanton vivisector than he;

but he claims a distinction:

Yes; but then I learn so much more from my experiments than he does! And the victims learn as much as I do. Thats where my moral superiority comes in.

Knowledge which is not used for human happiness falls, all the same, into the category of 'idealism' which Charteris professes to loathe. The inconsistency which renders the character comic is a necessary contrivance of the author, whose intentions are enacted not by one surrogate character, but by the whole play. We are the dramatist's victims, tormented not merely by the questioning of our opinions but by a gratuitous operation on the possibly diseased emotions which attach us to our moral values. At the end of the experiment we know as much as he does: the responsibility for further action in the light of it must be ours, and it is feeling that motivates us.

Shaw's choice of names for the Craven sisters, Julia and Sylvia, is a reminder of Shakespeare's *Two Gentlemen of Verona*, in which one of the heroines – Julia – puts on male disguise in order to seek out her errant lover, Proteus, whose own name suggests the fickleness of his affections. Shaw has taken the idea and redistributed its elements, so that his Julia assumes the conventional male role only in that she is the pursuer in the love chase; the male costume is worn by her younger sister, whose presence in the play is superfluous to the plot, but symbolically central. 'Who is Silvia? What is she?' – the questions of the Shakespearian song are not difficult to answer in the Shavian context. Though no ideal character but a gauche and often ridiculous adolescent, Sylvia's appearance and attitude, burlesque as they are, suggest an ideal: the androgyne as an image of perfect balance in human nature. The dramatist's ready admission of the identity of the typical Shaw heroine with the Shakespearian heroine makes sense if we see the succession of 'womanly women' and mother-images as vicious, or tragic, distortions of the true nature to which the Strange Lady of *The Man of Destiny*, Major Barbara and Saint Joan (all versions of the neoplatonic ideal) approximate.[1] It is the Shavian bias that society, in its self-adaptation, has been following recently.

The love-enmity between Julia and Charteris is thus exposed as the effect of an unhappy polarization of human nature into intellect and emotion. As he is not concerned with sex distinction alone, Shaw's view of this split cannot be impugned on biological grounds. His enquiry is into matters of conscience, not physiology. Though Julia is accepted by all as essentially a 'womanly woman', Charteris is very different from Cuthbertson's conventional and sentimental notion of a 'manly man', a creature who offers no challenge to 'womanly' values and morality. Charteris is the first example of the Shavian Don Juan to occur in the plays, and a difference from the Don Juan of tradition is already evident. Charteris does not run away from all women, but only from possessive women who threaten his self-containment. He does not regard women simply as objects, or seem to need continual conquests to bolster up his ego; his own vitality is sufficient for that:

GRACE. Oh, Leonard, does your happiness really depend on me?
CHARTERIS (tenderly). Absolutely. (She beams with delight. A sudden re-vulsion comes to him at the sight: he recoils, dropping her hands and crying) Ah no: why should I lie to you? (He folds his arms and adds firmly) My happiness depends on nobody but myself. I can do without you.

The lesson is one that Grace Tranfield hardly needs to learn; for her social circumstances, as a widow (a less unhappy one than Mrs Linde in *A Doll's House* or Mrs Alving) have already disposed her to acquire the virtues Charteris is defending: self-reliance, judgement and control, the values of sanity to stand against Julia's madness.

Although Shaw has avoided the danger of pressing an abstract social theory by presenting the denizens of the Ibsen Club as faddists, the setting and the bust of Ibsen, centrally placed, imply a particular criticism of society which serves to account for the incidence of Paramore's disease in the figurative sense. Julia's rages of frustration and jealousy and despair are the signs of a childish helplessness and fear of rejection, the insecurity of a creature who has never learnt independence of others. Like the spoilt child, Julia has acquired the cunning to use the appeal of her helplessness as a weapon of tyranny over others. Her father's testimony, 'She cant bear to be crossed in the slightest thing, poor child', is echoed with the severity of a schoolmistress in Grace's accusation:

You calculated to an inch how far you could go . . . You fall back on your natural way of getting anything you want: crying for it like a baby until it is given to you.

[1] See below, p. 183, in discussion of *Getting Married*.

Grace's cry 'These men: our lords and masters!' sums up Julia's more personal, more heartfelt complaint to Charteris:

> You might have made me good if you had chosen to. You had a great power over me. I was like a child in your hands; and you knew it.

Society as a doll's house, or perpetual nursery, for the childishness of women denied freedom and responsibility until they are incapable of both cripples its men too. Craven and Cuthbertson – and Paramore – are poor creatures, and their ideal of relations between the sexes, romantic love, is called into question. Don Juan, of course, is the villain of romantic love. *The Philanderer* justifies the focus of its title not only by exposing the sentimental illusions of romance (Craven, who married for money, was happier than Cuthbertson, who married for love, we may remember), but by revealing the intensity of romantic love as morbid and its beauty as deformity misjudged by a false aesthetic. (Shaw's view has a good deal in common with Chaucer's.)

Not that the ending of the play is, or could be, happy for Grace Tranfield and Charteris more than it is for Julia and Paramore. Shaw has cultivated the wryness of Shakespeare's 'black' comedies to match the negative resistance that is the most any of his characters can achieve in their given social situation. Only by remaining a widow can Grace retain her balance. (Her decision anticipates Vivie Warren's.) And the impoverishment implied was to be recognized by Shaw in his portrayal of a character Grace closely resembles: Mrs Clandon in *You Never Can Tell*. Both value order and control supremely; though Grace loves Charteris, whereas Mrs Clandon has never been in love, she brings in reason and the instinct of self-preservation to subdue the emotion, 'because I will not give myself to any man who has learnt how to treat women from you and your like,' she declares to Julia; 'I can do without his love, but not without his respect; and it is your fault that I cannot have both.' The imperfection of Mrs Tranfield is audible in her dressing-down of Julia. The effect is momentarily repellent, faintly echoing the blind, self-opinionated quality of Paramore and the self-conceit of Charteris; and it releases, briefly, an impulse of sympathy for Julia. For the contrary truth – that Don Juanism is responsible for women like Julia – has also been demonstrated in the play, though less forthrightly expressed: Julia's distress and rage are responses to Charteris's contemptuous treatment of her. Charteris's commentary on himself in the last line of the play, 'Never make a hero of a philanderer', is a warning that characters from the same mould in later plays, including Shaw's chief version of Don Juan, Jack Tanner in *Man and Superman*, need to be sceptically regarded.

Mrs Warren's Profession is the linking play between *Widowers' Houses* and *Major Barbara*, the second of three essays on the Ibsenite theme of social inheritance. In the first, Shaw had settled for a satiric treatment and conclusion: the pure ideals of the younger generation are dismissed as nothing but ignorance of the world; their common human appetites quickly bring them to terms with the prevailing system, the perpetuation of which is thus ensured. Superficially, *Major Barbara* presents a similar conclusion: after an interval of resistance, the young people agree to accept the money and go into the family business; but their decision is not a moral capitulation, and the motif of succession by adoption signifies a discontinuity, a possibility of change through free choice. An ironic tension is maintained at the close of the play in token of a struggle that has to be continued. Between the satire and the paradox, *Mrs Warren's Profession* gives a glimpse of uncompleted tragedy: Vivie Warren, in her Chancery Lane office, is trying to opt out, as surely as when she pulled the rifle Frank Gardner was aiming at the 'capitalist bully' round upon herself, at the end of Act III.

Shaw cannot be charged with having written the same play three times with variant endings. Sartorius, Mrs Warren and Andrew Undershaft are engaged in different businesses and, though all three exemplify the workings of capitalism literally and metaphorically, they are differently focused on their common subject and bring to attention different areas of human motive. The commodity of the trade has its own particular significance in each of the plays.

Slum-landlordism demonstrates, in general, the vicious exploitation of the poor; more precisely, it illustrates a socialist theory of rents and profits. In contrast to Sartorius, Andrew Undershaft is an industrialist, so that *Major Barbara* can explore the question of relations between employer and work-people as well as the ethics of investment in destruction. The 'amenities' for which Sartorius charges his victims are shoddy and injurious to health; the negative fact that his tenants are powerless either to demand better or withhold payment is underlined by the change of policy – the intention of improving the property for the sake of compensation – when a public authority, itself equipped with money and power, may start to bargain. It is power that Undershaft and Lazarus trade in, physical force – the weapons of war – a genuine product of labour and an efficiently organized society, with nothing shoddy about it; however, it is not force for peaceful, constructive uses, but for brigandage or defence against it, for the tenants against their landlords, or the workers against their bosses, if they can pay the fair price which is not just money but will (in the Schopenhauerian sense) – though Shaw does not forget that the control of money is an essential instrument of power in actual society.

By what may have originated as theatrical caution with an eye on the
Lord Chamberlain, Mrs Warren's profession is never named. Not that we
are in much doubt that the commodity she trades in is sex and that she has
graduated from common prostitution to become managing-director of an
international chain of brothels,[1] but the avoidance of plain terms has
helped to keep the range of the play's relevance open: this is a trade in
living human bodies and human virtue (whatever that may prove to be),
the resources for which the poor can make the rich pay, and for which
women (a 'poor' class traditionally) can get a reasonable market price by
hard bargaining with their 'lords and masters'. Kitty Warren's own career
has involved a shift from small-scale private enterprise to the employment
of labour in full-scale capitalism; it is generally analogous to Lickcheese's
progress – from picking up the crumbs by reluctant, enforced participa-
tion in a system that discriminates against the poor in favour of the rich –
to whole-hearted and profitable collaboration in the system. Mrs Warren
seems to be a model employer like Andrew Undershaft, a much more
effectively benevolent entrepreneur than Lickcheese was in his rent-
collecting days.

Very skilfully, Shaw tricks his audience, along with Vivie Warren,
into open-minded acceptance of Mrs Warren's self-justification. Most
theatre audiences are probably better disposed to be unprejudiced about
prostitution than about profiteering;[2] and, with an ease Ibsen might have
envied, Shaw exploits the irresponsible character of farce to subvert
normally accepted values and suspend the mechanism of inhibition.
Revelation follows revelation – the sentimentally viewed 'woman with
a past' turns into a promiscuous sensualist and a highly successful woman
of business with much more genuine pride and impudence than conventionally mannered shame. The tables of consanguinity are scattered,
so that parents cannot identify their children, or children their parents,

[1] J. T. Grein, *Dramatic Criticism, 1900–1901* (London: J. Long, 1902), p. 293,
records that the audience for the first production was largely mystified and embarrassed: 'It was an exceedingly uncomfortable afternoon . . . And, sure as I
feel that most of the women, and a good many of the men, who were present at
the production of "Mrs Warren's Profession" by the Stage Society, did not at
first know, and finally merely guessed, what was the woman's trade, I cannot
withhold the opinion that the representation was unnecessary and painful.' In
such conditions, the play would certainly have produced the 'unpleasant' tension
that a present-day production may miss through the support given to the farcical
aspect of the play by what is now a piling-up of really unambiguous revelation
after revelation.

[2] The publication of General William Booth's *In Darkest England and the
Way Out* (1890), which quickly became a best-seller, had prepared the way for
Shaw's play. Booth appealed to humanitarian feelings, not just horror, in his
accounts of the plight of London prostitutes.

or sisters know their brothers from their lovers; the old woman's marked taste for her daughter's young man diverts us as much as the old man's amorous advance to the young woman who might have been his daughter, and does not disgust us at all; children set themselves up in judgement on their parents; the futility, hypocrisy and stupidity of the church on earth make an easy target for blows dealt without the least scruple or compunction. Our reaction is mounting delight, not horror, until we relax as contentedly as Mrs Warren herself when all the pretensions are dropped. The most attractive characters in the play are the 'young scamp', with his happy-go-lucky gaiety, and the vitally energetic old reprobate and vulgarian, as natural as the rooks in the trees that, she knows, would find her out in a cathedral town, 'even if I could stand the dullness of it'. Customary morality is quite routed by stronger forces. Instinct prevails and without reservation acclaims the climax when revolutionary senti-ment is about to be translated into action. The rifle is trained on the repellent Crofts, and we can hardly wait to cheer. Then the reaction comes.

It was patently Shaw's intention to achieve a transference of the horror and shame conventionally associated with the sex-trade to its normally accepted and respected counterparts in the economic and social organiza-tion of society. His audience should watch its own gradual enlightenment enacted on the stage by Vivie Warren. Whether he did in fact succeed, or whether his own puritanical attitude to sex interfered and confused the issue has been disputed (e.g. by Eric Bentley[1]). The play needs to be carefully and thoughtfully followed: though Shaw has borrowed the broad theatrical methods of farce and melodrama, *Mrs Warren's Pro-fession* eludes both these categories in the fine precision of its insights.

Kitty Warren's appeal to her daughter, in Act II, is rationally per-suasive. 'Shame on you for . . . a stuck-up prude' is enough of a home-thrust to ensure a hearing for her case. The story she has to tell is crystal-clear in its implications, and the consistent logic of her mother's action, translated back now into logic of thought, inevitably wins assent from one who takes pride in the hard clarity of her own mind. The similarity between mother and daughter comes out in their acceptance of the same assumptions: of the value of self-respect and the importance to it of money; of the necessity of living sensibly and not in accordance with romantic ideals (Vivie has already revealed to Praed that she won her high honours at Cambridge for the sake of money); in their carelessness of convention, their energy and enterprise. In effect, her mother's exposition helps

[1] 'The Making of a Dramatist (1892–1903)', in R. J. Kaufmann (ed.), *G. B. Shaw*, Twentieth Century Views (Englewood Cliffs, N.J.: Prentice-Hall, 1965), pp. 57–75.

Vivie discard the unconsidered fragments of respectable opinion which she has taken over without recognizing their irrelevance to the kind of person she is and has chosen to be. The audience's self-identification with Vivie, in this scene, obscures the likelihood that an equally persuasive, but quite different case might be based on values Vivie dismisses with scant understanding. As it is, Mrs Warren's conclusions ring out with absolute authority:

> . . . where can a woman get the money to save in any other business? . . . Do you think we were such fools as to let other people trade in our good looks by employing us as shop girls, or barmaids, or waitresses, when we could trade in them ourselves and get all the profits instead of starvation wages? . . .

> . . . as if a marriage ceremony could make any difference in the right or wrong of the thing! . . .

> Of course it's worth while to a poor girl, if she can resist temptation and is good-looking and well conducted and sensible. It's far better than any other employment open to her . . .

> The only way for a woman to provide for herself decently is for her to be good to some man that can afford to be good to her.

Here is proof of the quality that has carried Mrs Warren to the top, and it can be seen in terms of that 'character' she so values: she argues with the clarity of conviction, faithful to the truth of what she is. She is obviously justified in advising her daughter, 'Dont you be led astray by people who dont know the world'; for its narrow, theoretical nature has been a weakness of Vivie's education, and money has protected her – and her Cambridge teachers – from knowledge of the brute facts of the industry by which that money has been made. Kitty's concession, 'It's not work that any woman would do for pleasure, goodness knows', is apt for puritan coldness. The generosities of sensuality and love are poor ground for a trade in sex. The money which passes is the guarantee of 'self-respect'; the term was Grace Tranfield's too, and in her mouth meant a refusal to be emotionally exploited by men, a determination to keep a seller's market. Though Praed is subjected to a teasingly satiric treatment and Frank Gardner plays the fool, each insists on a fragment of truth that Vivie has perilously ignored: her senses have not been educated and her young affections have been starved, so that she *over*-values money and is ripe for her mother's attentions. Something of the reformer lodges still in Mrs Warren's consciousness:

> It cant be right, Vivie, that there shouldnt be better opportunities for women. I stick to that: it's wrong.

So she has sent her daughter to Cambridge to learn how to make money in the way men do. The step was hardly radical enough, though it has made Vivie invulnerable to temptation by George Crofts.

Mrs Warren's Profession is quite as deliberately stagey as the two plays that preceded it: it is riddled with the coincidences and surprises of farce; it places and makes its points with all the force of melodrama; its tableaux and curtains have an unbelievable blatancy; and in Sir George Crofts it has the stock villain of melodrama. The element of farce modifies the realism of situation and characters and preserves the nature of the play as hypothesis. Shaw has used melodrama here to guy false emotion; it is the mode to which Vivie and Mrs Warren, both crippled natures, turn in their unused gropings after genuine feeling. And the melodramatic villain is a figure of evil recognizable by the most blunted perceptions. The association of Crofts with Kitty Warren keeps the audience aware of an unsavouriness that she hasn't explained away. Vivie's perceptions are not so blunted that she doesn't loathe herself at the thought that she might have 'the contaminated blood of that brutal waster in [her] veins'. But the melodramatic villain remains a concentration of evil external to the self and from which it is possible to run away; or which it is possible to kill.

The scene of Crofts's proposal to Vivie is amply illustrative of the words her mother had spoken in the previous Act:

> I'm sure Ive often pitied a poor girl, tired out and in low spirits, having to try to please some man that she doesnt care two straws for – some half-drunken fool that thinks he's making himself agreeable when he's teasing and worrying and disgusting a woman so that hardly any money could pay her for putting up with it.

The manner of Crofts's proposal is an index to what marriage with him would be like – for it is, of course, the 'respectable', i.e. hypocritical, form that he puts on for a 'lady'. Perhaps the most revolting aspect of Crofts is his stupid self-complacency. His self-description is a very broad stroke indeed on Shaw's part. The audacity of it takes the breath away and even inspires awe – at the human capacity for self-flattering delusion which alone can account for the survival of society as it is:

> You wont find me a bad sort: I dont go in for being superfine intellectually; but Ive plenty of honest human feeling; and the old Crofts breed comes out in a sort of instinctive hatred of anything low, in which I'm sure youll sympathize with me.

Of course we *do* sympathize with that feeling, which is ours – shared with Vivie – as we look at him; it is disconcerting, to say the least, to find the loathsome creature speaking our sentiments. What Shaw is here preparing is the emotional reaction which will swing Vivie out of the acquiescent state her mother has brought her to. In Crofts's mouth 'Believe me, Miss Vivie, the world isnt such a bad place as the croakers make out', is an obviously false and vicious distortion of the doctrine of the relativity and interpenetration of good and evil. Moral judgements and the force of moral horror are not redundant after all, in a world where Crofts survives and flourishes. Shooting him is too good for him: 'Much more sportsmanlike to catch him in a trap.' But Vivie's horror of life as she now sees it cannot be satisfied with that.

The shocks that irrationally trigger Vivie's self-directed violence are: first, the discovery that the Warren–Crofts business is still operating and that she, Vivie, had always lived off it (Harry Trench's discovery in different terms); and then, releasing her from the paralysis brought on by the first and greater shock, the (probably false) revelation in which Crofts takes his revenge:

> Allow me, Mister Frank, to introduce you to your half-sister, the eldest daughter of the Reverend Samuel Gardner. Miss Vivie: your half-brother.[1]

Crofts himself is the simple instinctual answer to the questions that remain to be reasonably answered: What is horrible about the continuance of the business? And what is horrible in the prevailing economic and social structure to which the business in fact conforms? Translated, Crofts stands for the principle of idleness and waste and callousness, which society not merely tolerates but rewards, and the bullying attitude that feeds on the subjection of workers and women and is the antithesis of genuine authority. The irony of his revenge lies in the fact he does not recognize (and perhaps the others don't either) that the two young people, between them, are tarred with all these vices, and Vivie's suicidal impulse is a passionate counterpart of the ne'er-do-well philanderings of Frank. The latter's derision for 'the gospel of getting on', and the sporadic gambling which expresses his scorn for its morality, are abstainer's methods; and his airy repudiation of 'the old woman's money' (hardly likely to be put within his reach by her or her daughter) is as facile as Harry Trench's initial reaction and very different from Cusins's attitude to the Undershaft inheritance in *Major Barbara*. He tries to console the distressed Vivie with their old lovers' game of Babes in the Wood: 'Come and be covered up with leaves again.' Vivie's flight, at that, is from the spectre of a false innocence, hiding from the knowledge of

---

[1] I part company from Bentley in my reading of the relation between Frank and Vivie's reaction to this and their apparent easy dismissal of the matter in the last act. I judge Shaw's use of the incest motif in this play to be coolly deliberate and not confused at all.

its complicity in the evil of the world. But the address she runs to, 'Honoria Fraser's chambers, 67 Chancery Lane, for the rest of my life', is an equally bad alternative: the puritan's retreat from life into abstractions.

A neat stroke in the first Act lingers in the mind to point the futility of this flight:

> In that month at Chancery Lane I had opportunities of taking the measure of one or two women very like my mother.

Mrs Warren's attempt to save her child from contact with her own kind of life and dependence on men ('She would deny that it ever had a father if she could') has ended by turning the girl into an efficient and conscienceless machine. The mother's compromise with society, which involved bringing up Vivie 'wrong on purpose', has worked well for that society, which needs machines for actuarial calculations and conveyancing. The version of 'independence' which threatens the system least is the self-sterilizing, secessionist version. Vivie may succeed in making money, but she has apparently rejected power and turned money into the token that conceals guilt. Her final gesture, the tearing up of the note ('Goodbye, Frank'), completes her ceremonial sundering of human ties, her refusal of responsibility.

Frank Gardner is more astute than Vivie and tries to preserve her, early in Act III, from the fallacy on which the proposition, 'To understand all is to forgive all', rests. Indeed, her violently negative reaction at the end of the act might have been averted if she had had time to absorb Frank's criticism of the nauseating sentimentality of her new attitude to her mother and his questioning of the basis of the change:

> VIVIE. . . . If you knew the circumstances against which my mother had to struggle –
> FRANK (adroitly finishing the sentence for her). I should know why she is what she is, shouldnt I? What difference would that make? Circumstances or no circumstances, Viv, you wont be able to stand your mother.

'What difference would that make?' is the question the whole play propounds; and it implies an answer in terms of action. But the warning to Vivie that she was still dealing with evil and needed to be alertly discriminating is also apt reminder of her resemblance to her Aunt Liz, who is at home in a cathedral town and at county balls and deplores her sister's vulgarity:

> Liz used to be angry with me for plumping out the truth about it. She used to say that when every woman could learn enough from what was going on in the world before her eyes, there was no need to talk about it to her. But then Liz was such a perfect lady! She had the true instinct of it . . .

It is the difference between Vivie and Mrs Warren in manners and tastes
that is emphasized in Frank's slangy insistence on the slovenly 'form' of
Mrs Warren and 'her crew'. The ladylike fear of vulgarity,[1] which
matches the puritan's fear of evil and the idealist's fear of life, has no
small part to play in the daughter's ultimate repudiation of her mother;
it is perhaps Vivie's fatal weakness. 'Decency', Tanner-Shaw was to
write in *The Revolutionist's Handbook*, 'is Indecency's Conspiracy of
Silence'; Vivie never does shout out those two words that describe what
Mrs Warren is: 'Acquired notions of propriety are stronger than natural
instincts. It is easier to recruit for monasteries and convents than to induce
an Arab woman to uncover her mouth in public, or a British officer to
walk through Bond Street in a golfing cap on an afternoon in May.'
(*The Revolutionist's Handbook* again.)

It is the vulgarity of Mrs Warren that emerges as her greatest attraction, and her line, 'Lord help the world if everybody took to doing the
right thing', is the last unchallengeable note of truth in the play.[2] To
maintain, as Shaw surely desired, the complete attractiveness of Frank
Gardner, who is *not* a cynical bounder or as stupid as his father, his
flirtatious teasing of Mrs Warren must, in performance, bear out his
assertion of a natural bond between them – which she seals with a kiss that
scatters the irrelevances of age and conventional social relations. (Shaw's
devotion to his mother – or to a very different image from the one his
actual mother showed – speaks out clearly here.) The old reprobate is
naturally fonder of the 'young scamp' than of Vivie, with whom she
enacts a maternal sentiment that is fictitious because it is void of any
affection at all, not because – as with Frank – it is not purely maternal.
It is no inconsistency of character-drawing that Kitty Warren exudes
friendly good humour and warmth to men. A ready response to men and
a coldness to women are psychological determinants of her initial choice of
profession and her pursuit of it in its later form; she is a renegade from
the woman's cause, and the youthful murderous impulse towards her
virtuous sisters was prophetic. Her sentimentality with Vivie is a sign of
straining after something she wants that is beyond her capacity, not just
beyond her reach. 'Sentimentality', declares *The Revolutionist's Handbook*, 'is the error of supposing that quarter can be given or taken in

[1] See Shaw, *Collected Letters*, Vol. I, pp. 412–15 (letter to Grein on *Mrs
Warren's Profession*) and p. 720, inc.: 'I have smiled and told her [Helen
Kinnaird] she is too nice for Mrs Warren. She objects, not to its morality, but to
its vulgarity. Not at *all* stupid, isnt Helen.'

[2] I should like to acknowledge the revelation of the charm of Mrs Warren I
received from a performance by Mary Kerridge at the Theatre Royal, Windsor,
in 1968 – and the way it was crowned with the line: 'Imagine m e in a cathedral
town. Why, the very rooks in the trees would find me out . . .'

moral conflicts.' In her own way, Kitty is seeking after righteousness;
but her way, isolating her qualities of energy and industry and strong-
mindedness from her sensual warmth and zest for life, and forming
her daughter's character on those chosen lines alone, is as tragically
misguided as Sartorius's spoiling of Blanche – and has produced another
kind of 'lady'.

Shaw's choice of Ibsen's social plays as a constructional model for
Mrs Warren's Profession determined the balancing of the retrospective
dialogue between mother and daughter in Act II by a second in Act IV,
which reaches a different conclusion. He wanted the second encounter
because the parting between mother and daughter was vital to his
conception of the play; he was concerned with the tragic implications of
such a parting – and the tragedy might be judged the mother's and the
daughter's. But it is doubtful whether he had left himself enough
material for a second debate between the two. Ibsen's dramatic re-
examinations of past incident and motive (as in *Ghosts* and *Rosmersholm*)
carry the analysis deeper and the social indictment further than the
original exposition has done. This is hardly true of the second discussion
here. Only at one point, in her reaction to 'taught wrong on purpose',
does Vivie seem about to gain some new insight. Though Frank and
Praed have raised expectations of a battle royal, Act IV offers a much less
forceful interchange than Act II, and it may be that Shaw's consciousness
of failing is responsible for some touches of false rhetoric that easily fall
flat (and are not psychologically justifiable, as is Vivie's 'you are stronger
than all England', in Act II, which can be a vehicle for her emotional
naïveté). The dramatic disappointment, in that the breaking of the family
bond does not provide a genuinely passionate scene, is the effect of Shaw's
misjudgement of the nature of what he had to portray. To go for a big
scene was a mistake; the relationship between Vivie and her mother
properly peters out, it doesn't violently break – because so little was ever
there. The hint of an interesting dramatic intention comes across in the
old woman's attempt to play the scene melodramatically and Vivie's
refusal to play at all; the theatrical lameness appropriately underlines the
apparently revolutionary act – throwing over the parent – which proves
to be only a failure of sympathy and shedding of responsibility.

The dramatist has been guilty of an irresolution all the same, a
reluctance to give Mrs Warren the full honours emotionally that ends in
offering the *truth* of her in melodramatic style:

> From this time forth, so help me Heaven in my last hour, I'll do wrong and
> nothing but wrong. And I'll prosper on it.

And the attempt to have it both ways, as tragedy and comedy, is not
quite brought off, either, in the clash between Frank's assertion

> Never see her again! Hang it all, be reasonable. I shall come along as often
> as possible, and be her brother . . .

and the weight the fall of the curtain gives to Vivie's final act, the tearing
up of his note. Frank's rejection of romantic finality has already modified
the effect of his previous statement, 'I withdraw gracefully . . . I'll just
send her a little note after we're gone.' Bringing the writing and receipt
of the note within the bounds of the scene is an instance of technical
error in a very good play. Shaw was clearly tempted to emulate the
double ending, in which problem play and tragedy are combined, that
Ibsen narrowly achieved in *Ghosts*. But Vivie's situation is not as desperate
as Mrs Alving's, and Frank has made the point too recently for her final
gesture of self-isolation to suggest anything more than that the dramatist
could not leave well alone. The play does not admit of a full tragic close:
there is something forlorn about Vivie at the end, but she is alive and
young and may still learn. She and Praed and Frank (and possibly Frank's
mother, who never appears but accounts for his superiority to the
Reverend Samuel) are capable together of reaching another conclusion.
The 'gospel of art' may be adapted to greater moral concern with social
issues. The rejection of Roman filial piety, on which Frank insists, gets
a different interpretation in *Major Barbara*, where the two generations
are reconciled in a wary tension.

3

Tales for the Nursery

Cleopatra's complaint to Caesar, 'Oh, it is you who are a great baby: you make me seem silly because you will not behave seriously', expresses an unease familiar to many readers of Shaw and not unknown even in the theatre, though, as Brecht wrote apropos of Shaw:

> What draws people to the theatre is, strictly speaking, so much nonsense, which constitutes a tremendous buoyancy for those problems which really interest the progressive dramatic writer.[1]

The combination of playfulness with intellectuality that is characteristic of Shaw's drama seems, indeed, to have been deliberately cultivated by Brecht himself on the Shavian model. But Brecht's freedom from puritan inhibition establishes a certainty that we are dealing with *faux naïf*, rather than *naïf*; an impatient judgement on Shaw would more probably go the other way, and often has done.

Admittedly, a play like *Baal* is quite outside Shaw's range; such common terrors as sickness, old age, death, cruelty, poverty, love and sex are turned into nursery bogies in his plays (death, in *The Doctor's Dilemma*, is an obvious example), or are kept at bay by the benevolent wisdom of some grown-up character that stands like Bluntschli, or Caesar, between us and the reality. The usual *mise en scène* for his drama is comfortingly and familiarly domestic. When it is not, it tends to be stage exotic, inviting to a game of make-believe with actors dressed up in funny clothes. A great deal of what happens on stage in *Caesar and Cleopatra* might have been kindly devised for the amusement of little Ptolemy. At the other end of Shaw's career as playwright, *Geneva* takes us into Madame Tussaud's and disposes the waxworks of the famous in a merry charade. Even the Passion play of *Saint Joan* takes off from the

---

[1] Quoted from 'Ovation for Shaw', trans. G. H. W. Zuther, in R. J. Kaufmann (ed.), *G. B. Shaw*, p. 16, where it is reprinted from *Modern Drama*, Vol. II (1959), pp. 184–7. Originally published in *Berliner Börsen-Courier* (25 July 1926).

basis of charmed hens, ogre and Principal Boy. Bluebeard is appropriately included, the Duchess de la Trémouille is an Ugly Sister, and the Dauphin is a Clown. The dramatist's remark, 'My stories are the old stories, etc',[1] is often quoted without the attention it deserves being given to the fact that what amused him *as a boy* made the basis of the entertainment he offered to adult audiences.

At this distance of time, the idea of connecting *Arms and the Man* with an actual and recent war must be one of the last to occur to any audience.[2] Bluntschli's view of warfare as, for the most part, dull and prosaic, comes as short of the whole truth as Raina's notion of it as romantically adventurous. One glimpse of squalid agony intrudes amid the laughter:

> Shot in the hip in a woodyard. Couldnt drag himself out. Your fellows' shells set the timber on fire and burnt him, with half a dozen other poor devils in the same predicament.

Even here, the affectation of clipped phrasing carefully limits the possibilities of emotional response; and it is finally a metaphor of war that we are left with, not a realistic description. And it is a fairy-tale view of love, its other main topic, that the play offers: instead of the patent fraud of romantic extravagance, something pleasant and simple, without sexuality or psychological complexity. In his mockery of Sergius's heroics and his affection for Raina, Bluntschli, the corrective to illusion, himself conforms to a recognizable folk-tale, or fairy-tale, type: the plain, simple man who makes good, the little tailor, or the old soldier, or the simpleton.

The swiftly paced incident is needed to carry the childish jokes:

> RAINA. . . . I am a Petkoff.
> THE MAN. A pet what?

> PETKOFF. I dont believe in going too far with these modern customs. All this washing cant be good for the health: it's not natural . . . It all comes from the English . . . I dont mind a good wash once a week to keep up my position; but once a day is carrying the thing to a ridiculous extreme.

---

[1] See Introduction, page 1, note 2.

[2] Shaw's rejected Statement prepared for the Select Committee on Censorship and published in the Preface to *The Shewing-Up of Blanco Posnet* contains the remark: 'In other countries I have not come into conflict with the censorship except in Austria, where the production of a comedy of mine was postponed for a year because it alluded to the part taken by Austria in the Servo-Bulgarian war.' A manuscript letter to Siegfried Trebitsch (16 Jan. 1905), quoted in Martin Meisel, *Shaw and the Nineteenth-Century Theater*, pp. 190–1, declares: 'The first version of the play had no geography – nothing but a war with a machine gun in it. It was Sidney Webb who suggested the Servo-Bulgarian war. However, I adapted it to the historical and social facts of the time very carefully.'

The by-play over the library and the electric bell, the idea and the naming of the 'chocolate cream soldier' are equally childish in their appeal. When we come down to it, every stage trick in the clockwork mechanism of the play, including the simplified version of psychological conflict given in Sergius's doll-like reactions, and the equally simplified treatment of the sub-theme of social inequality, suggests a puppet-play for human actors, or a moving toy-shop.[1] The whole thing is family entertainment, like a traditional Christmas pantomime or a Punch-and-Judy show. (Significantly, Shaw avoided the music hall as a model.) There is nothing in it to disturb the sensibilities of a protected child, and most of it is well within the range of such a child's actual or imaginative experience. Perhaps it is best enjoyed by adults in the company of children, which can sanction a simplicity, an innocence of entertainment, that our sophistication would otherwise reject. Taken that way, it is certainly a restorative experience, as it takes out some of the starch that gets into every adult personality. But a comparison of it with Strindberg's *Miss Julie*, early identified as a source of Shaw's themes here,[2] makes it doubly clear that *Arms and the Man* aims at an innocuous effect.

A rationale of the childishness of Shavian drama is suggested in the Preface to *Three Plays for Puritans*, which argues that the theatre has been vitiated by the average Englishman's inability to play: 'He cannot even play cricket or football: he has to work at them.' In his deliberate exploitation of the play aspect of theatre, the sense of make-believe, Shaw was in effect reviving a medieval and Renaissance concept; the degree of his personal fitness to do so may be the root explanation of his superiority to his predecessors in the English theatre for over a century and the general lift he gave to the status of modern theatre and the art of comedy in particular. Play, in Shaw's use of the word, is very different from amusement: 'The moment you make his theatre a place of amusement instead of a place of edification, you make it, not a real playhouse, but a place of excitement for the sportsman and the sensualist.' Amusement is the relaxation of adults, and implies a condescension or decline from some superior earnestness of mind and behaviour; 'sensualist' introduces connotations of adult vice. Play is a child's activity, a child's

---

[1] Cf. Bergson's proposition in *Le Rire* – 'Les attitudes, gestes et mouvements du corps humain sont risibles dans l'exacte mesure où ce corps nous fait penser à une simple mécanique' – and his elaboration of it to take in the effect of a group of human figures behaving like marionettes and, finally, the whole mechanical aspect of comic structure.

[2] See M. M. Morgan, 'Strindberg and the English Theatre', *Modern Drama*, Vol. IV (1964), especially p. 172: 'Massingham, in his notice of the A.P.S. *Miss Julie*, alluded to the common belief that *Arms and the Man* had been influenced by the play . . .'

way of learning, whole-heartedly pursued; 'edification' is a pedantic word that clashes with 'play' as it suggests the presence of a teacher, directing or encouraging proceedings to some end beyond the child's comprehension. The clash has generated much of Shaw's drama, as it reflects the co-existence of child and adult within the one personality. It is in the sub-plot of *Arms and the Man* and the characters of Louka and Nicola that the presence of the teacher makes itself felt most directly. Caesar overtly takes on the role of teacher to the young Cleopatra. But *Pygmalion* is not the only Shaw play which demonstrates that the teacher may sometimes be foolish and the child show superior wisdom.

It is well known that Shaw did not seek out the company of children and that he was not much at ease with them. He cannot immediately be classed with Edward Lear, or Lewis Carroll; adults found him excellent and zestful company; and, even with the testimony of *My Dear Dorothea*, there is little enough in his life or work to suggest the Lolita-syndrome. Yet the flourishing of children's literature in the nineteenth century is a relevant background to his art: it was a refuge from, or a safe protest against, a rigidly conformist, authoritarian society; not effectively subversive in any outward way, it provided an exercise for shy and timid souls that kept them alive and resilient. The ease with which Shaw regressed to childishness can be regarded as a sign of psychological weakness and emotional immaturity; his awareness of the negative and cowardly aspect of his attitude to revolt is one source of the irony that runs through his plays. But he was able, as an artist, to turn the weakness to account. In the popular theatre of his youth he found a medium that the adult world did not take seriously, that the pious considered immoral, and intellectuals judged vulgar. Going to the theatre implied a release from normal responsibility to which he himself responded ebulliently with a liberated sense of fun and a gaiety sufficient in itself to ensure the happy endings that encourage hopefulness and restore energy for action. The nature of the response was a bond with playgoers who were neither Ibsenites nor Wagnerites. In quality, its keenness, freshness, good humour and intelligence were extraordinary: released within the frame of the play, it is this childishness that constitutes Shaw's genius. He used it as a means of attacking insidiously and openly every form of humbug and pretentiousness, including the unnaturalness of moral virtue that children (and Petkoff) instinctively detect even in the social ritual of washing. It works through its appeal, beneath custom and prejudice, to the clear-eyed, unsentimental child that survives, however tenuously, in every adult, and is certainly nourished by the enjoyment of Shaw in the theatre. It is, in Shavian theory, the teachable part, which any reformer needs to engage. Whether he himself was less adult than the rest of us, or less concerned to conceal and repudiate his childish qualities, or more conscious of them and respectful towards them, is at least debatable.

The plays testify to Shaw's recognition of how much of adult life is spent in trying to escape the consequences of childhood upbringing, or to repair the damage it did. (Praed says, 'you must have observed, Miss Warren, that people who are dissatisfied with their own upbringing generally think that the world would be all right if everybody were to be brought up quite differently.') His high admiration for Bunyan recognized the rare unity of consciousness, at once naïve and adult, which could address itself equally to all conditions of humanity. The innocence of the fun in his plays is an assertion of the *virtue* of the infant in opposition to 'the farce of parental wisdom' (Don Juan's phrase, borrowed by the Statue). It is one ground of his affinity with the *faux naïf* Blake, this belief in the uncorrupt mind of the child and the suspicion that the notion of disciplining children into social beings might be the most pernicious ever conceived by the human mind.

Whether there can be power without corruption is one general question at issue in *Caesar and Cleopatra*. No power is more absolute and tyrannical than that wielded in the nursery, where the innocent are injected with the corruption of their elders, as the malignant nurse, Ftatateeta, has injected Cleopatra with her evil. Caesar's mildness, integrity, patience and spirit of forgiveness are New Testament virtues opposed to the revenge and cruelty glorified by Ftatateeta. But the greatest of his virtues is also the one form of Christian humility Shaw never rejects: 'Except ye become as little children . . .' there is no entering the Shavian heaven. (The phrase is a recurrent theme in his letters to Alice Lockett.[1]) The principle at work, which sets aside the subjection of the child, is radically and sweepingly egalitarian.

If we resist the temptation to dismiss Blake's doctrine as hyperbolical, or plain mad, there is no doubt that it is dangerous. It may be objected that the Shavian innocence is pale beside the sword-like radiance of Blake's innocents, powered by dark subconscious forces of which Shaw remained unaware. Yet the abstract recognition that childish passion contains all the emotions of adult experience in peculiarly intense form is certainly illustrated in the characterization of Julia Craven and Blanche Sartorius. There is hardly a Shaw play which is not centrally concerned with the dark shadows of parental authority threatening, or repudiated by, the younger generation. But the danger is half-smothered: the ambiguousness of the parent–child, teacher–pupil relationship, the unconscious nature of the conflict, especially the child's failure to identify

[1] *Collected Letters*, Vol. I, pp. 65, 71, 72 especially.

4 *Mrs Warren's Profession*. Theatre Royal, Windsor, 1967 (see pp. 38 and 41).

5 Romance and realism in *Arms and the Man*.

(a) Laurence Olivier as Sergius Saranoff.

(b) Cyril Cusack as Bluntschl

the antagonist, these things constitute a large part of what Shaw was concerned to reveal. Blake's vision of innocence is centrally linked with his anarchic doctrine of sexual freedom. The absence of sexuality from the Shavian world of innocence balances its association (by Gloria Clandon, by Eve, perhaps by Vivie Warren) with shame and guilt. *Mrs Warren's Profession* went some way towards severing the conventional association between guilt and sex and assigning guilt where it more properly belonged. But the puritan conviction that eroticism is not innocent, not fit for children, played its part in inhibiting the utterance of those 'two words', the violent challenge to an evil society, not just by Vivie Warren, but by the dramatist himself. The character of Mrs Dudgeon in *The Devil's Disciple* bears the marks of discipleship to Ibsen as well as to Dickens, and a rational acceptance of Ibsen's view of the repression of natural affection as the root of evil; but not until *Back to Methuselah* did Shaw come to a full-scale critical exploration of his own irrational puritan assumptions.

Meanwhile, in *Arms and the Man*, the shift was made from the method of the Unpleasant Plays to an exploitation of make-believe that can be seen as an extension of the philanderer-character over the whole play, which is now similarly disengaged from reality. It contains in itself the explanation for the change of method. The mechanical toy-shop quality of the entertainment is appropriate to the presentation of the Petkoff household, revolving about Raina, the young woman of twenty-three, who acts less than seventeen. It is a nursery play by virtue of its theme as well as its style, contrasting, in Raina and Sergius, the vital young woman with a genuine capacity for play and the man whose awakening from innocent illusion is so recent as to render all reminders of childhood painful to him.

The theatrical concepts of the role, the disguise, the pose are associated with both Sergius and Raina. The terms of abuse that express the hero's disillusion are the traditional ones hurled by literalists at art: 'lie', 'fraud', 'sham' – and 'farce'. His self-torture is the delayed effect of imperfectly distinguishing between real and ideal:

SERGIUS. . . . how ridiculous! Oh, war! war! the dream of patriots and heroes! A fraud, Bluntschli. A hollow sham, like love.

and of a failure to recognize that the truth of human personality lies in its protean nature:

Which of the six is the real man? thats the question that torments me. One of them is a hero, another a buffoon, another a humbug, another perhaps a bit of a blackguard. And one, at least, is a coward . . .

Raina needs no reconciling to the fact that living involves acting and the exercise of creative imagination; she has no bad conscience about her

c

lies. She is in an obvious sense the most childish character in the play, but this does not prevent her from being Bluntschli's aptest pupil and making the transition from nursery to marriage, ignorance to wisdom, spoilt infancy to maturity, with painless ease. She can take up her mask and drop it at a signal, without discomposure, because her play-acting is deliberate, gratuitous and self-delighting, not in the least compelled by fear or desperate necessity.

Sergius, on the other hand, *is* motivated by a kind of fear: of disappointing expectations, including his own. The pragmatic morality of Bluntschli (and Louka) – 'It's all a question of the degree of provocation' – is beyond him; he is less well adapted to survive, as – but for luck – he would *not* have survived the notorious cavalry charge. His heroics and his adherence to the rigidities of form (abiding by his word) betray him into the power of Louka, the social climber and the predatory woman, who will play a game without disguise when it suits her advantage. This unattractive side of Louka is akin to the narrow and complete realism of Nicola, joyless and unaspiring, except to what is convertible into material value: a figure of the servility of servitude.

The more general consideration behind the treatment of individual characters is lightly sketched, but emerges with the neatness of a similitude near the end of the play:

> SERGIUS. . . . Ah well, Bluntschli, you are right to take this huge imposture of a world coolly.
> RAINA (*quaintly to Bluntschli, with an intuitive guess at his state of mind*). I daresay you think us a couple of grown-up babies, dont you?
> SERGIUS (*grinning savagely*). He does: he does. Swiss civilization nurse-tending Bulgarian barbarism, eh?
> BLUNTSCHLI (*blushing*). Not at all, I assure you. I'm only very glad to get you two quieted.

Viewed as a paradigm of growth from a primitive state of nature towards a more advanced civilization, the play reveals a similarity of theme to that explored in *Caesar and Cleopatra*. And those childish jokes are relevant: hygiene – and the washing spread out on the hedge – divided barbarism from sophistication; the library and the electric bell are tokens of alternative values, alternative goals towards which the emergent civilization may move. And Sergius represents the unhappy stage of transition: self-conscious and losing touch with nature. The rise and fall of classes, the see-saw of social movement, which is the theme of Strindberg's *Miss Julie*, is reflected in the alliance of Louka and Sergius, a subtly different phenomenon from the union of Raina, the child, with Bluntschli, the egalitarian democrat, representative of the classless society. It is mechanistic process that Strindberg's play illustrates, and its relation to power: the shifting of social balance between relative strength and weakness. This is what Sergius and Louka reflect.

Bluntschli anticipates Caesar as a type of the good nurse; there is no obvious parallel to Ftatateeta in *Arms and the Man*, as the bogies which the historical play acknowledges – especially cruelty and revenge – are more thoroughly excluded from the earlier play. Yet there is a sinister element in it passed off as deceptively innocuous. Shaw was moving towards *Candida* in associating it with the mother, Catherine, handsome and attractive in her absurdity as she is. The brief passage between mother and daughter when they are alone in Act II takes us as far as anything in the play from the mild and 'pleasant' humour that is generally pervasive. This is one of the moments when the dramatist has supplied for his actors a hint of psychological realities beneath the conventional pattern of burlesque, a hint that the characters are to be played not just as puppets, but trembling on the verge between puppet and human creature:

> RAINA (*with cool impertinence*). Oh, I know Sergius is your pet. I sometimes wish you could marry him instead of me. You would just suit him. You would pet him, and spoil him, and mother him to perfection . . .
> I always feel a longing to do or say something dreadful to him – to shock his propriety – to scandalize the five senses out of him . . .
> CATHERINE. And what should I be able to say to your father, pray?
> RAINA. . . . Oh, poor father! As if he could help himself. . .
> CATHERINE (*looking after her, her fingers itching*). Oh, if you were only ten years younger!

It is a glimpse of a real family which gives a sour edge to the joke of the name, Petkoff. Raina's unsparing audacity exposes the nature of the treatment that has kept Colonel Petkoff (the most completely stock character of the play) a perpetual boy. The sense of rivalry between mother and daughter has been equally clear, beyond the laughter, when Catherine's choric aside to her husband punctures the effect of Raina's entrance to greet the returned warriors:

> PETKOFF (*aside to Catherine, beaming with parental pride*). Pretty, isn't it? She always appears at the right moment.
> CATHERINE (*impatiently*). Yes: she listens for it. It is an abominable habit.

Catherine, it seems, is jealous of Raina's hold on her father's affections as well as feeding narcissistically on the girl's relationship to Sergius.

Unused as she is to any but the mother–child relation, a matter of power and possession, Catherine has left herself vulnerable to the fever of romantic imagination, from which Raina began to liberate herself with her first encounter with Bluntschli. At the beginning of the play, mother and daughter had been at one in their enthusiasm for Saranoff, though even there it was evident that Raina's was a reflection of her mother's and undermined already by a healthy scepticism:

> CATHERINE. A great battle at Slivnitza! A victory! And it was won by Sergius. . . .
>   Cant you see it, Raina: our gallant splendid Bulgarians with their swords and eyes flashing, thundering down like an avalanche . . .
> RAINA. . . . it came into my head just as he was holding me in his arms and looking into my eyes, that perhaps we only had our heroic ideas because we are so fond of reading Byron and Pushkin, and because we were so delighted with the opera that season at Bucharest. Real life is so seldom like that . . . Only think, mother: I doubted him . . .

The significance of giving to Catherine the entrance which starts the play into action is becoming clear: '*imperiously energetic, with magnificent black hair and eyes*', runs the author's description, a possible first sketch for Orinthia in *The Apple Cart*; the spirit which leads to war for patriotism and glory is personified in Catherine, who does not fight but seeks the satisfaction of the ambition proper to her imperial name (*Great Catherine* was nearly twenty years off) vicariously through her menfolk. How she sees herself is unambiguously conveyed:

> PETKOFF. . . . What more could I do?
> CATHERINE. You could have annexed Serbia and made Prince Alexander Emperor of the Balkans. Thats what I would have done.
> PETKOFF. I dont doubt it in the least, my dear. But I should have had to subdue the whole Austrian Empire first . . .

It is from Louka that the most nearly similar note is heard:

> . . . if I were Empress of Russia, above everyone in the world, then!! . . . I would marry the man I loved, which no other queen in Europe has the courage to do.

Louka is closer than Catherine to an understanding of what Bluntschli represents: common humanity, the factor which all men and women, servants and masters, children and parents, share equally; but it is an understanding that bears critically on society, without irradiating and transforming her own personality at all. She will dominate Sergius, domesticate him, and keep her contempt for his servitude and his merely verbal courage:

> SERGIUS. . . . Oh, (*fervently*) give me the man who will defy to the death any power on earth or in heaven that sets itself up against his own will and conscience: he alone is the brave man.
> LOUKA. How easy it is to talk! Men never seem to grow up: they all have schoolboy's ideas.

Even Raina is not exempt from the dramatist's suspicion of the power of women over men. Apart from the unflattering view of her that

Louka's opinion gives, the image of the 'chocolate cream soldier', doubly associated with the sweet tooth of childhood through the fib of the ice pudding, contains, latent, an omen of the tigerish woman who devours her mate. But here it is Bluntschli's character as beneficent nurse, tending her growth in dispassionate enlightenment, that is threatened by her infant greed, as Cleopatra proves dangerous to Caesar.[1]

It is not often that a woman plays the role of teacher in Shaw's plays (cf. *Too True* and *On the Rocks*). Yet it is so in *Captain Brassbound's Conversion*, where the character of Lady Cicely is coloured by his response to an actual benevolent and very attractive person: Ellen Terry, for whom he designed the part.

Captain Brassbound's Conversion is one of the plays (*The Devil's Disciple* is another) in which Shaw's relish for the conventional mode he has borrowed comes near to swamping his originality. Not until half-way through Act II do we find adventure plot and Shavian theme knitting together, as they do throughout *Arms and the Man*. Before this, the dramatist relies almost entirely on the character of Felix Drinkwater to keep at bay the boredom of the *Boy's Own* adventure story; and if Drinkwater carries us a little further from *Beau Geste* in the direction of W. S. Gilbert, he remains very much a theatrical type: the Cockney rascal who lives by his wits, too lazy to work, but thoroughly at home in this world as a hypocritical parasite, existed in the comedy of Ben Jonson and, translated into Irish terms, survives in the comedy team of Captain Boyle and Joxer in *Juno and the Paycock*.

The fact that audiences today have little taste for the convention Shaw chose as his vehicle in this play is a considerable production hazard. The humour is broader, the wit rarer, the pace slower than in *Arms and the Man*, with the consequence that the later play can seem far more wooden, much more of an illustration of an idea with the aid of puppets than that first of the Plays Pleasant. To some extent the woodenness is deliberate: it is the mark of the *poseur*: in the ne'er-do-wells masquerading as brigands; in Brassbound's un-self-knowing pursuit of revenge, reflecting in reverse Sir Howard Hallam's equally un-self-knowing service of the ideal of justice. There are, indeed, three styles employed to relate these figures: conventional naturalism for Hallam, the norm accepted by the society to which the audience belongs; melodrama for Brassbound, the conventional antagonist who proves to be the mirror-image of that norm, with the evil and savage elements more blackly

---

[1] For some further discussion of *Caesar and Cleopatra*, see below, Chapter 14, especially pp. 241–4.

outlined; and the chorus which burlesques melodrama and prepares for
the deflation, first of the effigy, Brassbound, and then of the ultimate
focus of attention, the Judge.

Shaw had hoped to interest Irving in his play, as well as Ellen Terry;
and he not only created, in Brassbound, the kind of melodramatic role
that Irving was able to invest with tragic grandeur, he managed to
include some tones of an Irving production of Shakespeare. Lady Cicely
Wayneflete and Captain Brassbound, in relation to each other and the
general dramatic context, reflect two Shakespearian roles on which
Irving and Ellen Terry had left their mark most distinctively: Shylock
and Portia. Shaw's play shares the theme of justice with *The Merchant
of Venice* and Brassbound's wild justice of revenge, like Shylock's, opposes
to the official law a caricature of itself; though she leaves the seat of
judgement to the woodenest figure in the play, the American Kearney,
Lady Cicely as witness and prosecutor determines the verdict as surely as
Portia does, and her plea is Portia's: for mercy tempering justice. It is
the plea of New Testament Christianity exposing, in each case, the fraud
of an officially Christian society. The opening of the play, with its
presentation of Rankin, the Scots missionary, confronted by his sham
convert, Drinkwater, the pirate, anticipates the main exposure the play
moves towards. In place of Shakespeare's Jews, the counter-religion and
civilization here is that of the Moors, among whom Rankin has not been
able to make a single convert, though he has come to be known among
them for his virtue as 'the Christian who is not a thief'.

The very euphemism, 'gentlemen of fortune', applied to Brassbound's
crew, insinuates that they are intended as caricatures of those who
succeed within the law, in capitalist society. (They anticipate Mendoza
and his brigands of the Sierra in *Man and Superman*.) They give themselves away thoroughly in the last act when, invited to jump on the
glossy top hat that Brassbound has been wearing, their awe of the thing
prevails and puts an end to their fooling. The hat, and the rest of the
respectable gentleman's garb in which he has appeared in the court, has
been supplied by Lady Cicely from her luggage. The author's comment
on Brassbound's appearance in this garb corresponds neatly to his
observation, in other plays, of the taming effect women exert upon men:

> To an unsophisticated eye, the change is monstrous and appalling; and its
> effect on himself is so unmanning that he is quite out of countenance – a
> shaven Samson.

But the difference, here, is that the woman is acting as the dramatist's
delegate: putting Brassbound in the costume that will confuse the conventional morality of his judges; turning him, morality-play fashion,

into the kind of pirate – respectably dressed – that society accepts, without altering his inner nature: '*out of countenance*' shows a careful choice of words, and so does the sentence that follows:

> *Lady Cicely, however, is greatly pleased with it; and the rest regard it as an unquestionable improvement.*

She is pleased with the success of the illusion she has produced, knowing it illusion, and employing it as a trick to secure Brassbound's acquittal – as Shaw employs it for the moral enlightenment of the audience; her whole function in the play exonerates her from any suspicion of sharing that illusion or thinking it any improvement at all on the natural man.

For all the conceptual correspondence of the unmanning of Brassbound to Strindberg's Captain, calling for his lion skin and being given a shawl, Lady Cicely is as little like Laura as any character in Shaw's work. Essentially she does *not* 'unman' Brassbound, but the opposite: she restores the natural man to dominion. The 'unmanned' effigy reveals the price men themselves choose to pay for social acceptance. Reducing Brassbound to a child, shedding child's tears, is this time only a means of releasing him from the evil effects of his first childhood, which he finally admits was a hell of unhappiness with a drunken and crazy mother. There are shades in the dialogue between Sir Howard and Brassbound about the latter's mother which recall Old Werle with Gregers, in *The Wild Duck*, on the late Mrs Werle whose mind was often clouded. Lady Cicely becomes, in fact, the good mother through whom Brassbound is reborn. And it is as a consequence of her treatment that we hear from him, towards the end, an adult voice speaking with unrhetorical seriousness:

> . . . nothing makes a man so selfish as work. But I was not self-seeking: it seemed to me that I had put justice above self . . .
>
> You have taken the old meaning out of my life; but you have put no new meaning into it. I can see that you have some clue to the world that makes all its difficulties easy for you; but I'm not clever enough to seize it. Youve lamed me by shewing me that I take life the wrong way when I'm left to myself.
>
> . . . My uncle is no worse a man than myself – better, most likely . . . My mother would have opened anybody else's eyes: she shut mine. I'm a stupider man than Brandyfaced Jack even; for he got his romantic nonsense out of his penny numbers and such like trash; but I got just the same nonsense out of life and experience . . .

It is the same healthy and tranquil sobriety that we hear from Lady Cicely herself in the moments when she can afford to be honest in word as well as honest at heart. It is not the sense of being let down, but the sense of being given solid ground to stand on and clear light to see by that comes when she caps Sir Howard's 'You have made me your accomplice in defeating justice' with 'Yes: arnt you glad it's been defeated for once?'

Of course, the inner integrity is matched by an outer deviousness as considerable as Raina's. Though Lady Cicely's lies are altruistic, while Raina's are innocently egotistic, it is an altruism that works by compromise and conspiracy within the frame of established society. The point is driven home in the last act by the repeated trick of Redbrook, the gentleman-brigand, silencing Drinkwater: 'Shut up, you fool.' For Drinkwater at the farce of a trial is the fool from whose mouth the truth comes forth, or the child who threatens to expose the fiction of the Emperor's New Clothes. It is the same phrase as is used in Archer's version of *The Wild Duck* by Relling, the nurturer of life through illusion, to silence Mollvik's pious declamation over the death of Hedvig. The coincidence, or echo, whichever it is, reveals Shaw's intention of creating in Lady Cicely a similarly paradoxical figure, whose realism admits and works through creative imagination and make-believe.

The last line of the play ('LADY CICELY. How glorious! how glorious! And what an 'escape!') is, of course, the cry of the comic spirit at the final breaking of the illusion that is the play, as well as the philanderer's cry as the nets of love and marriage and responsibility fail to hold him (or her). But this time the escape is not onesided, an escape of the prisoner from the gaoler. For Lady Cicely has not refused marriage to Brassbound; the firing of his ship's guns has let him release her and drawn him away; a trance like that in which Tanner and Ann Whitefield are bound to each other is broken here by a call to action. It is Brassbound's escape, too, and seems less a running away than Marchbanks's escape at the end of *Candida*:

> BRASSBOUND (*He kneels and takes her hands*). You can do no more for me now: I have blundered somehow on the secret of command at last (*he kisses her hands*): thanks for that, and for a man's power and purpose restored and righted. And farewell, farewell, farewell.

The slight falseness of style, the return of stage rhetoric, exposes a certain gap between the idea of the fable and its imaginative realization. (Shaw understood more than he could feel and live out.) But the idea is plain: the good mother does not hold her child by outward bonds or emotional chains; and 'one of the Idealists – the Impossibilists!' who has been purged of false illusions will try a form of action that is not compromise. (He has already called out, iconoclastically: 'Stand by, all hands, to jump on the captain's tall hat.') When we meet Brassbound next, in his old age, his name will be Shotover, but he will remember his West Indian background, his old, unregenerate secret of command (force and terror) and will persist in his convention of nautical imagery:

BRASSBOUND. . . . I wasnt unhappy, because I wasnt drifting. I was steering a course and had work in hand . . .

BRASSBOUND. In my world a man can navigate a ship and get his living by it.

SHOTOVER. . . . Let a man drink ten barrels of rum a day, he is not a drunken skipper until he is a drifting skipper. Whilst he can lay his course and stand on his bridge and steer it, he is no drunkard . . .

Lady Cicely's secret, which Brassbound learns, is detachment from idolatry: 'I have never been in love with any real person; and I never shall.' Both, in fact, know the ideal for what it is and do not, finally, reject it because it is neither real nor realizable. But their worlds remain apart. Brassbound's simple statement, 'I dont like being patronized', is the child's statement of independence of its parents, and the poor citizen's rejection of the most benevolent of autocrats along with the worst. It is Lady Cicely, Hallam's 'deceased wife's sister' (something of a step-sister to lawful authority), the reformer who is not a revolutionary, who is ultimately the more bound:

In my world, which is now your world – ou r world – getting patronage is the whole art of life . . .

But she does not oppose, or decry, the other way.

Androcles and the Lion can be classified as a by-product of Shaw's work on *Major Barbara*. Ferrovius's methods of conversion recall Todger Fairmile's way with Bill Walker (see below, pp. 147, 154):

FERROVIUS. . . . A young man . . . scoffed at and struck me as you scoffed at and struck me. I sat up all night with that youth wrestling for his soul; and in the morning not only was he a Christian, but his hair was as white as snow . . .

It is conversion by force and terror, easy to contrast with Lady Cicely's guileful way of converting Brassbound, and easy to dismiss as no conversion at all. But the matter is not quite so simple. There is a principle of justice involved (as in *Captain Brassbound's Conversion*), the fulfilment of which leaves the offender free. Ferrovius, in effect, proposes to return blow for blow, though the return comes not in anger but in love and asks for acceptance:

> . . . try for yourself whether our way is not better than yours. I will now strike you on one cheek; and you will turn the other and learn how much better you will feel than if you gave way to the promptings of anger.

The Centurion's suggestion that the quarrel be compounded for money is treated by Ferrovius as only peripherally relevant: he throws the coin to a beggar as fulfilment in deed, though not intention, of the Christian precept, 'Give all thou hast to the poor', and at once returns to his mode of persuading Lentulus to value spiritual things more than the things of the body:

> I may hurt your body for a moment; but your soul will rejoice in the victory of the spirit over the flesh . . . I saved his soul. What matters a broken jaw?

The blow is not, in fact, given (the beating up of Bill Walker who has gone to seek it for the good of his soul is not visually presented): no harm is done; a little respect has been inculcated by playing on the young man's fear of bodily hurt, a natural fear. The stick is shown, but not used.

The incident is a minor, telescoped version of the principal action that the play presents: the victory of the Christians over Roman tyranny, acknowledged by a similar token conversion of the Empire to Christianity. Ferrovius and the lion contribute equally to this result through the Emperor's admiration for the first and fear of the second, that amounts to a valuing of force, the reality on which the Roman Empire was based. Ferrovius, of course, is a human lion with velvet paws: *not* tamed, in that his teeth and claws and fury remain ready in time of need. But the strength of the physically weak man, whom love and compassion and respect for the *nature* of every creature endow with courage, wins the friendly respect of the lion. It is the kind of strength Christianity itself opposed to Rome, but the courage Androcles and the lion share indicates that it *is* a strength. Much of the heartening laughter the play exacts is a response to the rejection of masochism, along with cruelty; a response to the surprising robustness and joyousness of Ferrovius's cry: 'Join us. Come to the lions. Come to suffering and death.' In his mouth it is a militant cry – to face life without fear and with exultation.

The 'romantic' element in the play is scaled down to the rest, yet is more than a cipher: the prospect of an alliance between Lavinia and the Captain has a similar value to the alliance of Barbara with Cusins, though it has not the same fullness of implication. And it is Lavinia who is made the spokeswoman for the idea in the play: the recognition of the spiritual thing that can make the suffering of life bearable and the striving more than naturally joyous, the sense of a reality greater than the mind of any man can conceive:

> What he would have called my faith has been oozing away minute by minute whilst Ive been sitting here, with death coming nearer and nearer, with reality becoming realler and realler, with stories and dreams fading away into nothing;
>
> If it were for anything small enough to know, it would be too small to die for. I think I'm going to die for God. Nothing else is real enough to die for.

Shaw has not complicated this play with a cry for the Superman. Lavinia is not reduced to mother-woman; and the Superman would be 'too small'. Neither she nor Barbara is egotistically fixated on the image of her individual mission and prepared to sacrifice all others to it. Lavinia is more properly one with the band of Christians.

Of course, it is Androcles, in the play's Prologue, who initiates the action that ends in reconciling Christ and Rome. He is the clown encountering the pantomime lion (and Shaw plays on his likeness to that other brave little tailor of fairy tale). Even at the first, his pathos is modified by his humour, his detached, frank, amused view of the situation that enables him to keep his end up, the satisfaction his mind gives him when he contemplates the miserable, stupid bullying of his wife:

> MEGAERA. A man ought to think of his wife sometimes.
> ANDROCLES. He cant always help it, dear. You make me think of you a good deal. Not that I blame you.
> MEGAERA. Blame me! I should think not indeed. Is it my fault that I'm married to you?
> ANDROCLES. No, dear: that is my fault.
> MEGAERA. Thats a nice thing to say to me. Arnt you happy with me?
> ANDROCLES. I dont complain my love.
> MEGAERA. You ought to be ashamed of yourself.
> ANDROCLES. I am, my dear.

Down to the last equivocation that is the kind of dialogue Shakespeare wrote for Touchstone and Audrey. The convention supports an unscrupulous delight in Androcles' shedding of this burden – and the dramatist's 'callousness' in telling us nothing of Megaera's ultimate fate – in order to dance with the lion right out of this world and its cares: for the pantomime dance, here, is also a paradisial image. The casual dismissal of the burden of torment has been necessary first, strengthening us in our ability to dismiss the worthless and miserable elements in ourselves, instead of hugging them to us in fearful self-love. And the childish joy in the absurd, uplifted right out of the everyday, is an emotion well matched after all to the contemplation of divine perfection.

Shaw cannot be accused this time of hiding from the children he addresses the horrors life may hold. The relation of force to sadism (a connection he will have recognized in *The Sign of the Cross*[1]) is admitted in the Captain's words:

> The men in that audience tomorrow will be the vilest of voluptuaries: men in whom the only passion excited by a beautiful woman is a lust to see her tortured and torn shrieking limb from limb. It is a crime to gratify that passion.

This is a condemnation of every cult of virgin martyrs and a recognition of something vicious in the submission to such torture as many virgin saints have been credited with. (There is irony in the immediate relevance of the word 'audience' in the theatre. Not all are there from worthy motives; some have to be restored to the pure feelings of childhood.) It is significant that the Roman gods who figure most largely in the text are Mars and Diana, to whom Ferrovius and Lavinia are human counterparts. Diana, to whom Lavinia could consider sacrificing, can serve as a symbolic figure of woman's integrity and independence of spirit. But Androcles does not forget that Diana is also the huntress. Shaw refrains from direct reference to the legend of Actaeon, torn to pieces at Diana's command; but this latent association is relevant to our sense of the possibility of perversion in every ideal. The statue of Mars, as Lavinia describes it, is very different from the true god of Ferrovius, a man of iron as his name proclaims him:

> . . . an iron statue that has become the symbol of the terror and darkness through which they walk, of their cruelty and greed, of their hatred of God and their oppression of man . . .

The Christianity of Ferrovius and Lavinia and Androcles is no worship of cruelty, greed, suffering, poverty, or death; it puts these in their place in a determined pursuit of the good. The Captain's understanding of things marks him as destined to be of their company:

> The hand that holds the sword has been trained not to come back from anything but victory.

What is implied is not only the value of determined perseverance, but a refusal to romanticize failure.[2]

Shaw's Cinderella play, *Pygmalion*, falls into the present category of Nursery Tales; but it is also organized as a problem play and will be

[1] See Meisel, op. cit., pp. 334–48.

[2] The moral is the same as was expounded through Anthony Anderson in *The Devil's Disciple*, like Ferrovius a Christian who discovers that his natural militancy cannot be subdued to any doctrine of submission.

discussed alongside *The Doctor's Dilemma* as an example of that type. For the present it will serve as a reminder that Shaw alternated between 'heavyweight' plays (such as *Man and Superman* or *Major Barbara*), embodying private conflicts and needing a battery of arguments to aid in their resolution, and limpid, relatively brief fable plays, in the early and middle years of his playwriting career. With Blake in mind, we may identify the distinction as between Plays of Experience and Plays of Innocence. The latter are not shallow, but they are fruits of a struggle that rages within the plays of Experience. As they are less taxing to audiences they have undoubtedly served to widen the range of Shaw's influence. In his old age, when it was more difficult for him to rally the power for major struggles, the simpler plays predominate over the complex type: but it is a strange and original simplicity, reflected in plots which are fantastic in a new and less predictable way.

4

The Virgin Mother

Though written close in time to *Arms and the Man*, *Candida* follows the naturalistic lines of *Mrs Warren's Profession* but with a more limited admixture of farce than operates in the earlier play. In some ways *Candida* is a bad play, with excruciatingly written passages. Yet its reputation as an important work in the Shavian canon is deserved. It nags at the reader's mind with the urgency of its author's deep involvement in his material and the elaborate strategy he adopted to stand free of it and get it under control. (The selective emphases of production may make it appear simpler than it does to the mind wrestling with its complexities in the study.) Finally it stands as a coherent structure that makes a rich, disturbing and wide-ranging communication. But the record of the author's struggle to explore, understand and objectively present the drama in his personal consciousness, involving the image of Woman and the idea of public responsibility, is built into the play.

The Preface to *Plays Pleasant* indicates Shaw's later recognition of what had taken place. The stress it lays on pre-conscious elements in the artistic process provides ground for questioning the common opinion that Shavian drama is an art of open statement, a rationally conceived and controlled didactic drama without any intimate, subjective resonance. Immediately, we are confronted by the perplexing and insufficiently discussed claim that *Candida* is in some sense a Pre-Raphaelite play:[1]

> To distil the quintessential drama from pre-Raphaelitism, medieval or modern, it must be shewn at its best in conflict with the first broken, nervous, stumbling attempts to formulate its own revolt against itself as it develops into something higher. A coherent explanation of any such revolt, addressed intelligibly and prosaically to the intellect, can only come when the work is done, and indeed *done with*: that is to say, when the development, accomplished, admitted, and assimilated, is a story of yesterday.
>
> (*Author's italics*)

---

[1] Recent exceptions to this neglect have been Elaine B. Adams, 'Bernard Shaw's Pre-Raphaelite Drama', *Publications of the Modern Language Associa-*

So far, this sets in perspective the conflict presented in the play between the middle-aged Christian Socialist parson, James Mavor Morell, and the young poet, Eugene Marchbanks. The phrase, 'its own revolt against itself', focuses attention on the close symbolic relation between the antagonists. Shaw goes on to write of art more generally in relation to the evolving consciousness of mankind:

> Long before any such understanding can be reached, the eyes of men begin to turn towards the distant light of the new age. Discernible at first only by the eyes of the man of genius, it must be focussed by him on the speculum of a work of art, and flashed back from that into the eyes of the common man. Nay, *the artist himself has no other way of making himself conscious of the ray: it is by a blind instinct that he keeps on building up his masterpieces* . . . He cannot explain it: he can only shew it to you as a vision in the magic glass of his artwork; so that you may catch his *presentiment* and make what you can of it.   (*My italics*)

The Preface then slides back from this consideration of the artist as maker of the play (the truncated quotation omits a mention of Ibsen) to the portrait of the artist *in* the play. The shift is a reminder that the relative degree of self-projection to ironic distancing in Shaw's presentation of the young poet is one critical question that must be raised in any discussion of *Candida*. But more immediately to the point is the implication that this play was written out of a 'presentiment' by 'a blind instinct', and that the truth it had to tell was only fully evident to the author himself at the end of the task.

Over three-quarters of a century later, the conventionality of *Candida* is more striking than the 'revolt' it contains. It is a domestic play, and its audacities are such in reference to the respectable manners and values of everyday life in late Victorian England. The plot reflects the popularity of such social intrigue drama as Sardou's *Divorçons*. The action is centrally devoted to a love triangle: a young intruder into a happy marriage presents his challenge and departs, leaving husband and wife to take up their relationship on a new basis of understanding. Instead of playing up the titillating possibilities of the adultery motif, Shaw has chosen to develop the thesis-character of the play in an analysis of the actual role of woman in contemporary English society. As he himself later pointed out, *Candida* presents a view antithetical to that of Ibsen's *Doll's House*:[1] instead of woman as the immature plaything of man,

---

tion, Vol. LXXXI (1966), pp. 428–58, and Louis Crompton, *Shaw the Dramatist* (Lincoln, Nebraska: University of Nebraska Press, 1969), especially pp. 32, 33, 39.

[1] Letter in the *Evening Standard* (30 Nov. 1944): '. . . the play is a counterblast to Ibsen's *Doll's House*, showing that in the real typical doll's house it is the man who is the doll.'

Shaw emphasizes her maternal aspect, her influence over men and their dependence on her strength. 'The hand that rocks the cradle rules the world' was hardly a revolutionary conclusion in itself, or any reason to support the cause of female emancipation – as long as the question of how well or ill the world was ruled was kept obscure.

It is raised quite plainly in *Candida* between Morell and his father-in-law, Burgess, but then seems to be thrust aside and forgotten. The Preface explains how the dramatist rejected the idea of a straight conflict between Christian Socialism and 'vulgar Unsocialism': 'In such cheap wares I do not deal,' he protested. Yet the character of Burgess, the petty capitalist, is retained in the play, unnecessary as he seems to the development of the action. Not only is he there as an element in the idea-plot; a fact largely ignored by commentators on the play is that Candida is Burgess's daughter, as well as Morell's wife. And, while similarities and contrasts to *A Doll's House* are in mind, it should be remarked that one character, though not here the wife, does leave the home for the world at the close of the play: the young poet, Eugene, whose heroics emphasize the importance of the moment, though they have a less impressive effect than the quiet decision of Nora's going:

> MARCHBANKS (*rising with a fierce gesture of disgust*). Ah, never. Out, then, into the night with me!
> . . . (*with the ring of a man's voice – no longer a boy's – in the words*) I know the hour when it strikes. I am impatient to do what must be done . . .
> I no longer desire happiness: life is nobler than that. Parson James: I give you my happiness with both hands: I love you because you have filled the heart of the woman I loved. Goodbye. . . . Let me go now. The night outside grows impatient.

At this point one is inclined to assent to the criticism Edward Carpenter made when Shaw first read the play to a group of friends at Henry Salt's: that it wouldn't do, that the central characters and the whole play rang false.[1] Certainly the conventional idiom of late nineteenth-century drama is not a sufficiently authentic language to disperse the falsities of late nineteenth-century attitudes and sentiments. Earlier in the play

---

[1] See Stephen Winsten, *Henry Salt and His Circle* (London: Hutchinson, 1951), p. 105. But it may be remarked that there is a resemblance between Eugene's rhetoric here and the rhetoric Ibsen wrote for Ulric Brendel, taking his leave of Rosmer and Rebecca. Ibsen uses the style simultaneously to carry off a satire of the speaker and to transport his play to an area of experience where naturalism is irrelevant. Improving on his 1894 draft, Shaw introduced near the end of Act I a touch that forcibly recalls the unsubtly symbolic words and gestures of Lona Hessel who is instrumental in recovering the true man within Consul Bernick in *Pillars of Society*: 'I'll force it to the light,' Eugene threatens Morell, and there the hysterical exaggeration of the words has a properly comic impact as they fit the gauche adolescent Eugene certainly is at that point.

Shaw has used the young poet's jibes to expose the unreal or inflated sentiment in Morell's rhetoric; but at the end his burlesque impulses were inhibited with the result that Marchbanks as hero is less convincing than he has been in his previous roles of innocent fool and mischievous imp. *Candida* here seems a less mature play artistically than *Mrs Warren's Profession*, possibly because the objectivity Shaw there preserved through the medium of Frank Gardner had to be given up for a confrontation of the forces limiting his personal maturity.

Candida has given Eugene the opportunity to play out his dismissal as his own rejection of what he is denied. The ambiguousness of his relation to her and what she represents is shown visually when, at her call, he kneels to receive her kiss, before leaving the stage to the final tableau: the embrace of husband and wife, alone together in their home. A modern actor can carry off Eugene's final lines without alienating a present-day audience, if he underplays them, perhaps half-humorously. But such a technique can hardly blend with the ritualistic effect in which naturalism is transcended, that Shaw seems to have been aiming at here: a weighted acknowledgment of the power of Candida over the youth in 'revolt' ('the higher but vaguer and timider vision, the incoherent, mischievous and even ridiculous unpracticalness' recognized in the Preface) as well as over the middle-aged man, acknowledging his weakness before her strength. The conflicts in which the play is rooted are not resolved in this ending, only distanced and stilled in an aesthetic transformation. The commonsense view of Candida expressed by Morell's secretary, Prossy, has no place here:

> She's very nice, very good-hearted: I'm very fond of her, and can appreciate her real qualities far better than any man can.

Realism has been abandoned for the iconography of a subjective truth.

The text of *Candida* as it originally appeared in *Plays Pleasant*, dated 1895, has the descriptive subtitle, 'A Mystery,' in place of the more straightforward designation, 'A Domestic Play in Three Acts', found in the autograph longhand version begun on 2 October 1894, and completed on 7 December of the same year.[1] To match this substitution Shaw added the allusion, in Eugene's final speech, to the 'better secret' in his heart and the final authorial comment on Morell and Candida: '*But they do not know the secret in the poet's heart.*' So he emphasized the enigmatic nature of his play and, punningly in that subtitle, the sacred character of the enigma.

He carefully and consistently cultivated uncertainties and ambiguous

[1] Manuscript in the British Museum (Addit. MS. 50603 A–C).

effects by other means. Simple stylistic devices do some of the work: the suspended sentence is an actor's tool for suggesting a more complex response than statement can convey (e.g. 'MARCHBANKS. Nothing. I—'; 'CANDIDA. Oh, James: did you—'), or raising questions in the spectator's mind which perhaps could be, but are not, simply answered (e.g. 'MORELL (*excitedly*). And she refused. Shall I tell you why she refused? I can tell you, on her own authority. It was because of—'). Walter King, in 'The Rhetoric of *Candida*' in *Modern Drama*, II (1959, 71–83), has noted Shaw's extensive use of verbal reiteration in this play. Among the single words that occur over and over again, in counterpoint, 'understand' is very prominent.[1] Understanding each other and the situation is a task the characters set themselves and often fail in. Their bafflement challenges the audience to do better, and the addition of a line spoken by Lexy to Morell to the first draft of Act I, as the first link in the chain of repetition, directs attention early to the central perplexity:

> LEXY (*smiling uneasily*). It's so hard to understand you about Mrs Morell—

The words 'lie' and 'truth', 'shy', 'dumb', 'secret' contribute similarly to the verbal patterning of the dialogue and sometimes make a thematic pattern with variant, synonymous expressions (e.g. 'cannot speak', 'cannot utter a word', 'talk about indifferent things', 'hold your tongue'). Such details fall into place against a background of Ibsenite naturalism in the European theatre, as they evoke the already conventional view (even if it was still an *avant-garde* convention) of a hypocritical society brazenly defiant of what men in their hearts know to be true and their own individual authenticity.[2] In the first moments of the play, Morell exposes a conventional form of doublethink that keeps truth at bay by not taking words seriously:

> MORELL. . . . You see theyre near relatives of mine.
> PROSERPINE (*staring at him*). Relatives of y o u r s!
> MORELL Yes: we have the same father – in Heaven.
> PROSERPINE (*relieved*). Oh, is that all?
> MORELL (*with a sadness which is a luxury to a man whose voice expresses it so finely*). Ah, you dont believe it. Everybody says it: nobody believes it: nobody.

The staple technique of verbal counterpoint presents us with a dialogue that is notably a game with words, a patterned fabric rather than a

---

[1] 'She said I'd understand; but I dont'; 'she will understand me, and know that I understand her'; 'I cant understand you, Miss Garnett'; 'What do you understand?' – 'I cant understand it'; 'how little you understand me'; 'you understand nothing', etc.

[2] See Maurice Valency, *The Flower and the Castle*, Universal Library Edition (New York: Grosset, 1966), pp. 106, 112–14.

transparent medium of communication. Words may conceal more than they reveal. What characters say may be at odds with what they think; and indeed nothing that is said can be accepted without question. The method is appropriate to naturalistic characterization as it implies that the *dramatis personae* have insides, that they are not just appearances; and the drama is borne on the current of their private thoughts and motives, and even on the interplay between conscious realization and unconscious self-betrayal. The discontinuity of Eugene's response to Candida's sybilline verdict ('CANDIDA (*significantly*). I give myself to the weaker of the two.') is as deliberately enigmatic: 'Oh, I feel I'm lost. He cannot bear the burden.' The subtle pair are communicating over Morell's unenlightened head. But within such a general use of dialogue even simplicities of statement invite the actor to add an emotional emphasis, or an ironic intonation, that reveals further possibilities of meaning.

Significantly, the two principal male characters are professional men of words, a preacher and a poet. Marchbanks's charge against Morell is that he is 'a moralist and windbag' who has lost his sense of reality in the practice of his 'gift of the gab'. Morell is vulnerable to self-doubt and responds quickly to the young man's insinuations that he has deceived himself with the same powers as have served him to hypnotize others, especially as his wife reinforces this view:

> James dear, you preach so splendidly that it's as good as a play for them. Why do you think the women are so enthusiastic? . . . Theyre all in love with you. And you are in love with preaching because you do it so beautifully. And you think it's all enthusiasm for the kingdom of Heaven on earth; and so do they.

The impressions of Marchbanks's poetry that are offered as indications of his particular talent can hardly be taken more seriously than the other characters take them.[1] Morell is impatient with the irresponsibility of such dreams; Candida, who admits to a limited appetite for poetry, calls them 'moonshine'; Burgess's sentimental opinion, 'very pretty', is the kindest remark they elicit; and Eugene's 'poetic horror' is regarded in

---

[1] One of the more striking examples of his fancy is: 'a tiny shallop to sail away in, far from the world, where the marble floors are washed by the sun.' It is a little unfair to Francis Thompson (whose first volume of poems was published in 1893) to suggest that his poetry, as well as the circumstances of his rescue by the Meynells and his devotion to Alice Meynell, can be compared with Eugene's poetry and his story. But the general parallel blends in with the dramatist's statement (in the letter quoted on p. 65, note 1), that he had De Quincey's adolescence in mind when he started to write the part of Eugene, to suggest that the aspect of the poet as a social drop-out should not be overlooked. Crompton, op. cit., pp. 29–32, associates the character with the younger W. B. Yeats.

much the same way as Morell's metaphoric Christianity – with faint indulgence, the most superficial kind of respect. What delights Candida at
least as much as his talent is the unworldliness and incompetence that she
associates with poets:

> Well, dear me, just look at you going out into the street in that state! You
> are a poet certainly.

Such defects are transformed into attractions in the nephew of a 'real live
earl'. (For Candida is a snob.) Though her remark to her father, 'Poor
Eugene hates politics', did not survive the 1894 draft of the play, it fits
in with such a general view of the poet as Shaw was to attack satirically
in Octavius of *Man and Superman*. Flatteringly, such negative qualities
could be summed up as 'innocence', and the action of the play carries
Eugene out of such a condition, as it shatters Morell's rather different
innocence.

Shaw has exploited the relativism of drama to keep sceptical enquiry
alive: no view and no character has entire authoritative endorsement, and
none is consistently perceptive or imperceptive. With a twist of irony, the
Voltairean title of his play directs attention on the woman, not the
ingénu. Eugene is certainly a version of Candide: innocent in the ways of
the world, he progresses quickly from being the unconsciousness through
which truth is revealed until he is in great part identifiable with the
sophisticated consciousness of the author; and Morell, in the days of his
self-confidence, orates with Panglossian optimism and unction:

> You will be married; and you will be working with all your might and valor
> to make every spot on earth as happy as your own home. You will be one of
> the makers of the Kingdom of Heaven on earth; and – who knows? – you
> may be a master builder where I am only a humble journeyman . . . I know
> well that it is in the poet that the holy spirit of man – the god within him –
> is most godlike . . .

But Candida, apart from her name, is Shaw's own and the focal point of
his evasive technique of presentation. True to her name,[1] she is certainly radiant and a figure of Victorian domestic purity above suspicion;
but as a character she is anything but open and candid to the enquiring
view, and anything but a satisfactory personification of honesty. The love,

---

[1] *The Oxford Dictionary of Christian Names* identifies CANDIDA (specifically
the name of a first-century saint) with BLANCHE. The entry under BLANCHE
includes the statement: 'There is . . . some evidence that St Candida was known
in England as St *Whyte* . . .' It seems that Shaw may have been strongly aware
of what there was in common in the conceptions of three of his heroines –
Blanche Sartorius, Candida Morell and Ann Whitefield. White is the colour
of innocence; the White Goddess – to anticipate subsequent discussion in the
present chapter – is a profoundly ambiguous figure.

praise and comradely familiarity of Morell towards her, the worship of
Eugene, the level-headed assessment Prossy makes, and the indulgent
irreverence of Burgess, combine to obscure and confuse the direct view
the audience, or reader, has of her. In fact, as a character she has a
double identity, partly realistic woman, partly idealization; and she
retains an opacity that neither of the principal male characters approaches.

The objective views of her that we receive are not balanced and
supplemented by an intimate subjective view: the woman sees only her
own mask and is not made to question it searchingly. To her husband she
ponders aloud:

> Suppose he only discovers the value of love when he has thown it away
> and degraded himself in his ignorance! Will he forgive me then, do you
> think? . . .will he forgive me for not teaching him myself? For abandoning
> him to the bad women for the sake of my goodness, of my purity, as you call
> it?

It is significant that the question with which she has started off is: 'I
wonder what he will think of me then.' The touch is softer than Ibsen's,
when he made Hjalmar Ekdal cry out on the death of Hedvig: 'Why hast
thou done this thing to me', but the question is equally self-absorbed.
This is a woman who dresses herself in the gazes of others and is incapable of catching herself out with a humorous perception; she laughs
only at others. Though Marchbanks exalts Candida's divine insight,
Shaw – wiser than his puppet – pointedly exposes the failures of her
ordinary human insight. Eugene has already spoken out to Morell, when
Candida says to the latter: 'Do you know, James, that though he [Eugene]
has not the least suspicion of it himself, he is ready to fall madly in love
with me?' Throughout the conversation that follows, she is totally un-
observant of Morell's perturbation, until Shaw with a final satiric touch
gives her the line: 'you, darling, you understand nothing.' Far from
feeling any burden of responsibility for an actual situation, she enjoys
what is to her a hypothetical situation.

Throughout the play, she belittles the ability of others to manage
without her. The curate, Lexy Mill, parroting Morell himself near the
beginning of the play, unconsciously supplies a critical caption for the
portrait of Candida:

> Ah, if you women only had the same clue to Man's strength that you have
> to his weakness . . . there would be no Woman Question.

The 'Woman Question' the play presents may well be interpreted as the
enigma an ambivalent attitude creates. Eugene Marchbanks comes to
distinguish between the actual woman and the ideal to which he still does

homage at the close of the play. For the audience the two are represented by the same figure, and the rational, objective distinction is still subject to blurring and confusion. If it were not so – if the dramatist had separated out cleanly and completely those warring elements which make up the total emotional response to a person – the play would lose its peculiar force and cogency.[1]

Shaw wrote in his blarneying way to Ellen Terry (6th April 1896):

> You have the wisdom of the heart which makes it possible to say deep things to you. You say I'd be sick of you in a week . . . But one does not get tired of adoring the Virgin Mother. Bless me! you will say, the man is a Roman Catholic. Not at all: the man is the author of Candida; and Candida, between you and me, is the Virgin Mother and nobody else.
>
> (*Collected Letters*, I, p. 623.)

He certainly had Ellen Terry's personal situation in mind: happiest, as he saw her, with her children about her in a household without a male head. But he was not just giving his play a gloss that would make it more enticing to a famous actress; the 1894 longhand text of the play introduces the heroine forthrightly:

> *A beautiful woman, with the double charm of youth and maternity. A true Virgin Mother.*

In the elaboration of this which appears in the published version, some less flattering hints have intruded – Candida is *'well nourished, likely . . . to become matronly later . . . a woman who has found that she can always manage people*, etc.', but the allusion to her as a *'Virgin Mother'* has been suppressed. It looks as though Shaw might have been avoiding direct offence to the pious; more probably he wanted the symbolism to remain entirely implicit in the naturalistic character, unselfconsciously acted. To James Huneker he wrote of his heroine in far less lyrical terms than were appropriate for Ellen Terry:

> Candida is as unscrupulous as Siegfried: Morell himself sees that 'no law will bind her'. She seduces Eugene just exactly as far as it is worth her while to seduce him. She is a woman without 'character' in the conventional

---

[1] Professor H. F. Brooks commented to me, after reading a draft of this chapter, that people who have trouble with their mother-images have trouble with Candida. This seems to me to indicate the level on which the play most potently works and the cause of the passionate disagreement of critics over the interpretation of the heroine. Shaw's own ambivalence, I contend, embraces equally the view put forward by Charles A. Carpenter in *Bernard Shaw and the Art of Destroying Ideals* (Madison, Milwaukee and London: University of Wisconsin Press, 1969), especially pp. 107–12, and that of Arthur H. Nethercot, *Men and Supermen: The Shavian Portrait Gallery*, 2nd ed. (New York: Blom, 1966).

sense. Without brains and strength of mind she would be a wretched slattern or voluptuary . . .[1]

Siegfried, of course, is a superman, so that the comparison sets Candida still beyond the range of ordinary human moral judgement. The rest of the account is as shrewd as Beatrice Webb's verdict on the character: 'a sentimental prostitute';[2] and one wonders if Shaw himself, in some moods, might not have applied that phrase to his character. As a variant for the 'Virgin Mother' it is startling, but not irreconcilable with the blasphemous humour indulged in by the male members of the Shaw household in Dublin.[3]

The attraction to religious themes and imagery and the impulse to deface them are evident in Shaw's juvenile and uncompleted Passion Play in verse (dated February 1878 in B.M. Addit. MS. 50593) which 'naturalizes' the Virgin Mary and presents her as the shrewish wife of a drunken ne'er-do-well and a capricious mother. (The adolescent misogyny that may be detected in this portrait comes out as more direct criticism in another unpublished play, *The Cassone* (B.M. Addit. MS, 50595A, B), when a character named Teddy rounds on the respectable women in his life:

You know as much about a man's wants and feelings as that cat does . . . Between the lot of you I had come to think that I had no right to consideration and no chance of affection; and for two mortal years after we were married I was sneak enough to think her better than myself, and be cowed by her airs, and when I wanted a kiss go dodging and hankering after her like a cur putting in for a bone that he's afraid to steal. And she knew that I felt small . . .)

A superbly comic chapter of *The Irrational Knot* presents the Rev. George Lind's reactions to an encounter with the actress, Lalage Virtue:

What interested him in her was her novel and bold moral attitude, her self-respect in the midst of her sin . . . there was a soul to be saved there, if only Heaven would raise her up a friend in some man absolutely proof against the vulgar fascination of her prettiness . . .

It is not necessary to follow the wild goose chase which the Rev. George's imagination ran from this starting-point to the moment when he was suddenly awakened, by an unmistakable symptom, to the fact that he was

[1] James Huneker, 'The Truth about *Candida*', *Metropolitan Magazine*, Vol. XX (August 1904), p. 635; also in *Iconoclasts* (New York: Scribner, 1905), p. 254. Reprinted in Stephen S. Stanton, *Casebook on 'Candida'* (New York: Crowell, 1962).

[2] See (e.g.) Christopher St John (ed.), *Ellen Terry and Bernard Shaw*, p. 99.

[3] See Preface to *Immaturity*, pp. xx–xxvi.

being outwitted and beglamored, like the utter novice he was, by a power
which he believed to be the devil. He rushed to the little oratory he had
arranged . . . and prayed aloud, long and earnestly. But the hypnotizing
process did not tranquillize him as usual. It excited him, and led him finally
to a passionate appeal for pardon and intercession to a statuette of the Virgin
Mother, of whom he was a very devout adorer. He had always regarded
himself as her especial champion in the Church of England; and now he
had been faithless to her, and indelicate into the bargain.

The Virgin Mother is featured here as a protective figure, inhibiting to
crude masculinity, and antithetically balanced against the 'novel and bold
moral attitude', the 'self-respect' of the actress. Now Shaw consistently
represents the heroes he approves of as 'original moralists', self-justified.
The Virgin Mother seems to be on the other side.

Virgin mothers, in another sense than the specifically Christian,
abound in Shaw's drama and range from Mrs. Warren to Lilith, in *Back
to Methuselah*. 'She's so determined to keep the child all to herself that
she would deny that it ever had a father if she could,' says Sir George
Crofts of Fanny Warren. 'No man alive shall father me' is Philip Clandon's
comically defiant boast; Brassbound's claim, 'I had a mother: that was all',
is a variant on it, familiar in conventional melodrama, which reappears
with the Gunner of *Misalliance*, who tries to assassinate his putative
father. Mrs Morell, of course, acknowledges a husband, but by the end
of the play he seems more like one of her children than her consort, her
equal in power (though she exacts from others a public respect for his
dignity). In view of our biographical knowledge of Shaw's mother-
fixation and the lack of respect which seems to have been accorded to his
father in the Dublin household, it would be easy to trace the recurrence
of the mother-dominated family group in his work to private obsession.
But what he made of this, in objectifying it, is possibly more interesting;
and the expansion of its significance seems to account for most of the
elaboration in the composition of *Candida*. By linking the sway of the
central female figure with a sacred Christian image on the one hand and,
on the other, with associations outside the Christian tradition, the
dramatist has transformed a private symbol into an emblem of a whole
society and the psychological pattern which he sees determining its
character.

The leitmotifs embedded in the dialogue communicate the two kinds
of association, Christian and non-Christian. Among the key words which
recur, and are developed in variant expressions of the same ideas, we find
the cluster, *heaven, hell, divine, prayer*; another group includes *mad,
drunk, (not) contain oneself* (cf. *giddy, laugh, hysterics*), words connoting
a dionysiac irrationality. The device is more significant, and probably

more effective, when repetition is given the deliberate formality of ritual. Eugene, anticipating a physical attack from Morell in Act I, cries 'Dont touch me'; 'Dont touch me' is Morell's own frantic protest against Candida's consoling embrace after the kiss she gives him in Act II, which he judges to be treacherous; in the first part of the next act, Eugene blissfully anticipates, 'I shall feel her hands touch me', and immediately explains to Morell 'why I shrank from your touch' – so that that previous incident and the present variation on the idea are closely linked; 'I did not mean to touch you' is Candida's cold response when her husband tries to assert his dignity and independence in the 'auction' episode; in culmination, the kiss she gives to the kneeling Eugene – and, perhaps, her embrace of Morell as the curtain falls – has the solemnity of a religious laying on of hands. Again, 'I shall stagger you if you have a heart in your breast', Eugene warns Morell in Act I; early in the next act, he 'staggers' Prossy with his talk of her heart's crying hunger, so that she rises *with her hand pressed on her heart*; the gesture recurs when Eugene himself *presses his hand on his heart, as if some pain had shot through it*, at Candida's mockery of her husband, and his words follow – 'I feel his pain in my own heart'; Morell's physical reaction to the kiss, just before, may not involve the same gesture – *'He recoils as if stabbed'* – but in a less mechanical way his words ('I had rather you had plunged a grappling iron into my heart than given me that kiss') bring it to mind with intensified impact. In the ecclesiastical context of St Dominic's Parsonage with its High Church pictures, the prophecy of Simeon to Mary may be remembered – and its later association with the lance of the Passion, when the kiss is the kiss of Judas –

(Yea, a sword shall pierce through thy own soul also,) that the thoughts of many hearts may be revealed.   (Luke 2.34)

Sitting with Eugene beside the fire, in Act III, Candida holds the brass poker – '*upright*', Shaw added to his original directions so that the audience might see the comic symbol[1] – '*looking intently at the point of it*'. Marchbanks makes a romantic image of knightly chastity out of it: 'my drawn sword between us'. The firelight is beyond it, and the sword becomes angelic, 'a flaming sword that turned every way, so that I couldn't go in'. The domestic hearth and the fire they are playing with turn to unquenchable flame, paradisial or infernal, as the image of exile from Eden is inverted: 'for I saw that that gate was really the gate of Hell . . . I was in Heaven already'.

Shaw's wish to emphasize Candida's symbolic elevation to divine status

[1] Of course, the upright poker is more outrageously phallic and a bolder comment on Candida's subconscious preoccupations.

continued to be operative after his original composition of the play was completed. In the 1894 longhand text, the last lines of Act I run:

MARCHBANKS. . . . I am the happiest of men.
MORELL. So was I – an hour ago.

In the published text, the word 'men' is replaced by 'mortals'.

Dominating the set and overlooking Morell's desk with its typewriter ('type' is another key word, punningly relevant to the play's symbolic figures) is the picture hanging above the hearth like an icon above the altar. It is supposed to have been Marchbanks's gift to the Morells, a compliment to Candida through a discernible likeness. Shaw originally instructed that this picture should be a '*Large photograph of the Madonna di San Sisto*'; when he completed his revised version in 1895 the instruction had changed to: '*a large autotype of the chief figure in Titian's Assumption of the Virgin*'. The gift of the picture is matched by the young poet's verbal description of Candida as he idealistically sees her:

her shawl, her wings, the wreath of stars on her head, the lilies in her hand, the crescent moon beneath her feet.

At this point Shaw's classification of his play as 'Pre-Raphaelite' seems apt, inasmuch as the young man's attitude to his benefactress is informed with just such a blend of erotic with religious emotion as Rossetti's pictures frequently communicate.

As an occasional visitor to Newton Hall, meeting-place of Frederic Harrison's group of Positivists, Shaw would have been familiar with the reproduction of the Sistine Madonna hanging there[1] as emblem of the Humanity on which Comte's Positive Religion centred. Comte's *System of Positive Polity* (trans. R. Congreve, 1877) proposed a Festival of the Virgin Mother 'to lay a foundation for the adoration, the collective adoration, of the representatives of Humanity, by instituting the abstract worship of woman' (vol. IV, ch. v). 'A satisfactory institution of the worship of woman is out of the question so long as the idea of maternity is incompatible with purity,' Comte argued, and he fantastically prophesied the Utopia of the Virgin Mother when woman would perfect herself by becoming self-fecundating. Meanwhile, 'the feminine Utopia becomes an inseparable part of the Positive religion, for all whose heart enables them to use it subjectively, without waiting till it is an objective fact.'

It is hard to believe that Shaw would not have agreed with John Stuart Mill that Comte's precise notion of addressing lengthy prayers three times

---

[1] See Warren Sylvester Smith, *The London Heretics 1870–1914* (London: Constable, 1967), p. 97, and below, Chapter 10, p. 184, note 1.

daily to the idealization of some actual woman, living or dead, was 'ineffably ludicrous' as a means of working up the feelings for the service of humanity.[1] *Candida* adopts Comte's notion of an idealization of the affective nature of humanity taking the place of supernatural religion, but the absurdity of worship projected on an actual woman is focused by Prossy and acknowledged in the presentation of Morell and Marchbanks as variant kinds of fool. The ambivalence determining the portrait of the heroine becomes the vehicle of Shaw's critical scepticism regarding the effect of Comte's prescription, and of his uneasy recognition that such a feminine ideal may work conservatively, even regressively, on society.

The replacement of the Sistine Madonna image by Titian's 'Assumption of the Virgin' is a shift towards a more powerfully beneficent concept. The Titian was described by Berenson in his essay on 'Venetian Painters', which first appeared in 1894 – a likely text for Shaw, who had been an art critic, to have read:

> . . . the Virgin soars heavenward, not helpless in the arms of angels, but borne up by the fullness of life within her, and by the feeling that the universe is naturally her own and that nothing can check her course.[2]

This sounds more to the taste of the playwright, naturalist and vitalist, than of the sickly Eugene, who cannot bear to think of a lovely woman in connection with boots that need blacking, onions to be peeled, or even paraffin lamps. (The fact that the picture is an Assumption also emphasizes the distance between symbol and actuality.) Berenson continues in Nietzschean terms, identifying qualities in the 'Assumption' with those of Titian's pictures on classical subjects, 'The Bacchanals' and 'Bacchus and Ariadne':

> They are truly Dionysiac, Bacchanalian triumphs – the triumph of life over the ghosts that love the gloom and chill and hate the sun.[3]

The metaphor used recalls Ibsen, and the whole view corresponds to Nietzsche's philosophical programme as stated in the Preface to *The Birth of Tragedy*: of countering the Christian ethical view with an aesthetic view that should be less life-denying.[4] Morell is associated by name and profession with the ethical approach, Eugene, the poet, with the aesthetic. Whatever we make of Candida as a naturalistic character, Shaw's association of her with the Titian suggests that, after his first

[1] J. S. Mill, *Auguste Comte and Positivism*, Ann Arbor Paperback edition (Ann Arbor: University of Michigan Press, 1961), p. 153.

[2] Quoted from Bernard Berenson, *The Italian Painters of the Renaissance*, Fontana Library edition (London and Glasgow: Collins, 1960), p. 29; first published New York, 1894.

[3] Ibid., p. 30.

[4] Quoted in Chapter 8, p. 138 below.

completion of the play, he conceived her as also being a personification of the Life Force, transcending both morality and art.

Candida's maid in the kitchen, who never appears on stage, is called Maria; the counterpart who does appear on stage is Morell's secretary, Proserpine Garnett. (The surname, etymologically associated with 'pome-granate', reinforces the classical reference.) Classical mythology had been employed by Swinburne in the sixties, within the Pre-Raphaelite tradi-tion, as a weapon against Christianity. In his 'Hymn to Proserpine' he invokes the goddess of natural death, powerful over Christianity as over the rest of creation, destined to triumph over the Virgin Mother as the latter had once usurped the place of Aphrodite:

> . . . thy kingdom shall pass, Galilean, thy dead shall go down to thee dead.
> Of the maiden thy mother men sing as a goddess with grace clad around;

> Not as thine, not as thine was our mother, a blossom of flowering seas,
> Clothed round with the world's desire as with raiment . . .

Proserpine, the poem acknowledges, is daughter of Demeter, the earth mother; in her symbolic identity as Demeter in eclipse, she still testifies to the splendour of physical life.[1]

The blending of the Demeter figure with that of the Virgin Mother distinguishes *Candida* from Swinburne's vision; it smacks more of the anthropologist's and comparative religionist's view. 'There is only one religion though there are a hundred versions of it', Shaw's Preface asserts; and the famous first chapter of *The Golden Bough* (first edition published 1891), entitled 'The King of the Wood', is essential background to the play. It is here that Frazer identifies Diana of Nemi with Diana of Ephesus and Asiatic goddesses of fertility and relates to them the Christian celebration of a Virgin Mother. Candida, whose image presides over the hearth while she occupies herself in trimming the lamps, is also Vesta; the room, though it serves Morell as a study, is essentially a temple of the domestic virtues. The typist (a spinster who has replaced a younger woman) is familiarly addressed as Prossy, a nickname that underlines her inferior relationship to Candida: not just Proserpine as the sacrificial aspect of Demeter, but the temple prostitute in a social and economic

---

[1] Proserpine was a potent image for other Pre-Raphaelites than Swinburne, notably for Rossetti who painted Jane Morris in the role. As a frequenter of the Morris household, Shaw was struck by the incongruousness of the actual character of the woman, who pressed him to eat suet pudding for his health's sake, with the idealization of her that strangely implicated the whole group of Rossetti, Swinburne, Burne-Jones and Morris himself. See Shaw's account of his associa-tion with Morris in May Morris, *William Morris*, 2 vols. (Oxford: Blackwell, 1936; New York: Russell and Russell, 1966), Vol. II, pp. ix–xi.

sense – and an emotional sense, too, as she gives the devotion from which Candida reaps the advantages:

> Why does Prossy condescend to wash up the things, and to peel potatoes and abase herself in all manner of ways for six shillings a week less than she used to get in a city office? She's in love with you, James.

Frazer's account of 'the Ephesian Artemis with her eunuch priests and priestesses' is recalled by the grouping of devotees about the central female image in the play: Morell and Eugene being supported by the yet more foolishly enthusiastic and incorrigibly second-rate curate, Lexy Mill, whose first name in its familiar form, may be a girl's name too;[1] with Prossy on the other hand, love-starved and compelled by her hopeless devotion to Morell to render her tribute of service to Candida.

The climax of the play's action, the show-down, when Candida makes her ceremonial choice between Morell and Marchbanks, is postponed – and gains more force from the consequent suspense – by the interruption of what the Preface intriguingly calls 'the drunken scene . . . much appreciated, I believe, in Aberdeen'.[2] Eugene has already been dancing about excitedly. His conversation with Morell has scattered the latter's self-possession ('. . . my head is spinning round. I shall begin to laugh presently'), when Lexy Mill and Proserpine Garnett come in with Burgess from a champagne supper: a chorus of revellers who attribute their ecstasy first to Morell's eloquence at the meeting and only then to the champagne Burgess has supplied. Shaw set the action of his play on the October day when he started to write it. It may have been no more than a happy coincidence that has left the drama for ever associated with autumn – and the season of the Eleusinian mysteries of Demeter: the Thesmophoria. The 'drunken scene' corresponds to the Bacchic revels associated with the abduction of Kore/Proserpine to the Underworld, in which the worship of Demeter and the worship of Dionysus/Iacchus were combined. We may see Burgess, in this context – if he is the ultimate villain of the piece – as Dis/Minos, Prince of the Dead, to whom Proserpine is subject. The 'madness' leitmotif now falls into place as a dionysiac manifestation, as does that image of Hebrew religious ecstasy, David dancing before the ark – but despised by his wife in her heart, which Eugene applies to Morell's public oratory.[3]

[1] One wonders if the curate's surname was not mischievously borrowed by Shaw from J. S. Mill as the author of *The Subjection of Women*.

[2] See *Collected Letters*, Vol. I, p. 795, for a reference to a stupid review of *Candida* which appeared in the *Northern Figaro* (7 Aug. 1897).

[3] The ritual gestures noted above (pp. 74–5) also contribute to the effect of a sacred dance, in which the characters are compelled to join, breaking out within the rational structure of the play.

Candida, it seems, is opposed to enthusiasm and the cries of the heart; she now reminds the others of 'our rules: total abstinence'. Whether she is thoroughly beneficent remains in doubt; the White Goddess has another aspect. Marchbanks protests at her 'cruelty' to Morell. But men suffer at the hands of the gods without feeling them to be any the less gods.

Frazer identified some of the youthful mortals of legend who are loved and destroyed by the Virgin Mother goddesses: Attis, Endymion, Hippolytus, Adonis, Virbius. Of the last he wrote: 'this mythical Virbius was represented in historical times by a line of priests known as Kings of the Wood, who regularly perished by the swords of their successors.' His chapter ends with a description of a double-headed bust found at Nemi which, he suggests, represents 'the priest of Nemi, the King of the Wood, in possession' and 'his youthful adversary and possible successor'. The one head is young, beardless, and with a steadfast expression; 'the other is a man of middle life with a tossed and matted beard, wrinkled brows, a wild and anxious look in the eyes, and an open grinning mouth.' Shaw's play presents an analogous version of Man in two persons, confronted by the power of Woman.[1]

At the end Eugene escapes – or does he only run away? – whereas Morell is left to his 'happiness', having been stripped of his pride, with his capacity for effective public action at least temporarily shaken. Yet the younger man, too, pays homage on his knees and receives Candida's kiss before he departs. Is she not the Life Force personified? But the dangerousness of submitting to her seductive blandness has been shown, and Lexy Mill's silly quip, 'How can I watch and pray when I am asleep?', now seems an apt cry from a society unconscious of the extent to which Candida governs it. The system allows art its place, as Burgess explains:

> BURGESS (*sentimentally*). He talks very pretty. I awlus had a turn for a bit of poetry. Candy takes arter me that-a-way. Huseter makes me tell er fairy stories when she was only a little kiddy not that igh . . .

---

[1] The admirable Jane Harrison, in *Prolegomena to the Study of Greek Religion* (Cambridge: C.U.P., 1903), comments instructively, but rather amusingly: 'The relation of these early matriarchal, husbandless goddesses, whether Mother or Maid, to the male figures that accompany them . . . seems to halt somewhere half-way between Mother and Lover, with a touch of the patron saint . . . With the coming of patriarchal conditions this high companionship[!] ends. The woman goddesses are sequestered to a servile domesticity, they become abject and amorous.' (p. 273). Although Arthur Evans was at Knossos (Candy) in 1894, the Cretan version of the White Goddess is not likely to have been generally known before his great exhibition of Cretan antiquities in London in 1903.

With an equally mischievous blandness, Shaw himself offers *Candida* as a pretty fairy story of Victorian domesticity – and its anti-revolutionary ideals.

'The gods', in Jane Harrison's words, 'reflect not only man's human form but also his human relations.'[1] Shaw's recognition of this enabled him to incorporate a dialectic of cultural change in a drama originally motivated by his personal difficulties in relating to women. By the time he came to write his Preface to *Plays Pleasant* he had kicked away the ladder that started in his private world – so determinedly that the heroine is not even mentioned there. But the material in Stephen Winsten's book, *Henry Salt and His Circle*, prefaced by a document from G. B. Shaw near the end of his life, enables us to look back at the growth of *Candida* out of a particular situation that exemplified a more constant psychological patterning.

In the days before his marriage, Shaw had been a frequent visitor to the Salts with his friend, Edward Carpenter. Archibald Henderson long ago supplied the information that the triangle aspect of *Candida* was based on the playful rivalry between the two visitors to be considered the 'Sunday husband' of Kate Salt.[2] In his account, included in Winsten's book, Shaw comments on Mrs Salt's lesbianism:

> She was a queer hybrid. I never met anyone in the least like her, though another friend of mine, the Christian Socialist parson Stewart Headlam, also had a wife who was a homo. (p. 9.)

(Headlam, of course, was the most obvious model for James Mavor Morell.[3]) It emerges that Edward Carpenter, himself a homosexual, encouraged Kate to regard herself as an Urnung, or hermaphrodite, as a superior type of humanity. The theory fits in with Comte's view of hermaphroditism, actual or metaphysical, as the utopian form of perfected womanhood. It was Kate's own fanciful view of herself as a mother to all helpless creatures (so that she needed no particular child of her own) that gave Shaw the bridge in actuality from Carpenter's *anima-*

[1] Jane Harrison, op. cit., p. 260.

[2] Archibald Henderson, *George Bernard Shaw: Playboy and Prophet* (New York: Appleton, 1932).

[3] Shaw's letter in the *Evening Standard* (see above p. 65, note 1) declares the nearest model to Morell was Stopford Brooke, with touches of Canon Shuttleworth and Fleming Williams. His habitual insistence on the syncretic way in which he used real life models seems to have been his method of asserting the independent identity of the fictive characters. It may be noted that the given names, James Mavor, are taken from an actual convert to socialism made by William Morris, of whom E. P. Thompson wrote: 'Any working-class comrade could tell he was not in the movement to stay.' See *William Morris: Romantic to Revolutionary* (London: Lawrence and Wishart, 1955) p. 421.

figure to his own; for Candida is certainly no Urnung (and the writing of *Saint Joan* was many years off). But still he wanted a figure of Woman entire. Kate Salt had another function in his life: she typed his manuscripts for him. It was an easy step to present Woman in two persons: as the dominant, maternal Candida and as the servant of the successful man, Prossy Garnett. Perhaps his uncertain, fluctuating view of himself is projected doubly too: on Morell, the able socialist preacher who is weaker than he suspects; and on the timid and gauche Marchbanks, who proves stronger than the world knows. In this connection the aged dramatist's reminiscent words, 'Kate [Mrs Salt] loved me as far as she could love any male creature' (Winsten, op. cit., p. 9), clash rather pathetically with a quotation from Kate herself on the subject of Shaw:

> He is always trying to show how advanced he is about women, but all the time he is conscious that he has to be nice because you are a woman. If he were not so amusing and clever I would not put up with him. I do it for Henry's sake. Henry is so sorry for him.   (Ibid., p. 72.)

We cannot now tell which was the more self-deceiving. Yet *Candida*, from one point of view, is certainly comprehensible as a fantasy defensive of the frail *amour propre* of an ambitious young man who had as yet tasted little recognition from women or the general public for which he wrote. (Eugene Marchbanks, an Orpheus in rags, has been sleeping on the Embankment with a seven-day bill for £55 in his pocket.) Its complex machinery of ideas and symbols conceals the author's fears of inadequacy; its hint that the woman-dominated male is defeated by regressive social elements in the service of capitalism may even have satisfied a vengeful impulse alternatively expressed in the poet's Shelleyan rejection of marriage and domesticity.

Candida stands finally as a critique of Victorian society focused, like Samuel Butler's, on the home. It works subversively – if it still needs to work in these days – through the touches of unease and revulsion with which it continually affects us. Only by such means, in such a society, can the process of revolt begin.[1] The fact that the heroine herself stands clear of burlesque humour and checks the ranging comedy of the play is a tribute to the contained power of the opposition, as the author sensed it, and also to the strength of the inhibitions he faced in his subjective knowledge of what he was writing about.

[1] See above, p. 13.

6 Katherine Cornell as Candida.

7 D. G. Rossetti: Jane Morris as 'Proserpine with the pomegranate' (see pp. 78–9).

8 Titian, 'Assumption of the Virgin' (see pp. 76–8).

5

Making the Skeleton Dance

You Never Can Tell not only *is* a comedy; it embodies a study of comedy, its traditions and its approach to life. Eric Bentley has argued that the critics who go least astray with Shaw are those who recognize the affinities of his work with popular conventions rather than attempting to relate him to the classic dramatists. Yet Shaw's recommendation to the young critic, Golding Bright, reflected the way in which he had educated himself:

> Read three or four of the most famous plays of Molière . . . Read all
> Goethe's plays and a lot of Schiller's . . . Read Aeschylus, Sophocles,
> Euripides, and Aristophanes, etc.
>
> (*Letters*, I, 570)

He was an experimental dramatist throughout his career, and his experiments were certainly deliberate and, the evidence suggests, informed. The success of his work owed much to his appreciation of the unliterary and unintellectual theatre of his youth in its authentic vulgarity. But he understood very well that popular, even vulgar, art has its own professionalism and that tradition and training count as much in the making of a great circus clown as in the making of a great tragic actor, dramatist or poet. As a self-made intellectual, he valued the knowledge he had acquired and the distinction it gave him over the average ignorant journalist.

The end of the nineteenth century was a period of active scholarly research into the history of theatre in all its forms. (The serious study of Commedia dell'Arte dates from about 1880; volumes I and II of Mantzius's *History of Theatrical Art* appeared in Danish in 1897, and William Archer wrote an Introduction for the English translation of the work; Gordon Craig was himself a researcher as well as a designer and a visionary.) The initiation of his long friendship with Gilbert Murray ensured that Shaw would be abreast of the speculations of classical scholars and anthropologists concerning the origins and significance of

D

ancient Greek drama. His own drama is a peculiar hybrid, a meeting-place of academic notions of earlier theatre and the remnants of such theatre which survived in more or less degenerate form in the unpretentious entertainments of Dublin and London in his own day. He united in himself the knowledge and tastes of both Count O'Dowda and the Savoyard (of *Fanny's First Play*), being as familiar with H. J. Byron, the writer of extravaganzas, as with Byron the Romantic poet, and, knowing the difference between 'a Louis Quatorze ballet painted by Watteau' and late nineteenth-century pantomime, was not averse to playing the earlier convention off against the later, not always to the detriment of either.

A remark in the Preface to *Plays Pleasant*, apropos of *You Never Can Tell*, keeps a faintly patronizing tone towards contemporary theatre:

> Far from taking an unsympathetic view of the popular preference for fun, fashionable dresses, a little music, and even an exhibition of eating and drinking by people with an expensive air, attended by an if-possible-comic waiter, I was more than willing to shew that the drama can humanize these things as easily as they, in the wrong hands, can dehumanize the drama.

Humanizing the drama meant infusing into its conventions the truth of human experience. But Shaw attempted more: to discover and restore to those conventions something of their original meaning and relevance to life.

It is not easy to write soberly about *You Never Can Tell* without giving a false impression of the kind of play it is: as serious as it is light-hearted; and with nothing melancholy about it, although it recognizes the pain and suffering that human beings have to meet in life. It is a festive play, a celebration of the perennial recurrence of summer; and through its action the characters move towards reconciliation with each other and with life itself. Shaw makes it abundantly clear that no one can enter into the general mood of happiness without abandoning personal grievances. This involves some kind of defeat for the individual; but he, or she, gains in the end through learning a balance between emotional involvement and detachment, between feeling and thinking in response to experience. It is a sweet-tempered play, reflecting the way in which the author's own emotion and reasoning power sweetened and freshened each other as he worked on his idea. As a reviewer, he had occasion to comment on Oscar Wilde's *The Importance of Being Earnest:*

> Unless comedy touches me as well as amuses me, it leaves me with a sense of having wasted my evening. I go to the theatre to be moved to laughter, not to be tickled or bustled into it. (*Our Theatres in the Nineties*, I, 42)

You Never Can Tell exemplifies the comedy Shaw himself was *moved* to write.

It was written between 1895 and 1897, when he was theatre critic for the *Saturday Review*. Of the six other plays he had already completed, only the first, *Widowers' Houses*, had been published; and he was still a largely unperformed dramatist. Although disappointment was in store and the play had to wait until 1899 for its first production, the prospects for *You Never Can Tell* looked at first brighter than had greeted any of Shaw's earlier plays. Cyril Maude planned to put it on at the Haymarket Theatre, and more than one leading American management was interested in it.[1] The encouragement came none too soon for a man of forty whose ability had been baffled in other careers before this. He can be heard speaking through Valentine in Act I. The audience (which knew him well from his reviews of other people's plays) is taken into the dramatist's confidence, as the eccentric dentist gives the show away to his patients:

> My conscience has been my ruin. Listen to me. Twice before I have set up as a respectable medical practitioner in various parts of England. On both occasions I acted conscientiously, and told my patients the brute truth instead of what they wanted to be told. Result, ruin. Now Ive set up as a dentist, a five shilling dentist; and Ive done with conscience for ever. This is my last chance . . . I'm eating and drinking on credit; my landlord is as rich as a Jew and as hard as nails; and Ive made five shillings in six weeks. If I swerve by a hair's breadth from the straight line of the most rigid respectability, I'm done for.

(No one had been prepared to risk even a private performance of *Mrs Warren's Profession*.) The approach is unconventional and disarming in its frankness. Shaw is in the commercial theatre now and going all out for success, making the gesture of throwing away principles and serious intentions of social or moral reform, in order to reassure a possibly apprehensive audience. Later in life he was inclined to dismiss *You Never Can Tell* as a potboiler;[2] but the critic may well conclude that he wrote better under pressure than he was willing to admit.

The whole of Act I, in the dentist's surgery, can be regarded as a

[1] See Cyril Maude, *The Haymarket Theatre* (London: Grant Richards, 1903), pp. 211–17 (chapter contributed by Shaw himself). The relevant chapter is reprinted in *The Bodley Head Bernard Shaw* (London, Sydney, Toronto: Max Reinhardt, 1970), Vol. I, pp. 797–803.

[2] See Hesketh Pearson, *G.B.S. A Postscript* (New York: Harper, 1950; London: Collins, 1951), p. 379, and *Collected Letters*, Vol. I, pp. 678, 735, 799. But there are few of his plays that Shaw did not similarly dismiss at one time or another, though in other moods he might describe them as works of genius. It is certainly incumbent on the critic to make his own assessments of quality, in every instance.

symbolic prelude to the main part of the play. Dentistry offers a farcical metaphor for the art of the comic dramatist:

'Pluck from the memory a rooted sorrow.' With gas, five shillings extra.

The laughing gas which Shaw's humour offers audiences is an anaesthetic under cover of which there is a necessary operation to be performed.

The grotesque appearance of the dentist's chair in the centre of the stage, as the main property of the scene, advertises the crudely physical action that is to be staged. It aligns the play at once with the repertoire of circus clowns and low comedians, or the Grand Guignol absurdity of Sweeney Todd with his barber's chair. A picture by F.-J. Watteau,[1] dating from 1798, represents a *parade*[2] of Harlequin as dentist. A well-known documentary comment on the medieval theatre, Fouquet's miniature of 'The Martyrdom of Saint Apollonia' (reproduced by Mantzius in *The History of Theatrical Art* and many times since), is peculiarly apposite to *You Never Can Tell* as it reflects the intersection of comedy with tragedy, terror with laughter. Against a background of scaffolds with angels at one end and devils at the other, Fouquet shows the enactment of the physical climax of a miracle play, the episode of extreme torment which leads to the death of the saint. She is helpless, with two tormentors hauling on the ropes that bind her, while a third drags at her hair; but the instrument of torture being applied by the fourth assailant is none other than a fantastically enormous pair of forceps gripping the teeth in her mouth: the frame to which she is bound in fact constitutes an improvised dentist's chair. As a version of tooth extraction the scene is a nightmare; as a martyrdom it is as irresistibly funny as it is violent (and the figure of the jester, scratching his backside, very effectively challenges the dignity of the balancing figure holding the book, in Fouquet's design). Altogether, it is a psychologically valid description of the relation between the minor ordeals of life and the supreme test of death or loss in extremest form, with which they may be subconsciously identified. Crampton, in Shaw's play, certainly faces the dentist's chair as if it were a rehearsal for worse trials in store: 'It's not the effect on the teeth: it's the effect on the character' that matters, he insists to Valentine.

The audience crowding round the actors, in the miniature, puts tooth-extraction and martyrdom alike into perspective as only make-believe.

---

[1] Reproduced in Léon Moussinac, *Le Théâtre des origines à nos jours* (Paris: Amiot, Dumont, 1957), p. 245.

[2] The *parade* was a farcical sketch played on a balcony at the Parisian fairs. 'They were meant to arouse the interest of the spectator in the play to be given inside the booth . . . and by the names of the characters show their affinity with the *commedia dell'arte*.' (*Oxford Companion to the Theatre*, under FAIRS.)

Yet, as mere lookers-on, they also mirror something like callousness in detachment from human suffering. The structure of *You Never Can Tell* similarly groups detached, emotionally unperturbed figures about a central situation that involves suffering. The contrast throws into relief a necessary element even in high comedy (which predominates over farce in Act I as later in the play). Though Shaw, rightly or wrongly, judged Wilde guilty of the triviality and evasiveness of laughing life off as a joke against other people, he self-critically acknowledged a pitilessness in his own art of comedy by his ultimately symbolic use of the 'toothache chair'. Laughter is harsh; but it is also tonic.

Valentine's first day in private practice as a dentist brings him two patients, strangers to each other, who turn out to be father and daughter, and makes him the agent of one of the oldest plots known to the comedy tradition: the chance encounter, mutual recognition and reunion of a long-separated family. Shakespeare used versions of this plot, which was also a favourite in ancient Greece. It occurs in *The Importance of Being Earnest*, which bears a particular burlesque relation to the *Ion* of Euripides. Its familiarity and traditional theatricality offered Shaw sufficient disguise for a more intimately autobiographical element, and in some ways *You Never Can Tell* can be regarded as among the most personal plays he ever wrote, the 'rooted sorrow' being his own. For the five members of this family – Crampton, the long-deserted father, broken down by over-indulgence in alcohol; the independent woman who left him and brought up his children under the name of Clandon; the beautiful and talented daughter, Gloria; and the gay twins, Philip and Dolly – show as a group and individually an insistent resemblance to the Shaw family: the father left in Dublin, when Mrs Shaw departed to London in 1873, taking her younger daughter, 'Yuppy', and soon to be joined by the other, Lucy, who became a singer and musical-comedy actress, then by her son, George Bernard Shaw, in 1876. After that date, twenty years before *You Never Can Tell* was written, none of them seems to have seen the father again. When he died in 1885, Lucy happened to be in Dublin but did not go to his funeral; G. B. Shaw saluted the news in a flippant note to a friend:

> Telegram just received to say that the governor has left the universe on rather particular business and set me up as
>
> An Orphan. (*Letters*, I, 132)

At the same time he seems to have shocked his Uncle Frederick by the offhand callousness of an immediate letter on the family's financial situation.[1]

---

[1] See *Collected Letters*, Vol. I, pp. 132–5.

It has been remarked (e.g. by St John Ervine) that Mrs Clandon was partly modelled on Shaw's mother (and, in her role as public reformer and authoress, on his friend, Annie Besant) and Gloria on his sister, Lucy.[1] The 'heartlessness' of the young G.B.S. is projected through the choric detachment of Philip Clandon, flourishing his protest, 'No man alive shall father me', and posing in his Harlequin fancy-dress to point out what he does not feel, with a certain grave irony:

> PHILIP. . . . Coming, dad, coming.
> (*On the window threshold he stops; looks after* **Crampton***; then turns fantastically with his bat bent into a halo round his head, and says with lowered voice to Mrs Clandon and Gloria*)
> Did you feel the pathos of that? (*He vanishes*).

But it is only when playing Harlequin that Philip is heartless; and Shaw (who laughed his way through his mother's funeral service, deeply attached to her as he had been) was certainly concerned, in staging the reconciliation that never happened in life, with what had gone wrong and what had been lost. He is not at all sentimental about what might have been; but he is concerned to do justice – to father as well as mother. But he chose to write about his own family situation only as it could be translated into general terms and seen in an impersonal perspective. The issues involved are lightly identified with favourite 'advanced' themes of the period[2] and tendencies at work in contemporary society: the late Victorian reaction against the family as a social institution; the Feminist Movement as a rejection of paternal dominance at the public level; the relations of the sexes as a Schopenhauerian power-struggle; and – less narrowly contemporary – the puritan tradition.

While he was at work on the play, Shaw had occasion to write to the actress, Janet Achurch (Mrs Charles Charrington). He had an acting role to dangle before her; but he was also concerned to use it as an instrument of moral pressure on a woman he admired and liked:

> There will be a good part – as heroic as Magda – for the younger woman, and a fine part for her mother . . . the tragedy will be between the father and the daughter. Now, no matter who plays the father, the daughter shall never during my lifetime be played by a woman who drinks brandy . . . There is only one physical crime that can destroy you – brandy . . .
> I cannot lock up the brandy – but I can poison it . . .   (*Letters*, I, 583)

His attempt to 'poison' Janet Achurch's brandy with threats and fore-

[1] See St John Ervine, *Bernard Shaw: His Life, Work and Friends* (London: Constable, 1956), pp. 322–3.

[2] Only in the theatre, McComas tells Mrs Clandon, would *her* ideas still be considered 'advanced' in England. Through this character, Shaw presents his own theme of socialism as more topical and urgent than Ibsen's themes.

bodings had no lasting success. This letter is dated 23 December 1895. In December 1897 he was writing again on the same theme:

> When I was a child of less than Nora's age,[1] I saw the process in my father; and I have never felt anything since. I learnt soon to laugh at it; and I have laughed at everything since. Presently, no doubt, I shall learn to laugh at you. What else can I do? (*Letters*, I, 828)

Later on, he wrote more publicly of his father's drinking habits, notably in the Preface to his novel, *Immaturity*, which reaches the conclusion: 'If you cannot get rid of the family skeleton, you may as well make it dance.' Though he certainly succeeded in distancing himself from the situation by laughter, it is worth noting that Shaw never fully escaped the sense of shock. There is no reason why a child should be traumatically affected by the mere sight of a parent under the influence of drink; the decisive element is usually the valuation of the incident by adults, which the child absorbs emotionally. George Carr Shaw was, as his son later stressed, 'a *miserable* drunkard', overwhelmed in shame that reflected his wife's contempt. Within the play, when the defence of Crampton has been made and some part of the responsibility laid at the door of Mrs Clandon's failure to offer him any sympathy in their marriage, her pre-eminence remains unchallenged. 'Oh, if your mother were only a widow!' says Valentine to Gloria, 'She's worth six of you.'

This is the playboy's tribute to the genteel puritanism in which Shaw himself had been brought up, and which regarded intemperance as the cardinal sin. The negative follies of puritanism are exposed in caricature through Crampton's responses in Act I. And puritanism is allowed to evoke its opposing spirit in the gaiety incarnate in Valentine, Philip and Dolly, and diffused throughout the play. Shaw's treatment of Crampton's alcoholism is far removed from Zola's (in *L'Assommoir*) or George Moore's (in *Esther Waters*) or even Dickens's view of the drunkard (one thinks of 'Mr Dolls') in the context of an uncontrolled capitalist economy which left the artisan population of the great industrial centres free to starve or to survive – but to survive only on terms of the most rigid control of the instinct for pleasure. The general fabric of the play is too delicate – in a way too flimsy – to carry anything like a straight political or sociological approach; and this is in itself a likely reason for Shaw's later deprecation of it as a 'pot-boiler'. But it seems significant that his way of dealing with the demon drink in later plays was to mythologize it: to associate it with Dionysus and make it symbolic of subversive force or prophetic vision.[2]

---

[1] Nora Charrington, Janet Achurch's daughter, was born in Melbourne in 1890.

[2] The tendency had already begun with *Candida* (see above, p. 79).

His own flight from emotion ('I have never felt anything since') takes
positive form as the gift Valentine claims: 'Lightness of heart'. 'And
lightness of head, and lightness of faith, and lightness of everything that
makes a man,' retorts Gloria, only to have her accusation turned into
affirmation: 'Yes, the whole world is like a feather dancing in the light
now; and Gloria is the sun.' This is an echo of Nietzsche's assault on
puritan moralism:

> He who climbeth on the highest mountains, laugheth at all tragic plays
> and tragic realities.
>
> And to me also, who appreciate life, the butterflies, and soap bubbles,
> and whatever is like them amongst us, seem most to enjoy happiness.
> To see these light, foolish, pretty, lively little sprites flit about – that
> moveth Zarathustra to tears and songs.
> I should only believe in a God that would know how to dance.
> And when I saw my devil, I found him serious, thorough, profound,
> solemn: he was the spirit of gravity – through him all things fall.
> Not by wrath, but by laughter, do we slay. Come let us slay the spirit
> of gravity!
>
> Now am I light, now do I fly; now do I see myself under myself. Now
> there danceth a God in me.[1]

That affirmation, 'Now there danceth a God in me', helps towards an
understanding of Shaw's intention in designing *You Never Can Tell* as
he did.

The appearance of Philip and Dolly as Harlequin and Columbine in
the last act, is full acknowledgement that these young visitors to late
nineteenth-century England are characters stylized to the verge of pure
fantasy. They are twins ideally in harmony with each other; and a
natural tendency for thought and speech to chime together, which sympathy and habit may breed in actual life, has been formalized by Shaw
into a swiftly paced choric style: not verse, but certainly speech with
wings. They are uninhibited by convention, and their sunny good
humour is abnormally difficult to disturb. These signs mark them out as
free beings, not creatures of society as Gloria and her mother are, and
hardly subject to the laws of this world at all. The harlequinade convention of nineteenth-century pantomime, which revealed the characters
of the specific story in their perennial, innermost Commedia dell'Arte
form, is employed in Act IV of the present play, forcing us to recognize
that Philip and Dolly have been Harlequin and Columbine all the time,

---

[1] *Thus Spake Zarathustra*, trans. Thomas Common, I, vii, in Friedrich
Nietzsche, *Complete Works*, ed. Oscar Levy, 17 vols. (London and Edinburgh:
J. Foulis, 1909–11; reissued New York: Russell and Russell, 1964), Vol. XI.

and that their contemporary dress – not this – was the disguise. The sing-song repetitiveness of the Waiter's speeches underlines the intimate connection between him and the twins, especially Dolly: together they sum up the whole span of life as Age and Youth eternally poised; they are magic presences, gods in disguise, in the setting of a nineteenth-century seaside hotel.

The artistic justification of Shaw's concern with archaic forms of theatre lies here: in that it enables him to suggest the immortal shining through temporal forms. The implication is that actual men and women fulfil themselves through a shadowy realization of the ideal quality at the heart of their individual being, and that their lives are an acting out of variations on a universal, changeless dance of life. The griefs and pains of personal experience and the conviction of personal failure evaporate, as they become aware of the greater pattern, and give themselves up to it. Careless of 'the trifles that wreck you at the harbour mouth', all the characters are swept up into the Fancy Ball '. . . for the benefit of the Life-boat'.

Harlequin was the most various, and ultimately the most popular, of the Commedia dell'Arte roles. His traditional bat was the instrument of a peculiar power: in pantomime it might be used as a magic wand; its older associations were with fertility, in keeping with its supposed descent from the symbolic phallus worn or carried by Roman comedians and linked even earlier with crude religious rites. It was no trivial chance that made sexual love the favourite theme of traditional comedy plots. Columbine was the chief nineteenth-century representative of a number of female figures associated with Harlequin at earlier periods. She was originally a serving maid, but had long been more of an ideal Girl than a low-life character. She and Harlequin were traditionally lovers as well as fellow conspirators. But Shaw emphasizes the detachment of Dolly and Philip from the play of emotions that they survey, by presenting them as brother and sister, not lovers. They are adolescents exempt from human weakness as they are less than fully human, and their partnership defends them both from sexual commitment. They are as buoyant and gay as they are invulnerable. It is true that Bohun foretells Dolly's ultimate marriage, but no one anticipates marriage for Philip.

We can see Valentine and Gloria, whose very names associate them with the springtime and blossoming of life, as more fully drawn and particularized counterparts of the token figures of Youth and Maiden. (Dolly's tooth-filling, which does not trouble her at all, is a token equivalent of the suffering in store for Gloria.) Their place in the pattern is that of the unmasked lover and lady of the Commedia dell'Arte plots, who have always worn the costume of the day. From this recognition we can move on to see the similarity of other characters to the traditional masks: Crampton is Pantaloon in a new disguise, and of the family of Molière's crabbed old men; the lawyer, McComas, mutual confidant of Crampton and Mrs Clandon, is a version of the learned Doctor; the stoutness and thick eyebrows of Bohun, Q.C., and the grotesque false nose, in which he makes his first entrance, constitute a physical resemblance to Mr Punch as well as to Mr Jaggers of *Great Expectations*; William the Waiter stands in the middle of the group, benign, and seeming to be and know more than meets the eye: a Watteauesque Pierrot.

The success of the play in the theatre depends largely on the Waiter, a part which has attracted star actors from Cyril Maude to Sir Ralph Richardson. There is a good deal more to it than caricature: William's ambiguous social position, as the servant who simply does not choose to assert his equality with, or superiority over, his masters, is token of a latent power more considerable than any of the other characters can exert. (Barrie's Admirable Crichton and P. G. Wodehouse's paragon, Jeeves, are comparable types.) Dolly has nicknamed him William, after Shakespeare, and puts her trust in his benevolent providence. There is, indeed, an important sense in which the Waiter controls the play, although he may not seem to do anything very effective. His unassertive, undogmatic philosophy supplies the mood and tone within which the whole range of emotion, from unshadowed gaiety to disillusionment and despair, can be safely contained. William makes comic mistakes and trembles in the presence of his more obviously eminent son; but this behaviour is like a wilful disguise to his universal wisdom that gives the final answer to mere rational prudence, as he caps the summary, 'It's unwise to be born; it's unwise to be married; it's unwise to live; and it's wise to die', with characteristic courtesy: 'Then, if I may respectfully put a word in, sir, so much the worse for wisdom!' And his final line does not so much close the play as throw it open to the surprises, uncertainties and possibilities of life: 'You never can tell, sir: you never can tell.'

The fact that Bohun is the son of William is a reminder that there are many kinds of power and that men have worshipped some very different gods. Bohun erupts into the play in his grotesque mask, 'dropped on us out of the clouds'. (The lowering of gods by stage machinery was, of course, a popular trick in pantomime as it had long before been a feature of ancient Greek drama.) Like the classical *deus ex machina*, he is blatantly employed to round off the plot by delivering his formal judgement, pronouncing the fates in store for the other characters, and ushering them into the final dance.[1] Shaw's description of him suggests an

---

[1] Cf. the role of the sybilline Mrs George in *Getting Married*. (See below, p. 179.)

infinitely more powerful version of Sir George Crofts (in *Mrs Warren's Profession*):

> *Physically and spiritually a coarsened man: in cunning and logic a ruthlessly sharpened one. His bearing as he enters is sufficiently imposing and disquieting; but when he speaks, his powerful menacing voice, impressively articulated speech, strong inexorable manner, and a terrifying power of intensely critical listening, raise the impression produced by him to absolute tremendousness.*

It is absurd to suppose that this is the dramatist's favourite deity, or that he expects audiences to like him. The supernatural Bohun is the false god of Comedy, a kind of demon, offered less for worship than for criticism. Shaw's respect for a spirit of comedy that has regard for feeling as part of the truth of any human situation is negatively implied and should be understood more clearly by the end of the play, as a result of the embodiment of the vices of unfeeling comedy in Bohun: callousness, arrogance, intellectual abstraction, cold indifference, insensitivity. William's presence is a persistent token of the humaner ideal, all along.

The *deus ex machina* is associated with Euripides more than any other Greek dramatist; and we can interpret Shaw's attitude to Bohun in the light of what Gilbert Murray said about this classical dramatist in his *History of Ancient Greek Literature*, published in the year (1897) when Shaw completed *You Never Can Tell*:

> His age held him for a notorious freethinker, and his stage gods are almost confessedly fictitious. Yet it is a curious fact that Euripides is constantly denouncing the inadequacy of mere rationalism. There is no contrast more common in his plays than that between real wisdom and mere knowledge or cleverness. (*Greek Literature*, p. 265)

The same contrast distinguishes William from Bohun.

You Never Can Tell as a whole makes a plea for sympathetic understanding as the better part of justice. At the centre, surrounded by the comedy chorus, stand Gloria and Crampton, united by their human vulnerability to emotion. Shaw touches only lightly on the potentially tragic passions involved, but marks their centrality with McComas's formal speech in Crampton's defence:

> . . . how would you feel . . . wont you make some allowance for his feelings? in common humanity . . . There are men who have a good deal of feeling, and kind feeling too, which they are not able to express. What you miss in Crampton is that mere veneer of civilization, the art of shewing worthless attentions and paying insincere compliments in a kindly charming way . . . Where the whole system is one of false good-fellowship . . . we say bitter things in a sweet voice: we always give our friends chloroform when we tear them to pieces . . .

It helps put the whole play in perspective. The final metaphor ('give our friends chloroform when we tear them to pieces') recalls Act I and conveys something like remorse in the dramatist for the violation that the art of comedy does to human beings, in however good a cause. Valentine's sunny mockery of Crampton, which the audience enjoys, is inseparable from his use of the forceps; and the phrase, 'tear . . . to pieces', helps to connect Crampton's martyrdom with the sacrifice that was part of the ancient ritual to which the art-form of Greek tragedy is still commonly traced back: the symbolic tearing-asunder of the god in one form as prelude to his resurrection in another.

Gilbert Murray contended that the ancient rites belonging to the worship of Dionysus (god of irrational forces) had left their clearest traces in the plays of Euripides. It is an amusing exercise to analyse the development of *You Never Can Tell* in terms usually applied to Greek plays. Thus Act I moves through the stages of the first part of an Attic comedy: the Exposition (between Valentine and Dolly); the entry of the Chorus (with Philip joining Dolly); and the Contest (when the children turn on Mrs Clandon demanding knowledge of their father), on which the rest of the play hangs. The dentistry, the lunch, the arrival of Bohun and the final ball correspond to the principal rites lying behind both tragedy and comedy: the Sacrifice; the Feast (at which the dismembered representative of the god was either literally, or symbolically, devoured); the subsequent Resurrection, or manifestation of the god in a new form; and the celebratory Komos, the procession of dancers in which the whole community joined – and that has its equivalent in the dance into which Shakespeare's comedies pass at the final curtain.[1]

We can go further in tracing equivalents of the possibly less essential elements of ritual origin that Murray found regularly combined in Euripidean drama, e.g. the Messenger (McComas), Pathos and Lamentation (Crampton's wail of 'a father robbed of his children. What are the hearts of this generation like?. . .'), Discovery and Recognition (acted out principally by Crampton and Gloria, in whom a new self-knowledge emerges from their shared sense of defeat by life). The chief of the play's violent reversals (the Greek *peripeteia*) takes the form of Gloria's turning, at the end of Act II, against her mother and her upbringing: the death of an old attitude and birth of a new one.

This is all evidence of the careful planning that went into Shaw's often apparently careless playwriting. It also brings out the fact that he was writing, as Shakespeare was supposed to have written, on different levels to suit the tastes and capacities of different sections of his audience. Thus

[1] The typical features of comedy are noted here in accordance with Gilbert Murray's account in his *Aristophanes* (Oxford: Clarendon Press, 1933, etc.).

the 'exhibition of eating and drinking by people with an expensive air', answering to the tastes of the ordinary Haymarket audiences of the nineties, might have a more esoteric appeal to the sophisticates who identified it as an opportunity for William and his assistants to perform their *lazzi*, the traditional skilled routines of Commedia dell'Arte clowns; and there was irony to be savoured by any who caught the allusion to the cannibalistic rites of ancient religion. It is amusing to recognize such simultaneities; but there is a taint of pretentiousness about the method – as though Shaw was safeguarding himself against the criticism of *cognoscenti* who might find him naïve. The whole much-advertised tendency of his work to invert or distort popular conventions is open to the same suspicion of fear that he might be found out sharing common tastes and sentiments; and yet his actual strength as an artist may be closely related to the fact that he *did* share them.

Gilbert Murray's observation of how the acts and suffering attributed in myth to a god might be distributed among different characters in an Euripidean play is also relevant:

> Dionysus did not die. He seemed to die, but it really was his enemy, in his dress and likeness, it was Pentheus or Lycurgus who died . . .[1]

What dies through suffering in Crampton and Gloria is his Scrooge-like quality, the negative side of puritanism at enmity with all happiness, and her false rationalizing, defiant of emotion. These are evil things, and something very like them is 'resurrected' in the figure of Bohun. There are qualities in Mrs Clandon and Valentine, too, that do not die in the course of the play, but which Shaw discriminates against by isolating and magnifying them in the same monstrous figure.

Crampton himself is restored when he is able to accept the situation as it is and join willingly with the group in its carnival. But it is only within the dance that the imagined reconciliation of the Shaw family is valid. It is possible to believe that his children might maintain some friendly communication with Crampton, but Mrs Clandon allows him no more than a faltering moment of pity and the impersonal courtesy that social convention exacts. It is her cool poise and independence of spirit that Gloria's early stand-offishness reflects; Valentine, who defeats this attitude in the daughter, also takes its measure in the mother.

Mrs Clandon testifies nobly:

> Let me tell you, Mr Valentine, that a life devoted to the Cause of Humanity has enthusiasms and passions to offer which far transcend the selfish personal infatuations and sentimentalities of romance . . .

---

[1] 'Excursus on the Ritual Forms Preserved in Greek Tragedy', included in Jane Harrison, *Themis* (Cleveland: Meridian Books, 1962), p. 362.

and only the fulsomeness of the phrasing hints at something a little false
here. Her accusation 'Mr Valentine: you are one of those men who play
with women's affections' is then met by the retort she deserves: 'Well,
why not, if the Cause of Humanity is the only thing worth being serious
about?' It is not the dramatist who is undervaluing the feelings of the
individual here. Indeed Shaw has related Mrs Clandon's admirable
altruism to its ground in personal deprivation:

> My case is a very common one, Mr Valentine. I married . . . the result was a
> bitter disappointment . . . So you see, though I am a married woman, I have
> never been in love; I have never had a love affair; and, to be quite frank with
> you Mr Valentine, what I have seen of the love affairs of other people has
> not led me to regret that deficiency in my experience . . .

and he pointedly directs the sceptical glance with which Valentine greets
this.

The latent tragedy of Mrs Clandon is her failure to live tragic experience through to the point of insight. When she says to Valentine, 'you
are very clever . . . And you have taught me – nothing', the words
Gloria flung in her face at the end of Act II echo ironically with a quite
contrary meaning. Whereas they expressed the daughter's sense of a
revolution in her life, the mother uses them to defy change.

Valentine, too, seems unmodifiable, as Gloria is not, and by his happy-
go-lucky nature secure from ordinary trouble. Philip's fantastical description of him as 'the man of ivory and gold' reinforces the fact that
Valentine is his *only* name to suggest that he is another mask, or mythic
figure: an embodiment of eros, or the springtime of life, eternally in love.
It is significant that he is more like Philip in this than Gloria is like
Dolly. For Philip and Valentine (anticipated by Frank of *Mrs Warren's
Profession*) are both projections of the author as he saw himself in early
and middle life: the professional comedian, gay, ironic, uncommitted, an
amorous but heartless Don Juan.

Shaw's consistent view of the male lover is of one striving to preserve
his independence in a balance between sexual involvement and detachment: he may be caught in intrigues, but his heart is never deeply
engaged. Women characters do his suffering for him as his victims, since
he is incapable of suffering himself. Luck is fancy-free, and Valentine
preserves his luck – his safety, in fact – by virtue of his intellect (the
opposite of 'heart'), 'a masculine speciality', as he reminds Gloria. It is
in this respect that Bohun is his god, hailed by him as 'the very incarnation of intellect'.

Valentine contends that 'Twentieth-Century Woman' can no more
escape subjection to Man than the traditionally submissive woman, and
Gloria is driven to confess the inescapable laws of her female nature:

I am one of those weak creatures born to be mastered by the first man whose eye is caught by them; and I must fulfil my destiny, I suppose.

Indeed the play seems curiously anti-feminist and conservative in its endorsement of the old order of relations between the sexes. Ostensibly it is a far remove from Ibsen in its attitude. Yet something like a re-miniscence of Ibsen is embedded in the play and modifies its explicit statement. The holiday atmosphere of the seaside town, Crampton's pro-fession of yacht-builder, and his navy blue coat like a pilot's coat, Gloria's sea-green silk blouse, not only point forward to the sea-symbolism of such later plays as *Heartbreak House* and *The Simpleton of the Unexpected Isles*, but direct attention to further resemblances between *You Never Can Tell* and Ibsen's *Lady from the Sea*: the estrangement (not long separation) between Dr Wangel and his second wife is reflected in his habitual drinking; Dolly's adolescent insouciance faintly echoes the all-but-inhuman mockery of the adolescent Hilda; and William the Waiter has a counterpart in the factotum, Ballested (a Harlequin figure himself, left behind by a theatrical troupe) with his choric refrain on the theme of acclimatization. Such trifling similarities combine significantly in the light of the general theme of *The Lady from the Sea*: the balance of human freedom and responsibility, in specific relation to the freedom-loving woman who learns to accept the bonds of responsibility. Change-ability is a primary quality of the sea on which the 'Life-boat' is adven-turously launched. Association with it helps endow the character of Gloria with a shimmering life that contrasts with the inhuman change-lessness Shaw's masks suggest; and it makes a background for the sym-pathetic treatment, a little sad, that is generally extended to the character.

There is something mechanical about the reversal whereby, when Valentine is 'caught', Gloria repels us by vengefully reasserting her power over the man, in a manner much more brutal and bullying than her mother's:

GLORIA (*peremptorily to Valentine*). Get up. (*Valentine gets up abjectly.*) Now let us have no false delicacy. Tell my mother that we have agreed to marry one another.

To dispel any suspicion that the dramatist didn't realize the effect he was creating, there follow the Waiter's words in the closing speech of the play:

Every man is frightened of marriage when it comes to the point . . . *I* never was master in my own house, sir: my wife was like your young lady: she was of a commanding and masterful disposition, which my son has inherited.

The 'Nature' which, Valentine declares, 'was in deadly earnest with me when I was in jest with her' is finally revealed as the matriarchal principle, a projection of the woman in control over her own feelings, or with personal feelings endorsed as universal law, subduing the male.

This does not seem to be the logical conclusion that *You Never Can Tell* has been driving towards. We may judge it to be a compulsive irony which sacrifices the unity of the play, and the unity of the character of Gloria, to the comedian's need to punish the aloofness of his own pose, his own detachment from emotion. It is not the capitulation of art before life which is enacted here so much as a superstitious awe of the female and an ultimate inability – after all his efforts – to see her as anything but the tyrant.

When Valentine pours scorn on Gloria's Higher Education and on her pretensions to intellect, his protestation that his worship is something greater than respect can hardly be accepted as true balm for her wounded feelings. For worship is appropriate to the man-created image, the idea, not to the individual woman. There are, indeed, two Glorias in the play, and it is instructive that the Gloria of Valentine's imagination is contrasted by the woman herself with: 'The real Gloria, the Gloria who was shocked, offended, horrified – oh yes, quite truly – who was driven almost mad with shame by the feeling that all her power over herself had broken down at her first real encounter with – with – (*the colour rushes over her face again*)'. It is the image he himself entertains, the image of the woman like Mrs Clandon who does not lose control, that asserts itself at the end and defeats him. For it is with the mother, rather than the daughter, that Valentine really struggles for power in the 'duel of sex'.

It is the prominence of Mrs Clandon in this play which distinguishes it from the Commedia dell'Arte plots. Despite the addiction of these to twins, and to family reunions, they have little room for mothers. Allardyce Nicoll's suggested explanations of this are particularly interesting here:

> This spirit of love . . . mirrors a dream rather than a reality; . . . its atmosphere . . . distinctly avoids the domestic.[1]

Again:

> In these plots the girls need to be free; their own emotions, although fervent, harmonize with the wider comic pattern; were a mother's sentiments to intrude, that comic pattern might well be shattered and confused.[2]

Mrs Clandon is not an obviously motherly mother; but her presence corresponds to the inbred and inherited tendencies that limit Gloria's freedom and, through her, Valentine's freedom too. So much is predetermined. Crampton and Mrs Clandon remain apart in the play to its end as a permanent token of the fact that marriages can fail and fail

---

[1] Allardyce Nicoll, *The World of Harlequin* (London: C.U.P., 1963), p. 140.
[2] Ibid., p. 141.

tragically for both sexes; the marriage of Gloria and Valentine may not be like that, but the prospect has ceased to look idyllic when the final curtain falls. 'You never can tell': there *is* freedom in human life; but it would not be as precious as it is, if the odds against it, the odds against the future being happier and better than the past, were not so great.

6

Man and Superman:
Verbal Heroics

Worst of all, I have been accused of preaching a Final Ethical Superman: no other, in fact, than our old friend the Just Man made Perfect: This misunderstanding is so galling that I lay down my pen without another word . . .   (1903 Postscript to Preface, *Man and Superman*)

The crux of *Man and Superman*, is the relation of the Hell scene in Act III to the rest of the play. Without it, as F. P. W. McDowell has observed,[1] the title Shaw gave the whole is reduced to a mere quip: 'Superman' could only have reference to the woman who overrules the man. Certainly Shaw conceived and wrote the play *with* the philosophy; there is no sign that Act III was an afterthought, an addition for publication, like *The Revolutionist's Handbook*. It brings in what, for Shaw, was an essential and fascinating part of Mozart's *Don Giovanni:* Don Juan's encounter with the supernatural, in the form of the Statue. And the scene, as we shall see (below, p. 104), is an important part of the panto-mime sequence the whole play follows. Yet the practical man of the theatre in Shaw recognized that *Man and Superman* would normally have to be played without the Hell scene and was at least moderately content to have it so. It looks as though we are confronted by an element that was essential to the dramatist's conception of the work, perhaps even essential to its composition, yet became a detachable segment of the finished art-object.

The Preface (anticipating the Preface of *The Doctor's Dilemma* in this) suggests that the idea for the play had a casual and superficial origin: in Walkley's challenge to Shaw that he should write a Don Juan play. There is, of course, more to the matter: Trefusis/Smilash in *An Un-*

[1] F. P. W. McDowell, 'Heaven, Hell and Turn-of-the-Century London: Reflections upon Shaw's "Man and Superman"', *Drama Survey*, Vol. II (1963), pp. 245–68.

social Socialist had been a Don Juan figure; Shaw also had behind him *The Philanderer*, which drew to some extent on his own amatory triflings; and Valentine in *You Never Can Tell* had been an idealized Don Juan whose fate it was to be captured and mastered by a woman. As the essential drama of *Candida* involved a confrontation of the author's *personae* as socialist and as artist by the figure of Woman, this new play was the occasion for the donning of another mask to meet the same antagonist: not quite the mask of lover – to himself John Tanner appears as a revolutionary socialist and a man of ideas – to us he is certainly a political pamphleteer and orator, but the Hell scene emphasizes what the comedy plot demonstrates: that the play turns on the fact of his sexuality and the relation to Woman that sets up, that he cannot break. Different degrees of consciousness are represented by revisions and final comments on the original writing of *Candida*; the same can be said of the modern dress comedy, the comedy with the interlude, and the published text with *The Revolutionist's Handbook*, in this later instance, though it is not a steady progress from faint intuition to full illumination that these divisions show. Rather, the interlude offers a dialectical counterpoint to the comedy, and the *Handbook* is a belated yet considerable strengthening of Juan's armoury.

Byron, selecting an anti-hero for his mock-epic, proclaimed a suitably trivial origin for the Don Juan he chose:

> We oft have seen him in the pantomime
> Sent to the devil somewhat ere his time.

Shaw's pre-eminent Don Juan play is a kind of epic, too, one of his first plays to adopt a cosmic range. 'I sing, not arms and the hero, but the philosophic man', he has Juan himself announce in the Hell interlude. The comedy he offers – and it is very close to farce – turns on the clownishness of this same 'philosophic man', whose silly-cleverness fails to save him from the trap. Through Jack Tanner, the most combative of all his characters, Shaw browbeats his audience with assertive argument and supplies a dogmatic interpretation of the action. Yet he makes game with the obtuseness of Tanner in certain directions and shows him up as, to some ill-defined extent, a shadow-boxer, unable to distinguish good causes from bad, defending others when the threat is to himself, wasting his energies in a kind of self-infatuation, vaunting the superiority of his opinions, his superior insight, over the stupidity, conventionality, or deceitfulness of everyone else.

The audience, liable to feel itself included in Tanner's generalized attack, is given its revenge in laughter. The impresario, Charles Frohman, commented on Shaw's wiliness in letting the boy get the girl in the end.

It is worth noting, not simply that the formula is reversed in this play – to girl gets boy – but that the 'happy ending' is a vindication of popular tastes and feelings: against the superior individual, against the eccentric and detached, even against reason and principle. Though still protesting, still playing his familiar role, Tanner is assimilated in high good-humour into the conventional group. The anti-intellectual impulse can be a healthy one, and Shaw's constant recognition of this is a major source of his strength. But the theoretical socialist is the only socialist with any serious claim to attention in this play; and it is an odd phenomenon that the socialist playwright, perhaps satirizing a weakness in his own party, should run so great a risk of leaving a philistine audience happily complacent. Conventional society wins hands down *in* the play; in the theatre, an audience pleased by the infectious comic mood completes what is remarkably like a ritual celebration of the *status quo*. The surface quieting of alarm this entails may possibly allow some of the things that have been said on the way to go on working without resistance in lay minds. It is likely enough that the men in the audience react with a touch of comic chagrin (such as the endings of conventional farce can evoke), modifying the sense of triumph. Sympathy with Ann Whitefield, whose own attitude to her social role is mixed, may awake rueful reflections in female minds. Yet any direct linking of these emotions with left-wing political attitudes is avoided. For the convinced and aware socialist, on the other hand, the pleasantness of the play may well leave a quite sourly unpleasant aftertaste. Once more, Shavian drama – if it works in a serious way at all – operates more subtly than criticism has been inclined to allow, and differently upon different sections of its audiences.

A degree of objectivity in the characterization of John Tanner must be accepted. It is well known that Shaw took the lineaments of the character from H. M. Hyndman of the Social Democratic Federation, though Granville Barker, playing the part, was made up to look like the dramatist himself.[1] On the other hand, it can hardly be denied or forgotten that analytical psychology recognizes the syndrome of Don Juanism and connects it with a mother-complex.[2] So the identification of Tanner with Don Juan can be read as an acknowledgement that the objective view the play presents is determined by a subjective bias. (There is, of course, not the slightest reason for valuing the work of art less on that account. Indeed we may be close to the springs of its power.)

Man and Superman is steeped in theatrical tradition. The idea of

[1] See Stephen Winsten, *Henry Salt and His Circle* (London: Hutchinson, 1951), pp. 64, 65, on Shaw's view of Hyndman, and Louis Crompton, *Shaw the Dramatist*, pp. 82–3.

[2] See Chapter 18, p. 338, note 1 below.

interpolating Jack Tanner's dream into Act III of the play can be traced back to the theatre of the masque. As in many an Elizabethan play, the main action is arrested, while an unrealistic, spectacular interlude, out of time, and either unlocalized or localized in some magic realm, gives another perspective on the theme of the containing play. The shift of scene from an English country house to some wild exotic spot, surprisingly inhabited by urban types, including a poetaster who carves his beloved's name on trees, and whose excruciating love-rhymes entertain us, is comparable to the shift from Duke's Court to Forest of Arden, where the principals reappear in disguise and where truth is found through dreams and fantasies. Disguise is the essence of the masque; but a disguise that reveals what is usually overlaid and obscure.

Writing to Charles Ricketts, the designer, after the interlude had been separately performed at the Court Theatre, Shaw commented on 'the artistic significance of our Don Juan experiment' with the words:

> William Morris always used to say that plays should be performed by four people in conventional costumes, the villain in a red cloak, the father in a bob-wig, etc. etc. etc., and I have always loved Harlequin, Columbine, Sganarelle, etc. in eighteenth century Italian comedy and French Champêtre painting. If only we could get a few plays with invisible backgrounds and lovely costumes like that in a suitable theatre, with fairy lights all round the proscenium . . .[1]

This suggests a double derivation: from the elegant refinements of Commedia dell'Arte offered by Watteau and Goldoni; but also the 'fairy lights all round the proscenium' would have been a familiar decoration of nineteenth-century pantomime (revived in more recent years in Zeffirelli's production of *Much Ado About Nothing*), and it seems likely that Morris had in mind something more rumbustious than would have pleased the Count in *Fanny's First Play*. In the main structure of *Man and Superman* the character of Octavius, the love-sick poet, is close enough to be identified with Ottavio, one of the stock romantic young lovers of the more courtly developments of Italian comedy (included in *Don Giovanni*, as Shaw's Preface reminds us). But Shaw makes capital of the fact that Octavius, if he is the *jeune premier*, is not central to the play but overshadowed by the true star performer from a coarser mould: Harlequin John Tanner, he might have been called in traditional pantomime formula. By a slight witty development of the convention, Shaw has varied his own device as used in *You Never Can Tell* and replaced the harlequinade interlude of older pantomime, in

[1] C. B. Purdom (ed.), *Bernard Shaw's Letters to Granville Barker* (London: Phoenix House, 1956), pp. 90–1. (This collection will later be referred to as the *Shaw–Barker Letters*.)

which the main figures of the specific story (the Don Juan legend it
might be, or a fairy tale) appeared transformed into the perennial
theatrical types, with an interlude in which his modern characters of the
Edwardian social comedy appear in the guise appropriate to the older
frame-tale. He has added a further dimension: Tanner is Don Juan, but
Don Juan is also Harlequin. Ironically enough, Tanner dreams of
himself as Juan, but not as clown, though the dream is an episode in the
chase across Europe, which is Shaw's equivalent of the chase which was
the *pièce de résistance* of the harlequinade. And the Hell scene itself is a
version of the Underworld scene of classical extravaganza, or the dark
scene that persisted in pantomime as an occasion for the Demon King
(here the Devil) to gloat over his victims.

Of course, the chief distinction between the scene Shaw offers and the
masque, or transformation ballet, lies in the shift of emphasis from visual
interest to the voices of the players. Visual pleasure there is in the
costumes he imagined: picked out by subtle lighting from the surrounding
darkness, they help give symbolic value to the figures, isolated from
plot or setting. But Mozart has intervened, as the Statue music reminds
us, and the old mimes have turned into opera singers. The appeal remains
aesthetic.

In reading the text it is too easy to lose sight of this fact and be wearied
by Shaw's undramatic verbosity if one is no longer engaged by what
Eric Bentley, in *The Theatre of Commitment*, has classified (perhaps not
quite accurately) as the only straight political propaganda in all Shavian
drama. For the debate form is a sham; there is no real conflict. The
Devil opposes Juan 'for the sake of argument', and his sustained tribute
to the death-instinct balances statically Juan's celebration of the Life Force.
Aña and the Commander make only occasional minor contributions.
Unlike the debating in the last act of *Major Barbara* this seems academic
and unconnected with the necessities of action; no tussle for Aña's soul is
proceeding, comparable to the tussle for Barbara's soul. It is no use
trying to accept their talk as a dimension of the characters, except in the
case of Juan. The 'characters' of the other three are so tenuous or conventional that they can hardly be said to exist. Juan is the only member of
the quartet who bears a significant resemblance to the main-plot figure
played by the same actor. Aña may look like Ann, but is much duller
and sourer; the Commander provides a strong contrast in manners to
Roebuck Ramsden; and we may look in vain for similarities between the
Devil and Mendoza. This helps establish the dream as Tanner's primarily:
the consciousness of the dreamer and, even more, the intention of the
dramatist, is the familiar element that links it with the main fabric
of the play. It is not inappropriate that the debate should prove, on

closer examination, to be more like a Platonic dialogue, a continuous exposition in which the speeches of the others, even the Devil's, are chiefly springboards for Juan's next oration, or merely pauses for him to get his breath. The ideas presented are generally too familiar to the present-day reader of Shaw to seem other than tediously outmoded: these are not the terms of current thinking; what have they to do with *our* problems? – and what else has the scene to offer? In the theatre, our ears give us the answer, when Juan is in full spate: we are caught up and carried along with a sublimated passion; words and ideas are alike instruments of its expression, their substance is rationalization.

Knowledge of the power of words is defined by Don Juan as 'the family secret of the governing caste'. Not only the orator, but the dramatist, can succumb to his own gift; the play's demonstration of this theme may be judged at once voluntary and involuntary, It must be said again: the involvement of Shaw with Tanner is very great indeed. The dialogue offers clues enough to indicate that the dramatist knew what he was doing, even if he could not stop himself from doing it. Tanner and Straker, together near the end of Act II, recall Beaumarchais's aphoristic remark 'that what was too silly to be said could be sung'. This prepares directly for Mendoza's rhapsodies on the name of Louisa, but more slyly it alerts us to listen sceptically to the whole of Act III. The allusion to Beaumarchais tacitly carries another: to Figaro. And surely something very like the garrulousness of the Beaumarchais–Rossini Figaro can be heard in the elaborate recitative of some of Juan's speeches:

> . . . your friends are all the dullest dogs I know. They are not beautiful: they are only decorated. They are not clean: they are only shaved and starched . . . they are not loyal, they are only servile; not dutiful, only sheepish; not public spirited, only patriotic; . . . not disciplined, only cowed; and not truthful at all: liars every one of them, to the very backbone of their souls.

The other characters bring against such speeches the charges 'mere talk', 'nothing but words'. Even in what look on the pages less like mechanical exercises in rhetoric, the thought (and the thoughtful distinctions are precise enough) is in fact being forced into patterns and grooves under a rhythmical and musical impulse. Tanner, on his first entrance into the main play, is described by Shaw as '*exaggerative*' and '*prodigiously fluent of speech*'; '*all his moods*', the direction runs '*are phases of excitement*'. In the dream these qualities are liberated from normal restraints, as the character finds himself in his ideal form. The immensely lengthy, cumulative speeches require great vocal power, variety and elocutionary skill for their delivery; the part demands an actor vocally trained as precisely as a classical singer. Though the Devil complains that Juan

'never sings for us now', this is surely part of the hallucination of the
dream: what may seem to the dreamer like rational prose sounds in the
theatre like a musical Triumph.

The locale, after all, is Hell, and Beaumarchais's thought is presented
again in Goethe's words: 'the poetically nonsensical here is good sense'.
Juan's epigram, 'Music is the brandy of the damned', is not an indictment
of music – the puritan in Shaw striking back at Corno di Bassetto – but
an indictment of the way it is abused by those who are happy in Hell.
Juan is not happy there; but for some reason obscure to him he *is* in Hell:

> . . . that is the enigma on which I ponder in darkness. Why am I here?
> I, who repudiated all duty, trampled honor underfoot, and laughed at
> justice!

The dream, one may guess, is a paradox: Juan's denunciations of Hell
are an indulgence of his chief vice, which marks him as a true denizen of
the place; and it is on the wings of eloquence that he takes flight for
Heaven, leaving Aña and the rest behind – and wakes up, not in Heaven,
as Jack Tanner about to be caught. On behalf of the author, Juan defines
the condition of Hell:

> the home of the unreal . . . here you escape this tyranny of the flesh . . .
> here there are no hard facts to contradict you . . .'

It is the condition of the dream and, being in the dream, Juan cannot help
but illustrate his definitions in his own person:

> You are a ghost, an appearance, an illusion, a convention, deathless, ageless:
> in a word, bodiless.

It seems very like the dream of an idealist, even a puritan idealist.

The words would serve also to describe any character in a work of
art. Shaw was certainly familiar with the Renaissance Christian connotations of the *dream* metaphor, especially as used by Shakespeare. All
the illusion–reality debate in his work reflects a traditional belief that the
value of human life is contingent on its relation to some infinite. In *Man
and Superman*, Shaw does not identify the puppet-master behind the
scenes ('If the play still goes on here and on earth, and all the world is a
stage, heaven is at least behind the scenes') as the Christian God; though
the paraphernalia of a Christian heaven and hell provide images for the
play's metaphysics, the throne of heaven is never glimpsed, nor any
figure on the throne. The divine Will to which Juan gives testimony in
the energy of his speech, even more than in his argument, is the Schopenhauerian irrational. His warning that 'Man . . . can only be enslaved
whilst he is spiritually weak enough to listen to reason' may strike the
audience with peculiar irony. Is it reason or irrational energy that

dominates in Tanner/Juan himself? And is the dramatist praising this as the Life Force, or warning against it, in this play as a whole?

Shaw claimed that William Poel's production of the morality play, *Everyman*, suggested to him the idea of making the heroine of his new play Everywoman.[1] But the specific character of Ann Whitefield, who incarnates Everywoman, is by no means generally representative; not even every Shavian heroine is of her type, predatory and uninterested, if not rather stupid, where anything beyond her narrow personal range is concerned; Ann's social and economic circumstances are certainly not Everywoman's. Yet the unity of main play and interlude depends on Tanner's identification of Ann with Woman and Woman with Will. In the dream of Hell (where there is no objective reality, only subjectivity), Jack's comic fear of Ann is projected in Juan's cosmic vision of a Will greater than his own:

> I had come to believe that I was a purely rational creature: a thinker! I said, with the foolish philosopher, 'I think; therefore I am.' It was Woman who taught me to say 'I am; therefore I think.'

The technique of the morality play may have encouraged the dramatist to build into the conventionally realistic fabric of his play an allegorical conflict between abstractions. Ann and Jack stand as female and male personifications of Will and Intellect, undifferentiated Energy and Individuality, though the characters resist total simplification into such terms. To a limited extent, the dramatist's identification of Ann with the Life Force endorses his hero's. An authorial direction describes her as '*one of the vital geniuses*', and Ann's play with her boa, falling in with Tanner's metaphor of the boa-constrictor, must have been linked in Shaw's mind with the legend of Lilith, though he has taken no pains to ensure that the audience should make the same association.

Lilith presided emblematically over nineteenth-century evolutionary theory, which regarded male organisms as later and 'higher' developments from more primitive female forms (the idea is reiterated by Strindberg); in *Back to Methuselah*, the matriarchal goddess, Lilith, fills the role assigned traditionally to God the Father, creator of Adam and Eve, and she is linked by association with the Serpent in the Garden of Eden. The serpent as emblem of Lilith belongs to ancient (Rabbinical) tradition; J. B. Kaye (*Shaw and the Nineteenth-Century Tradition*) has noted that Lilith is given by Blake as the name of one of the serpents – Good – in his Laocoön engraving. In line with this, the Lilith of *Back to Methuselah* is a figure of Wisdom whom it is possible to equate with creative imagination. More pointedly relevant to Shaw's presentation of

---

[1] *Man and Superman*, Epistle Dedicatory, p. xxviii.

Ann is the place occupied by Lilith in Pre-Raphaelite iconography. Rossetti's Lilith is a siren, snarer and potential destroyer of men: 'her enchanted hair was the first gold' implies a link between sex feeling and social acquisitiveness borne out by his comment in a letter: 'The idea which you indicate (viz. of the perilous principle in the world being female from the first) is about the most essential notion of the sonnet.' It is an idea that may owe something to Goethe's *Faust*, the Walpurgisnacht scene, as Harry Geduld has observed,[1] quoting Shelley's translation:

> Lilith, the first wife of Adam.
> Beware of her fair hair, for she excels
> All women in the magic of her locks;
> And when she winds them round a young man's neck,
>   She will not ever set him free again.

Now gold, or wealth, is undoubtedly an important consideration in the main play of *Man and Superman*. The action begins with a will – was this Shaw's central, strategic pun? – that leaves Ann an heiress. Of the guardians appointed for her, Roebuck Ramsden is '*a Chairman among Directors*', an inhabitant of the business world of Dickens's Veneerings, allied politically to Broadbent of *John Bull's Other Island*; the second guardian, Jack Tanner, is a millionaire whose name has the ring of common coin in it. The play does not tell how the Whitefield money was made, but Ann's mother bears the signs of lower-middle-class origin. The society Ann moves in is a plutocracy, where wealth buys idleness – and breeds a certain kind of art and idealism. Shaw remarked, in a letter to Granville Barker, on the 'peculiar intimacy of the Whitefield–Robinson family circle'.[2] Violet Robinson's husband, Hector Malone, is named with the same irony as Hector Hushabye of *Heartbreak House*: his uxoriousness promises to defeat his insufficiently strong impulse to be self-supporting by his own work, and he is doomed to parasitism on the vast commercial empire of his self-made, Irish-American father. 'What is the use of having money if you have to work for it?' asks Violet. Even Violet's self-effacing brother, the poetically inclined Octavius, will inherit enough to justify the form in which Ann consoles him:

> A broken heart is a very pleasant complaint for a man in London if he has a comfortable income.

Shaw has been at pains to demonstrate that these people are not aristocrats. Malone senior has come in search of something better, and

[1] Harry M. Geduld, 'The Lineage of Lilith', *Shaw Review*, Vol. VII (1964), pp. 58–61.
[2] *Shaw–Barker Letters*, p. 85.

Violet, though she carries her fashion with hauteur, has to meet his objections to her lack of a title:

VIOLET. . . . My social position is as good as Hector's, to say the least. He admits it.

MALONE. . . . Hector's social position in England, Miss Robinson, is just what I choose to buy for him. I have made him a fair offer. Let him pick out the most historic house, castle, or abbey that England contains. The very day he tells me he wants it for a wife worthy of its traditions, I buy it for him, and give him the means of keeping it up.
. . . she must be born to it.

Tanner, of course, styles himself a socialist as well as 'Member of the Idle Rich Class', and he has published a *Revolutionist's Handbook,* but it seems as much a rich man's toy as his motor car, the sign of technological progress and ruthlessness which Shaw wants brought on to dominate the stage in Act II. He is certainly the potential traitor within the group, until captured by Ann in a slavery that gives scope only to talking – a safety valve that helps keep the money secure. The cry of 'Superman', 'A father for the Superman', with which Aña in the dream sets out on her hunt, coincides with Tanner's awakening but has little genuine bearing on the real Ann's arrival in another motor car. If this Act was omitted we'd not have the cry to associate with the match between Ann and Jack. They are two very vital people, but their child will be no specimen of eugenic breeding across class barriers; on the other hand, it will be the heir to a double accumulation of what Ruskin called Illth.

None of this belongs to the Don Juan story – except in the general way that Don Juan tries to escape from conventional *mores* – and it has only the most negative relation to the Vitalist doctrines that Tanner, as Juan, expounds. The interpretation of the play's action that is offered by Tanner as *persona* of the author simply won't do.[1] It is the character's philosophical self-justification; but the author contrives to be as detached from Tanner as he is from Broadbent,[2] though it may be more the detachment of self-irony here. In the playing of the part there is room for a hint that Tanner/Juan's eloquence is the bluster of a timid man, or the self-assertiveness of a vain man, for the play does not entirely forsake naturalistic conventions except in the dream. How untrustworthy is this philosopher's practical judgement is made clear in Act I: his idealism

[1] This is not to say that Shaw deliberately and consistently intended the discrepancy. As with *Candida,* the baffling ambiguousness of the play which invites a variety of interpretations, as does life itself, is the effect of unresolved conflicts preventing the dramatist from maintaining full conscious control of his material.

[2] In *John Bull's Other Island,* see Chapter 7 below.

rushes him into a chivalrous defence of Violet, when a moment's reflection on her actual character, as he has long known it, would have made him see the absurdity of his suppositions. This is the clown's first tumble, and the audience, not having seen Violet before, feels the let-down as he does: there is nothing generous or unconventional about this priggish young woman except her cool-headed determination. It was a skilful device of Shaw's to establish Tanner's clear-sightedness on general issues first; the impression is not quickly destroyed, and so an ambiguous attitude to the character is established and maintained to the end of the play: Tanner is a clown, but he is also the nearest thing to a just man and a visionary in sight; and there is something depressing, if not actually tragic, contained in his ultimate comic defeat. As a satirist and social critic Tanner can be trusted; but his understanding of what happens in the play is more limited than the dramatist's. Jack's assumption that Octavius is Ann's quarry, incredulously mocked by his chauffeur, Straker, is another instance of his blindness: it is, indeed, a manifestation of his more general failure to make the right sort of practical application of his theory of civilization as a conflict between artist-man and mother-woman.[1] That might have served as an interpretation of *Candida*, where the artist's was a fighting role. Even if we suppose that Tanner himself plays the artist's role in such a confrontation (that he is Marchbanks in the mask of Morell), the maternal drive, the Will in Ann that momentarily overcomes her will, is not – even in the negative aspect of female cannibalism – the most important element in the opposition that finally captures him. It is his own idealistic obsession with maternal creativity that delivers him bound into the power of his enemies. His crowning delusion is the dream of escape to reality.

Juan's choice of Heaven is balanced by the Commander's decision to quit Heaven for Hell. Or, rather, it is the Statue of the Commander, as ostentatiously a symbol of authority as possible, authority not vested in any human being. (Appropriately, the Statue commends the conception of the Superman as 'statuesque', but is sceptical of his ever being created; and here, surely, is the view of the future author of *Back to Methuselah*.) The figure represents Aña's father, but Ramsden substitutes for White-field in the role, leaving the identity of Whitefield as enigmatic, his existence as problematic, as the identity and existence of the absent Hastings Utterword will be in *Heartbreak House*. It is not necessary to

---

[1] It is my contention that, if Shaw the philosopher shared in the error, Shaw the artist knew better and revealed what he knew in the total structure of his play. One needs to remember that he specifically linked parental indulgence, passionate family feeling, with capitalist ruthlessness in his very first play, *Widowers' Houses*; but such feeling is presented there as an extension of egotism, not as an *evolutionary* appetite.

read the play in anthropological terms in order to identify Whitefield with *patriarchal* authority; we may see him as as a non-entity like Veneering, a faceless personification of money, the accumulated wealth of middle-class England. The death of Whitefield is the significant fact that presides over the interview of Octavius and Ramsden, with which the play opens. The question it raises can be phrased in general terms as: who is to inherit the authority? A paternalistic authority is implied; for Whitefield, we gather, was a generous protector to all the young people in the play and a *paterfamilias* whose family was not limited by blood-relationship. Roebuck Ramsden, the old-fashioned liberal, sees himself as the natural successor to Whitefield as guardian of Ann and her fortune and he is, indeed, appointed as one guardian. But Ramsden is the Pantaloon in the harlequin-plot of *Man and Superman*, as bumblingly inadequate as Polonius in the government of Denmark. Tanner claims unwittingly to have influenced Whitefield's choice of a second guardian. In the play's final crisis Ann does the same and gets the response: 'The will is yours then! The trap was laid from the beginning.' Despite the weight their placing gives the words and despite Tanner's fatalistic recognition of the primacy of the female will, the shadowy figure of Whitefield is not simply exposed as a puppet; for there has been no earlier hint that his own judgement was ever overborne. Behind the dramatic structure of the play is an ironic consciousness. Starting with Whitefield as maker of the Will is a way of gesturing towards it.

The other character we hear of, who never appears, is Ann's younger sister, Rhoda, who supplies the legal pretext for the appointment of guardians and thus points up the oddity that Ann does not need a guardian, being of age to do what she wishes with her fortune and to choose a husband for herself. The fact that all the talk is of guardians for Ann, not for Rhoda, implies acknowledgement of the importance of that fortune. Ann's insistence on having guardians is part of the woman's pretence of being weaker than she is. The motive Jack attributes to her is the only one that makes sense in the context:

> . . . she has plenty of money and no conscience. All she wants with me is to load up all her moral responsibilities on me, and do as she likes at the expense of my character. I cant control her; and she can compromise me as much as she likes.

He adds: 'I might as well be her husband.' Running away to escape marriage involves an attempt to elude the permanent burden of such responsibility. In the play, as allegorical struggle between Will and Intellect, he is shirking the problem of learning to control Ann, allowing irresponsible force to usurp the authority that properly belongs to moral conscience. In the more specific terms of the political allegory, the new socialism joins the older liberalism in slavish subservience to established society, a subservience caricatured in the devotion of the artist, Octavius. A third view can reach a further conclusion: that the trouble has its source in the timidity of good women, their belief in their own weakness, which drives them to deviousness and prevents them from assuming the responsibility of social equality with men.

Tanner's verdict in Act I, 'You seem to me to have absolutely no conscience – only hypocrisy; and you cant see the difference', is a better clue to the character Ann demonstrates than is the identification of Woman with the Life Force. The *lie* is the dominant motif of the play, reiterated throughout the text, even audible in the Brigand's name, Mendoza; and the action includes a serial demonstration of Ann's mendacity and duplicity. What we see in Ann is not a sexual drive which would be genuinely subversive, reckless of social conventions and economic security, but conventionality hand-in-hand with calculation, a combination in itself as repellent as Violet's go-getting bitchery, but set in a more attractive temperament. Mrs Whitefield agrees with Jack's view of Ann – one of many Shavian daughters who show at their worst with their mothers. The climax of his indictment reiterates the initial charge: 'I can stand everything except her confounded hypocrisy.'

It is, of course, the vice traditionally associated with English society. Miss Ramsden's censorious attitude to Violet in Act I, Violet's own self-righteous revenge ('I have borne your hard words because I knew you would be sorry for them when you found out the truth'), Ann's affectedly priggish manner ('I do not think any young unmarried woman should be left quite to her own guidance'; 'Miss Ramsden would not like to speak about it before me, Granny. I ought not to be present.') and Mrs Whitefield's refusal to admit her hatred of Ann[1] – the behaviour of all the women in the play, including the snobbish, morally self-complacent Aña of the dream, comes to suggest a composite female image very like the legendary Mrs Grundy.

Both Ramsden and Octavius conform to the fraud of womanly morality, though it is based on weakness and cowardice, as Ann will admit to serve her purpose:

All timid women are conventional: we must be conventional, Jack, or we are so cruelly, so vilely misunderstood.

---

[1] Unacknowledged hate in family relationships, especially between parents and children, is a Shavian obsession that often helps to complicate the plays. Of course, it is a deep form of hypocrisy in Mrs Whitefield that makes her protest in horror: 'Do you mean that I detest my own daughter! Surely you dont believe me to be so wicked and unnatural as that . . .'

Even the would-be iconoclast is vulnerable to their moral blackmail through his tender-mindedness:

> You had acquired by instinct that damnable woman's trick of heaping obligations on a man, of placing yourself so entirely and helplessly at his mercy that at last he dare not take a step without running to you for leave . . . If we try to go where you do not want us to go there is no law to prevent us; but when we take the first step your breasts are under our foot as it descends: your bodies are under our wheels as we start.[1]

Whether or not it is the dramatist's sentimentality as well as the character's, Tanner's capitulation, in the last Act, to Ann's claim that she is herself a victim of the Life Force, risking in childbirth a death he does not risk, is another instance of his enslavement by theory: by a plea out of a primitive past fast losing its validity by the beginning of the twentieth century. It is his unacknowledged acquiescence in her view –

> I am too feminine to see any sense in destruction. Destruction can only destroy . . .

– that defeats him. What avoidance of destruction is reduced to, in Ann's code of behaviour, is tact and diplomacy, superficial conformity and social compromise, the system condemned in *Widowers' Houses*, where 'tact' is a key word. (Logically, Shaw is now ready to write *Major Barbara* and examine the value of destructive power.)

Yet Ann *is* very different from her friend Violet. In part, it is a matter of theatrical descent of the two characters: Violet's from the elegant lady, the contemporary figure, of the later, literary modifications of Commedia dell'Arte (though the name, Violette, is given to a servant of Don Juan in Molière's *Festin de pierre*, it is more frequently associated with the romantic heroine), Ann's from Columbine, a soubrette type, with still about her more than a little of the robust serving-maid who lives by her wits and is a true companion for Harlequin. Ann is exposed as virtually a pathological liar, so consistently outrageous as to beggar our judgement; she does, in fact, endear herself to audiences as a comic type, almost a picaresque character, by her *nature* challenging what Tanner calls the 'pious English habit of regarding the world as a moral gymnasium' more effectively than all his preaching does. Of course, the fact that Ann is lovable (whereas Violet's power depends on the physical beauty that leads infatuated men to idealize her out of recognition)

---

[1] Shaw wrote of Robert Loraine's playing of Tanner in 1907: 'He wanted to deliver the great speech about the tyranny of mothers enthroned in the motor car, with Lillah somewhere under the wheels with her back to the audience. I immediately saw the value of the idea, and put Lillah in the car in a fascinating attitude with her breast on the driving wheel, and Loraine ranting about on the gravel . . .' (*Shaw–Barker Letters*, p. 85.) See fig. 9.

contributes largely to her dangerousness: the part that Woman holds in her is less easy to reject and defy. Certainly she bears a kinship to Raina of *Arms and the Man* and chooses Jack, as Raina chooses Bluntschli, because he has found her out and can regard her as a human being, not an idol. The play thoroughly exposes the worst side of Ann; but there are other aspects to her character:

> Getting over an unfavorable impression is ever so much easier than living up to an ideal. Oh, I shall enrapture Jack sometimes!

There is insight and seriousness, at last, not just vanity and cruelty at play, in her attitude to Octavius:

> You have offered to tell Jack that I love him. Thats self-sacrifice, I suppose; but there must be some satisfaction in it . . . it seems quite simple. But *I doubt if we ever know why we do things*. The only really simple thing is to go straight for what you want and grab it. I suppose I dont love you, Tavy; but sometimes I feel as if I should like to make a man of you somehow. You are very foolish about women.   (*My italics*)

This is truth, not hypocrisy now. 'I doubt if we ever know why we do things'; that line gives a perspective on Tanner and the complexity of the play as a whole: on the fallacy Tanner represents, of supposing that reason alone is the best equipment for facing life, or that moral conscience is the prerogative of the philosopher.

Act I provides some evidence that Shaw, composing the character of Ann as an individual girl, not Everywoman, or Britannia, had elements of *Hedda Gabler* in mind. The memories of childhood she shares with Jack are comparable to Hedda's girlhood association with Eilert Lövborg:[1]

> TANNER. . . . You were insatiably curious as to what a boy might be capable of . . . You lured me into a compact by which we were to have no secrets from one another . . . I didnt notice that you never told me anything . . . And I found myself doing all sorts of mischievous things simply to have something to tell you about.

This suggests that Ann, like Hedda, was driven to seek vicarious satisfaction of her appetite for life. (It is his own closeness to British middle-class feeling that makes Shaw put these incidents further back in his characters' lives – at a time previous to adult sexual consciousness – than Ibsen does.) Her aspiration, too, was for a quality of life missing from the middle-class conventional world where 'people don't do such things', and she similarly missed her aim:

> I never wanted you to do those dull, disappointing, brutal, stupid, vulgar things. I always hoped that it would be something really heroic at last.

---

[1] *Hedda Gabler*, Act II.

9 Alan Badel as John Tanner in *Man and Superman*.

10 *Don Juan in Hell*. The operatic effect.

But *Man and Superman* is a play without a hero in that epic sense; and Ann never seems remotely likely to assume the role herself, as Hedda at last resolutely does in the suicide that is a dismissal of middle-class values.

Hedda's rejection of motherhood (though it is specifically a rejection of Tesman's child) links her with the negative aspect of New Womanhood, the aspect Shaw had portrayed in Vivie Warren. Though Tanner introduces his chauffeur, Straker, as the New Man, signs of the New Woman are quite curiously absent from *Man and Superman*. In a wider social setting, Ann might appear to be fighting a rearguard action against progressive movements in general and female emancipation in particular; but the social scene has been very carefully confined to avoid direct social contrasts: there are not even any poor to contrast with the rich – only a caricature of general political and economic issues, and political personages, in the Mendoza episode of Act III.[1] The only employee allowed on stage, Henry Straker (the Leporello of *Don Giovanni*), shows a startling independence of manner, based on his indispensability in the running of the industrial system: he is the skilled mechanic, in short supply still, and he has not yet made up his mind which side of the political fence it will best pay him to be on. Straker's relative prosperity and freedom may be contrasted with the image of poverty that haunts the mind of the elder Malone (as the image of his mother haunted Sartorius):

> His granmother was a barefooted Irish girl that nursed me by a turf fire . . .
> Me father died of starvation in Ireland in the black 47 . . . and I was starved
> out to America in me mother's arms.

No doubt the Whitefield money was amassed in those times, but its present redistribution seems less than urgent in the context presented by the play: the need for revolution seems almost as theoretical as Tanner's revolutionist doctrines themselves. In this context, the men are merely playing politics – as a drawing-room talking game, or as a variant of cowboys and Indians. What the play altogether embodies is the smothering sense of security, comfort and complacency that can resist all change. It is the sense the mother supplies to the child, and Tanner is convinced of the need to rebel against mothers – but not clear enough that it is not a woman's need alone.

> Always the mother! . . . to lie and slander and insinuate and pretend . . .
> That is what obeying your mother comes to . . . this vile abjection of youth
> to age! . . . The law for father and son and mother and daughter is not the
> law of love: it is the law of revolution, of emancipation, of final supersession
> of the old and worn-out by the young and capable.

---

[1] The comedy of this episode would have been much richer for a contemporary audience that could identify the originals of Shaw's caricatures.

E

Ann pleads her love for her mother, but she can afford to, as in her case
the tables are turned and the younger generation has the upper hand;
so that it is left to her mother to demonstrate the dislike and resentment
that largely define her relation to the daughter who, in fact, disregards
her as neither of the young Robinsons nor Jack is inclined to do. Precisely
because it is against violence, aggression, outspokenness, the dominance
of the mother-image is opposed to the disturbance of change and the
fruitful conflict of opposites. We may see Ann's own character as a victim
of the matriarchal ideal: though she may seem free, she is not creatively
and heroically free. Ann will not destroy herself, but also she will have no
adventures outside the biological hazards even conventional women are
subject to: the seeds of a Hedda Gabler have died within her, and her
dangerousness is of a diametrically opposite kind from what Laclos
discerned in his eighteenth-century precursor of the emancipated woman
at war with men: Mme de Meurteuil of *Les Liaisons dangeureuses*.

Not creativity but sterility is apparent in most areas of the play.
The once-progressive Ramsden lives a bachelor existence with his spinster
sister, a dragon of conventional morality. Octavius is equally destined
for bachelordom and is even less embroiled with life than the others.
Violet's supposed pregnancy, on which most of Act I turns, finds no
later mention in the play. The Violet we see has insufficient generosity
or passion, it would seem, to conceive a child except for dynastic reasons;
and she makes no use of the news of an imminent grandchild in her
dealing with Hector's father or Hector himself. Indeed, Violet's triumph
is the defeat of old Malone's idealism of *social* profit. Ann is different,
more vulnerable, more capable of emotional warmth; but her attitude
to her mother and her younger sister still leaves it likely that her children
would, in part at least, be means for binding Tanner to her and to the
family which is her realm, as he foresees.

Shaw chose to represent the final bout in the match between the two
as an embrace symbolic of the sexual act. It is Tanner who initiates it,
admitting the division in his own will: 'I have the whole world in my arms
when I clasp you. But I am fighting for my freedom, for my honour, for
my self, one and indivisible.' At the climax Ann is as much affected as he:

ANN (*panting failing more and more under the strain*). Jack: let me go. I have
   dared so frightfully – it is lasting longer than I thought. Let me go: I cant
   bear it.
TANNER. Nor I. Let it kill us.
ANN. Yes: I dont care. I am at the end of my forces. I dont care.

At this point, the individual woman is no more the controlling Will than
the man, but she recovers in time to assert her social hold over him –

ANN (*reeling, with a supreme effort*). I have promised to marry Jack.

Of course, Shaw is associating two quite distinct things which Tanner insists on identifying. It is not sexual passion but social discipline that traps him into marriage. To what extent the association – the need to associate the social and political subjection of the man with his sexual submission – was compulsive is hard to judge in the isolated context of this play. Comparison, for instance, with the end of *You Never Can Tell* suggests that it may have been. There is a formal resemblance to the mock-happy ending of *The Philanderer;* but this play has been pleasanter all along, and geniality wins over bitterness at the final curtain too.

Man and Superman is concerned with the deathliness of compromise and the betrayal (or self-betrayal) of men through women, but also with the shoddy romanticism of revolution presented in the inset burlesque of the brigand group. Despite the opinions they profess, and though it is the motor cars of the rich that they ambush, Mendoza's band caricatures capitalist society (as Brassbound's does) in a mirror image. The meeting with Tanner makes the point:

MENDOZA. . . . I am a brigand: I live by robbing the rich.
TANNER (*promptly*). I am a gentleman: I live by robbing the poor.[1]

The anarchist of Mendoza's 'parliament' wears the top-hat which Shaw commonly employs as the badge of capitalist respectability (e.g. in *The Perfect Wagnerite*). The identification is clinched by the eventual absorption of the band in a common commercial enterprise with the plutocrat, Malone.

Mendoza himself is a send-up of the melodramatic type of broken-hearted lover. In the character-plot of the play he seems most obviously reflective of Octavius; but his speech-making and his concern with politics give him a pointed relevance to Tanner himself. It is Ann, speaking to Jack in the final moment of the play, who echoes Mendoza's instructions to his followers at the end of Act III:

MENDOZA (*between his teeth*). Go on. Talk politics, you idiots: nothing sounds more respectable. Keep it up, I tell you.

ANN. . . . Never mind her, dear. Go on talking.

So Tanner becomes Ann's ally, as Octavius is Violet's – 'romance' and hard-bitten self-seeking hand-in-hand – in the social conspiracy that can easily absorb a little amateur socialism. The 'romantic' background of the Sierra is satirically appropriate to the unreality of the whole pretence of civilization.

But, of course, one character stands apart, contemptuous of words,

---

[1] Compare the ironic meeting of the Master of the Mine and the Master of the Campo in Conrad's *Nostromo* (1904).

self-reliant, clear-sighted: Straker, the engineer who maintains and drives the car. To Straker, H. G. Wells's New Man, most of what goes on around him is irrelevant. He is the only character in the play who *works* for his living and is to that extent careless of inherited fortunes, as he is careless of traditional class-divisions. It does not matter that Tanner's praise of him is also a way of making game of him; he knows his superiority to his tutelar master. The play at least admits the possibility that even Ann's will may count for little, if Straker continues to drive the car.

By virtue of Act III, *Man and Superman* must be classified as the first example in Shaw's work of the play of ideas that may be considered his most characteristic invention. In its general structure, the work does not anticipate the strong dialectical patterning to be found in *Major Barbara*, but illustrates a contrary tendency in Shavian drama: away from clear organic unity and the self-containment of art. The interrupted plot, the variation of style, the shifting locale, and even the proliferation of ideas, represent a struggle away from rationally determined form and order. The common perplexities about Shaw's ideas are proper and significant in such a dramatic context. What are they worth? How committed to them is he? Through Tanner/Juan he expounds those doctrines of the Life Force, the struggle between artist – man and mother – woman, and the Superman so commonly associated with him; yet to a certain extent, through plot and structure, he makes game of them. They are certainly useful pegs to hang the play on. As hypotheses, Tanner's theories are ridden for all they are worth – but in a spirit of scepticism, on the dramatist's part, about the absolute validity of any theories at all. The pleasure *Man and Superman* gives is one with what it demonstrates: that ideas are good to play with. They are suggestive; the exercise is healthful and may be corrective. But one may sense a stirring of speculation on whether abandonment to reason alone may not lead to a special kind of anarchy. It emerges in lines and phrases here and there: 'weak enough to listen to reason'; 'I doubt if we ever know why we do things'; more positively in 'It was Woman who taught me to say "I am; therefore I think" '. Shaw closes no doors in the mind to prove anything finally; he is artist more than philosopher in this.

7

John Bull's Other Island

When the Vedrenne–Barker tenure of the Court Theatre was running out, in 1907, Shaw wrote to Vedrenne:

> I have given you a series of first-rate music hall entertainments, thinly disguised as plays, but really offering the public a unique string of turns by comics and serio-comics of every popular type. Calvert as Broadbent and William, Gwenn as Straker, Lewis as B.B., Yorke as Bill, with the sisters Clandon and the Irish character turns and the newspaper man have done for the Court what George Robey and Harry Lauder have done for the Halls . . . that is the jam that has carried the propaganda pill down.
>
> (*Shaw–Barker Letters*, p. 77.)

Though it is a far from complete account of the technique used in *John Bull's Other Island* – or in any of his other plays – the statement is notably relevant to it. It is a good play for a repertory company if only because of the chance it gives every member of the cast for a personal triumph. The character-turns are the essential elements in the dramatic structure which allow the dramatist to get away with a casualness of plot and looseness of texture that, in turn, create an almost spontaneous effect. The very fact that the play was so far from being conventionally well-made was surely as important as the topicality of the Home Rule issue in breaking through the artificial barriers between actors, author and audience in the Edwardian theatre. A comparable effect was achieved fifty years later in the Court Theatre, when John Osborne let Jimmy Porter's diatribes shatter academic play-structure, button-hole the audience in their seats and shake them out of their complacent detachment.

The sprawl of a middle-period Dickens novel, in which interest is constantly renewed through the rich succession of fantastic characters, is the obvious non-theatrical model for Shaw's plays in this kind; and even *Heartbreak House* remains a variation on the kind. The influence of narrative can be detected in more negative ways in *John Bull's Other Island*: the breaks and scene-changes in Acts II and IV fragment the dramatic shape and seem to tie it unduly to chronology. There is little sense of the *scène-à-faire*, the inherently dramatic situation within an action, behind Shaw's choice of episodes for presentation on stage. The occasions they represent are generally unremarkable: commonplace moments of preparation, arrival, an after-breakfast pause, an after-tea walk. But the characters are gathered in their groups, large or intimate, and become the means of generating an immediate, almost arbitrary theatrical interest, not much dependent on setting or context. Variations of setting and the ordering of the loosely connected items are obviously as important to the success of the whole entertainment as in those other rather loosely constructed theatrical forms of pantomime and opera. (Shaw's plays could be considered as anticipations of Brechtian 'epic' drama, on these grounds.) It is more than usually important for a reader of the text to remember that Shaw's brain-child was the theatrical performance that could be based on that text; criticism has to involve the judgement of possibilities and not a finally defined achievement.

Shaw's objections to unauthorized cutting of his plays have been much publicized; he was far from blind to the fact that the text *could* be cut harmlessly, even advantageously, as long as the work was done responsibly. His Irish play, written for a National Theatre programme (though it outran the capacities of the Irish Abbey Theatre, it took its place in a repertory designed to show what an English national theatre could do) was an ambitious project,[1] and he approached it fresh from the *tour de force* of *Man and Superman*. The result was an overabundance that alarmed him even when he was preparing the new play for Granville Barker. 'The theme is a huge one; and it can't be cut down to Court size,' he wrote to the producer. He and Barker both worked on a drastic reduction of the text for performance, but Shaw remained aware of having tried to get too much in: 'there are five separate tragedies in the thing besides the Broadbent comedy.'[2] Of course he wanted an epic sweep: to present Ireland *vis-à-vis* England; not Dublin, but the Ireland of small country towns. And, as far as the theatre could accommodate the method, he wanted to give it through a Dickensian range of characters that would acquire a not-so-limited autonomy in the acting: a stage-Irishman, Tim Haffigan; an authentic Irish exile in England, Larry Doyle; an Irish saint, the immemorial pilgrim, deeply European in culture, Peter

---

[1] Shaw first mentioned writing a play for the Irish Theatre 'on the contrast between Irish and English character' as early as March 1900. See Allan Wade (éd.), *Letters of W. B. Yeats* (London: Rupert Hart-Davis, 1954), p. 335. The play proved beyond the resources of the Irish company and was therefore first performed in England. See also *Shaw–Barker Letters*, pp. 22–5.

[2] These quotations are taken from the *Shaw–Barker Letters*, pp. 45 and 39 respectively.

Keegan;[1] a decent Irish priest, Father Dempsey; the small-holders, Matthew Haffigan, ex-peasant labourer, and the more substantial ex-land-agent, Cornelius Doyle; a traditional, relatively prosperous artisan, Barney Doran, the miller; a reputed half-wit, the put-upon lad, Patsy Farrell; the colleen-heiress, Nora, chaperoned by the motherly old maid, Aunt Judy, in the interests of Irish propriety. They are cleverly balanced by the single English type-figure, Tom Broadbent, Shaw's John Bull, a Gladstonian Liberal, assisted by his valet, Hodson. This can be properly seen as a document of the Irish Dramatic Movement, a contribution to national drama which is concerned with the religious and political identity of Ireland, with its legends and its day-to-day life.

The Ireland of O'Casey's plays and Yeats's greatest poetry, the Ireland of the Easter rebellion and the black-and-tans, was still more than a decade away. But the Fenians, the hungry forties and subsequent famines, the land question and the Home Rule issue are part of the history implied in the play, and there is even an echo from Cromwellian Ireland. The temperament of the 'bould Fenian' is represented in Larry, though his old political alignment has vanished with his removal to England. The grimness, poverty and hardship of peasant life are recalled by the dour presence of Matthew Haffigan and the comments others make on his experience:

> LARRY. . . . That man's industry used to make me sick, even as a boy. I tell you, an Irish peasant's industry is not human: . . . Matthew Haffigan and his brother Andy made a farm out of a patch of stones on the hillside: cleared it and dug it with their own naked hands and bought their first spade out of their first crop of potatoes . . .
>
> . . . the landlord put a rent of £5 a year on them, and turned them out because they couldnt pay it . . .
>
> You know very well that Billy Byrne never paid it. He only offered it to get possession . . .
>
> AUNT JUDY. That was because Andy Haffigan hurt him with a brick so that he was never the same again. Andy had to run away to America for it.

The anecdote serves as a paradigm of more recent Irish history. Its content of suffering and violence is summed up in Larry's protest:

> . . . whats the good of the man thats starved out of a farm murdering the man thats starved into it?

---

[1] This character shows marked resemblances to George Tyrrell, the eminent Catholic Modernist (and Shaw's fellow Dubliner in origin) who was to be expelled from the Society of Jesus in 1906 and refused Catholic burial in 1909. See M. D. Petre, *Autobiography and Life of George Tyrrell*, 2 vols. (London: Edward Arnold, 1912). The young Tyrrell was noted for a tenderness for tiny creatures such as insects (cf. Keegan and the grasshopper).

Broadbent's instruction to Hodson to pack his revolver and cartridges for a visit to Ireland not only opens the play smartly by surprising the audience with an absurdity. It is an alert to the emotional antagonism important in the play, not only in the grating of one character against another, but in the pattern of emotional relationships set up between the characters and the audience. Opposition of opinion in debate, what Shaw described as the 'superficial political' element in the play, is revealed as a mere parliamentary exercise, a sham, by contrast.

The engaging humour of the stage-Irishman is rejected in Act I as a preliminary to the main business of the play. Tim Haffigan's attempt to act the part lacks both artistry and conviction. What is amusing in his scene with Broadbent is supplied by the other, whose assurance and expansiveness throw into relief the near-pathetic inadequacy of his visitor. In isolation, Tim would be merely dispiriting; as he projects no strong and clear emotion, but only uncertainty, he attracts little sympathy from the audience. This is not a portrait in any depth, but it is realistically and unsparingly observed: Tim's thirst for spirits, his only genuine interest, shows up as the poor joke it is. Broadbent's determinedly persistent admiration for him is the source of the comedy, and arouses wonder. It is an interesting variation on the traditional theatrical confrontation of knave and gull: the genial, well-fed, prosperous gull, on his own ground, is so surely impervious to any threat from this knave, poorly endowed by nature and by fortune alike. The direct impression of Broadbent's personal superiority to Haffigan conveys a sense of English power, which can afford a careless patronage of hangers-on and poor relations. The Englishman's sunny humour extends beyond this scene over the whole play. It is attractive, as nothing else in the play is – but across the distance that the spectacle of blatant folly creates. Rich in feeling, null in insight and intellect, the character calls out a double response; a variation on the effect is presented by his man-servant Hodson, in which the smooth, null surface of the conventional valet is temporarily discomposed to reveal the intransigent Cockney who owns no master.

The role of Larry is the one Shaw might have been expected to identify himself with most readily, from which he might have needed to distance himself most carefully: the exile reluctant to return to his native district after eighteen years. Indeed, in revising, he reported to Granville Barker, whom he had wanted for the part, that Larry had become an unsympathetic character. Larry's dominant mood throughout the play combines guilt and depression – at his inability and reluctance to bridge the gulf between his busy and successful life in England and his origins that he meets again in the Irish landscape and its people, in the father who now seems of little consequence and the girl who has been passively and constantly waiting for him all this time. For though Shaw makes Larry jibe at the imaginative Irishman who can only be interested in Ireland when it is personified as Kathleen ni Hoolihan, his play straightforwardly approaches patriotism (whatever particular sentiment for the homeland the term may cover) as the public, diffused sentiment which corresponds to the emotional tie with his family and early friends and the relations of his mature self to his boyhood. Larry has, in fact, run away from narrowness, boredom, inactivity and ineffectuality, 'The torturing, heartscalding, never satisfying dreaming, dreaming, dreaming, dreaming'. His growth into manhood has involved a revulsion from this kind of idealism, and its unbalance is clear in his insistence on the real, solid qualities of his busy English life. A Sergius who has tried to turn himself into a Bluntschli, he recommends the same cure to Nora:

> Play your new part well, and there will be no more neglect, no more loneliness, no more idle regrettings and vain-hopings in the evenings by Round Tower, but real life and real work and real cares and real joys among real people: solid English life in London, the very centre of the world. You will find your work cut out for you keeping Tom's house and entertaining Tom's friends and getting Tom into Parliament: but it will be worth the effort.

Larry's bias is slily underlined by the information, conveyed by Tom, that his taste in women is for animated beefsteaks. It is Larry who provides the shrewdest diagnosis of Ireland's economic and political ills and proposes the most realistic remedy; but he approaches the situation as an abstract problem of little personal concern to him: 'Youre all children: the big world that I belong to has gone past you and left you.' The individual psychology of the character is apparent in his ready estimation of his friendship with Broadbent above his relationship with Nora. Though he says to her, '*I* want you; and I quarrel with you and have to go on wanting you', the line helps establish Nora's figurative value, suggestive of the 'soul' of Ireland, but is otherwise little supported as testimony to Larry's feeling. What does clearly emerge is that his preference is not purely a choice between individuals: giving priority to friendship between man and man amounts, in this case, to a preference for the business partnership over the purely personal relationship. The portrait is consistent in that it is Larry who speaks as Keegan's main antagonist (and the only character in the play who shows no respect for him). Larry is ruthless:

> Pah! what does it matter where an old and broken man spends his last days . . . I say let him die, and let us have no more of his like . . .

and, forgetting the effect of grinding poverty, puts his trust in impersonal efficiency:

> our syndicate has no conscience . . . In the end it will grind the nonsense out of you, and grind strength and sense into you.

Keegan indicts what he calls 'this foolish dream of efficiency'; but Larry keeps up his scorn of fine words and fine sentiments, Irish or English, to the end of the play.

Pairing Larry with Broadbent was a principal means whereby Shaw brought something like tragi-comic balance into the composition of *John Bull's Other Island*. The relationship has the imaginative and philosophical closeness of the Mephistopheles–Faust doubling. But his diagnostic of the situation in terms of political morality draws also on Voltaire's *Candide*: Broadbent is Shaw's Pangloss as well as his foolishly unimaginative Faust, and in this role it is Keegan who proves to be his necessary antagonist. The first part of Act IV is. devised to communicate the tension of opposed moods through the expedient of dividing the stage into two areas occupied by emotionally separate groups: on one side Barney Doran is the centre of attention recounting to a group convulsed with laughter, as he is himself, the tale of Haffigan's pig in Broadbent's motor car. It is a laughter calculated to infect the audience, irrespective of what the figures on stage are laughing *at*; but, sitting apart and inviolate from the crowd emotion, is Keegan, and his grimness combats the hold of Barney and his cronies on the audience's mood. He is supported by the quietness of Nora and the composure of Aunt Judy; but Shaw risks a complete withdrawal of audience sympathy from Keegan here, more than from Barney. His soliloquy with the grasshopper, in Act II, predisposes us to like him and respect his wisdom. Yet he is now so far from genial, so puritanically disapproving in his rejection of the humour of an affair that certainly had more than one aspect, that we cannot feel complete authorial endorsement of his attitude. Temperamentally, Keegan emerges in this scene as very like Larry: bitter and rejecting. He is the Brother Martin of the *Candide*-pattern here. Both Keegan and Larry are capable of the cold savagery of Irish wit. In view of what eventuated, the relief Doran and the rest find in laughter is natural; Keegan's protest seems high-flown and overstated:

> There is danger, destruction, torment! What more do we want to make us merry? Go on, Barney; the last drops of joy are not squeezed from the story yet. Tell us again how our brother was torn asunder.

The stage picture, with its clashing emotions, represents two forcibly separated halves of a truth. And the validity of Keegan's half rests, finally, on the fact that the pig was terrified and was killed; this is the climax of one of the play's leitmotifs – the theme of the little things, flowers or grasshoppers, towards which Keegan (a Saint Francis of Ireland) shows respect and consideration, and the imagery of efficient little things – bees, coral insects, even caterpillars, to which Broadbent's symbolic motor car is tacitly opposed.

The value of sensitiveness and delicacy is thus asserted in the play, claiming recognition alongside other values. It is realized and embodied in Nora, whom Shaw has drawn with great tact and careful neutrality. It would have been easy to make the character pathetic, miserable, or faintly ridiculous: a woman nearing thirty-six, who came for a visit and stayed for good, who has been constant to the image of a girlhood sweet-heart for half her life with no encouragement from him, a woman without purpose or occupation, so ignorant of the world that she thinks the wealthy Englishman wants her 'fortune' of forty pounds a year. (This is, of course, Shaw's way of measuring the poverty of Roscullen and its powerlessness against the capital Broadbent represents.) Before she appears in the play, Larry's description of her to Broadbent focuses on her pride, which could be interpreted as a stoic submissiveness to convention:

> Nora would wait until she died of old age sooner than ask my intentions or condescend to hint at the possibility of my having any . . . and if I had to choose between wounding that delicacy in her and hitting her in the face, I'd hit her in the face without a moment's hesitation.

Nora is a far cry from Ann Whitefield, then, as well as from Violet Malone. Larry explains her 'Irish charm' in terms of her diet – of tea and bread-and-butter. The Nora we see and hear could, possibly, be classified as a decayed gentlewoman, but so pejorative a term is hardly likely to occur to an audience confronted by the simple integrity of the woman. As a portrait of a gentlewoman, the character has been drawn with consider-able understanding and quite unpatronizingly. The note of Shaw's approach is precisely struck in the direction before her first entrance, when Broadbent's and Larry's estimates of her are followed by the anti-dogmatic statement: '*These judgements have little value and no finality.*' It is as good as an assertion that human beings are not to be summed up so easily, that they are other and more than they may mean to any single beholder:

> For Tom Broadbent . . . an attractive woman whom he would even call ethereal. To Larry Doyle, an everyday woman fit only for the eighteenth century, helpless, useless, almost sexless, an invalid without the excuse of disease, an incarnation of everything in Ireland that drove him out of it.

The actress who has to play the part must, obviously, render it capable of these diverse interpretations; but it is a human being, not specially enigmatic, yet also not set and typed into caricature, but with wavering uncertain outlines, that she has to present.

The sympathy between Nora and Keegan contributes to the characteriz-ation of both, underlining a quality of toughness that helps sustain her delicacy and, in him, modifying the harshness with a gentle, ap-preciative response towards another person; the authority of Keegan is stern, but not unloving. Arguably the most acutely conceived and best-written scene of the play is the second 'love-scene' between Broadbent and Nora, which comes in Act IV. The most considerable imaginative achievement of the play lies in its presentation of the 'innocence' of Broadbent, which Keegan carefully distinguishes from hypocrisy:

> I know that you are quite sincere. There is a saying . . . Let not the right side of your brain know what the left side doeth . . . this is the secret of the Englishman's strange power of making the best of both worlds.

The two worlds, as verbal reiteration throughout the dialogue serves to insinuate, are not this world and the next, but heaven and hell. Keegan's definition of hell consists of a Blakean catalogue of evils which are not directly presented in *John Bull's Other Island*, and the speech could as well have been placed in the Interlude in Hell of *Man and Superman*:

> a place where the fool flourishes . . . where men and women torture one another in the name of love; where children are scourged and enslaved in the name of parental duty and education . . . where the hardest toil is a welcome refuge from the horror and tedium of pleasure. . .

Its dramatic point lies in the fact that it passes so completely over Broad-bent's head and disturbs him not at all in his conviction that the world is 'rather a jolly place', where he feels at home: 'I find the world quite good enough for me.' Too amiable and too good-tempered to be a devil, he has immunized himself against suffering, so that he cannot tell hell from heaven, and he cheerfully passes on the farcical prescription to Keegan: 'Try phosphorous pills.' Shaw's presentation of idealism recalls Voltaire's impugnment of Leibniz, as Broadbent echoes Pangloss's doctrinaire insistence that 'All is for the best in the best of all possible worlds.' The world Keegan sees, like the world of Brother Martin, is bewilderingly different.

Broadbent is the most attractive character in the play by reason of his ebullient spirits, his expansiveness, his soft-heartedness in immediate response to others, even the transparency of his motivation, the straight-forward simplicity of his vanity and self-delusion. The Tim Haffigan episode of Act I establishes his tendency to think well of others – a natural disposition that overrides all the facts of experience and observa-tion. While his folly invites derision, his generosity of attitude keeps the audience's liking for him. The absence of any sceptical habit of mind blinds him to his own nature, too, and makes him unable to comprehend irony. He takes at their face value Keegan's words:

> when I come here in the evenings . . . to break my heart uselessly . . . over the dead heart and blinded soul of the island of the saints, you will comfort me with the bustle of a great hotel, and the sight of the little children carrying the golf-clubs of your tourists as a preparation for the life to come.

And it is a similar quality of comfort that he offers to Nora, in equal insensitiveness to the chagrin he is causing her:

> BROADBENT. . . . There! (*swinging her round against his breast*) thats much more comfortable for you.
> NORA (*with Irish peevishness*). Ah, you mustnt go on like that. I don't like it.
> BROADBENT (*unabashed*). Youll acquire the taste by degrees. You mustnt mind me: it's an absolute necessity of my nature that I should have somebody to hug occasionally. Besides, it's good for you: itll plump out your muscles and make em elastic and set up your figure.

Even his cynicism is hardly recognizable as such, as his verbal protests are merely conventional accompaniments of a failure to see anything wrong or morally unsatisfactory in the behaviour he expects from others and practises himself:

> BROADBENT. Just wait and say something nice to Keegan. They tell me he controls nearly as many votes as Father Dempsey himself.
> NORA. You little know Peter Keegan. He'd see through me as if I was a pane o glass.
> BROADBENT. Oh, he wont like it any the less for that. What really flatters a man is that you think him worth flattering. Not that I would flatter any man: don't think that. I'll just go and meet him.

Broadbent in isolation would be an eighteenth-century comic figure, a John Bull from the workshop of Voltaire. But Larry Doyle acts as his sardonic shadow; and the close personal attachment, so obviously working through the attraction of opposites, strengthens the effect of a deep-laid reciprocity. This is not one of Shaw's plays of conversion, and we have no chance of seeing what a Broadbent emerging from his Faustian ignorance into the knowledge of good and evil might become. (The half-wit, Patsy Farrell, seems to benefit more than Broadbent from Fintan, the salmon of knowledge, which he has to carry.) The separate presence of Larry in partnership with him is, indeed, the necessary condition of Broadbent's invulnerable optimism; the theatrical method of morality drama makes a point that is both philosophically and psychologically valid here: it is the separation out of elements and values, that more naturally would blend and modify each other, that is the source of evil. It follows logically that

Keegan, taking up his stand between the other two, should preach a gospel of the unity of life and consciousness:

> a country where the State is the Church and the Church the people: . . . a commonwealth in which work is play and play is life: . . . a godhead in which all life is human and all humanity divine: three in one and one in three.

It is Shaw's version of Saint Patrick's great hymn of praise to the Trinity, the *Lorica*, and captures something of its rhythm:

> I bind unto myself the Name
> The strong Name of the Trinity.
> By invocation of the same
> The Three in One, and One in Three.
> (trans. C. F. Alexander)

Again like *Candide*, this play associates a critique of religion with its critique of optimism: not just a superficial tilt at the false relation of Irish State to Catholic Church, but a more radical attack on dualistic Christianity. Broadbent himself identifies Keegan's faith with its nineteenth-century manifestation in the moral tradition of Carlyle and Ruskin.[1] A similar identification of medieval and modern images is at work in the animal (and especially insect) motifs – caterpillar, grasshopper, coral insects, bees, Billy Byrne's cow, which Haffigan with traditional peasant superstition and parsimony 'once paid a witch a penny to put a spell on' – which, in the central instance of Haffigan's pig, merge with the emblem of Benthamism, the unacknowledged utilitarian religion of Broadbent.[2]

As for the Faustian group of Broadbent and Larry, it derives its connotations from Keegan's vision of the perpetual choice between heaven and hell and from the allusions to his legendary confession of a black man who laid a spell on his wits – a note of black magic that comes in again with the reference to the witch Haffigan resorted to. In this context Nora (certainly a figure of Ireland here) is the betrayed Marguerite, and the scene in the parlour, where the death of the pig is effectually re-enacted, is a Walpurgisnacht. If the play transcends its narrow political theme to become universal, in part by its conformity to the Faust legend, it does so also by virtue of the background supplied for Keegan: his Catholicism of outlook is linked with his journeyings that recall by their nature (he walked through Europe) the missionary journeys and pilgrimages of the medieval Irish saints. And, like these predecessors,

----

[1] Act IV, Broadbent: 'Too true, Mr Keegan, only too true. And most eloquently put. It reminds me of poor Ruskin . . . Dont sneer, Larry: I used to read a lot of Shelley years ago . . .'

[2] I am assuming that Carlyle's indictment of Utilitarianism as the 'pig-philosophy' was too familiar to Shaw for the animal on which Irish economic hopes were based not to have had this other association in the contextual linking with Broadbent's Liberalism.

he is a messenger of human equality – the equality of souls: a man who knows more Latin than Father Dempsey, one trained in the ancient strongholds of Christian culture, who lives as simply as the peasant and speaks the peasant's vernacular. Even the fact that he is not now officially a priest, though regarded as a saint, puts him alongside earlier Celtic monasticism (with its organizational looseness), not the contemporary Catholic church. Keegan goes on foot, not in a motor car – he is a figure out of time, whose solutions have to be worked out by men *in* time in terms of actual life.

Settings help carry out the implications of spiritual choice conveyed through action and dialogue. The number of outdoor settings is unusual in a Shaw play of the first half of his career (though he was always fond of the garden scene, perhaps just for a shift of visual interest, or always as a reminder of *natural* values); and, in view of the nature of the first scene played against such a background (Keegan and the grasshopper), the choice of locales gives a hint of nature mysticism. Evening and sunset play their part. The Round Tower, like Stonehenge in Hardy's work, suggests immemorial religious consciousness and a spiritual sense that accommodates a sturdily realistic phallicism. The great stone may be the kind of object myths or secular legends grow up around; it is also surely the bare rock itself, to which Peter's name corresponds, and the icon recalled in Larry's words, startling in the context of Act II's political debate:

> St Peter, the rock on which our Church was built, was crucified head downwards for being a turncoat.

The retort (which *does* turn on the idea of conversion) has little relevance[1] except as it helps define the symbolic value of the stage-rock. The game of backgammon in which Keegan and Nora are engaged during Barney's recital, in Act IV, is a key to the formal patterning of that scene and the play of opposites involved. It is a contrast to the use of the basket as a seat, in Act II, which helps establish the impromptu nature of the public meeting.

Shaw, the playwright as musician, has been as active in *John Bull's Other Island* as in *Man and Superman*, though he does not so noticeably flaunt himself in this character, as careful attention has been given to changes of tone and grouping and variations of voices as to the patterns of attraction and repulsion set up by the characters in their relation to the audience. Duets and trios have been carefully varied with ensembles: in Act I, Hodson, the valet, is used to prevent the dialogue from settling into two duets, first Broadbent and Haffigan, then Broadbent and Doyle.

[1] It is one of the trail of hardship and suffering and torture images that recall *Candide*. Of course, the figure standing on its head is emblematic of paradox, too.

In each instance the dramatist was obviously out to exploit the contrast between an Irish (or mock Irish) voice and Broadbent's English boom. Act II opens boldly with a slightly camouflaged soliloquy, the sound of the grasshopper being used as a musical punctuation to Keegan's lines.[1] After the bridge-passage with Patsy Farrell, there follows a lyrical duet between Keegan and Nora, whose tones, sufficiently alike, never blend again outside passages of ensemble writing. The first, rather casually dispersed ensemble passage follows, with the arrival of Broadbent; and the first encounter of Nora with Broadbent (contrasting with her earlier duet with Keegan). Act III is largely an ensemble composition which, in its central part, gives way to a design of chorus and arias – from Larry Doyle's nervous tenor and Broadbent's baritone. As with parts of *Man and Superman*, the rhetoric of this section may be repugnant, even boring, to a reader; the scene demands to be *heard* in the larger context of the play's composition. The coda to the act is supplied by the brisk surprise dialogue of Hodson, in Cockney character, with Andy Haffigan. The fourth act opens with the most elaborately orchestrated section, dominated by Barney Doran, but with a counterpoint in the minor from Keegan, giving way to another aria from Broadbent (full of dignity, compared with the racy hilarity of Doran's), then a duet – between Keegan and Broadbent with interpolations from other voices; this is followed by an unbroken sequence of contrasted duets between Larry and Nora and Broadbent and Nora, a romantic emotional strain continuing through them, though harsh and comic themes are constantly interwoven with the lyricism. This makes way for the final trio, in which debate is sublimated into a singing match.

Shaw's skill in handling the detail of an evolving scene can be illustrated from the Act IV interchange of Nora and Broadbent (which recalls, yet varies from, their duet in Act II). It is a scene that brings out very clearly the fact that Broadbent is not a copy of Pangloss but a living exemplar of the optimism that is the theoretical doctrine of Pangloss; he is not a Candide either. (Voltaire's double motif of the earthly paradise and the garden, which Shaw was to use more prominently in *The Simpleton*, is echoed in the Garden City metaphor of *John Bull's Other Island*. 'Have you ever heard of Garden City?' Broadbent asks Tim Haffigan. 'D'ye mane Heavn?' is the doubtful reply. Broadbent's conception of a Garden City is very like Undershaft's Perivale St Andrews,[2] but to Keegan the cleanliness and order promised suggest nothing more heavenly than 'our poetically named Mountjoy prison'.)

[1] In production, the use of a violin might meet the case most satisfactorily. But see *Shaw–Barker Letters*, p. 97, for a more ingenious suggestion.

[2] See Chapter 8, p. 137, note 1.

Broadbent comes in to find Nora in tears, and is at once moved to sympathy. His way of comforting her is also a way of comforting himself, and it establishes his well-fed physical presence. (The born healer B.B. of *The Doctor's Dilemma* is anticipated: pain and suffering must be vanquished by Broadbent, likewise, because they are so alien to his nature.)

> Cry on my chest: the only really comfortable place for a woman to cry is on a man's chest: a real man, a real friend. A good broad chest, eh? not less than forty-two inches.

His adaptability is evident when she wants a handkerchief and he assumes that hers is a tiny useless ornament. The protective emotion doesn't waver but just adroitly accommodates the unimportant facts to itself:

> Of course it's a common cotton one – silly little cotton one – not good enough for the dear eyes of Nora Cryna . . .

The mispronunciation that makes her laugh despite her misery, is an indication of his bemused liking for conventional sentimentalities about Ireland. Because it is the easiest thing to do, and quite agreeable, he starts making love to her:

> Nora darling – my Nora – the Nora I love . . .

But Nora is not at all disposed by *her* upbringing to take the easy way. Her dignity and self-control reassert themselves at the recognition of his lack of control. Again Broadbent falls in with her mood, as far as his nature will let him, and proceeds portentously and moralistically without a touch of humour. He moves into the 'correct' routine – the routine of a proposal now – insensitive as an unthinking automaton to the particularities of the situation. He is blithely unaware of the nonsense he inadvertently exposes in the convention:

> I am prepared to wait as long as you like, provided you will give me some small assurance that the answer will not be unfavorable.

Nora remains sharply realistic in her awareness, though this does not prevent her admitting that Broadbent's emotion is genuine and sincere enough. The comic spectacle of self-delusion gets an easy effect in his humourless talk about his 'strong sense of humour' and his emotional insistence on being 'a plain unemotional Englishman, with no powers of expression'. Indeed, when emotion seizes him, he behaves like a baby, almost choking in a conflict of rage and grief. When Nora remains unaffected ('Whatever may be the matter with you, it's not want of feeling' implies the corollary: it is want of thought, conscious awareness and understanding), he turns sulky. Reassured (however unintentionally) by her, he flies to the opposite extreme of '*immense relief and triumph*'; his insensitiveness to the way *she* feels is conveyed in the '*crow*' Shaw directs him to give at this point: Broadbent has the blind vanity and egotism associated with the cock. However, Nora's scruples mean something to the idealist in him – 'thats really most delicately womanly'. Being once more on an emotionally even keel, he now shows his own capacity for realism too. He sees Larry shrewdly enough:

> Larry's taste is just the opposite: he likes em solid and bouncing and rather keen about him.

In a rather lordly manner – he is sure of his superiority to her in the 'real' world – he can talk Shavian good sense, quite free of romantic notions:

> First love is only a little foolishness and a lot of curiosity: no really self-respecting woman would take advantage of it.

But immediately Shaw lays it on more thickly until the good sense becomes altogether too much of a good thing:

> Love affairs always end in rows. We're not going to have any rows: we're going to have a solid four-square home: man and wife: comfort and common sense – and plenty of affection, eh?

There's nothing exactly wrong with this – except that the complete exclusion of the other side of life, darker, uncertain – the life of the Haffigans, of the crucifixion of Saint Peter – makes it all wrong: human life on earth is just not like this; to live as if it was is to live self-complacently, unimaginatively, in a fool's paradise, while the evil in the rest of the world goes on breeding. This is mental and moral sluggishness; but the physical vigour and zest remain infectious:

> By George, Nora, it's a tremendous thing to be able to enjoy oneself. Lets go off for a walk out of this stuffy little room. I want the open air to expand in . . .

Incorrigible as he may seem, this attractive natural bounce makes it impossible for despair to creep in.

While there is life in such crude abundance, there is hope. The one indication that Broadbent may be more conventionally a hypocrite, not just a protraction of innocence unpenetrated by experience, is in the start of surprise he shares with Larry at Keegan's prognosis of their business policy:

> I do every justice to the efficiency of you and your syndicate. . . . You may even build the hotel efficiently if you can find enough efficient masons. . . . When the hotel becomes insolvent . . . your English business habits will secure the thorough efficiency of the liquidation . . . you will liquidate its second bankruptcy efficiently . . . you will get rid of its original shareholders efficiently after efficiently ruining them; and you will finally profit

very efficiently . . . you will foreclose your mortgages most efficiently . . .[1]
and . . . when at last this poor desolate countryside becomes a busy mint in
which we shall all slave to make money for you, with our Polytechnic to
teach us how to do it efficiently, and our library to fuddle the few imaginations your distilleries will spare . . .

The sustained recitative proceeds to a crescendo and then a full close:

For four wicked centuries the world has dreamed this foolish dream of
efficiency; and the end is not yet. But the end will come.

The moral determination, on which the satire is based, sounds unmistakably in the prophetic tone of this, though it is hardly the *efficiency*
of British capitalism that Ireland has seen since the play was written.

[1] Cf. the methods expounded by Mangan in *Heartbreak House*.

8

Major Barbara

Major Barbara has been generally acclaimed as one of Shaw's finest plays. The impact it made on Brecht is indicated by the extent to which it inspired *St Joan of the Stockyards*. Francis Fergusson's account of it as a 'farce of rationalizing',[1] however denigratory in tone, is true to the quick-silver brilliance and buoyancy of the play, as careful analysis cannot be. To attempt such analysis would be misguided if it were not necessary to show that the intellectual intricacy of the dramatic structure is precise, not confused, and that Shaw now handles his ironies with a clarity and control lacking in the comparably ironic *Candida*.

The mainspring of the play seems to have been provided by Shaw's response to Blake, reinforced by a reading of Nietzsche where he is closest to Blake. The dialectical terms of *The Marriage of Heaven and Hell* provide the intellectual perspectives of the drama:

> Without contraries is no progression. Attraction and repulsion, reason and energy, love and hate, are necessary to human existence.

> From these contraries spring what the religious call good and evil. Good is the passive that obeys reason; evil is the active springing from energy.

> Good is heaven. Evil is hell.[2]

Conventional moral distinctions are annihilated as the antinomies prove to be complementary. Like *The Marriage of Heaven and Hell*, *Major*

---

[1] See Francis Fergusson, *The Idea of a Theater*, Anchor Books edition (New York: Doubleday, 1953), pp. 192–4.

[2] The self-evident relationship of these quotations from *The Marriage of Heaven and Hell* to *Major Barbara* is objectively confirmed by Shaw's comment in the Preface to *Three Plays for Puritans*: 'Let those who have praised my originality in conceiving Dick Dudgeon's strange religion read Blake's Marriage of Heaven and Hell; and I shall be fortunate if they do not rail at me for a plagiarist.' This is the starting-point of I. Fiske's essay, *Bernard Shaw and William Blake* (Shavian Tract No. 2), reprinted in R. J. Kaufmann (ed.), *G. B. Shaw*, pp. 170–8. The link with *Major Barbara* is not noted there.

Barbara employs the shock tactics of paradox to induce a more comprehensive understanding of the world. The means used involve insistence on both literal and metaphoric meanings, simple and ironic readings.

Shaw's original intention of calling the play *Andrew Undershaft's Profession* implied the reworking of the pun already employed in *Cashel Byron's Profession* and *Mrs Warren's Profession*, so as to bring out the relation between a trade or occupation and the creed implicit in its pursuit. In each instance (and this also applies to *Widowers' Houses*), practice of the occupation is permitted, or even relied on, by society, while official morality disapproves. On the realistic level, the munitions firm of Undershaft and Lazarus and Bodger's whisky firm represent capitalist enterprise exploiting human weakness for pecuniary gain and producing further social evils, destructive to humanity. In theory, Christians reject war; they are answered by the 'Voice of the Devil' (Blake's phrase) issuing from Andrew Undershaft, in whom Blake's view of Satan and Nietzsche's Dionysus unite to form one of Shaw's most impressive characters. Imaginative vision, it seems, can use the devil as a friend who has important truths to tell: gunpowder, fire and drink have positive value as symbols of elemental power, revolutionary, cleansing, inspirational. Indeed they are symbols in the Coleridgean sense, marked by a translucence of the general in the particular and of the eternal in the temporal; they are true symbols of power for change because, as material objects, they can bring about change. Together they represent the general Blakean category of Energy. Shaw associates with them – as society does – money, capitalist profit (or Illth), which can also be positively seen as a token of natural abundance translated into the commodities of civilization and *human* power, which reason can master and wield.

Certainly nowhere else in Shaw's work do we come so close to the imaginative sense of Blake's propositions:

1. Man has no body distinct from his soul . . .
2. Energy is the only life, and is from the body; and reason is the bound or outward circumference of energy . . .

and, above all, the sense of:

3. Energy is eternal delight.

Undershaft, the manufacturer of armaments, is in a different relation to society from Sartorius, the slum landlord of *Widowers' Houses*, or Mrs Warren, owner-director of an international chain of brothels. Whereas those earlier creations remain prisoners of society, outcasts from respectability, and in presentation are touched with the pathos of melodrama, the nature of the commodity Undershaft traffics in puts him in mastery over society and gives him the confidence and authority to set up his sign: 'UNASHAMED', implying a total rejection of (puritan) guilt on all fronts. In this play Shaw grasped the basic nature of the threat offered to the intellect by the actual world: the challenge of undifferentiated force and mass in the physical universe to the essentially sole and individual; the ruthless and mindless violence that 'can destroy the higher power just as a tiger can destroy a man'. But man naturally has a tiger in him, too, which can match the violence of the elements. Active, aggressive, this force is translated into social terms under the image of an army. The literal fact of the Salvation Army is essential to the realistic fabric of the play. Traditional metaphors of Christian life as warfare are already implicit in the uniformed figures of men and women, marching with banners, bearing the sign 'Blood and Fire', to a drum that beats out a quickened pulse of life. As interpreted through Cusins, Major Barbara's fiancé, it takes on the more general significance of the Church Militant of a universal religion: organized humanity, active, purposeful and joyous in its onslaughts against misery and darkness. The play as a whole demonstrates its theme by the physical exhilaration and the optimism it generates through its explosions of condensed thought and the aggressive release of laughter.

As in *Mrs Warren's Profession*, the basic conflict of opposites is again enacted within a child–parent relationship: the innocence of society's dupes is confronted with the disillusion of its exploiters. But this time the parent and the child are of opposite sexes, and experience does not simply destroy innocence; it complements it and produces new strength. The simple dialectical plan, in which Barbara's heavenly counsel and Undershaft's hellish counsel fight it out, was complicated in the process of writing, when Shaw transformed the heroine's fiancé from a young man-about-town comparable to Charles Lomax (for so he is characterized at the beginning of the longhand version) to a Professor of Greek. I think we can assume that Cusins was at first envisaged as playing a minor, or choric, role comparable to Frank's in the earlier play: that of an observer and commentator who also sets the comic tone of the drama. In his character of observer, the Professor of Greek is qualified to identify for us the philosophical issues and the mythopoetic analogues as they arise. His intellectual quality does not entirely obscure the lineaments of the clown; but he plays the ironical fool to Lomax's 'natural'. As a more considerable and distinguished member of society, he is also fitted to become one of the main pivots of the dramatic scheme. The extension in the play's significance which has followed from this later conception of the character culminates in a scrap of dialogue inserted as an after-thought in the longhand text of Act III (B.M. Addit. MS. 50616 A–E).

UNDERSHAFT. . . . Remember the words of Plato.

CUSINS (*starting*). Plato! You dare to quote Plato to me!

UNDERSHAFT. Plato says, my friend, that society cannot be saved until either the Professors of Greek take to making gunpowder, or else the makers of gunpowder become Professors of Greek.

To the opposition between Undershaft and Barbara there has been added an independent opposition between Undershaft and Cusins. Of course, these are various examples of a single basic conflict between idealism and realism. But the placing of the two in the progress of the drama must absolve Shaw from any charge of tautology: Barbara, the indubitable protagonist of Act II, subsides into watchfulness in Act III, while Cusins takes over from her, is put to the test and makes the crucial decision; her endorsement of this in the last moments of the play lends strength to the impression that he has indeed been deputizing for her. It is dramatically necessary, after her defeat by Undershaft in Act II, that the initiative should pass from Barbara. Cusins carries the play into its final movement, as he makes his pact with Undershaft. This has the effect of restoring Barbara to her proper centrality, though now in alliance with her former opponents. As the representative of spirituality, she returns to inform and bless the compact between reason and energy and the paradox of good *in* evil, heaven *in* hell. Cusins's function has been to introduce the dialectical synthesis. The reconciliation he proposes between power and service, realism and idealism, corresponds, of course, to the Platonic advocacy of the philosopher-king.

The peculiarly Shavian variety of Ibsenite dramatic structure, imitated from the Platonic dialogues, is evident in the verbal debates, rationally conceived and conducted to a great extent – especially in the last act – in abstract terms. This is the drama of ideas in exemplary form. But there is much more to the play than this. The realism of its settings – the library in Wilton Crescent, the Salvation Army shelter in Canning Town, and the especially topical Garden City[1] – establishes it as a critique of actual society that reveals the spectrum of class and its cruel contrasts, as *Man and Superman* did not. Changes of setting are matched by changes in dramatic style. Wealth, aristocracy and the culture that goes with them play out a comedy of manners in Act I; Dickensian realism verging on melodrama invades Act II, in the Salvation Army Shelter, bare and chill, with its horse-trough as derisive comment on the poorly dressed

---

[1] The fact that Ebenezer Howard, as originator of the Garden City idea, was an exponent of the Smiles's Self-Help attitude to the working class, drawing the teeth of revolt, is relevant to the interpretation of Shaw's play. Perivale St Andrews is still more suggestive of the philanthropy of George Cadbury, founder of Bournville. See Warren Sylvester Smith, *The London Heretics* (London: Constable, 1967), p. 248.

wretches at their free meal; Act III presents a Utopia designed by contemporary paternalism, and theory reigns there – a front for the Satanic
mills that produce the wealth of Wilton Crescent, or that, differently
directed, could blow the whole unequal system sky-high. Metaphysically,
Perivale St Andrews represents the spiritual cosmos, heaven and hell and
the battlefield of the world (in its fort with dummy soldiers), corresponding to the emotional range – touching tragedy and ecstasy – that the play
embraces. The action of *Major Barbara* contains thinly disguised versions
of folk-lore quests and divine rituals, as well as sharp clashes of personality, to set off the philosophy. The dialectical scheme is strongly supported by mythopoetic patterns and humanized by a rich assortment of
characters. The second act in particular with its centrally placed sub-plot,
involving Barbara with a character from a sub-group, Bill Walker, is
highly exciting in the pace of its symbolically weighted action and the
intense sense of crisis it conveys. Energy, one is reminded, is the stuff of
drama.

Energy, of course, is the power that Nietzsche called dionysian and
regarded as the antithesis of the Socratic poise he defined as apollonian.[1]
'The business of the Salvation Army is to save, not to wrangle about the
name of the pathfinder,' declares Cusins. 'Dionysos or another: what does
it matter?' The protest was anticipated by Nietzsche himself in the
passage from his Preface to *The Birth of Tragedy* already mentioned in
relation to *Candida*:

> It was *against* morality, therefore, that my instinct, as an intercessory
> instinct for life, turned in this questionable book, inventing for itself, a
> fundamental counter-dogma and counter-valuation of life, purely artistic,
> purely *anti-Christian*. What should I call it? As a philologist and man of
> words I baptized it, not without some liberty – for who could be sure of
> the proper name of the Antichrist? – with the name of a Greek god: I
> called it *Dionysian*.[2]

---

[1] Louis Crompton has taken up the point of Shaw's debt to Nietzsche and his
concept of Dionysus in 'Shaw's Challenge to Liberalism', *Prairie Schooner*,
Vol. XXXVII (1963), pp. 229–44, reprinted in R. J. Kaufmann (ed.), op. cit.,
pp. 88–9 (see Louis Crompton, *Shaw the Dramatist*, pp. 105–22), which I read
after writing this chapter in draft. I have let my discussion of the matter stand,
as its direction and emphasis are different from Mr Crompton's. I compared
Shaw's use of his source in *Major Barbara* with Yeats's in *The Resurrection*
in 'Shaw, Yeats, Nietzsche and the Religion of Art', *Komos*, Vol. I (English
Department, Monash University, 1967), pp. 24–34.

[2] See above, Chapter 4, p. 77. I have quoted W. A. Haussmann's translation
of *The Birth of Tragedy* (Edinburgh and London: Foulis, 1909), as this version,
in manuscript at least as early as 1901, is the one Shaw is most likely to have
known when he wrote *Major Barbara*. For the text, see Friedrich Nietzsche,
Complete Works, ed. Oscar Levy, Vol. I, p. 11. The facts concerning Shaw's early

In fact, Dionysus is mentioned in the dialogue with sufficient frequency to justify entirely the critics Shaw attacked in his Preface for labelling his play as derivative from Nietzschean philosophy. Barbara Undershaft, the evangelist, represents the orthodox Christian attitude that Nietzsche described as 'a libel on life'. Her father, whom Cusins nicknames 'Prince of Darkness' and 'Mephistopheles', as well as 'Dionysos' and 'Machiavelli', challenges her with the 'fundamental counter-dogma and counter-valuation of life':

> Leave it to the poor to pretend that poverty is a blessing: leave it to the coward to make a religion of his cowardice by preaching humility;
> I had rather be a thief than a pauper. I had rather be a murderer than a slave. I dont want to be either; but if you force the alternative on me, then, by Heaven, I'll choose the braver and more moral one.

In adding to these two the figure of a Professor of Greek, Shaw had supplied his play with a representative of that dispassionate and philosophical Hellenic consciousness upon which Nietzsche saw the originally Asiatic religion of Dionysus as having broken in, at a critical point in the history of civilization. The passage in *The Birth of Tragedy* that supplies the fullest account of this event and its consequences can be related illuminatingly to *Major Barbara*:

> On the other hand, we should not have to speak conjecturally, if asked to disclose the immense gap which separated the *Dionysian Greek* from the Dionysian barbarian. (p. 29)

Already this hints at the rationale of supplying Undershaft with a double opposition in, first, the aptly named Barbara, and then Professor Cusins. The famous essay goes on:

> From all quarters of the Ancient World . . . we can prove the existence of Dionysian festivals, the type of which bears, at best, the same relation to the Greek festivals as the bearded satyr, who borrowed his name and attributes from the goat, does to Dionysus himself . . . the very wildest beasts of nature were let loose here, including that detestable mixture of lust and cruelty which has always seemed to me the genuine 'witches' draught'. (pp. 29–30)

Now Shaw has almost entirely dissociated these forces from his principal characters. They are symbolically represented in the play by Undershaft's explosives and the wars in which they are used: 'the men and lads torn to pieces with shrapnel and poisoned with lyddite! . . . the oceans of blood . . . the ravaged crops!' – by 'Bodger's Whisky in letters of fire against the sky', by the drum that Cusins beats, and by the Salvation

familiarity with Nietzsche's work are discussed in my article, 'Shaw, Yeats, Nietzsche and the Religion of Art', pp. 25–6 and 33.

Army motto of 'Blood and Fire!' More directly, they are present in the physical violence with which Bill Walker disturbs the shelter, in Act II, and for which he has prepared himself by drinking gin:

> Aw'm noa gin drinker . . .; bat when Aw want to give my girl a bloomin good awdin Aw lawk to ev a bit o devil in me.

Returning to Nietzsche, we find the immunity of Shaw's principal characters, the educated and the aristocratic, accounted for:

> For some time . . . it would seem that the Greeks were perfectly secure and guarded against the feverish agitations of these festivals . . . by the figure of Apollo himself rising here in full pride, who could not have held out the Gorgon's head to a more dangerous power than this grotesquely uncouth Dionysian. It is in Doric art that this majestically-rejecting attitude of Apollo perpetuated itself. (p. 30)

The production note which prepares for Cusins's first entrance on the stage refers to his *'apalling temper'*. The character described is that of a man who has obtained mastery over his own passions and thus, according to Socrates, fitted himself for the task of governing others:

> *The lifelong struggle of a benevolent temperament and a high conscience against impulses of inhuman ridicule and fierce impatience has set up a chronic strain . . . He is a most implacable, determined, tenacious, intolerant person who by mere force of character presents himself as – and indeed actually is – considerate, gentle, explanatory, even mild and apologetic, capable possibly of murder, but not of cruelty or coarseness.*

Cusins has his proper place in Lady Britomart Undershaft's library. Its decorum, reflecting her own majestic rejection of all licence, is an essential adjunct to its perfect security; she is herself prepared to recognize the dependence of the standards of a gentleman upon the tradition of classical education.

The significance of Cusins's crucial decision to accept a directorship in the Undershaft firm, in order to 'make war on war', can be explored in terms of the rest of the passage from *The Birth of Tragedy*, which grows now even more closely analogous to the play than in its earlier sentences:

> This opposition became more precarious and even impossible, when, from out of the deepest root of the Hellenic nature, similar impulses finally broke forth and made way for themselves: *the Delphic god, by a seasonably effected reconciliation, was now contented with taking the destructive arms from the hands of his powerful antagonist.* This reconciliation marks the most important moment in the history of the Greek cult: wherever we turn our eyes we may observe the revolutions resulting from this event. It was the reconciliation of two antagonists, with the sharp demarcation of the boundary-lines to be thenceforth observed by each . . . in reality, the chasm was not bridged over. But if we observe how, under the pressure of this conclusion

of peace, the Dionysian power manifested itself, we shall now recognize, in the Dionysian orgies of the Greeks, as compared with the Babylonian Sacaea and their retrogression of man to the tiger and the ape, the significance of festivals of world-redemption and days of transfiguration. Not till then does nature attain her artistic jubilee; not till then does the rupture of the *principium individuationis* become an artistic phenomenon. (pp. 30–1)

The dramatic crisis, towards which the play moves, is related to the action of Barbara Undershaft, granddaughter of the Earl of Stevenage, daughter of a millionaire capitalist, leaving the established church of the established social order to join the Salvation Army. The inheritance of power (the 'destructive arms') is kept in the family through the resolution and audacity of her fiancé, who makes his pact with 'Dionysos Undershaft', though asserting still: 'I repudiate your sentiments. I abhor your nature. I defy you in every possible way.' The 'transfiguration' which ensues has its appropriate setting in the Garden City of Perivale St Andrews, blueprint for the millennium of social welfare, and its individual enactment in Barbara's change of mood: 'She has gone right up into the skies,' says Cusins.

Proleptically, the new festivals are represented in the play before Cusins's decisive gesture is made. He himself is ritually prepared for the crisis by an evening spent with Undershaft (shown in the film version, alluded to in the stage play): 'he only provided the wine. I think it was Dionysos who made me drunk'; by implication, the drunkenness was spiritual and inspirational, not crudely orgiastic. And the values the dramatist associates with the Salvation Army are multiple, the morality of the soup kitchen, which Nietzsche–Undershaft rejects, being only tangential to it. The spirit of the Salvation Army, as it has attracted Barbara Undershaft, is itself dionysiac and revolutionary; but it is an enlightened and purified version of older, cruder enthusiasms, which the Hellenistic mind is already able to approve and associate with from the start of the play; for Cusins too, though in pursuit of Barbara, has joined the Salvation Army. In his apologia to Undershaft, he declares:

> I am a sincere Salvationist. You do not understand the Salvation Army. It is the army of joy, of love, of courage: it has banished the fear and remorse and despair of the old hell-ridden evangelical sects: it marches to fight the devil with trumpet and drum, with music and dancing, with banner and palm, as becomes a sally from heaven by its happy garrison. It picks the waster out of the public house and makes a man of him: it finds a worm wriggling in a back kitchen, and lo! a woman . . . It takes the poor professor of Greek, the most artificial and self-suppressed of human creatures, from his meal of roots, and lets loose the rhapsodist in him . . .

In fact the reconciliation of Dionysus and Apollo enacted dramatically in Act III is, in non-dramatic form, imaged from the first, already achieved.

Music itself is the sublimation of dionysiac energy. (The full title of Nietzsche's famous essay is, of course, *The Birth of Tragedy from the Spirit of Music*.)

Shaw actually stages the beginning of one triumphal procession and accompanies it with a shadow-play of the supersession of one religion by another. The form in which the climax, in Act II, is presented may be related to another extract from *The Birth of Tragedy*:

> Schopenhauer has described to us the stupendous *awe* which seizes upon man, when of a sudden he is at a loss to account for the cognitive forms of a phenomenon, in that the principle of reason, in some one of its manifestations, seems to admit of an exception. Add to this awe the blissful ecstasy which rises from the innermost depths of man, ay, of nature, at this same collapse of the *principium individuationis*, and we shall gain an insight into the being of the *Dionysian*, which is brought within closest ken perhaps by the analogy of *drunkenness*. It is either under the influence of the narcotic draught, of which the hymns of all primitive men and peoples tell us, or by the powerful approach of spring penetrating all nature with joy, that those Dionysian emotions awake, in the augmentation of which the subjective vanishes to complete self-forgetfulness. So also in the German Middle Ages singing and dancing crowds, ever increasing in number, were borne from place to place under this same Dionysian power. In these St John's and St Vitus's dancers we again perceive the Bacchic choruses of the Greeks, with their previous history in Asia Minor, as far back as Babylon and the orgiastic Sacaea. There are some, who, from lack of experience or obtuseness, will turn away from such phenomena as 'folk-diseases' with a smile of contempt or pity prompted by the consciousness of their own health: of course, the poor wretches do not divine what a cadaverous-looking and ghastly aspect this very 'health' of theirs presents when the glowing life of the Dionysian revellers rushes past them. (pp. 25–6)

With his presentation of the Salvation Army as a recrudescence of dionysiac fervour, Shaw extended Nietzsche's medieval analogues to the bacchic chorus into modern times. The image suggested in the last lines of Nietzsche's paragraph may have provided the hint for the episode in which Barbara, who has just witnessed the triumph of Undershaft at which her faith, as it seems, has crumbled, remains a still figure amid the animated scene as the Salvation Army band, caught up in the exultation with Undershaft, marches off with music to the great meeting:

> CUSINS (*returning impetuously from the shelter with a flag and a trombone, and coming between Mrs Baines and Undershaft*). You shall carry the flag down the first street, Mrs Baines (*he gives her the flag*). Mr Undershaft is a gifted trombonist: he shall intone an Olympian diapason to the West Ham Salvation March. (*Aside to Undershaft, as he forces the trombone on him.*) Blow, Machiavelli, blow . . . It is a wedding chorus from one of Donizetti's operas; but we have converted it . . . 'For thee immense re-

joicing – immenso giubilo – immenso giubilo.' (*With drum obbligato*.) Rum tum ti tum tum, tum tum ti ta—

BARBARA. Dolly: you are breaking my heart.

CUSINS. What is a broken heart more or less here? Dionysos Undershaft has descended. I am possessed . . . Off we go. Play up, there! Im m e n s o giu bilo. (*He gives the time with his drum; and the band strikes up the march, which becomes more distant as the procession moves briskly away*.)

MRS BAINES. I must go, dear. Youre overworked: you will be all right tomorrow. We'll never lose you. Now Jenny: step out with the old flag. Blood and Fire! (*She marches out through the gate with her flag*.)

JENNY. Glory Hallelujah! (*flourishing her tambourine and marching*).

UNDERSHAFT (*to Cusins, as he marches out past him easing the slide of his trombone*). 'My ducats and my daughter'!

CUSINS (*following him out*). Money and gunpowder!

BARBARA. Drunkenness and Murder! My God: why hast thou forsaken me?

She sinks on the form with her face buried in her hands. The march passes away into silence.[1]

The exclamatory dialogue contributes to the excitement; the syntax of logical speech has little place here. The crescendo of sound is intensified by the gathering in of themes, the drawing together of the various symbolic perspectives in which Shaw presents his fable during the course of the play. Cannon and thunder, elemental and divine, as well as the strong pulse of life, are to be heard in the beating drum. But the sense of emotional and mental violence communicated at this point comes chiefly from the harshly ironic intersection of moods: exhilaration set against agony. Horror at the contemplation of destructive power is transformed through identification with that power; pity is rejected for recognition of agony as a further inverted celebration of violent energy. Shaw had perhaps remembered that comedy and tragedy alike have been traced back to the satyr chorus of the Dionysiac festival. There is no doubt that audiences are infected by the exhilaration. The conventional reaction to the sentimental appeal of a deserted heroine is pressed into service to give a keener edge to Cusins's brutal denial of sympathy and emphatic reassertion of unmixed joy. We should like to recoil from him, but cannot. The experience is a brilliantly conceived vehicle for the loss of self-possession in a transport of irrational feeling. Shaw is demonstrating something very like a physical law: the superior power of volume of sound, weight of numbers, releasing energy under the pressure of an intensifying rhythm. And the march remains a wedding march as the gentle-mannered Cusins confronts the chagrin of a subdued Barbara with a bridegroom's self-regarding exultation.

Yet the impression of the single figure in its stillness persists: there is

[1] The text is drawn from Bernard Shaw, *Six Plays* (London: Constable, 1962).

strength of another kind in this maintained integrity and isolation. It is the apollonian will in Barbara that holds out now. And with the shock of recognizing in her final cry, 'My God: why hast thou forsaken me?', the words of the Christian divine saviour, the audience is returned to thoughtfulness.[1]

'There are mystical powers above and behind the three of us,' declares Undershaft in the screen version. The shadows of Dionysus and Apollo are to be glimpsed shiftingly behind Undershaft himself, Cusins and Barbara, but Barbara alone is the Christ figure of the play:[2] its action represents her ministry, her betrayal and abandonment by her disciples, and her agony; leaving off the uniform of the Army is a kind of death; visiting the munitions factory of Undershaft and Lazarus, she harrows hell. The multiple symbolism of the play's final setting suggests, as Shaw chooses to bring the various implications dramatically to life, Golgotha, in the dummy corpses of mutilated soldiers; the exceeding high mountain of the Temptation; the mount of the Ascension, with a view of the New Jerusalem itself, where Peter Shirley has been given the job of gatekeeper and timekeeper.

Shaw, indeed, introduced a valid criticism of Nietzsche when he identified the Salvation Army not only with the worshippers of Dionysus, but also with the Church Militant of the risen Christ. His representation of Christianity as a variety of dionysiac religion corrects Nietzsche's exaggeration of its 'subjective' quality, which made possible his over-schematic view of the opposition between Christianity and Dionysus–Antichrist. The Preface to *Major Barbara* distinguishes between true Christianity and Crosstianity, the religion of negation, of sin and guilt, suffering and death, submission and deprivation. Within the play, a process of redemption is enacted through a bargaining for souls and a vicarious sacrifice. It is a redemption of Christianity itself. Undershaft does not destroy the Salvation Army; he is ready partly to identify himself with it, more ready to identify it with himself, as, in order to win Barbara, he buys it with his cheque to Mrs Baines, the Commissioner. Barbara's spiritual pilgrimage takes her through disillusion and despair to a rebirth of hope and a new vision. Her private emotional experience enforces the recognition that 'the way of life lies through the factory of death', that destruction has its proper place in a healthy scheme of things, and even

---

[1] Shaw had rehearsed the effect obtained in this scene in Act IV of *John Bull's Other Island*, where the stage is divided into two areas, one dominated by the passionate grimness of Keegan, the other occupied by a group contorted with mirth at the story of Haffigan's pig. See above, p. 124.

[2] She is the daughter of Britomart, which being interpreted is 'the sweet virgin', and, when the play opens, she does not know her father.

religion and morality must change in order to survive.[1] Her spiritual death and resurrection contain the promise of a new social order: the money for which she was betrayed bought the freedom of Bill Walker's soul. What this freedom implies is given rational definition in Cusins's declaration of his own new-found purpose:[2]

> I now want to give the common man weapons against the intellectual man. I love the common people. I want to arm them against the lawyers, the doctors, the priests, the literary men, the professors, the artists, and the politicians, who, once in authority, are more disastrous and tyrannical than all the fools, rascals and impostors.[3] I want a power simple enough for common men to use, yet strong enough to force the intellectual oligarchy to use its genius for the general good.

The purging of obsolete and unworthy elements in Barbara's Christian faith is accompanied by revision of its liturgy. This process begins in Act I, when the household, except for Stephen, is seduced from family prayers to the more original and vital form of service conducted by Barbara in the drawing room. It opens to the strains of 'Onward, Christian Soldiers, on the concertina, with tambourine accompaniment'. The emblematic sword, which Undershaft has referred to as the sign of his works, is already at least as appropriate as the cross in the insignia of Barbara's religion; and Shaw certainly expected his audience to supply the remembrance of Christ's words, 'I came not to send peace but a sword.' Cusins's excuse to Lady Britomart is unserious in manner and may easily be taken as simple camouflage; but rejecting, as it does, the terms of the General Confession, it at least calls into question the common sense of perfectionism and the morality of self-abasement and excessive emphasis on guilt:

> . . . you would have to say before all the servants that we have done things we ought not to have done, and left undone things we ought to have done, and that there is no health in us. I cannot bear to hear you doing yourself such an injustice, and Barbara such an injustice. As for myself, I flatly deny it: I have done my best.

Undershaft later proposes a revision in the Church Catechism to admit that 'Money and gunpowder' are the 'two things necessary to Salvation'. His account of the works of mercy follows from an identification of the deadly sins with the burdensome material necessities of 'Food, clothing,

---

[1] Among the best-known lines in the play are Undershaft's: '. . . you have made for yourself something that you call a morality or a religion or what not. It doesnt fit the facts. Well, scrap it. Scrap it and get one that does fit.'

[2] There are here some parallels of thought and idea with Yeats's *Calvary*, also indebted to Nietzsche.

[3] The Platonic view seems to have been adopted in order to be abandoned.

firing, rent, taxes, respectability and children.' Stephen, in Act I, supplies the address of the Undershaft business as 'Christendom and Judea'.
This serves as a warning note of a half-hidden movement in the play from
the Old Testament (and ancient Greek) morality of just exchange to the
New Testament morality of forgiveness and love. In effect, these are
reconciled through the rejection of false and facile interpretations of the
New Testament admonitions. Cusins's point of agreement with Undershaft, 'forgiveness is a beggar's refuge. I am with you there: we must pay
our debts,'[1] is the necessary counterpoise to that repudiation of irrational
guilt in Act I (quoted above). Cunningly Undershaft confounds his
daughter in answering her charge, 'Father do you love nobody?', by
carrying the meaning of love to the extreme of 'Love your enemies':

> UNDERSHAFT. I love my best friend.
> LADY BRITOMART. And who is that, pray?
> UNDERSHAFT. My bravest enemy. That is the man who keeps me up to
> the mark.[2]

Cusins's admiring response to this, 'You know, the creature is really a
sort of poet in his way', does more than acknowledge the Socratic unfolding of neglected truth in a paradox; it conveys a recognition of beauty in
the healthy ambivalence of strong emotions, an admission very necessary
in the lover of Barbara that aggression need not be ugly and mean. His
repudiation of beggarly forgiveness prepares for her new version of the
Lord's Prayer:

> I have got rid of the bribe of bread. I have got rid of the bribe of heaven.
> Let God's will be done for its own sake: the work he had to create us to do
> because it cannot be done except by living men and women. When I die,
> let him be in my debt, not I in his; and let me forgive him as becomes a
> woman of my rank.[3]

---

[1] Cf. Bill Walker: 'Let wot Aw dan be dan an pide for; and let there be a end
of it.' This is one point where the professor can appropriately point out that
the modern Cockney thinks and acts like an ancient Greek. But Bill's attempt
to buy his way out of obligations to practise the virtues of mercy and forbearance
is no denial of those virtues. (Cusins and Barbara do not cease to value them,
and indeed they are implied in Shaw's blueprint for the millennium, as presented
in the last act of the play.) This is just a stage in the process of his rehabilitation.

[2] Cf. Blake's 'Opposition is true friendship'. Shaw is certainly fulfilling
Blake's promise: 'NOTE. This Angel, who is now become a Devil, is my particular friend: we often read the Bible together in its infernal or diabolical sense,
which the world shall have if they behave well.' (*The Marriage of Heaven and
Hell.*) But Shaw may also have had Burke in mind: 'He who wrestles with us
strengthens our nerves and sharpens our skill. Our antagonist is our helper.'
(*Reflections on the Revolution in France.*)

[3] Cf. *The Marriage of Heaven and Hell*: 'God only acts and is in existing
beings and men.'

11 *Major Barbara*. Difficult but not impossible.

12 *John Bull's Other Island*. Kingsway Theatre, 1912.

13 *Getting Married*. Haymarket Theatre, 1908. A fine symbolic tableau.

This is so different from conventional humility, it could unkindly be termed arrogance and found unattractive.[1] For the most part, Shaw manages to endear us to a heroine whose actual living counterpart might well repel us. He does so by suffusing the portrait with his own warm appreciation of the type and setting it off by contrast with a minor sketch of a more conventionally admirable woman.

Orthodox Christianity has a truer representative in Jenny Hill, the Salvation Army lass, than in Barbara Undershaft, and Jenny's Christian spirit is a sublimation of her womanly nature. Jenny is the natural victim of the bullying male; turning the other cheek in response to Bill Walker's assault, offering forgiveness instead of revenge and treating her suffering as matter for joy. She merits her place in the triumphal band, bearing her tambourine, for she has positive qualities that Shaw admires: genuine courage and cheerfulness and industry in the cause she has at heart; this is a credible instance of the 'worm . . . in the back kitchen' become a woman, a daughter of the Highest. But Jenny's morale (she is only eighteen) is fed by her admiration of Barbara, and there are weaknesses in her that lessen her appeal. Her conventional expressions of piety often strike a false note; her insistence on *love* is too facile; her pity is equally sentimental. Neatly, Shaw demonstrates something unpleasant in her excessive sympathy; Barbara's sense of the ridiculous, like Undershaft's antagonisms, conveys a truer respect for human dignity, for the independence and privacy of the soul:

> BILL (*with sour mirthless humour*). Aw was sivin anather menn's knees at
> the tawm. E was kneelin on moy ed, e was . . . E was pryin for me: pryin
> camfortable wiv me as a cawpet. Sow was Mog. Sao was the aol bloomin
> meetin. Mog she says 'Aw Lawd brike is stabborn sperrit; bat down urt is
> dear art.' Thet was wot she said. 'Downt urt is dear art!' An er blowk
> thirteen stun four! – kneelin wiv all is wight on me. Fanny, ain't it?
> JENNY. Oh no. We're so sorry, Mr Walker.
> BARBARA (*enjoying it frankly*). Nonsense! of course it's funny . . .
> JENNY. I'm so sorry, Mr Walker.
> BILL (*fiercely*). Downt you gow being sorry for me: youve no call . . . Aw
> downt want to be forgive be you, or be ennybody . . .

If Shaw was concerned to attack the morbid sentimentality of late Victorian Christianity, he was – he needed to be – ready likewise to attack the womanly ideal associated with it. The imbalance between Jenny's emotional and intellectual development has made her the dupe of society, unawake to realities, assisting the millionaire's daughter in collecting the pennies of the indigent in her tambourine, as the wealthy

---

[1] Yet it is a repellent quality, an aggressiveness, far from unfamiliar in the militant virgin saints of Christian tradition.

F

good-for-nothing Lomax takes them in his hat. There is an analogy to be drawn between her and Barbara, who, with the same power of work and need to expend herself in a cause, has to be cured of a similar blindness to things as they are, saved from an equal frittering away of her quality in a cause unliberated from a capitalist economy. Certainly G.B.S. does not repudiate wholesale the Christianity that Barbara and Jenny share; it is its vulnerability and self-betrayal that he rejects. So, in the symbolic structure of his play, he has replaced Christ by the Female Warrior, an androgynous type presiding over the new religion. In the setting aside of the old interpretation of woman's role, along with other forms of masochism, an ideal of sexual equality is implied.

The whole play is flagrantly concerned with money. The first scene, set in the luxurious and stately library of the house in Wilton Crescent and dominated by the opulent physical presence of Lady Britomart, laps us round in an atmosphere of womblike security. The unreality of material need and adversity, in this context, comes through all the more clearly for Lady Britomart's talk of economy. If it were anxious talk, the whole effect would be destroyed; but there is no anxiety in Lady Britomart's make-up: she is the abundant and never-failing earth-mother of the peak of the golden year. In explaining to Stephen their financial situation, she is merely eliciting the moral approval she thinks due to her; she knows the easy and comfortable solution to her problems – such as they are! – and will apply it quite unscrupulously and without false pride; for she is free of the personal uncertainty that needs to worry about pride. In the first few minutes of the dialogue, we learn of the money available: the Lomax millions (though Charles will not inherit for ten years); the 'poverty' of the Earl of Stevenage on 'barely seven thousand a year' and her own personal income, enough to keep one family in its present luxury. The date is 1906,[1] and the value of the pound is high. Anyway, Shaw has thoughtfully provided a cost-of-living index within the play: thirty-eight shillings a week is the standard wage paid by that model employer, Andrew Undershaft; in the first scene itself, her mother's standard of 'poverty' can be measured against the reference to Barbara discharging her maid and living on a pound a week – a gesture with more of eccentricity about it than real asceticism, for she still lives in Wilton Crescent and, when we see her, is the perfect representative of physical well-being – plump with nourishment, rosy-cheeked and 'jolly' with health, brisk with energy. The immediate prospect is, perhaps, a

[1] January 1906 is the date given in the preliminary directions to Act I of the published (stage) version. No year is given in the original longhand MS. The first performance of the play at the Court Theatre took place on 28 November 1905.

little more serious for Sarah Undershaft and Charles Lomax, 'poor as church mice' on £800 a year, as they are less richly endowed by nature. But there is always the comforting thought of the unseen providence who has only to be supplicated: the absent father, 'rolling in money', 'fabulously wealthy'. Not a hint of the uncertainties of great wealth creeps into the dialogue, no shadow of sudden losses and bankruptcies, only of the chances of picking up a fortune. In every generation since the reign of James I some foundling has succeeded to the vast Undershaft inheritance; and 'they were rich enough to buy land for their own children and leave them well provided for', apart from the main bequest. Through the centuries the wealth has been accumulating without a break, it seems. This play is certainly not haunted by the Malthusian nightmare.

In this respect, its world is that of folklore and fairy tale, of Dick Whittington and Jack and the Beanstalk; a world of inexhaustible hoards of treasure, where straw can be spun into gold and geese lay golden eggs; a world ruled over by luck and indulgent to its favourites: the young, the beautiful, the cheerful, the quick-witted and, not least, the hopeful stranger who carries off the prize from the legitimate heir. The conditions of the will made by Charles Lomax's father establish the genre: 'if he increases his income by his own exertions, they may double the increase.' They reveal a principle of economic distribution that could be called natural, though it is also familiar in Christian terms: 'To him that hath shall be given'; the proposition is that the naturally endowed are fittest to control the resources of civilized society. *Major Barbara*, in its unfolding, extends the principle beyond economic bounds: power to the strong; authority to the commanding.

The fictional situations on which Shaw's plays turn are often absurd and fantastic. Their remoteness from credible actuality works curiously in alliance with the excessively rational element. The arbitrariness of the fable, as an excuse for the play, is flaunted: Shaw is not dramatizing a story with a moral, but creating a dramatic image of his conflicting emotions and ideas. The blatant casuistry with which Cusins matches the doubtful relevance of the test – claimants for the Undershaft inheritance must prove that they are foundlings – communicates the dramatist's sense of logic as a game, his mind's self-delight in its own free play, and a scorn for the plodding literalist. More seriously, it communicates his sense of the slipperiness of all attempts to interpret life rationally. Casuistry is a common element in fairy tales. But the foundling motif is not without serious significance.[1] In relation to Shaw's own psyche, the foundling

[1] It may be noted here that Lady Britomart and the foundling had had fairly recent theatrical precursors in Wilde's Lady Bracknell and the child mislaid in a

figure is here interestingly linked with the images of providential bounty and the blueprint for a benevolent paternalism.

The conversion of Barbara, on which the play turns, is essentially conversion to the acceptance of wealth.[1] As part of Shaw's campaign against idealism, or more precisely 'Impossibilism' as it was currently termed among the Fabians, *Major Barbara* sets itself against false pride in unrealizable commodities. Beyond the temptation to refuse tainted money lies the more pernicious temptation to keep out of the market-place altogether. The position from which Cusins has begun to emerge in pursuit of Barbara, when the play begins, represents the negation from which he and Barbara have to be saved: the retirement of the intellectual, poet, or saint, possible only as a form of privilege (Oxford – surely it is Oxford? – being in 1906 no more an exposed position in society, no less comfortable than Wilton Crescent, as Lady Britomart's acceptance of Cusins recognizes; scholars are gentlemen, and 'nobody can say a word against Greek'). Shaw uses Cusins's intellectual clarity to make explicit, near the end of the play, the realist's view of selling the soul in compromise with the world:

> It is not the sale of my soul that troubles me: I have sold it too often to care about that. I have sold it for a professorship. I have sold it for an income. I have sold it to escape being imprisoned for refusing to pay taxes for hangmen's ropes and unjust wars and things that I abhor . . .

Before we reach this point, our acceptance of the statement as a truism has been prepared by Shaw's confrontation of the Faustian theme of the bargain with its connotations in the central Christian myth.

Undershaft as Mephistopheles, *Doppelgänger* to Cusins's Faust, is presented as a sham villain in a sham conflict. He is more like Cusins than at first appears probable, the stage 'heavy', but intellectualized, no more dionysiac in temperament and character than Cusins, the self-confessed apollonian. The two together provide the play with twin foci of ironic consciousness, mutually comprehending; Undershaft merely reveals to Cusins what he already knows, in order to elicit admission of the knowledge: intellectually they are from the start equally free of illusions. They watch each other's manœuvring for the winning – or betrayal – of Barbara; they may talk of rivalry, but the total view they present is more like complicity.

It is in Act II, where Undershaft and Cusins observe the working out

---

handbag. T. S. Eliot, remembering *The Importance of Being Earnest* in *The Confidential Clerk*, recognized that it was a farce on classical themes.

[1] But this wealth connotes more than money or power; it is fullness of life, too.

of the sub-plot, or inset play, involving Barbara and Bill Walker, that Shaw concentrates awareness of the Christian analogues:[1] the price received by Judas for the betrayal of Christ and the sanctified bargain of the Redemption, the sacrifice which ransoms human souls. The act begins with the frauds, the minor characters of Rummy Mitchens and Snobby Price ('Snobby's a carpenter,' says Rummy, so preparing for our recognition of the fullness of Bill Walker's pun: 'Wot prawce selvytion nah? Snobby Prawce! Ha! ha!').[2] Both are unscrupulous in their readiness to benefit from the providence of the Salvation Army. (Rummy and Lady Britomart, it seems, are sisters under their skins.) They epitomize a natural way of regarding wealth, opposed to Peter Shirley's and Bill Walker's legalistic way. Peter talks conscientiously in terms of paying for what he gets and being himself paid a just price for what he gives. Bill, attempting legalistically to buy the natural freedom of his soul, throws his sovereign on the drum, where it is followed by Snobby Price's cap; Snobby, the instinctive, unregenerate socialist, is a parasite on legality, as well as the self-justified petty thief preying on such master-thieves as Undershaft and Bodger. Barbara, alluding to Bill's 'twenty pieces of silver' and suggesting that her father need contribute no more than another ten 'to buy anybody who's for sale', gives the gesture its ironic ambiguity: in the miniature play, the ostensible object of the bargain is Bill's soul and Barbara is both tempter and cheapjack working up the bidding – 'Dont lets get you cheap,' as she works up the collection at Army meetings; the greater price paid for Barbara herself, in the cheque handed over to Mrs Baines by Undershaft, cancels out Bill's payment and is the token of his release from his bond;[3] the second payment is not only a magnified reflection of the first, but its sacramental transfiguration.

The folk law, to which the Undershaft tradition adheres, bears a genuine relation to the mythology at the centre of the play and to the ritual of the Dionysiac festivals in which Attic drama is believed to have originated, ritual celebrations of the rebirth of God in a divine foundling.

[1] Mrs Glenys Stow has pointed out to me that Shaw's description of the set for Act II, if followed closely, would give a cruciform design dominating the action. Furthermore, the shed to one side, the horse-trough to the other are potentially suggestive of a Bethlehem (waiting for the 'rough beast' of 'The Second Coming'?); or the shape and stone colour of the horse-trough could suggest to the eyes a tomb, even more than a manger: the extremes of the messianic life on earth.

[2] His full name is Bronterre O'Brien Price, commemorating the Dublin Chartist, editor of *The Poor Man's Guardian*. (Incidentally, Bronterre > Brunty > Brontë + Romola + Shirley suggests that Shaw's mind was running on women novelists and women of genius in general.)

[3] Another modern dramatic model comes to mind here: Yeats's Countess Cathleen pledging her soul in exchange for the lesser souls bought by the devils.

In the present Shavian context, official Christianity is certainly reborn as natural religion after the symbolic 'death' of Barbara. (Cf. Proserpine's descent into the Shades.) But there is also present the suggestion of a foundling Apollo inheriting from Dionysus.[1] The transmutation of this into the fairy-tale of the boy from Australia who takes up the challenge and proves himself worthy of the kingdom and the hand of the princess, that traditionally go together, does much to save *Major Barbara* from pretentiousness. It might limit its power to disturb, if the ironic ambiguity of the end of the play was not realized – a realization important also to the success of the play in performance (for, without the edge such an interpretation gives, Act III, so exciting to read, could well fall dramatically flat after Act II – as it did when the play was first produced at the Court Theatre).

Major Barbara is no exception to the tendency of Shaw's plays to reflect the pantomime form of fairy-tale, or mythological material, while relying on the fundamental unity in such different forms of imaginative construct. Britomart, Barbara and Undershaft are Edwardian incarnations of Demeter, Persephone and Dis/Minos (more easily recognizable as such in the years just following Arthur Evans's first exhibition of finds from the Knossos site[2] than their counterparts in *Candida* had been); but also there is a touch of that sham villain, the demon king, about Undershaft, and in the grouping of Britomart and Barbara an intriguing resemblance to the association of the pantomime Dame with the Principal Boy.[3] In the course of the play, a number of references are made to Barbara's self-evident likeness to her mother. The most broadly comic is assigned to Lady Britomart herself in the opening scene:

[1] Cf. Note 1 to Gilbert Murray's 'Excursus on the Ritual Forms Preserved in Greek Tragedy', in Jane Harrison, *Themis* (Cleveland: Meridian Books, 1962), p. 341: 'It is worth remarking that the Year-Daimon has equally left his mark on the New Comedy. The somewhat tiresome foundling of unknown parentage who grows up, is recognized, and inherits, in almost every play of Menander that is known to us, is clearly descended from the foundling of Euripidean tragedy who turns out to be the son of a god and inherits a kingdom.' Jane Harrison herself (ibid., p. 443) suggests that Apollo and Dionysus 'are Kouroi and Year Gods caught and in part crystallized at different stages of development'.

[2] Evans paid his first visit to Crete in 1893, and A. C. Merrian published 'Discoveries in Crete' in *The Nation* (August 1894), p. 81. Excavations at Knossos began in 1900 and continued until 1905. An article by M. Galloway, 'Labyrinth of Crete', appeared in *The Nineteenth Century* (July 1901), pp. 96–102, and a note by Evans himself, 'Labyrinth and the Palace of Knossos' in *The Athenaeum* (26 July 1902), p. 132. An exhibition of reproductions of the Knossos finds was held in London in 1903. (See *Cornhill* (March 1903), pp. 319–32). From all this the prominence of a mother-goddess in Cretan worship was made very clear, one of her names perhaps being Britomart (known to Pausanias).

[3] See Chapter 14, p. 251.

Ever since they made her a major in the Salvation Army she has developed a propensity to have her own way and order people about which quite cows me sometimes. It's not ladylike: I'm sure I dont know where she picked it up.

The whole of this scene is an emphatic demonstration of Lady Britomart's matriarchal domination of her son, Stephen. She accuses him of fiddling first with his *'tie'*, then with his *'chain'*, and the objects are certainly emblematic of his relations with her. The trick is later repeated in her scene alone with Undershaft:

LADY BRITOMART. Andrew: you can talk my head off; but you cant change wrong into right. And your tie is all on one side. Put it straight.
UNDERSHAFT (*disconcerted*). It wont stay unless it's pinned (*he fumbles at it with childish grimaces*).

Here Andrew takes on the aspect of Jove in a nineteenth-century classical burlesque, bullied by his consort. The parental reconciliation which seems implied in the last act denotes more than the acceptance by society of an unpalatable truth, the reconciliation between power and the 'incarnation of morality'. When Undershaft has won his daughter, his wife sweeps in to appropriate the empire he has built up.[1] The last glimpse we are given of Barbara represents her clutching *'like a baby at her mother's skirt'*.

In retrospect, the action of the play, initiated by Lady Britomart, can be been as the working-out of her purpose: to absorb and assimilate the potentially hostile forces, adding them to her own strength. Nations are revitalized in this way; and who else but Britannia at her most imperial have we here? But the persistent victory of the mother over her children, her power always to *contain* them, is more ambiguous in its value. Barbara claims to take a less narrowly domestic and material view than her mother –

I felt like her when I saw this place – felt that I must have it – that never, never, never could I let it go; only she thought it was the houses and the kitchen ranges and the linen and china, when it was really all the human souls to be saved . . .

– but she is equally possessive, and her similar tendency to treat men as children implies that the pattern will continue in the next generation. She addresses her fiancé invariably by the pet name of 'Dolly' (Lady Britomart, with the formality of her period, calls him reprovingly 'Adolphus'); even when he has seemingly passed the test of manhood by accepting Undershaft's challenge, he remains to Barbara 'Silly baby Dolly', and she can cry exultantly: 'I have my dear little Dolly boy still;

[1] Cf. the ostentatious ease and sang-froid with which the attractive, but indolent, Sarah seats herself on the cannon.

and he has found me my place and my work.' The child keeps the doll,
the mother keeps the child, the Stevenages maintain their ascendancy
through the instrumentality of the strangers they annex.[1] The Earl of
Stevenage, Lady Britomart claims, suggested the inviting of Andrew to
Wilton Crescent. Whether we take this eponymous ancestor of the conventionally philistine Stephen[2] to be a smokescreen or an actual presence
in the background, the sense of ulterior motivation remains, and the
sense of a consciousness, like the author's, foreseeing and embracing the
whole dramatic development. Bill Walker warns Cusins of the fate
before him, as he relates his own experience of Barbara to what may
be in store for her 'bloke':

> Gawd elp im! Gaw-aw-aw-awd elp im! . . . Awve aony ed to stend it for a
> mawnin: e'll ev to stend it for a lawftawm.

Martin Meisel has classified Barbara's wooing of Bill Walker's soul as an
example of the reversed love-chase (in which the woman is the pursuer).
Certainly it offers a reflection of, or insight into, Cusins's fate. It is in
relation to Bill that we chiefly see demonstrated Barbara's capacity for
chivvying and bullying, and Shaw leaves us in no doubt of the hidden
pressures on her side: her self-confidence is the manner of her class, the
product of money, of social prestige and the habit of authority, the certainty of police protection and support. What subdues Bill, before ever
Barbara appears to him, is the information that she is an earl's granddaughter; when her millionaire father turns up, he involuntarily touches
his cap; the brute force and skill of Todger Fairmile, already won over
to Barbara's faith, are her final weapons.

Male vulnerability to the woman's ethic of respect for weakness, shame
and guilt is recognizably caricatured in the boastful 'Snobby' Price, whose
official confession, 'how I blasphemed and gambled and wopped my poor
old mother', is balanced by his private admission to Rummy, 'She used
to beat me', and who runs out the back way when his mother arrives at
the gate. Bill's blow to Jenny Hill's face is his repudiation of this ethic;
making reparation for the act, in preference to being forgiven, is the next
stage in his discovery of a morality that does not rob him of his self-
respect and self-responsibility. Class distinction no longer cows him when

---

[1] Cf. Shaw's letter to the *Evening Standard* (30 Nov. 1944), concerning *Candida*:
'the play is a counterblast to Ibsen's *Doll's House*, shewing that in the real typical
doll's house it is the man who is the doll.'

[2] Stephen, of course, is the name of the first martyr and thus both this character and his grandfather, the Earl of Stevenage, form part of the mythological
machinery of *Major Barbara* as a play about the emergence of a new religion
and a new cultural epoch. It may be appropriate to observe here that Undershaft's first name brings him also within the fold of Christianity. One wonders
who decided to give his son the name of the first martyr.

he has paid his debt. Before his exit, near the end of Act II, he is able to take his leave of the desolate Barbara with the magnanimity and good humour of an equal, restored to freedom. He checks his instinctive gesture towards his cap, and he does not take the hand she puts out to him – that would be acceptance of middle-class manners, and Bill can now afford, as he prefers, to keep proudly to his own: 'Naow mellice. Sao long, Judy.'[1] It is a recognition of an integrity in her that matches his own. Her 'Passion', as well as her betrayal by the rest, has thus played its part in saving his soul – from guilt, gloom, slavery and negativism.

Fergusson's critique of *Major Barbara* refers to the Wilton Crescent setting of Act I as though it was retained throughout the play. His interpretation of it as 'the London version of the bourgeois world's appearing to Shaw 'as stable and secure as the traditional cosmos of the Greeks or Elizabethans', is not simply an affront to Lady Britomart's aristocratic breeding; it disregards the extent to which Shaw has fantasticated the locale through the characters he gathers there and the dialogue they speak, not least by introducing 'Salvation' music among the games of the young people. In fact, the play destroys any possible illusion that this is a naturalistic interior and not a richly furnished stage to accommodate the superhuman stature of Lady Britomart and Andrew Undershaft, sprung from the gutter to become secular master of the world. But Fergusson's mistake can be related to the impression other critics have got from the end of the play. Alick West, seeing in it Shaw's capitulation to bourgeois values and decisive desertion of Marxist socialism, ended serious consideration of Shavian drama, in *A Good Man Fallen Among Fabians*, at this point. Indeed there are sections of Marcuse's 1966 Preface to *Eros and Civilization* on the actualities of our 'advanced industrial society' which it is useful to place beside the situation Shaw has brought his characters to, in Perivale St Andrews. Marcuse is concerned with the difficulty, in an affluent society, of breaking 'the fatal union of productivity and destruction, liberty and repression' and learning 'how to use the social wealth for shaping man's world in accordance with his Life Instincts, in the concerted struggle against the purveyors of Death':

> The very forces which rendered society capable of pacifying the struggle for existence served to repress in the individuals the need for such a liberation

---

[1] I owe the observation of this nice point of stage business to my colleague Mr Dennis Douglas. The film of *Major Barbara* included a shot of Bill Walker as a newly prosperous citizen of Perivale St Andrews, thus confusing what is clear in the play: that Bill, at least, achieves a kind of heroism and is not bought up and assimilated to the Establishment. Cusins, who understands and sympathizes with Bill, need not be assimilated either; but he has a life-long siege to withstand.

. . . In the affluent society, the authorities are hardly forced to justify their dominion. They deliver the goods; they satisfy the sexual and the aggressive energy of their subjects. Like the unconscious, the destructive power of which they so successfully represent, they are this side of good and evil, and the principle of contradiction has no place in their logic.

Only in the name of Undershaft and perhaps the Wedding Chorus that reminds us that *Major Barbara* is, like *Widowers' Houses*, in part a marriage play, does Shaw take sexual energy into account. Otherwise Marcuse's diagnosis is uncannily close to the terms in which Shaw has resolved the philosophical dilemma of his play. Undershaft has successfully induced Barbara to abandon the principle of contradiction for the faith that 'There is no wicked side: life is all one', and the question must be asked, whether she has truly gone *beyond* good and evil, or whether the unity of vision beyond moralistic duality has been achieved at the cost of a vital distinction. Perhaps she and Cusins *have* lost their way and been subtly tricked by the older generation ('The odds are overwhelmingly on the side of the powers that be,' Marcuse remarks).[1] The political Preface to *Eros and Civilization* takes a historical perspective:

> This situation is certainly not new in history: poverty and exploitation were products of economic freedom; time and again, people were liberated all over the globe by their lords and masters, and their new liberty turned out to be submission, not to the rule of law but to the rule of the law of the others. *What started as subjection, by force soon became 'voluntary servitude', collaboration in reproducing a society which made servitude increasingly rewarding and palatable. The reproduction, bigger and better, of the same ways of life came to mean, ever more clearly and consciously, the closing of those other possible ways of life which could do away with the serfs and the masters, with the productivity of repression.*[2] (My italics.)

I do not think Shaw was confused or uncertain, but fully conscious of the perilous ambiguity of the situation. The last line of his text is an alert:

UNDERSHAFT (*to Cusins*). Six o'clock to-morrow morning, Euripides.

And the undercutting of the dramatic resolution in the reduction of Cusins and Barbara in the last moments is functional in referring the

---

[1] 'As to the triumph of Undershaft,' wrote Shaw to Gilbert Murray, 'that is inevitable because I am in the mind that Undershaft is in the right, and that Barbara and Adolphus, with a great deal of his natural insight and cleverness, are very young, very romantic, very academic, very ignorant of the world. I think it would be unnatural if they were able to cope with him.' Letter of 7 October 1905, published in Gilbert Murray, *Unfinished Autobiography* (London: Allen and Unwin, 1960), pp. 155–7.

[2] The text is quoted from the Sphere Books edition of Herbert Marcuse, *Eros and Civilization* (London: Sphere Books, 1969; Boston: Beacon Press, [1966]), pp. 11–13.

problem back to the audience. It implies a recognition (which Brecht later shared) that the true resolution of socialist drama belongs not in the work of art but outside it in society. Cusins's choice is a resolution in terms of plot; as a total structure of ideas the play remains a paradox in which antitheses retain their full value and cannot be resolved away. The many churches in Perivale St Andrews are not only confirmation of the comparative mythology built into the play; they represent rival visions and issues undecided. There is nothing static about this New Jerusalem: snobbery and the sense of hierarchy survive, but they are confronted by the principles of the William Morris Labor Church. Barbara is aware that the efficient industrial society, however prosperous, is not the fulfilment of her vocation but its opportunity. Her purity of intention, what the nineteenth century called 'character' and what *On the Rocks* was to call 'conscience', is relied on still to find its way through a perspective of infinitely proliferating ironies. Singleness of purpose is necessary to action; but conversely, Shaw's drama now implies, the purity of the action needs to be safeguarded by a matching scepticism, an understanding of things that has moved beyond the defensive self-irony of *Candida* to become a well-forged weapon of assault against 'the purveyors of Death'.

9

Problem Plays

Shaw's Preface to the play, audiences' delight in the doctors, and critical recognition of the dramatist's debt to Molière's *L'Amour médecin*[1] have combined to establish the view that *The Doctor's Dilemma* is primarily a satire on the medical profession. But Shavian plots are commonly parables, and the metaphor of disease and cure had already played a defining part in *The Philanderer*; it was to be used again in *Too True to be Good*. The word *dilemma*, in the title and the dialogue of the present play, gives warning of an abstractly conceived theme and a syllogistically organized action. The retired doctor, Sir Patrick Cullen, is a socratic figure who surveys the situation and propounds the question:

> Well, Mr Savior of Lives: which is it to be? that honest decent man Blenkinsop, or that rotten blackguard of an artist, eh?

He makes it clear that the case is to be regarded as typical; the decision is a test of principle:

> Suppose you had this choice put before you: either to go through life and find all the pictures bad but all the men and women good, or to go through life and find all the pictures good and all the men and women rotten. Which would you choose?

It is essentially an unreal question, demanding a choice between extremes as though they were mutually exclusive and life was lived, or could be lived, in terms of absolutes. The artificiality of the mental categories involved, and their falseness to experience and the facts of natural history, is self-evident. Yet they give moral definition to the entirely practical charge that Sir Patrick lays on his middle-aged colleague, Ridgeon:

> Youve to hold the scales between Blenkinsop and Dubedat. Hold them fairly.

---

[1] See A. Hamon, *The Twentieth Century Molière: Bernard Shaw* (London: Allen and Unwin, 1915) and James Bridie, 'Shaw the Dramatist', in S. Winsten (ed.), *G.B.S. 90* (London: Hutchinson, 1946), esp. pp. 84–8.

Thinking over a hypothetical problem gives exercise in weighing values and recognizing responsibilities – abilities eminently desirable in those who hold power within an actual human context.

The metaphor of the scales is a reminder of the Shakespearian proto-type of such 'problem plays' as *The Doctor's Dilemma*: *Measure for Measure*. There the action turns on an unreal choice between chastity and charity, lightly masking the more fundamental – but still unneces-sary – choice between justice and mercy. The fact that it *is* unnecessary, and undesirable, is the chief lesson the play has to teach, and the whole ironic basis of the design is a means of teaching it. For the test is set up and applied by a delegate of the author hard to accept as an ideal char-acter: the Duke's authoritative role does not quite obscure an objective view of him as a self-opinionated fool, and the test he devises bears marks of folly and an insensitive grossness of moral imagination. Sir Patrick Cullen does not invent the situation in Shaw's play, as the Duke does in Shakespeare's; he is not so much of a fool in meddling with lives, only the kind of fool every philosopher submits to be in the practice of his vocation. Still, Sir Patrick *is* biased, and his bias corresponds to the fault revealed in Shakespeare's Angelo by the test for a just judge. It is puritan moralism.

The meddler with lives, in *The Doctor's Dilemma*, is the younger doctor, Ridgeon, whose discovery of a cure for tuberculosis gives him – he thinks – the keys of life and death, absolute power over the fates of those who need his help. 'Mr Savior of Lives', gibes Sir Patrick at the other's assumption of a messianic role. Though a much more likeable character than Dr Paramore in *The Philanderer*, Ridgeon shares Paramore's dominant fault: greater concern for the disease and the art of healing than for the patient; a personal vanity stronger than his social conscience. His choice of a bachelor dinner party at Richmond (a symposium?) as the occasion for judging Louis Dubedat's worthiness to be rescued from death, is a very neat stroke on Shaw's part to throw into relief the absence of sympathetic imagination in such morality-mongering devotees of science. Ridgeon's embarrassed protest to Blenkinsop, 'the most tragic thing in the world is a sick doctor', ricochets with full irony when he corrects himself, in Act IV: 'The most tragic thing in the world is a man of genius who is not also a man of honor.' Ostensibly a judgement of Dubedat, it is equally applicable to the doctor who has knowingly handed his patient over to an incompetent bungler because he is in love with the patient's wife. Whether Ridgeon's precise motive is a desire to marry Jennifer, or a desire to protect her from disillusion, his treatment of Dubedat is as little honourable as Angelo's readiness to trade Claudio's life for Isabella's virginity. He has, indeed, consulted Sir Patrick about

symptoms he has observed in himself and received the other's diagnosis
of middle-aged foolishness. Perhaps it shows itself in his infatuation with
Jennifer's beauty and innocence; more monstrously, it prompts him to
play God with the lives of men – and enjoy the sense of power. 'Physician,
heal thyself . . .' is all the more thunderously implied because the words
are never spoken.

What keeps Ridgeon attractive is his boyishness, very apparent in the
eager enthusiasm with which he recognizes that he is up against the
Kantian test:

> RIDGEON. . . . I'm not at all convinced that the world wouldnt be a better
> world if everybody behaved as Dubedat does than it is now that everybody
> behaves as Blenkinsop does.
> SIR PATRICK. Then why dont you behave as Dubedat does?
> RIDGEON. Ah, that beats me. Thats the experimental test. Still, it's a
> dilemma. It's a dilemma . . .

He might as well call out: 'A game! A game!' He is, indeed, behaving
more like Dubedat than he sees. Though Shaw's writing of a whole fifth
act seems hardly justified to get a single point across (it is really an
epilogue, except that tragedies traditionally run to five acts), the realization Ridgeon comes to, 'I have committed a purely disinterested murder!',
is certainly the logical conclusion that follows from his initial stance: the
healer, priest, king, or Duke, who is more conscious of his power *over*
other beings than of his opportunity to serve them, is likely sooner or
later to find his acts entangling him in the paradox of judicial murder.

Dubedat, the ironist in the play, recognizes this when he puts the
doctor's top hat on the lay figure in cardinal's robes – with hour glass in
hand and scythe on back. The gibe at 'proud man, Dress'd in a little
brief authority' takes into account the doctors' pretentious investment of
themselves with the gravity of Death and the irresistibility of Time.
Like Hamlet with Yorick's skull, Dubedat plays with the symbols of
mortality. In his role of the doomed man, he affronts the seriousness of
the others by playing the antic death's head.[1] Inviting an illiterate
newspaper reporter to attend the final scene turns it into a burlesque of
their conventional attitudes, to which his persisting impishness contributes the unwavering comic mood. He can afford to take this attitude,
not only because he recognizes – as they do not wish to recognize – that
death is the common fate, to which doctors themselves are not immune
('It is in questionable taste under any circumstances or in any company
to harp on the subject of death; but it is a dastardly advantage to take of a

---

[1] One is reminded of the image in *Richard II*, III. ii: '. . . within the hollow
crown / That rounds the mortal temples of a king / Keeps Death his court, and
there the antic sits, / Scoffing his state and grinning at his pomp.'

medical man,' protests B.B., when Dubedat has put it to them that they none of them know that they are not going to die within six months), but even more because he is an artist – and art is a better answer than medicine to the fact of man's mortality. He is not 'intimidated', and this is why. The curtain gives emphasis to Ridgeon's line at the close of Act III: 'Death ends everything, doesnt it? Goodbye.' Dubedat disproves the statement by living on through Jennifer even more spectacularly than in his other works of art. Ridgeon can only kill; but Dubedat, like Pygmalion, can create a living goddess, turn a naïve country girl into a queen. The concept of art is extended beyond the range of finite, if perdurable, achievements to include all creativity which enriches life and is absorbed into its endless flow.

The protean character of Dubedat is the real 'ginger' in the play. The analogous figure in *Measure for Measure*, though less centrally placed, is the irreverent Lucio, who pulls the hood off the Friar-Duke. Both, in their respective plays, are the means whereby Shakespeare and Shaw maintain their comic perspective on the whole and keep their audiences healthily sceptical about the terms in which the philosophical lesson is presented. They represent the dramatist's own freedom from the illusion he can create for others; and Dubedat, who certainly relishes the conspiracy to kill him more than he resents it, mirrors his author's aesthetic pleasure in the design of his play, as Ridgeon with less self-awareness mirrors Shaw's delight in the idea, the classically perfect dilemma, he has hit upon. For much of the particular pleasure *The Doctor's Dilemma* offers is unabashedly intellectual: it arises from a completely lucid awareness of the abstract scheme being logically worked out, and a sense of the play as a game and a contrast with life, as the rules which define it are clearer-cut, less complexly modified. The simplification is a relief; the mind is exercised, but in a way that never threatens its poise and control.

Dubedat is not an example of the Shavian villain with a heart of gold (like Brassbound, or Blanco Posnet). He is a self-respecting rogue, an out-and-out individualist, who rejects all the moral assumptions on which society operates. He is the true amoralist in that he has no moral sense; from the physician's point-of-view he is defective. 'I feel perfectly convinced that this is not a moral case at all: it's a physical one,' declares Cutler Walpole. 'Theres something abnormal about his brain.' He is the exceptional case that makes nonsense of the whole notion of panaceas (each of the doctors has his own favourite) – and of universally applicable rules of conduct.

St John Hankin's *The Return of the Prodigal* had been put on at the Court Theatre in 1905, the year before *The Doctor's Dilemma*. Hankin's

hero, Eustace, is an anticipation of Dubedat: a ne'er-do-well, who stages
a pathetic return from Australia to lie in sham exhaustion on his family's
doorstep, proceeds to play on the pity and affection of those who have
them to give, on the stupid sycophancy of the doctor, and on the social
ambitions and concern for respectable appearances in the rest, until he
wins himself a sinecure. Eustace's bold and cool blackmailing technique,
and his deliberate employment of a code that binds others but not himself, is a useful medium for social criticism. But he is not entirely a comic
character. Hankin gives glimpses of sad psychological realities, as the play
develops, and Eustace's bleak, fatalistic self-knowledge finally bites
deeper than the social satire. His talents are not the ones his society
values, and he does not believe in that society's goals. So his roguery
shows up as a defensive means to survival within a system in which he is
unfitted to live otherwise. In so far as Hankin's play remains social in its
ultimate concern, it has to be interpreted as a plea for tolerance and a
more open form of society with room for dissentient minorities.

Shaw's close personal association with the Court Theatre makes it
certain that he knew Hankin's play before ever it was performed, and he
may have owed to it the new variation on the 'Wyndham part', cool-as-
a-cucumber, that Dubedat represents. The character is, indeed, related
to Shaw's other philanderer types and perhaps most closely to Frank
Gardner; but the range of his rascality is new and, though Frank's dis-
respect for 'the usual arrangements' made him a gambler, nowhere else
in the plays do we come across such a magnificent cheat in money
matters as Dubedat. The more typical Shavian Don Juan (Charteris, or
Valentine, or Tanner) is highly respectable in his social behaviour, however startling his opinions may be: they are sham revolutionists, whereas
Dubedat is genuinely subversive, like Brecht's Azdak (or Baal) after him.

Sir Patrick Cullen's aphorism, 'There are two things that can be wrong
with any man. One of them is a cheque. The other is a woman,' provides
a programme for the showing up of Louis Dubedat. When it has run its
course, B.B. concludes:

> He had only two failings, money and women. Well, let us be honest. Tell
> the truth, Paddy. Dont be hypocritical, Ridgeon. Throw off the mask,
> Walpole. Are these two matters so well arranged at present that a disregard
> of the usual arrangements indicates real depravity?

However just as a criticism of society, it is only an excuse for the individual. Dubedat's claim to be a disciple of Bernard Shaw is a provisional
truth that gets a quick laugh. Sir Patrick's common sense checks the
supposition that here is another devil's disciple, upholding a true morality
against the falseness of orthodox morality:

SIR PATRICK. I assure you, young man, my father learnt the doctrine of deliverance from sin from John Wesley's own lips before you or Mr Shaw were born. It used to be very popular as an excuse for putting sand in sugar and water in milk. Youre a sound Methodist, my lad; only you dont know it.

The other's reaction, '*seriously annoyed for the first time*', is an admission that Sir Patrick has the right of it:

It's an intellectual insult. I dont believe theres such a thing as sin.

The dramatist will not go that far, and neither does Dubedat when faced with the practical test. Forcing up the price of the sketch he has made of Sir Patrick, he becomes the biter bit:

LOUIS. . . . May I send it to your house, Sir Patrick, for twelve guineas? . . .
B.B. . . . Twelve guineas? Thank you: I'll take it at that . . . I neednt settle with you now, Mr Dubedat: my fees will come to more than that. (*He also retrieves his hat.*)[1]
LOUIS (*indignantly*). Well, of all the mean -- (*words fail him*)! I'd let myself be shot sooner than do a thing like that. I consider youve stolen that drawing.
SIR PATRICK (*drily*). So weve converted you to a belief in morality after all, eh?

On ethical grounds, Dubedat has to be judged the direct antithesis to the good man, Blenkinsop; though he can be used as an indictment of evil in society, his egotism and irresponsibility are not morally exonerated thereby. The question of what is to be done with the Dubedats remains unsolved. Ridgeon's answer – extermination – is hardly endorsed by the author, who mocks the principle of cutting bits out of the body politic, under a variant paradigm, in the figure of Cutler Walpole, obsessed with the 'nuciform sac'; he rationally rejects it in the one argument Dubedat puts forward that gains Sir Patrick's hearty support:

The criminal law is no use to decent people . . . itll punish him. Itll punish not only him but everybody connected with him, innocent and guilty alike . . . You may put the criminal law out of your head once for all: it's only fit for fools and savages.

Sin without deliverance – to accept Sir Patrick's terms – is ineluctable in the human community, as far as this play's vision can reach.

But Shaw's vocabulary of values is larger. Holding the scales between Blenkinsop and Dubedat, and holding them fairly, involves more than Sir Patrick is allowed to see. There is more than one kind of good to be taken into account. Dubedat's self-respect is saved by a virtue that is not

[1] From its perch on the lay figure's head. The gesture demonstrates silently that he has ceased to be Dubedat's gull.

moral at all but æsthetic and is even identifiable with his moral viciousness. For his propensity for lying and faking is the source of his main and
undeniable gift to society,[1] the art which the puritan in Shaw, fed on
Plato, regarded as the biggest fake of all in its romantic presentation of
ideal beauty: the naïve Jennifer apotheosized as Guinevere.[2] The tension
which remains in the play is connected with an unsettled doubt as to
whether or not it is a poisoned gift.

Shaw had styled *Candida* his Pre-Raphaelite play and there translated
the Pre-Raphaelite double image of woman into thoroughly bourgeois
naturalistic terms as Mrs Morell and Prossy Garnett. Rossetti and Morris
had exalted Jane Burden as Guinevere. (Rossetti painted her as Proserpine
too.) Rossetti's poem, 'Jenny', is at once a tribute to the 'Queen of
kisses' betrayed by gold, the country girl become London prostitute, and
an exposure of the ambiguous relationship between art (the aesthetic
principle) and commercialism in nineteenth-century English society.
Dubedat, it seems, is a Pre-Raphaelite artist in the counterbalancing of
his portraits of Jennifer's beauty with his bigamous marriage to the
necessary Minnie Tinwell (Fanny Cornforth to Jane Burdon and Elizabeth Siddal) with the vulgarly chinking name. The Victorian artist-
socialist's need to reconcile the dichotomy between art and morality is
reflected in the steady grasp of the scales in *The Doctor's Dilemma*.

Dubedat, we gather from Jennifer's own innocent lips, would have
treated her as he treated Minnie Tinwell:

> He came to me like a child. Only fancy, doctor: he never even wanted to
> marry me . . . I had to propose it myself. Then he said he had no money.
> When I told him I had some, he said 'Oh all right,' just like a boy.

Jennifer's own weakness is a preference of beauty to truth, an incapacity
to see factual truth. She remains at the stage of Ellie Dunn repudiating
Hesione's suggestion that Marcus Darnley is a liar:

> Hesione: don't say that you don't believe him. I couldn't bear that;[3]

'If I lost faith in him,' says Jennifer, 'it would mean the wreck and
failure of my life. I should go back to Cornwall and die. I could show
you the very cliff I should jump off.' In fact, Ellie discovers her strength

---

[1] Walpole appreciates another in Dubedat's 'dazzling cheek', essentially the
quality of the comedian, the harlequin.

[2] Shaw wrote to Lillah McCarthy, who was to play Jennifer: 'I wish you would
suggest a name for yourself in this new play. I cannot very well call the lady
Lillah. Provisionally I have called her Andromeda; but Mrs Andromeda Dubedat
is too long. Here in King Arthur's country the name Guinevere survives as
Jennifer . . .' Lillah McCarthy, *Myself and My Friends* (London: Thornton
Butterworth, 1933), pp. 79–80.

[3] See Chapter 12, p. 218.

through disillusionment. The Jennifer who supports and protects Louis is surely capable of equal strength, for all her talk of suicide. The error of the doctors is their failure to trust her strength, the timidity that keeps them silent about the Louis they know and makes Ridgeon resort, instead, to virtual murder of Dubedat, his second motive – to protect Jennifer's blissful ignorance – being no better than the first – his wish to marry her.

The trouble with the doctors is that they are such perfect gentlemen. One of the first points made in Act I is the citation of Ridgeon in the Birthday Honours: it is on this that the others gather to congratulate him ('Welcome to the order of knighthood!' is B.B.'s greeting); and the report of it brings Jennifer, a damsel in distress, to seek his aid. The hideous Emmy, who connives in her attempt to see the doctor and win his support, suggests not only the reality principle which inspires a Rembrandt ('a fellow who would paint a hag of 70 with as much enjoyment as a Venus of 20' – *Man and Superman*), but, more mischievously, a Morgan le Fay, plotting the destruction of the Round Table and the fall of Arthur.[1] As Shaw saw it, the socialism of the Pre-Raphaelites got lost in their dream of fair women; and that other revolutionary socialist of the forties, Richard Wagner, betrayed his faith and his genius when he turned to the Arthurian world in *Parsifal*.

There is a special appositeness in the fact that the creed recited by the dying Dubedat is derived from Wagner:

I believe in MichaelAngelo, Velasquez, and Rembrandt; in the might of design, the mystery of color, the redemption of all things by Beauty everlasting, and the message of Art that has made these hands blessed.[2]

Despite *Parsifal*, Shaw remained a Wagnerite; and it is not the irony of uncertain faith, but a perception that truth is not simple and onesided, but diverse and complex, that makes the final image of Jennifer triumphant genuinely enigmatic and challenging. It represents the victory of illusion and a selling-out to beauty, no doubt; but it also signifies the defeat of the doctors, and the creative power of the imagination which can move men to try to shorten the distance between the world as it is and as they feel it ought to be. Dubedat, the pathological liar, is also the most thoroughgoing realist of the play, and the image is his creation. (The mirror, '*mostly disabled from reflection by elaborate painting . . .*', belongs not to him but to Ridgeon.)

Eduard Bernstein identified Edward Aveling of the Socialist League

[1] Merlin's magic was one of the supports of Arthurian power; Ridgoon is conscious of his reputation as a magician, and B.B.'s cures act 'like magic'.

[2] See Richard Wagner, 'An End in Paris', *Prose Works*, trans. W. Ashton Ellis (London: Kegan Paul, 1898), Vol. VII, pp. 66–7.

and National Secularist Society, scientist Fellow of University College, London, and common-law husband of Eleanor Marx, as Shaw's model for Dubedat, and the identification sticks. 'He has his good points, has Edward,' wrote Shaw to Ellen Terry in 1898:

> For instance, he does not deny his faiths, and will nail his atheism and socialism to the masthead incorruptibly enough. But he is incorrigible when women or money or the fulfilment of his engagements (especially prepaid ones) are in question . . . For some years past he has been behaving well, because Marx's friend Engels left Eleanor £9,000. But the other day he tried the old familiar post-dated cheque on Sidney Webb – in vain . . . Must I really not tell anyone? If you only knew how utterly your delicacy is wasted!

Henry Salt's judgement on Aveling was: 'a nature in which there was an excess of the emotional and artistic'; and Bernstein himself commented on the embarrassed mixture of reticence and effusive enthusiasm with which English socialists talked to the uninitiated about the Avelings. It is of no small interest that Shaw chose to write the play he did around this figure, well known to himself,[1] and close to the centre of the English socialist movement. (At the time of Eleanor Marx's suicide, he commented on the stronger fascination the task of writing about Edward would hold for him.[2]) What has emerged is Aveling as Harlequin, the living prototype explored and understood through his approximation to a traditional stage type: the individualist whose socially deviant behaviour may find a convenient religion in socialism, yet consorts so oddly with it. The sense Shaw made of the character reconciled the inner lack of respect for conventional standards, the common dishonesty and the preying on women, with the courage proper to a convinced socialist and freedom from authoritarian pressures. Though far from using psychological realism in the presentation of his characters, Shaw seems to have elaborated the whole play out of psychological insights, not least out of the perception that morality is somehow related to fear of death, and that complete freedom from either gives a personality an inhuman (or

---

[1] Under the pseudonym of Alec Nelson, Aveling was prominent in the *avant-garde* amateur theatre of the period, too, and among the pioneers of Ibsen's and, later, Strindberg's work in England. For background to *The Doctor's Dilemma*, see C. Tzuzuki, *The Life of Eleanor Marx* (Oxford: O.U.P., 1967) and Lewis Feuer, 'The Marxian Tragedians', *Encounter*, Vol. XIX (1962), pp. 23–32. I am inclined to think that Eleanor Marx contributed something as a model to Ellie in *Heartbreak House* too.

[2] A letter of 4 April 1898 to Charlotte Payne Townshend records 'the news of Eleanor Marx's suicide in consequence of Aveling having spent all her money' (perhaps a characteristically Shavian interpretation of motive). Shaw adds: 'Massingham wants to write about her. *I* want to write about Aveling.' The original letter is in the British Museum Collection (Addit. MS. 46505).

pathological) invulnerability. As for the readiness to exploit, rather than idealize, women, it is contrasted with the quality of devotion to women that seems to frustrate the socialist impulse in Pre-Raphaelite art. Shaw commented to Lillah McCarthy, who was preparing to play Jennifer in the first production, that she would have her work cut out to make the character fascinating, as she should be, since he himself disliked such women.[1] But his ambivalence – to women and to art – emerges less as evasiveness than as subtle and intricate understanding of motive in the lucidity of *The Doctor's Dilemma*, remarkably successfully conveyed by the flaunted two-dimensional scheme.

The description of *The Doctor's Dilemma* as a tragedy is, of course, acceptable only in relation to the meaning of the play, not its form. Ridgeon's statement, 'Life does not cease to be funny when people die any more than it ceases to be serious when people laugh', interprets the relation between the idea of the play and its presentation. If we are concerned with categories of style, this is farce, based on wit, coincidence, improbability and caricature. But Dubedat's death-scene, which Archer challenged Shaw to write,[2] is a more subtle affair than this suggests, and an indication of his claim that he could, when he judged it appropriate, write movingly, and that his comedy is not characteristically unemotional at all, but a detached and delicate handling of genuinely pathetic or sombre, as well as sometimes serenely happy, themes. Admittedly, Shaw did not have much success when he tried to write poetically, though he could write both gravely and gaily and produce an effect like poetry. In the present play, and the death scene in particular, his choice of quotations is effective. It is certainly the emotions responding to the ear, without reference to the brain, that are worked on by B.B.'s hash of famous Shakespearian lines:

> To-morrow and to-morrow and to-morrow
> After life's fitful fever they sleep well
> And like this insubstantial bourne from which
> No traveller returns
> Leave not a wrack behind.

He organizes harmony in every situation, as he recurrently calls in the other members of the chorus:

Tell the truth, Paddy. Dont be hypocritical, Ridgeon. Throw off the mask, Walpole.

Believe me, Paddy, we are all mortal. It is the common lot, Ridgeon. Say what you will, Walpole, Nature's debt must be paid. If tis not today, twill be tomorrow.

---

[1] Lillah McCarthy, op. cit., p. 78.

[2] See Archibald Henderson, *George Bernard Shaw*: *Man of the Century* (New York: Appleton-Century-Crofts, 1956), pp. 606–7.

His disarming innocence of any intention to insult and patronize keeps the others from protesting. As a characteristic, it neatly bridges the gap between Jennifer's incredible innocence and Dubedat's conscienceless blatancy, and it is nearer than the simplicity of Blenkinsop or the outspoken plainness of Sir Patrick Cullen to the core of the play. Bloomfield Bonington is the baby, with the baby's attractiveness, the baby's irresponsibility, the baby's vanity and insouciant lack of self-knowledge or effective knowledge of the world: his ego is in the way of his seeing anything else clearly; the touch that completes the portrait is his awe of his wife – and her motherly, if sometimes indulgent, authority:

> EMMY (*looking in*). Come on, Sir Ralph: your wife's waiting in the carriage.
> B.B. (*suddenly sobered*). Oh! Goodbye. (*He goes out almost precipitately.*)

> B.B. In moments of domestic worry, I am simply Ralph. When the sun shines in the home, I am Beedle-Deedle-Dumkins.

Dubedat's epitaph, spoken in B.B.'s sincere tones and nonsensical words, does not lose touch with farce but works also as a genuine emotional tribute to something in Dubedat that cannot simply be dismissed. It is the quality that comes through in the latter's description of the burning bush:

> . . . we looked through the window and saw the flames dancing in a bush in the garden.
> LOUIS. Such a color! Garnet color. Waving like silk. Liquid lovely flame flowing up through the bay leaves, and not burning them.

This is something out of the moralist's reach. And the passage is followed by words to Jennifer in which Louis's egotism is abandoned:

> I used to think that our marriage was all an affectation, and that I'd break loose and run away some day. But now that I'm going to be broken loose whether I like it or not, I'm perfectly fond of you, and perfectly satisfied because I'm going to live as part of you and not as my troublesome self.

But the seal of strength and dignity is placed on the scene by the magnificently sombre biblical lines given to Sir Patrick and his following comment which sets the problem-play element aside, as it deserves:

> Aye! that is how the wicked die.
>   For there are no bands in their death;
>   But their strength is firm:
>   They are not in trouble as other men.
> No matter: it's not for us to judge. He's in another world now.

That is a positive tribute to the wickedness in which genius inextricably inheres; and it confirms the image of the garnet flames in the flourishing green bay tree as an emblem of the unified life, beyond good and evil. This is life as Barbara Undershaft was brought to understand it. The Jennifer of the death-scene is no weak sentimentalist and no Mrs Bloomfield Bonington. When she returns after Dubedat has breathed his last, she is completely transformed from the type of woman Shaw dislikes to a splendour of the imagination that only the unified life beyond innocence could have brought into being. It is Shaw's tribute of loyalty to the socialist movement in all its vagaries – including the rascality of Aveling, the suffering of Eleanor Marx, the dreams of the Pre-Raphaelites, the robust humour and power of work of William Morris, his public dedication and private unhappiness, and the magnificence of Jane Morris at her husband's funeral – all absorbed into a remarkable aesthetic affirmation.

The classical legend of Pygmalion supplies an image of the artist, or dreamer,[1] that challenges too ready an acceptance of Shaw's play as a version of *Cinderella*. The title insists on recognition that the thematic importance of Higgins at least equals that of Eliza: the experimenter is a vital part of the experiment.

Like *The Doctor's Dilemma*, *Pygmalion* has been designed strictly on Problem Play lines.[2] The social question it sets out to examine can be formulated in Higgins's terms: What creates 'the deepest gulf that separates class from class and soul from soul?' Taking more than a hint from Dickens's late novel on the class system and the cash nexus in Victorian society, *Our Mutual Friend*, Shaw has worked out two hypotheses: in the fantasy of the girl taken from the gutter and given a superficial education – a veneer of culture and fashionable manners – and the second fantasy of her father, the dustman, suddenly endowed with wealth. In Doolittle he presented a conflation of two Dickensian characters: Boffin, the honest serving man who inherits a vast fortune made out of dust (the dust-heaps which neighbour his house being at least as symbolic as they are actual), and the villainous Silas Wegg, parasite and self-styled philosopher; the expansive humour which makes Doolittle finally an attractive character is Shaw's own contribution, and the value it represents in the play can hardly be overestimated. In *Our Mutual*

---

[1] Shaw reverts to this mask of the artist in *Back to Methuselah*, Part V.

[2] Shaw published the screen version in the Constable Standard Edition of his plays. Where any variants on the original (1913) are mentioned or quoted in the present discussion, the source is noted. The textual differences are discussed in Milton Crane, '*Pygmalion*: Bernard Shaw's Dramatic Theory and Practice', *Publications of the Modern Language Association*, Vol. LXVI (1951), pp. 879–85. The variant texts are printed in Donald Costello, *The Serpent's Eye: Shaw and the Cinema* (Indiana: University of Notre Dame Press, 1965), Appendix C.

Friend, Boffin himself plays Pygmalion's part in the ingeniously contrived education of Bella Wilfer into a true lady, on the principle of
'gentle is as gentle does'. It is an education of the heart which the more
humbly born Lizzie Hexam, in the same novel, does not need; and the
seal is set on Lizzie's natural virtue by her ultimate marriage, across all
class barriers, with the regenerated Eugene, formerly a wealthy idler.

The natural virtue of Eliza Doolittle is of another kind from Lizzie
Hexam's: it is the spirit that makes her commandeer a taxi, when she
has been thrown a handful of money, the spirit that takes her to Higgins
to ask for lessons and to propose to pay for them an amount that fires
his interest in her case:

> She offers me two-fifths of her day's income for a lesson. Two-fifths of a
> millionaire's income for a day would be somewhere about £60. It's handsome.
> By George, it's enormous! it's the biggest offer I ever had.

Boffin is designated the Golden Dustman; the gold dust from which
Higgins's Galatea is made is a natural inheritance from her original and
only parent. (The point that Eliza has no mother is made three times
over in the play.) Neither simple acquisitiveness nor vulgar ambition to
rise in society inheres in its substance. Eliza is in quest of some more
real value, a richer and finer quality of life.

The way in which Doolittle's two appearances intersect the chronological development of Eliza's story is reminiscent of the Ulrich Brendel
episodes in *Rosmersholm* and the way they function dramatically. True,
there is a precedent in Shaw's own drama in the appearance of Lickcheese, first as poor man, then as plutocrat, in *Widowers' Houses*; but
Lickcheese's part in the main plot, which keeps him on stage nearly to
the end of the play, robs his entrances of the special significance that
Brendel's and Doolittle's have: checking the main plot, and distancing us
from it while we consider its meaning in the light of this new, compelling figure that has usurped the centre of the stage. Doolittle's appearances first as poor man, then as rich man, mark the beginning and the
zenith of Eliza's social ascent. The paradox of Brendel's more prosperous,
if grotesque, outer appearance, signifying his spiritual bankruptcy, is
reflected in the top-hatted misery and defeat of Doolittle, which underlines the emptiness of Eliza's social success, and the irrelevance (as it
then appears) of Higgins's experiment with her.

What has happened, so far, is a mere selling-out to social convention.
The Professor in the haven of his laboratory, absorbed in the fascination
of his special study and careless of any other concerns, appears to his own
mother as a baby playing with its toys, with the peculiar irresponsibility
of the baby, not realizing that its 'doll' is a human being with human

feelings who has to go on living in a bigger, more complicated world outside the laboratory. The imperative implied is that every man *ought* to see what he is doing in relation to the whole society in which he lives, in the context of its values and his own. (Bringing most of his characters together, at the start, under the portico of Inigo Jones's church in Covent Garden – 'the handsomest barn in England', according to its creator's description – was Shaw's visual statement of the interrelatedness of these souls, implying such an ideal of society as Peter Keegan had expressed: 'a country where the State is the Church and the Church the people . . . in which all life is human and all humanity divine'.)

But what Higgins learns from his experiment outruns what he foresaw. The discovery that teaching Eliza is not just a matter of phonetics comes first in the realization that she has to be taught grammar as well. The meeting with the Eynsford Hill family, at Mrs Higgins's At-Home, demonstrates plainly that 'you have to consider not only how a girl pronounces, but what she pronounces'; and Eliza's conversation at this stage is nothing but the utterance of an automaton that betrays its lack of individuality, first in the scientific precision of the weather report ('The shallow depression in the west of these islands . . .'), and then, with more semblance of life, in its voicing of the ignorance and melodramatic imagination of the slums:

> What call would a woman with that strength in her have to die of influenza? What become of her new straw hat that should have come to me? Somebody pinched it; and what I say is, them as pinched it done her in.

At last comes the individuality of Eliza speaking out:

> Walk! Not bloody likely . . . I am going in a taxi.

The revelation corresponds to her teacher's latest conception of his task: 'watching her lips and her teeth and her tongue, *not to mention her soul, which is the quaintest of the lot.*'

Higgins's role as *raisonneur*, in addition to principal actor, is clear in this scene. His understanding of the vulnerability of conventions to honest naturalness ('what they really think would break up the whole show') leads on to reflections on the superficiality of the culture that passes in polite (conventional) society. These undercut his insistence on the 'advantages' he has given Eliza and prepare for Mrs Higgins's summing up:

> The advantages of that poor woman who was here just now! The manners and habits that disqualify a fine lady from earning her own living without giving her a fine lady's income! Is that what you mean?

The identification of 'that poor woman' hangs in the air: it is Mrs Eynsford Hill, her daughter, and Eliza herself in so far as her part in this act has been to present a travesty of the 'lady' in this pejorative sense, the individual intimidated by the pressures of society.

The experiment with Doolittle demonstrates that money without manners is sufficient to elevate a man in the social scale, especially if he is naturally endowed with self-confidence. Higgins, even better able to elucidate the implications of what has happened in the last act, makes this point:

> Eliza, it's quite true that your father is not a snob, and that he will be quite at home in any station of life to which his eccentric destiny may call him.

The similarity between Doolittle and Higgins himself is established. Money and genius allow Higgins, also, to infringe protocol and keep to his natural manners. But Higgins is protected from 'intimidation', as Doolittle is not, by his attachment to a wise, benevolent mother.

An inveterate bachelordom characterizes Pygmalion in Ovid's version of the legend: the sculptor's disgust with women as they are is the ground of his love for the ideal woman he models. Shaw accepted the motif, and his resistance of all persuasion to end his play with Eliza's marriage to her teacher testifies to the importance he gave it. Higgins is not one of the more obvious Shavian philanderers, but he does belong in the general category, among the theoreticians. His bias is presented in realistic psychological terms admitted in a conversation with his mother:

> MRS HIGGINS. Well, you never fall in love with anyone under forty-five. When will you discover that there are some rather nice-looking young women about?
> HIGGINS. Oh, I cant be bothered with young women. My idea of a lovable woman is something as like you as possible. I shall never get into the way of seriously liking young women: some habits lie too deep to be changed.

He has, in fact, a second mother in his bachelor establishment in the person of the housekeeper, Mrs Pearce (comparable in her role with Emmy in *The Doctor's Dilemma*). It is she who takes him rigorously to task for his swearing, his slovenliness, his bad table manners, leaving Mrs Higgins, however aware she may be of such things, without direct responsibility for checking him, without cause for exasperation, free to give accepting affection and detached advice: to be, as perhaps no other mother is, throughout Shaw's plays, the embodiment of benevolent wisdom, a personification of the good society. Higgins's bullying manner may be symptomatic of his childish dependence:

> HIGGINS. You know, Pickering, that woman has the most extraordinary ideas about me. Here I am, a shy, diffident sort of man. Ive never been

able to feel really grown-up and tremendous, like other chaps. And yet shes firmly persuaded that I'm an arbitrary overbearing bossing kind of person.

This play is not concerned with Higgins's weakness, however, but more with the way good mothering licenses irresponsible childishness and the creativity inherent in it. Higgins plays with his doll, but reacts as the good teacher and good parent, when by throwing the slippers at him she violently rejects the Cinderella part and her place in the Doll's House:

LIZA. . . . I can do without you: dont think I cant.
HIGGINS. I know you can. I told you you could.

His work is successfully done only when his charge is self-reliant and independent of him. Society and marriage being what they were, and to some extent still are, Eliza's self-liberation could hardly be shown in marriage to Higgins, but only in good fellowship with him. The umbilical cord has to be cut between the artist and his work of art; the dream is idle until the dreamer abandons his special attachment to it and lets it work itself out in the world as it can, and be changed and modified as it must. This is the moral that the play *as fable* drives home in ending as it does.

Though Higgins has seemed to demonstrate the usual way of a man with a woman in this society, educating Eliza to suit his own convenience, camouflaging the fact by training her in a few useless accomplishments, and treating her as an unpaid servant, he is quite free of the motivation Doolittle betrays in his comment to Higgins and Pickering:

I been the victim of one woman after another all my life; and I dont grudge you two getting the better of Eliza.

For the Professor's indulgence by women has not really spoiled him. He is the lucky exception that illuminates Shaw's theme of what men have made of women by the discipline of the strap, by keeping them economically dependent and subjugated, and what such women in instinctive revenge have made of men, through the discipline of the chain. Doolittle's proposal to sell his daughter to Higgins matches the latter's initial assumptions that the girl has no feelings and no power of understanding. Playing with his doll educates Higgins to the stage where he can say:

I think a woman fetching a man's slippers is a disgusting sight . . . I think a good deal more of you for throwing them in my face. No use slaving for me and then saying you want to be cared for: who cares for a slave? If you come back, come back for the sake of good fellowship . . .

The logic of *his* way of treating women catches out Doolittle and makes him a sadder man, enslaved to the task of providing for others, bound for his wedding in Hanover Square, 'tied . . . up and delivered . . . into the hands of middleclass morality', which is the morality of the drawing-room where women make the laws. He ends up as nothing else than an older Jack Tanner, Member of the Idle Rich Class.

To use Shaw's own terms, the judgements of this play are not, finally, moral judgements but vital judgements. It moves (as *Our Mutual Friend* does, in its much greater complexity and subtlety) beyond a view of democracy that depends on equalizing the advantages of wealth and education, to one that recognizes self-respect and independence of spirit (to which money and education can contribute) as the only reliable bases for an egalitarian society; it is again Higgins who sees:

> The great secret . . . is . . . having the same manner for all human souls . . . behaving as if you were in Heaven, where there are no third-class carriages, and one soul is as good as another.

But saying this is not enough: the play's vital judgements are distinctly not puritanical judgements. The validity of the unregenerate Doolittle's criticism of women is implied in his statement, 'she's only a woman and dont know how to be happy anyhow'. He recognizes women as the devotees of the official Victorian virtues of prudence and thrift, and his praise of 'Undeserving Poverty' is a plea for happiness and fullness of life as against prudence and thrift and security:

> Dont you be afraid that I'll save it and spare it and live idle on it. There wont be a penny of it left by Monday . . . Just one good spree for myself and the missus, giving pleasure to ourselves and employment to others, and satisfaction to you to think it's not been thrown away. You couldnt spend it better;
>
>   . . . Undeserving poverty is my line. Taking one station in society with another, it's – it's – well, it's the only one that has any ginger in it, to my taste.

Tastes differ, but Eliza likes a little ginger, too, and can recognize from her experience the need all human beings have of it and the extent to which 'respectable' morality denies it:

>   . . . my mother used to give him fourpence and tell him to go out and not come back until he'd drunk himself cheerful and loving-like. Theres lots of women has to make their husbands drunk to make them fit to live with . . . If a man has a bit of a conscience, it always takes him when he's sober; and then it makes him low-spirited. A drop of booze just takes that off and makes him happy.

Finally, what saves Higgins himself from social intimidation is the genuine, human security, for which money is a substitute, that lets him spend his time in work that, to his taste, is 'fun'. (It is not the barbarian's taste.) He insists that his freedom is creative freedom and appeals to Eliza to join him in it:

> LIZA. What am I to come back for?
> HIGGINS (*bouncing up on his knees on the ottoman and leaning over it to her*). For the fun of it. Thats why I took you on.

Becoming a real woman, instead of a conventional woman, seems to involve abandoning prudence and security and the bonds of morality, and learning the value of fun and the enjoyment of freedom. It makes possible, in turn, a new, unconstrained, affectionate relation between the sexes:

> HIGGINS. . . . By George, Eliza, I said I'd make a woman of you; and I have. I like you like this.
> LIZA. Yes: you turn round and make up to me now that I'm not afraid of you, and can do without you.
> HIGGINS. Of course I do, you little fool. Five minutes ago you were like a millstone round my neck. Now youre a tower of strength: a consort battle-ship. You and I and Pickering will be three old bachelors together instead of only two men and a silly girl.

In fact, he has made Eliza the first young woman of his acquaintance who is like his mother:

> MRS HIGGINS. . . . you were surprised because she threw your slippers at you! *I* should have thrown the fire-irons at you.

As for the prognostication, in Shaw's Afterword, that Eliza will marry Freddy, it can be accepted as a device to avoid the suggestion that she (like Vivie Warren) is destined for a confined and sterile existence, after all.[1] In fact, the possibilities of life are open to the New Woman at the end of the play.

---

[1] The Afterword was a final attempt to combat the Cinderella interpretation of the play. But Gabriel Pascal resisted this proposal and ended his film with an indication that Eliza would become Higgins's slipper-bringing wife. In fact, marriage to Freddy, like the suggestion that Eliza might make her living by teaching phonetics, implies taking over the role of the stronger, or the teacher, that was Higgins's with her. There is, of course, something less than satisfactory in the prospect of a marriage on these terms, especially as Freddy has shown little sign of equalling Eliza's natural genius and ability to learn.

10

The Greek Form Again:
Getting Married

On 7 May 1908 *The Daily Telegraph* published an interview with Shaw on the subject of his new play due to open at the Haymarket Theatre five days later. It is one of his most viciously histrionic performances. To the insulting portrait of a journalist he had included in *The Doctor's Dilemma* he now added a description of dramatic critics in terms of 'their arrant Philistinism, their shameless intellectual laziness, their low tastes, their hatred of good work, their puerile romanticism, their disloyalty to dramatic literature, their stupendous ignorance, their insensibility to honour, virtue, intellectual honesty, and anything that constitutes strength and dignity in human character.' No doubt this was a publicity stunt, and recognition that the dramatist was a public entertainer, clowning in this way, may have robbed the remarks of some of their offensiveness. Yet it looks as though Shaw was anxious about the reception his latest play might get and was attempting to forestall adverse notices by appealing beyond the press to the superior judgement of the audience. In particular, one may scent an appeal – of a rather gross kind – to the classical *cognoscenti*: *Getting Married* observed the unities; it was written without act or scene division (in line with theories of Greek comedy); far from being a wilful aberration, it was a return to the 'Greek form' which, Shaw claimed in another context, became almost inevitable at a certain stage in the evolution of drama.

Looked at as an exercise in stagecraft, *Getting Married* works simply and, on the whole, extremely effectively. Although there is very little plot or action in the conventional sense, this is compensated for by the evident pattern and a strong sense of direction. There are two major climaxes: the entrance of Mrs George Collins and her subsequent prophetic trance. Progress towards the first is steady and cumulative. The play starts off with a series of duologues, the transition from one to another being marked by the withdrawal of one of the two speakers and the entry of another character. In this way we are gradually introduced to Mrs Bridgenorth, the Bishop's wife, and the greengrocer, William Collins, who is supervising preparations for a wedding breakfast, then to General Bridgenorth and to Mrs Bridgenorth's sister, Lesbia Grantham; and each duologue makes its thematic points: the first, most significantly, interweaves talk about marriage with the topic of social position, knowing one's place in the social hierarchy and being recognizable for what one is. After these conversational episodes, Shaw proceeds to gather his cast on the stage, one by one: first, the General, Lesbia and Mrs Bridgenorth, then Reginald Bridgenorth, then his ex-wife, Leo, followed by the Bishop himself. The entrance of each of these last three constitutes a minor dramatic climax. In a play where little else happens, appearance on stage is established as an event.

The respect the others show to the Bishop establishes his importance and, anyway, it is his episcopal Palace that provides the scene. Now a temporary withdrawal of the women leaves the three brothers alone and so emphasizes their representative character: the three estates of Church, Army and Landed Gentry. The trio becomes a quartet with the arrival of Sinjon Hotchkiss, the declared snob, and the volatile comedian of the piece; and the cumulative process continues with the appearance first of the bridegroom, Cecil Sykes, then of the bride, Edith, and so to the return of Mrs Bridgenorth, Lesbia and Leo. All this time, the shift from passage to passage has been managed more naturally through the comings and goings of Collins, intent on his business. When all nine of the characters who represent the wedding party are assembled (some of them prematurely), it is the greengrocer's turn to make his own formal entrance in alderman's robes. The whole group now takes on the role of the chorus, awaiting the manifestation of the protagonist – or is it the god? – Mrs George Collins, whose story was told soon after the play began. The General is sent, in the grandeur of his full-dress uniform, to summon her on the Bishop's behalf, and in the sign of the episcopal ring; and the Bishop's Chaplain, Soames, who prefers to be called Father Anthony, is brought on, so that all the rest of the cast is introduced before the audience is allowed to see Mrs George, announced by her Beadle, in the glory of her mayoral robes. The civic authorities and the church dignitaries meet.

Shaw does not prolong this climax into an extended scene. Instead, he has Mrs George marshal the women and lead them off in procession. How effective this is seems doubtful: the stage has been set for a judgement, and this avoidance of it could seem a mere anti-climax. It does serve to identify the division of the cast into something resembling a Chorus of Women and Chorus of Men (as in Greek New Comedy, not

separate from the actors); and it marks the entry of illogicality and
arbitrariness as principles underlying the later development of the play.
For, after this, the pattern is less clear. A more irregular manipulation of
the characters' movements produces a frequently dissolving scene, and
the ensemble gives way once more to duologues interspersed with trios,
a further, incomplete ensemble, more exits, and so to the final ceremonial
ushering out of Mrs George and Hotchkiss by Collins and the Beadle,
leaving the Chaplain on stage, writing, as the curtain descends.

The visual interest of a fantastic assemblage of costumes[1] – the
General's uniform, the Bishop's apron and gaiters, an alderman's robes,
the cassock and biretta affected by Soames, the ceremonial splendour of
the Beadle and the Mayoress, combined with the more ordinary wedding
finery of the other guests and Edith's pretty *déshabillé* – against the
monumental simplicity of the Norman kitchen, gives significance to the
stage movement throughout the piece. And the effect is paralleled by
the skilful orchestration of the dialogue: whereas 'talk, talk, talk' might
indeed be aesthetically dry and boring, the subtle interweaving of so
many different voices brings out the variety of temperament represented,
and the variety of personal situation conveyed in anecdote, without
weakening the organic unity of the play. The total effect is delightfully
absurd and a tribute to the richness of imagination that even the conventions of modern life embody. The distinctness of the types shown is
enhanced by their official garments, as it could not have been enhanced,
in so colourful a way, by the use of masks. Yet they work like masks in
wiping out the casual and idiosyncratic and giving ideal status to
individual character. Leo, Mrs George and Lesbia, in their different ways,
all know the value of a 'Sunday husband', and the Bishop approves
idealizations such as Dante's Beatrice. In effect, all the robes of office
worn on stage are Sunday clothes, not destructive of the individual's
humanity, but carrying that humanity to the pitch of transcendence.
And Soames has adopted a Sunday name to match the spiritual identity
he has chosen.

In this respect, *Getting Married* shows less affinity with the comedy of
humours, or morality drama, than with the classical burlesque, that
nineteenth-century genre that presented the gods in carpet slippers,
eating muffins and reading *The Times* – an apt form of popular entertainment for a period and a theatre-going public that identified education
largely with a knowledge of the classics. The dramatist's awareness,
and enjoyment, of the absurdity of his supernatural figures (not just
social types and not personified abstractions) gives the play its burlesque

---

[1] Cf. the use of fantastic costumes by Aristophanes, perhaps especially in *The
Acharnians*.

14 'Death watching a combat', *c.* 1485–90 (see pp. 160–1).

15 *The Doctor's Dilemma.* Mortality *v.* art.

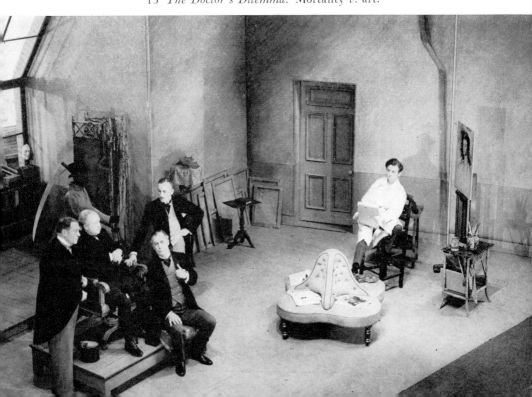

16 Conventional representation of the head of Dionysus on a
pillar at the altar.

17 *Misalliance*. The 'altar' and the Turkish bath from which the Gunner's head emerges.

tone. It comes nearest to the bare convention in its presentation of the woodenest of the figures, the General, whose 'charmed life' is touched with a pantomime, or stage illusionist, kind of magic:

Bayonets bent on my buckles. Bullets passed through me and left no trace.

Shaw had used such a character before in the more repellent guise of Bohun, in *You Never Can Tell*, with which *Getting Married* is otherwise comparable.

As a stage presence, and a focus of the expectations of the rest, Mrs George recalls Bohun, though she is pre-eminently an attractive character and a woman – or goddess – of passion, whereas he personifies rationality in its more repulsive forms.[1] The rounding-off of such action as there is, the bringing about of the marriage and the general reconciliation, in a celebratory social occasion, is made arbitrarily dependent, in both plays, on the appearance of these influential figures. Collins, the greengrocer, appears to be a descendant of William the Waiter: counting the table linen, bearing in the wedding cake, ushering on the guests; and the evening dress he wears at Curtain-up is the Waiter's, too. In Greek comedy (or in Plautus) the preparation of the feast would have brought on that stock comic type, the Cook (concerned with the wedding feast in Menander's *Women of Samos*), and possibly the Charcoal Burner, whom Shaw may have remembered when he gave the trade of coal merchant to Collins's brother, George.[2] The introduction of Collins as a greengrocer is made deliberately tantalizing. Few people are enlightened by the early line:

They joke about the greengrocer, just as they joke about the mother-in-law. But they cant get on without both.

Of course, there is a long tradition of 'green' and 'salad' jokes,[3] and the fertility figure of a green man is sufficiently in place in a marriage-comedy; as a symbol of youthful, growing nature, he might well be counterbalanced by a coal merchant figure,[4] associated with the wasting fires of passion that show their effect in his wife's face:

her beauty is wrecked, like an ageless landscape ravaged by long and fierce

---

[1] I realize that others find Bohun more genial than I do. Perhaps I am unduly influenced by the author's description of the character, but I certainly think the role and the play can take my interpretation without distortion.

[2] The fragmentary *Epitrepontes* of Menander, published in 1907 from the Cairo papyrus found in 1905, contains both Cook and Charcoal Burner.

[3] And Euripides seems to have been a butt of greengrocery jokes. Gilbert Murray, *Aristophanes* (Oxford: O.U.P., 1933), pp. 110–11, n. 1, writes: 'It was for some reason a joke to pretend that Euripides' mother, Cleito, was a greengrocer, and that her greens were "wild", not the proper garden variety.'

[4] Perhaps there is a hint of Vulcan here.

G

war . . . her cheeks are wasted and lined, her mouth writhen and piteous. The whole face is a battle-field of the passions . . .

As in *You Never Can Tell*, Shaw has taken pains in this play to revive a sense of the ritual origins and original social import of comedy. This is demonstrated in the choice of occasion for which his characters are brought together: it is a wedding-day and, though matters do not go according to plan, the young couple are married and reappear to receive the congratulations of the rest before the play finishes.[1] The reminder that this is a feast day stands on the table from the first moments: the wedding cake in all its glory. Shaw has included the common detail of ancient comedy, the arrival of unwelcome guests, in his introduction of Reginald and then Hotchkiss. And the primitive symbolic phallus itself is borne reverently in by the Beadle, in the form of the mace.[2] It is a beautiful stroke of theatre: the gorgeously dressed functionary appears simply to display the staff of office; then he and it are dismissed – the magic symbol, having been acknowledged, is withdrawn from the public gaze. (Sinjon Hotchkiss's embarrassment at the proposal that he should accompany the Beadle has more comic point if it can express not only a sense of the paradoxes of social class but a realization of what the mace actually is, in this context.)

The scintillating line that directs its removal gleefully concentrates in itself the play's multiplicity of relevance:

MRS GEORGE. . . . Take away that bauble, Joseph.

This implies a reversal of the situation recalled a few minutes earlier by the Bishop's Chaplain: 'that most terrible curse of the priest's lot, the curse of Joseph pursued by the wife of Potiphar'.[3] (The story told about Mrs George gives her a role like that of Potiphar's wife: she flings herself at men other than her husband, but they oftener than not reject

[1] The cast list Shaw wrote in his notebook, when first he started work on this play at Llanbedr in August 1907, includes two engaged couples and so provides for a double wedding, suggestive of a more general social ritual. The list contains no equivalent of Reginald Bridgenorth and so no couple 'reeking from the divorce court'. Lesbia was then to be the name of the Bishop's daughter and Edith the name of her aunt; Boxer Hotchkiss was one of the bridegrooms. In the finished play, Boxer is the General's name, and Hotchkiss's first name of Sinjon contributes to the stock of Christian images and allusions. Another significant omission from the original cast is Soames, who fills the role of ascetic saint. The greengrocer was to have been called Worsnop, and Mrs Nina Ferryman, if she was the original of Mrs George Collins, was not apparently related to him.

[2] Cf. Aristophanes' *Acharnians*, where a slave carries in the symbolic phallus processionally. Otherwise, the Herald in the *Acharnians* corresponds to Shaw's Beadle.

[3] Potiphar's wife troubles Joseph Percival in Shaw's next play, *Misalliance*, too.

her and bring her back to George with 'no harm done'.) The giving of a personal name to the Beadle draws him into the company of the other characters who are presented as dual personalities, with private and official selves. It is a name representative of the Hebraic-Christian system of religion and sexual ethics brought here into incongruous juxtaposition with Hellenic fertility ritual. With the sending away of the obscene 'bauble', Mrs George as Potiphar's wife gives way to the image which is the impregnable defence of Father Anthony (baptized Oliver Cromwell) against such women:

> Do you think that a man who has sung the Magnificat and adored the Queen of Heaven has any ears for such trash as that or any eyes for such trash as you . . .

The play's obscene climax is, in fact, also a climax in the use of the counter-theme of chastity and parthenogenesis: the inspired Mrs George is to speak for Woman in all her aspects, even the values for which the Virgin Mary stands.[1]

The Magnificat combines the glorification of virginity with a triumphant hymning of revolution: the subversion of earthly order by heavenly power. Though her garb is far removed from Cromwellian plainness, Mrs George's gesture is as formidable and radical in its implications as the historic dismissal of regal authority her words echo. Evidently the crossing of the play's debate on marriage with discussions of snobbery and class distinction is not casual but integral to Shaw's meaningful design. This accounts for the emergence of Sinjon Hotchkiss into greater prominence than the initial situation promised. As Cecil Sykes's best man, he is first employed as a messenger, when both bridegroom and bride are inclined to call the wedding off. On his first appearance, he introduces himself with a farcical anecdote, as a professed snob; his place in the final group, arm-in-arm with his coal merchant's wife, is the sign of his conversion, one of the chief events in the second half of the play. Shaw did, after all, base his *Case for Equality*, a socialist case for equality of income,[2] on eugenic grounds of the importance, as he saw it, of ensuring complete freedom of choice in marriage for the sake of the human quality of future society. Hotchkiss, while still unregenerate, voices the orthodox opinion:

> If he's not a gentleman, I dont care whether he's honest or not: I shouldnt let his son marry my daughter. And thats the test, mind.

---

[1] The companionship of the Queen of Heaven and the lowly carpenter of Bethlehem is another image of the spiritual equality Shaw — and the Bishop — is concerned with.

[2] Published as Shavian Tract No. 6 (London: The Shaw Society, December 1958), the text of an address given to the National Liberal Club, 1 May 1913.

For Shaw, a play about marriage *had* to be a play about the organization of society.

His family's pet name for the Bishop is 'The Barmecide', a term relevant to the illusory nature of the feast on stage: the wedding break-fast is not eaten, but instead we have a symposium in the transferred, metaphoric sense, a feast of talk. Somehow the wedding itself is like the wedding breakfast: it doesn't take place as planned, but after the con-gregation has left the church, the music is over and the organist has gone home – and the wedding dress is not worn; the ceremony is accom-plished off stage, not really as an event *in* the play at all; but, on stage, the manifestation of divine power in Mrs George's trance operates as a substitute climax – or perhaps it is the spiritual reality to which the natural fertility rite and the civic undertaking correspond. By such devices Shaw facilitates the shifting and extension of his main theme to what Soames, at the end, calls 'Christian fellowship', a social ideal that actual marriage, legal and civil, with its property basis, its exclusiveness and domestic narrowness, simply mocks.

For roughly the first half of the play, the rational approach to marriage is given its head. We are offered spasmodic criticism of the existing laws of marriage and divorce, more fundamental criticism of the limita-tions and difficulties of the married state, and an attempt by most of the assembled characters to draw up a rationally based marriage contract (not a very logically or seriously pursued attempt), which they exasperatedly abandon. All the arguments have been exposed as futile and threadbare rationalizations. Into this situation sweeps Mrs George Collins to domin-ate the play, as an image of power transcending reason. The marriage of Cecil and Edith, now able to take place, happens (like all marriages, Shaw implies) in defiance of reason. 'Marriage', Collins has remarked, 'doesnt bear thinking about.' The presence of the Bishop and Father Anthony as witnesses to the supreme climax of Mrs George's trance – the miracle which answers the legal contract – conveys the view that human relationships, sexual and communal alike, necessitate some kind of religious approach; nothing else is adequate. The tension of attitudes presented in *You Never Can Tell* –

> BOHUN. . . . all matches are unwise. It's unwise to be born; it's unwise to be married; it's unwise to live; and it's wise to die.
> WAITER. . . . so much the worse for wisdom,

– recurs in *Getting Married*; but the later play communicates a more mystical perception.

It is offered in the comically exaggerated form of Father Anthony's extremist view:

My advice to you all is to do your duty by taking the Christian vows of celibacy and poverty. The Church was founded to put an end to marriage and to put an end to property.

His response to Mrs Bridgenorth's question, 'But how could the world go on, Anthony?' remains uncompromising:

Do your duty and see. Doing your duty is y o u r business: keeping the world going is in higher hands.

Clearly, he is not only rejecting a form of marriage that is characteristic of a corrupt social system; he disdains a human world that is not a commonwealth of saints where miracles are part of the normal order of things and parthenogenesis is the established mode of procreation. This is hardly Anglo-Catholic orthodoxy; and we may note the paradox – and the satirical point against the marriage laws – that it is not the Bishop but the lawyer who takes so spiritually lofty a view. But Cecil Sykes's parents would have understood it. Shaw plants the allusion deftly through the Bishop's explanation:

They were Positivists. They went through the Positivist ceremony at Newton Hall in Fetter Lane after entering into the civil contract before the Registrar of the West Strand District. I ask you, as an Anglican Catholic, was that a marriage?

The audience laughs at Cecil's horror, and it may be that Shaw intended that their answer to the Bishop's question should be 'Yes'.

A. J. L. Busst's essay, 'The Androgyne',[1] traces the association of the image of the hermaphrodite with French radicalism in the nineteenth century, most particularly from the French Revolution to about 1850. (This may be the place to observe that several of the male characters of *Getting Married* show a hermaphrodite aspect, inasmuch as they wear some kind of skirt). It images the socialist ideals of Saint-Simon and Fourier, the ideals of social equality and the emancipation of women, as well as being the central icon of Comte's Religion of Humanity:

Since positivism represents the synthesis of the spiritual and material, of theology and science, the hermaphrodite resumes Comte's philosophy; and, precisely, Comte points out that woman's ability to fecundate herself would depend on the marriage within her of mind and body, spirit and matter.[2]

Shaw is certainly not preaching Comtism as such; as a system it is a comic peg on which to hang his play. He fully recognizes that Comte's

[1] Included in Ian Fletcher (ed.), *Romantic Mythologies* (London: Routledge, 1967), pp. 1–95.
[2] Ibid., p. 4.

Utopia of the Virgin Mother is a religious concept,[1] a dream that must change its nature if it is to be translated into reality. But *Getting Married* is more concerned with the converse: that all social contracts (which the marriage contract exemplifies), all programmes of reform, are unworkable except as articles of faith to be mediated through the common human realities of affection, respect and honesty. Marriage truly 'doesn't bear thinking about', but it can be lived. Shaw has used it as a subject of dispute which throws into relief differences of temperament and opinion; as an abstract idea, hovering over the play, it represents a harmony able to contain the self-assertive quarrelsomeness of human beings.

The marriage of the Bishop and his wife is one that works, and the matching fact may be noted that the ease between the greengrocer and the Bishop's wife, at the beginning of the play, suggests equality even while their words express acceptance of inequality. (It makes the point more convincingly, because less theoretically and obtrusively than the Bishop's declaration, 'I have to do such a terribly democratic thing to every child that is brought to me . . . I'm not allowed to make any class distinction.') The dramatist has been careful to guard against any interpretation of Mrs Bridgenorth as a personification of domesticity by making her the recipient of the greengrocer's confidences about his own wife, who never appears on the stage:

> . . . she's what you might call a regular old hen . . . She's a born wife and mother, maam. Thats why my children all ran away from home. . . You see, family life is all the life she knows: she's like a bird born in a cage, that would die if you let it loose in the woods . . . You see, she's such an out-and-out wife and mother that she's hardly a responsible human being out of her house . . .

Mrs George is the antithesis of Mrs William Collins; and Mrs George as 'Incognita Appassionata' figures as the ideal love in the Bishop's life

---

[1] See Auguste Comte, *System of Positive Polity*, trans. R. Congreve, 4 vols. (London: Longmans, Green, 1875–7; New York: Franklin, 1967), Vol. IV, ch. III, pp. 212–13 and ch. V, pp. 357–9. Shaw's connections with Positivism have already been touched on in relation to *Candida* (see pp. 76–7, 81 above). Edward Pease, *The History of the Fabian Society* (London: Allen and Unwin, 1925; with new introduction by Margaret Cole, London: Cass, 1963), wrote: 'One man there was who professed to offer us an answer, Auguste Comte . . . Most of the free-thinking men of that period read the *Positive Polity* and the other writings of the founder and spent some Sunday mornings at the little conventicle in Lamb's Conduit Street, or attended on Sunday evenings the Newton Hall Lectures of Frederic Harrison.' See also Warren Sylvester Smith, *The London Heretics*, pp. 84–104, who notes that the young Beatrice Webb learnt from Frederic Harrison 'the economics of trade unions and factory legislation'.

that balances yet corresponds to the actual Alice, his wife (as King Magnus's Orinthia, in the later *Apple Cart*, balances Queen Jemima).

In the 1933 Postscript to his Preface to *Getting Married*, Shaw defended the play against criticisms that it was out of date with the assertion that in nearly every respect 'British marriage is what it was' in 1908. At the present time, attitudes to marriage have certainly changed and several of the type figures in the play are remote in their manners and their views from an average present-day audience. Where the play anticipates amused shock and depends on a precise judgement of the degree of outrage that will titillate but give no real offence, it runs the risk of failure; only the very unsophisticated would spare a gasp at Leo's views today, or at the story of Mrs George's carryings-on, if that were not saved by its fantasy style. The Bishop's broadmindedness in the face of what was unconventional in 1908 may strike us now as more facile than when Henry Ainley played the part. (As nothing comes of the revolutionary impulses of the rest, his calm is not really put to the test.) Yet Shaw does comment on his complacency. Probably no audience would ever have recognized itself in the General, Shaw's figure of the public as booby, the fiction of sentimental stupidity which he seems to have invented in order to expose it. Yet the character works as an element in the structure of the comedy: the foolish clown stands eternally at one end of the comic spectrum, and the familiarity of the type is solid ground from which the more specific and unusual deployment of fantastically costumed *personae* takes off. Lesbia Grantham is an effective portrait of the Edwardian old maid, proud of being a lady, precise and dogmatic. Such self-justified old maids are rarer now; but Lesbia's priggishness is not so unfamiliar. One has the uneasy sense that the playwright may not have expected reader or audience to find her out as quickly as we do. Indeed, Lesbia seems to have taken over the writing of parts of the Preface to the play. Yet, in the dramatic context, Shaw keeps her in perspective clearly enough. The ignorance of Lesbia and the limitations of Soames are condemned out of the mouth of Mrs George, as the sentimentalities of the General are criticized by Lesbia herself and Hotchkiss. And the Bishop, as a married man, though he names no names, puts the play's two rejectors of marriage firmly in their place:

> When you meet a man who is very particular about his salvation, look out for a woman who is very particular about her character; and marry them to one another: theyll make a perfect pair.

Shavian drama owes its force and liveliness to the practice of letting every devil, and every biased human being, have his due; and here the human bias is one fabric with the symbolism, as the narrower theme remains intrinsically connected to the greater: Lesbia, who advocates the Wellsian social reform of endowing maternity and recognizing the mother and child as the family unit, is another distorted, human reflection of the divine androgyne.

11

Shaw on the Tightrope: *Misalliance*

As surely as Pirandello, Shaw deserves credit for shattering the old theatre of illusion and the tight structure of the well-made play to let in more life. In the series of plays that continues from *Misalliance*, through *Heartbreak House* to *Too True to be Good* and *The Simpleton of the Unexpected Isles*, he jests among the ruins he has made. But he is a cunning jester, only apparently irresponsible; like Pirandello again, he offers a personal and meaningful dramatic form where convention-dimmed eyes see only chaos. Max Beerbohm's comment, in *The Saturday Review*, on *Getting Married*, anticipated what many objectors have said of this later group of plays:[1]

> . . . the fun does not seem to be integral: it seems to have been foisted in for fear lest we should fidget.

By conventional standards, *Misalliance* is a rag-bag of a play, haphazardly developed; the 'fun' is even more fantastic than in *Getting Married*, and the events appear even more sharply divorced from the discussion element. Eric Bentley's remark about the incidents in Pirandellian drama is completely apposite to the incidents and characters in *Misalliance*:

> They erupt on the instant, arbitrarily, just as his characters do not approach,

---

[1] The charges of untheatricality and poor articulation are constantly mixed with praise in St John Ervine's *Bernard Shaw*, which is in tune with the generality of older Shaw criticism; K. H. Gatch, 'The Last Plays of Bernard Shaw: Dialectic and Despair', in W. K. Wimsatt, Jr (ed.), *English Stage Comedy*, English Institute Essays, 1954 (New York: Columbia University Press, 1955), discusses a supposed breakdown of form; Edmund Fuller's generally sensible book, *George Bernard Shaw* (New York: Scribner, 1950), judges the late plays to be so much rubble; Edmund Wilson, 'Bernard Shaw at Eighty', *The Triple Thinkers*, 2nd ed. (London: Lehmann, 1952), makes the odd defensive remark that *The Simpleton* is 'the only play of the author's which has ever struck me as silly'.

enter, present themselves, let alone have motivated entrances; they are suddenly there, dropped from the sky.[1]

An androgynous aviator, who crashes into a vinery and demands a Bible and six oranges, and a would-be assassin, who emerges from a Turkish bath, could be simply the mischievous inventions of an author bored with the task of developing a plot logically and plausibly. The author of *Widowers' Houses* who, having been supplied by William Archer with a plot for a play, complained that he had used it all up in Act I and asked for more, might well be suspected of improvisation: throwing in unlikely irrelevancies at intervals to galvanize a dragging play into new life. There is more to the design of *Misalliance* than that, however. A closer look at it establishes a new basis for judging the whole group to which it belongs.

The unity and coherence of *Misalliance* may be shown most clearly if the play is approached through the theatrical context for which it was written. It was first produced at the Duke of York's Theatre in 1910, as part of the repertory season directed by Granville Barker for Charles Frohman, the American impresario. Eleven of Shaw's plays had been performed during Barker's previous seasons at the Court Theatre; his nearest rival was Euripides, with three plays. Shaw had been virtually a partner in the Court Theatre enterprise, concerned with the whole programme, not just with his own contributions as dramatist (*Major Barbara*, *The Doctor's Dilemma* and *Getting Married* had been written specifically for this undertaking). The friendship between Shaw and Barker was very close at this time, and the stimulus each gave to the other's work can be demonstrated from their dramatic texts.[2]

Granville Barker's play, *The Madras House*, opens with two visitors listening to a maid's warning that the family may be home late from church, if it is the third Sunday of the month and therefore Holy Communion; when she leaves, they go on, as if with an interrupted argument:

> PHILIP. Very well then, my dear Tommy, what are the two most important things in a man's character? His attitude towards money and his attitude towards women.

This statement of theme was picked up from *The Doctor's Dilemma*:

> SIR PATRICK. There are two things that can be wrong with any man. One of them is a cheque. The other is a woman. Until you know that a man's sound on these two points, you know nothing about him.

---

[1] Introduction to Luigi Pirandello, *Naked Masks* (New York: E. P. Dutton, 1952).

[2] See further Margery M. Morgan, *A Drama of Political Man: A Study in the Plays of Harley Granville Barker* (London: Sidgwick and Jackson, 1961).

Accordingly to Lillah McCarthy, who was Barker's wife and the leading lady of the Company, Shaw retaliated in kind by attending the first reading of *The Madras House* and then departing to write *Misalliance*.[1] Although the latter play went into the bill on 23 February and *The Madras House* on 9 March, there is no doubt that priority must be conceded to Barker's play. In July 1909 he had written to Gilbert Murray, asking if he might send him the first draft, just finished.[2] In October 1909 Shaw wrote to Barker:

> The play, now longer than Getting Married, has at last reached Lillah's entrance – consequently not yet the beginning of the play.[3]

(Other letters make it clear that the part of the acrobat, Lina Szczepanowska, was written for Lillah McCarthy, who, in the event, was not available to play it.)

The two works contain a number of cross-references. Towards the end of *Misalliance* Joey Percival taunts his future father-in-law:

> Arnt we getting a little cross? Dont be angry, Mr Tarleton. Read Marcus Aurelius.

Tarleton's habit of literary allusion echoes Barker's philosopher of commercialism, Eustace Perrin State, whose appearance on stage is heralded by a telephone call:

> PHILIP. Yes? Well? . . . Who . . . Mark who? . . . Aurelius. No. I've not been reading him lately . . .

State excuses his departure in the words:

> I have to meet a man about a new system of country house drainage that he wants me to finance. I can hardly hope for another Transcendental Discussion upon that.

'Why not?' is the response he gets from Constantine Madras; and indeed the audience could come another night of the season and hear Mrs Tarleton and her daughter, Hypatia, on precisely that topic. Constantine has already made reference to 'my friend Tarleton', and the published text comments: '*All one gathers from this cryptic allusion is that* MR HUXTABLE *at any rate reprobates Tarleton and inferentially Niet[z]sche.*'

Such hints were evidently directives to the audience which came regularly to see the drama of Shaw and Barker – and Euripides – that

[1] See C. B. Purdom, *Harley Granville Barker*, pp. 102–3.

[2] The letter is quoted in ibid., p. 94.

[3] *Shaw–Barker Letters*, p. 158. An undated postcard (ibid., p. 156), apparently written in the late summer of 1909, refers to the start of work on the new play, 'Something like Getting Married in construction'. The role intended for Lillah McCarthy is described (p. 159) as that of a 'professional athlete'.

Misalliance and *The Madras House* were truly companion-pieces, which might fruitfully be considered together. In fact Shaw has taken Granville Barker's argument, his themes and his symbols and composed a set of variations upon them, as original in its way as a musical composition of similar origin may be.

Among other things, it *is* a musical composition, for the dialogue is written in the contrapuntal style which is usual in Barker's plays and is certainly a feature of *The Madras House*. The first scene, in each of the two plays, is an exposition in the musical sense: themes are introduced which will be repeated, varied and interwoven through the rest of the dialogue. The principal themes to be traced in the opening pages of Barker's text are: religion (Holy Communion), food, commerce, women, talk (first introduced in the form of 'moral precepts'), animal life ('ants on an ant heap') and revolution (muted at first in '. . . it's bread people want, and not either cake or crumbs'). Shaw uses all these themes. The first passage of *Misalliance* yields some obvious examples (my italics):

> JOHNNY. Hallo! Wheres your luggage? . . . whos to fetch it?
> BENTLEY. Dont know. Dont care. *Providence*, probably. If not, your mother will have it fetched.
> JOHNNY. Not her *business*, exactly, is it?
> BENTLEY. . . . Lets *argue* about something *intellectual* . . .
> JOHNNY. . . . go over to the Congregationalist minister's. He's a nailer at *arguing* . . .
> BENTLEY. You cant *argue* with a person when his *livelihood* depends on his not letting you *convert* him. And would you mind not calling me *Bunny*?

The first physical gestures of the two plays are also related: one of Barker's characters gives his hat to the maid, who '*backs through the door, entangling the hat in the handle*'; Bentley Summerhays, on entering, '*goes to the hat stand and hangs up his hat.*' Shaw was thoroughly practised in the method of analysis he brought to Barker's text; when William Archer first saw him in the British Museum, he was alternating between reading *Das Kapital* and tracing the leitmotifs in Wagner's *Tristan*.[1]

The subject of *The Madras House* is contemporary Western civilization, presented through the image of the drapery trade, with which all the characters are in some way connected. *Haute couture* represents a decadent culture and an art that is the luxury of a few. The commercial principle is associated with prostitution. Imperialism and the dominant

---

[1] According to Archer in *The World* (14 December 1892), an account included in the Author's Preface to the first edition of *Widowers' Houses*, reprinted in *Complete Prefaces*, p. 667. On Shaw's study of counterpoint, see Archibald Henderson, *George Bernard Shaw: His Life and Works* (London: Hurst and Blackett, 1911), p. 233.

male attitude to women as 'choice morsels' come within the orbit of the
play, identified with an oriental imagery, contained in the name Madras
itself, most strikingly presented in the setting of Act III in the Moorish
Room of a Bond Street emporium, taken up in metaphors of the seraglio
and the turban (a variant of the *hat*), and sharply focused by the promiscuous character of Constantine Madras, who has made a moral
principle of his natural susceptibility and adopted the Mohammedan
religion. Complementary to the symbolism of the Madras House is that
of the Crystal Palace and its miniature counterpart, the conservatory of
Act I; though certain of the characters view both in the glow of fairy-tale
and legend, the link between them is their association with a ruthless
Victorian commercialism; together they suggest that exotic growth and
death-like sterility (the conservatory contains a dead frog!) are poles of
one condition. The theme of Christian communion and charity runs
through the dialogue as an ironic accompaniment to the observed facts;
for Barker judges by a standard derived from Ruskin, as the text obliquely
acknowledges.[1] An anecdote related in the last act sums up the idealist's
unhappy consciousness of a world as far removed from true civilization as
from the simplicity of nature, and reflects his doubt whether the poet is
ever anything other than an ineffectual angel:[2]

> I remember once travelling in the train with a poor wretch who lived . . .
> so he told me . . . on what margins of gain he could pick up by standing rather
> incompetently between the cornfield and the baker . . . And he was weary
> and irritable and unhealthy. And he hated Jones . . . because Jones had done
> him out of a half per cent on two hundred and fifty pounds . . . and if the
> sum had been bigger he'd have sued him, so he would. And the end of
> Prometheus was running in my head: This like thy glory, Titan, is to be
> Good, great and joyous, beautiful and free . . . and I thought him a mean
> fellow. . . .

The correspondences are easily detectable in *Misalliance*. The portable
Turkish bath, so incongruous in the hall of a mansion at Hindhead, picks
up the oriental theme of the other play. The glass pavilion, in which
Johnny Tarleton takes his ease, is Shaw's equivalent for the Crystal
Palace, and there is a greenhouse just off stage. Tarleton senior, who has
made his money in Underwear, is notorious for his amours, and prides
himself on his ideas and his literary culture, unites aspects of three of
Barker's characters: Constantine Madras, Eustace Perrin State and the
domesticated and sympathetic Henry Huxtable. His son, Johnny, the
Philistine who boasts of being 'a natural man' and is accused by Lina

---

[1] The chimneys of Ruskin's house are among the landmarks pointed out to the
visitors in Act I.

[2] The doubt had been raised for the later nineteenth century in various ways
by Ruskin, Ibsen and Tolstoy.

Szczepanowska of being a domesticated brute, is a less attractive version of
Barker's *homme moyen sensuel*, Major Thomas. The argument between
Thomas and his intellectual friend, Philip, serves as a prologue to *The
Madras House*; its counterpart is the opening duologue between Johnny
Tarleton and the 'philosopher', Bentley Summerhays.

Granville Barker's experiment of excluding dramatic action from
The Madras House was vital to what he had to say. His play has no hero.
The unheroic character of Philip Madras, the central figure, is the
ultimate object of the author's criticism. For Philip, whose consciousness embraces the whole play, is the earnest intellectual who judges,
yet lacks the power to act. His inadequacy is emphasized by the theme of
the tame animal, usually recurrent in allusions to the farmyard and its
fowls. The rabbit is Shaw's favourite version of the same motif:

> TARLETON. . . . say what you like, provided the moral is a Welsh rabbit for
> my supper.
> LORD SUMMERHAYS. British morality in a nutshell!

It figures in Lina Szczepanowska's climactic tirade:

> . . . this Englishman! this linendraper! he dares to ask me to come and live
> with him in this rrrrrrrabbit hutch, and take my bread from his hand . . .[1]

Here, as always with Shaw, the domestic smacks of the apolitical; and
we may be sure that, when Hypatia protests against the endless talk and
cries out for something to happen, it is political action her creator has in
mind.[2] The sharp division between the fantastic incidents and the debate
element in *Misalliance* has the same significance as Barker's exclusion of
action; and the end of *The Madras House*, which presents Philip gazing
into the domestic fire, has a Shavian analogue in the final return to the
status quo, with the motherly Mrs Tarleton in command. The theme of
talk *versus* deeds, linked with the theme of religion, is the last to be heard
in *Misalliance*:

> TARLETON. Well, sufficient unto the day is the evil thereof. Read the old
> book.
> MRS TARLETON. Is there anything else?
> TARLETON. Well, I-er (*he addresses Lina, and stops*). I-er (*he addresses
> Lord Summerhays, and stops*). I-er (*he gives it up*). Well, I suppose-er-I
> suppose theres nothing more to be said.
> HYPATIA (*fervently*). Thank goodness![3]

---

[1] Note the recurrence of the *food* theme in both these passages.

[2] Charles Bradlaugh's daughter was called Hypatia. The name owed its revival
to Charles Kingsley's novel.

[3] The Shavian symphony ends with an effect commonplace in music: the
repeatedly broken phrase, at last extended, then clinched with the emphatic
final notes.

Its importance in the formal design is an indication that this is Shaw's ultimate theme, as it is Barker's.

There is no equivalent to Lina Szczepanowska among the characters of *The Madras House*. This, Barker's most hilarious play, is also his most pessimistic; Shaw's introduction of Lina, on the contrary, is his forceful affirmation of the power for change. Indeed, she is a (burlesque) personification of the Positivist ideal suggested allusively in *Getting Married*. Her theatrical origin, on the other hand, seems traceable to Euripides. In 1908, while Barker was in Ireland, Lillah McCarthy had persuaded William Poel to put on a production of *The Bacchae* in Gilbert Murray's translation, at the Court Theatre. She herself played Dionysus. Shaw rehearsed her for the part, writing to Barker:

> Poel doesn't understand Lillah technically, and doesn't understand Dionyseus [*sic*] temperamentally.[1]

(He also had a hand in the direction of the chorus.) In *Major Barbara*, the fiery spirit of Bodger's whisky has its place alongside gunpowder and cannon as a symbol of power; 'Dionysos Undershaft has descended. I am possessed,' cries Cusins at the climax, dinning out divine thunder on his drum. Now the aeroplane crashes into Tarleton's vinery and out steps Lina, dressed in man's clothing and – as the dramatist intended – in the impressive person of Lillah McCarthy. In the day of the militant suffragettes, it was especially appropriate for Dionysus to be incarnate as a woman.

The pavilion of Tarleton's house is an arched semicircle and contains a series of pillars, surmounted by elaborate pottery urns; the presence of a sideboard with '*every convenience for casual drinking*' implies that this temple of false art is a temple of Bacchus too.[2] Johnny Tarleton's act of sacrilege, in taking the punchbowl from the altar and smashing it, is answered, in a delayed echo, by a greater smash, as the aeroplane crashes into the greenhouse and the god emerges from the machine. The dialogue leaves small doubt of Lina's divine nature:

> LINA. Nothing that we Szczepanowskis do is usual, my lord.
> LORD SUMMERHAYS. Are you all so wonderful?
> LINA. It is our profession to be wonderful.

Lord Summerhays recognizes her as a tightrope-walker; she talks of life on the flying trapeze, where 'there is often another woman; and

---

[1] *Shaw–Barker Letters*, p. 159. Lillah McCarthy's own account of the episode appears in *Myself and My Friends*, pp. 293–5. See also Gilbert Murray, *Unfinished Autobiography* (London: Allen and Unwin, 1960), p. 160.

[2] This type of allegorical setting was anticipated in *An Unsocial Socialist*, in the description of Trefusis's study in 'Sallust's House': the antique statues in their niches are used by Trefusis for pistol practice, and there is a trapeze alongside his books.

her life is in your hands every night and your life in hers'; she wants
her six oranges for a juggling act; but, repudiating any association with
the pantomime, she explains to Tarleton:

> In our family we touch nothing but classical work. Anybody can do lamps
> and hatstands. *I* can do silver bullets.

Her arrival sets off a number of otherwise unrelated strange events.
On a mundane level, the Gunner makes his assault on Tarleton's house
and person; eventually, under the influence of sloe gin (the Bacchic cup),
he loses his proletarian accent and idiom, swells up and delivers prophecies:

> The strength of a chain is no greater than its weakest link; but the greatness
> of a poet is the greatness of his greatest moment. . . . This is my day. Ive
> seen the tenth possessor of a foolish face carried out kicking and screaming
> by a woman . . . [1] Ive read more than any man in this room. . . . Thats
> whats going to smash up your Capitalism. The problems are beginning to
> read. . . .

In maenadic abandonment, Hypatia Tarleton pursues Joey Percival
through the heather. The other men, each in turn, cast prudence to the
winds and declare their passion for Lina. At the end of the play, after a
scene of blackmail and counter-menaces, the goddess prepares to re-
ascend, taking the philosopher with her.

The Bacchae, specifically, appears to have been plundered in the
same way as *The Madras House*; but it is incident, rather than argument,
that Shaw has taken from this source. Dionysus, come to avenge the death
of his mother, Semele, upon Cadmus and the city of Thebes, is oddly
caricatured in Julius Baker, who sees himself as the avenger of his dead
mother, Lucy Titmus,[2] on her 'betrayer', Tarleton, and threatens:
'Rome fell. Babylon fell. Hindhead's turn will come.' The Turkish bath,
in which he conceals himself, is a focal centre for the stage action,
rather as the tomb of Semele is, in Euripides' play. Tarleton himself is
Cadmus, boasting of his youthful spirit in an aged frame and joining with
the rest in the ritual celebrations. Like Tiresias, the other old man,
Summerhays, comes to his door and joins him in confessing the god's
power. Johnny Tarleton's smashing of the punchbowl sets events in
motion as does Pentheus' refusal to honour Dionysus; but it is the Gunner,
watching the frenzy of Hypatia from the Turkish bath, who corresponds to
Pentheus spying on the Bacchic orgies. The descent of the aeroplane,
shattering the glass in the pavilion and destroying the greenhouse, is

[1] An inverted reminiscence of the suffragettes and the police? It may be worth
recalling that Elizabeth Robins's play, *Votes for Women*, was among Barker's
most highly praised productions at the Court Theatre.
[2] To what less could a figure of myth be reduced? Cf. the name Minnie
Tinwell, in *The Doctor's Dilemma*.

Shaw's version of the shaking of the Theban palace and the destruction
of its outbuildings. The binding of the god, on the orders of Pentheus, is
represented in the capture and intimidation of the Gunner.

The chase of Joey by Hypatia, daughter of Tarleton, is a condensed
recapitulation of the chase of Tanner by Ann Whitefield. Hypatia, too,
seems destined to give birth to the Superman, as Semele, daughter of
Cadmus, gave birth to the god (according to the prologue to *The Bacchae*).
The 'inspiration' of the Gunner when he has drunk the gin, and the
departure of Lina in the machine with the (live) body of Bentley, which
is in prospect at the end of the play, are features generally Euripidean or
'Greek', for which there is no exact model in *The Bacchae*. As for the
tragic catastrophe of that drama, there is no room for it in *Misalliance* –
unless the motherly bullying of Mrs Tarleton, which ensures that
nothing does happen, seemed to Shaw as terrible as Agave's ritual murder
of her son!

The absence of act and scene divisions from the play and its organization, instead, into a succession of episodes (in duologue), each terminating
in an incident which brings other characters upon the stage for a choric
interlude, are mechanical features of 'the Greek form', which Shaw,
presenting *Getting Married* to the public, had declared 'inevitable when
drama reaches a certain point in poetic and intellectual evolution',
The first duologue, between Joey and Bentley, functions less as a Euripidean
prologue than as a *parade*, farcically introducing the theme of the play
as the dentistry episode did in *You Never Can Tell*.

By making the contrast between brain and brawn more prominent
in this first episode than it is in *The Madras House*, Shaw indicates the
first possible application of his title, *Misalliance*. However, Bentley's
giant brain in a pigmy body is only one of numerous incongruous associations contained in the play. Lina's 'Bible and six oranges' brings together
the sublime and the absurd, spiritual and physical sustenance. The play
introduces further variations on familiar misalliances: between parents
and children, age and youth, rich and poor, appearance and reality,
idealism and realism, talk and action, body and soul; but most prominent
among the verbal themes and most relevant to the symbolic action,
including the character of Lina, is the misalliance between beast and god.[1]

[1] It is more than likely that Shaw had in mind the traditional imagery of
political man, found in Hobbes as in Plato. A. J. L. Busst, 'The Androgyne',
in Ian Fletcher (ed.), *Romantic Mythologies* (London: Routledge, 1967), p. 30,
quotes Leroux, *De l'humanité* (1840) on the decomposition of the androgynous
nature of Man as the origin of all social evils, especially inequality: 'cette dualité
qui a divisé et rendu si malheureuse l'espèce humaine, sous les formes diverses
de *riche* et de *pauvre*, de *fort* et de *faible*, de *tyran* et de *sujet*, de *maître* et
d'*esclave*, de *noble* et de *roturier*, d'*aîné* et de *puîné*, etc.'

Teaching the other characters to pronounce her name, Lina sets them to
repeat the words 'Fish church', and the combination of beast and god
suggested is also a punning reference to the primitive Christian community
and its symbol of the fish. The final alliance of the play is made between
'Bunny' and the goddess – or, more precisely, the divine androgyne,
emblem of human nature restored to unity.

Humanity, in Nietzsche's striking metaphor, is a tightrope stretched
between beast and Superman. The aviator, Joey Percival, seems to
represent the extremes without the tension between. His advantage over
the rest of having had 'three highly intellectual fathers' does not show
in terms of wisdom or attractiveness.[1] As a gentleman, Percival is a
perfect hypocrite; as a Superman, he is only a perfect brute. ('Papa: buy
the brute for me,' is Hypatia's demand.) Tarleton himself has a more
heroic spirit than his daughter's narrowly realistic young man:

> TARLETON. I suppose, to an athlete like you, I'm pretty awful, eh? . . .
> I'm ashamed of myself. I could do nothing on the high rope.
> LINA. Oh, yes: I could put you in a wheelbarrow and run you along, two
> hundred feet up.
> TARLETON (*shuddering*). Ugh! Well, I'd do even that for you. Read The
> Master Builder.

The popular notion of the Superman is always treated by Shaw as a bit
of a joke, but Percival has his serious aspect. He is heaven-sent to the
country house at Hindhead in order to deal with the Gunner and his
demand for justice. It is, as Tarleton demonstrates, an absurd, futile and
'romantic' quest that the Kipps-like figure of Julius Baker pursues. Yet
Shaw has another moral to point. Under Percival's direction, the weekend
party turns on the failed assassin, conspires against him, bullies him,
intimidates him, shows him up as a perfect fool – but can't alter the fact
that he is in the right. Though his language is a tissue of clichés, he is
superbly eloquent. The voice rises and falls, as he is emboldened or
dismayed; the tones remain authentic, and the inept melodramatic
gestures convey passionate conviction, while the others smoothly lie and
coldly threaten. Lord Summerhays, experienced in the government
of barbarians, recognizes a typical situation:

> Men are not governed by justice, but by law or persuasion. When they re-
> fuse to be governed by law or persuasion, they have to be governed by force
> or fraud, or both. I used both when law and persuasion failed me. Every

---

[1] Cf. *The Simpleton of the Unexpected Isles*, where the Children are finally
rejected as unsatisfactory products of a eugenic and social experiment. This may
be more pertinent to a critical interpretation than Shaw's statement, in *Sixteen
Self Sketches*, p. 14, that he himself, like Joey Percival, 'also had a natural father
and two supplementaries'.

ruler of men since the world began has done so, even when he has hated both fraud and force as heartily as I do.

Indeed, Summerhays's disinterested benevolence prompts him to give the Gunner advice that would stand him in good stead before the force and fraud of Percival and his like:

It is as well that you should know this, my young friend; so that you may recognize in time that anarchism is a game at which the police can beat you.

The dramatist's own stance seems equally disinterested: with a measure of affection (endorsed in Mrs Tarleton's sympathetic protection of the Gunner[1]), he exposes the folly of the proletariat, and at the same time communicates his approval of the good sense and the vital qualities of the upper class, both aristocracy and new rich.

The idealists in *Misalliance* are all to some extent recommended to the audience's affections: the ruthless realists who counterbalance them, Hypatia and Joey, are distinctly less attractive. The line drawn between these two types does not correspond exactly to that dividing talkers from men of action. The Gunner, whose attempt at action fails, is one type of idealist, nourished on the falsities of romantic literature; Lord Summerhays, one of the old talkers, has been an effective governor of barbarians, but has decayed into a condition 'on the shrink' from reality; Tarleton, the most richly likeable character in the play, is an able, self-made man, who knows that ideas have creative power. Johnny Tarleton, certainly no idealist, is the worst talker of the lot: democratic man. Bentley Summerhays, who begins unpromisingly, 'Lets argue about something intellectual', ends in an alliance with the personification of heroic action. The initial duologue poses the question of how intellect (Bentley) is to resist the stupidity of physical force (Johnny). It is a question in the same line of thought as *Major Barbara* explored, though the burlesque victory of brain over brawn, with which the episode ends, is very different in style from the earlier play. In *Misalliance*, too, it appears that Shaw backs the philosopher-king, for whose apotheosis he provides. Percival as he is may be Hypatia's choice, but Hypatia is a singularly unprepossessing young woman. The inversion of the romantic

---

[1] I have suggested above that Mrs. Tarleton may be as fatal to her child as Agave. The usual ambiguousness of Shaw's Candida-figure is present in this character. Mrs Tarleton incarnates the domestic virtues that the play as a whole assaults; yet her husband's affection for her is approved by Lina, the ideal figure of equality, independence and heroic action. Her protection of the Gunner, whose social background she knows well as it was her own, entails giving the whole upper-class show away, exposing the conspiracy by simple disbelief. Her maternal nature leads her to reject her children when they are strong, and to protect them when they are vulnerable. She is certainly least sympathetic to Hypatia.

approach in Shaw's presentation of the engagement of this young man to this young woman – largely a matter of hard financial bargaining – is not only a kick in the teeth for domestic sentimentality, it is a reminder of the hard facts of the actual social situation, the nastiness that keeps company with political domination by birth and wealth. The crassness of youth and the ruthlessness of action need to be allied to other values, such as sympathy and social responsibility.

The general nature of the play reflects the movement of Tarleton's mind and invites similar criticism:

> JOHNNY. . . . I dont set up to have as many ideas as the governor; but what ideas I have are consecutive, at all events. I can think as well as talk.
> BENTLEY (*to Tarleton, chuckling*). Had you there, old man, hadnt he? You a r e rather all over the shop with your ideas, aint you?

In one sense, very little of *Misalliance* is Shaw's own. Its elements were thought out in Granville Barker's densely packed and finally introvert drama. The richness of the Shavian play is due first to the completeness and respect with which Shaw has comprehended the other's intention; but then to the quite distinctive colouring of the borrowed material by his own temperament. The ease with which his play flashes from idea to idea is as impressive as Barker's wrestle to embody the whole of a complex argument in dramatic form; but it is a very different kind of display. *Misalliance* is founded in the practice of burlesque: it has burlesque's relation to its models; the allusive style of its dialogue and the farcical quality of its action also mark the type. It is an excellent· example of Shaw writing at his best when the fun of the play carries him along. It is brilliant writing on the level of farce; it is more brilliant because of the play of thought and feeling going on simultaneously, which enables it to be at once very funny and very serious. Though the financial collapse of the season in which it was first presented did something to delay recognition of the play's quality, later revivals have amply demonstrated that *Misalliance* belongs with Shaw's very best work. As in *Arms and the Man* so here, his boyishness in maturity proves to be not a weakness but a powerful asset.

Insignificant burlesque contrives to empty out the original meaning and aesthetic value of the elements it juggles with. That is not the effect of the change of key from *The Bacchae* to *Misalliance*, however. Euripides' play is a tribute to the validity of irrational violence as part of the spectrum of human life. It presents, for our assent, one of the fundamental truths of human nature: that lack of respect for natural human feeling leads to an accumulation of frustrated emotion liable suddenly to manifest itself like the fury of a divine visitation upon individuals and cities – in murder or revolution; or ordinary vandalism, assault and rape; in the smashing of crockery, the pulling of hair and the boxing of ears, these last being the common forms in which farce makes its testimony to a universal mode of human response that survives, even under prohibition, within civilized society, and that the more civilized art-forms tend to ignore, evade or transcend. Summerhays's presence in the play (like the image of Hastings Utterword to be conjured up in *Heartbreak House*) is finally less important as a means of bringing British colonialism within the range of the discussion than as a means of keeping in mind that authority has to be held over the savagery within all men, which may be dormant mostly, but is always liable to wake under extreme pressures. The ex-governor is acutely aware that society itself channels and utilizes this savagery for the enforcement of law: 'anarchism is a game at which the police can beat you', in fact.

Farce, the mode of Shaw's choice, concentrates on the mechanistic process of violent action and plays down or disregards its emotional content. It turns an aspect of mature experience (which in melodrama retains its content of horror) into something we can accept as childish tantrums, or schoolboy behaviour, and that as such does not trouble us too deeply. This works as an emotional de-fusing of a frightening subject and makes possible cool, relaxed thinking about its implications.

Yet the rhythm of the play's unbroken development and the bound of its energy correspond to the impulsion intense emotion gives to a chain of berserk activity. Tarleton's Underwear, its manufacturer reflects, is after all the soul.[1] And emotional seriousness has been absorbed into the dialogue – in the cogency with which ideas are expressed and in the imaginative resonance of recurring images:

> TARLETON. . . . Look at me! Look at these wrinkles, these grey hairs, this repulsive mask that you call old age! . . . if you want to understand old age scientifically, read Darwin and Weismann. Of course if you want to understand it romantically, read about Solomon . . . .Theres no such thing as decay to a vital man. I shall clear out; but I shant decay.
>
> BENTLEY. And what about the wrinkles and the almond tree and the grass-hopper that becomes a burden and the desire that fails?
>
> TARLETON. Does it? by George! No, sir: it spiritualizes.

The figure of Solomon is fragmentarily reflected in Constantine Madras; it is a more central symbol of the consciousness expressed in *Misalliance*. The Philanderer, who becomes Don Juan, here enters into his ripeness, a figure of the grave poise of serious comedy holding the balance of judgement in matters of life and death.

[1] An idea he may have owed to *Sartor Resartus*.

12

Heartbreak House:
Shaw's Dream Play

> Time and space do not exist. On an insignificant background of reality, imagination designs and embroiders novel patterns: a medley of memories, experiences, free fancies, absurdities and improvisations. The characters split, double, multiply, vanish, solidify, blur, clarify. But one consciousness reigns above them all – that of the dreamer; and before it there are no secrets, no incongruities, no scruples, no laws.
>
> August Strindberg, *A Dream Play*,
> trans. Edwin Björkman (London: Duckworth, & Co., 1912)

Heartbreak House, begun in 1913 and completed in 1916, is a play of the night, reigned over by the triple Hecate. The action begins as the clock strikes six in the evening light and the volume of Shakespeare falls from the slumbering Ellie's lap. Hesione has also fallen asleep, while putting the final touches to her guest's room; the light fades gradually throughout the first act, and the transition to Act II is heralded by the Captain's cry, 'Give me deeper darkness'; for much of Act II, the centre of the stage, lit by hurricane lamps, is occupied by the sleeping figure of Mangan; Ariadne is in the hammock and Captain Shotover asleep on the garden seat, when the curtain goes up on Act III, and Randall and Mazzini Dunn have gone to bed in the house – though Mazzini soon comes on, like a sleepwalker, in his pyjamas and dressing-gown. No moon shines on this last act, but the characters' talk of the beauty of the night conspires with the arc light, '*which is like a moon in its opal globe*', to flood the scene with the moonlight of the imagination. The characters are outside the house now, but there is no earth under their feet, though there might be the deck of a ship; their suspension in space matches the suspension in time until the play ends amid the glare of fires and the blinding flash of explosions. There can be no natural moon, as Heartbreak House itself, at once strange and familiar, is the underworld of dreams and symbols. Its people have an immensity, a grotesqueness, a symbolic resonance that make them comparable to Blake's mythopoetic images, whose cosmic relevance similarly includes a pointed political allegory.

The comment of Robert Brustein that 'the work seems peculiarly unplanned, as if it had been snatched from the top of the author's unconsciousness without much effort or organization',[1] does less than justice to the coherent strength of the play: its randomness is a calculated illusion. Shaw's technique is nowhere more brilliant, assured and purposefully directed, and the play makes a clear rational statement to the attentive mind. But this is not an instance of reason imposing logic on the plot; the core of the play is imaginative, and the argument is part of the harmony of the total concept.

There is a continuity of social and economic interest, certainly. As surely as *Major Barbara*, *Heartbreak House* is about money and power. Dialogue and action review the possibilities: to make money, to save money, to marry money, or to steal money. Mangan, the capitalist, represents financial success; Mazzini Dunn, the liberal humanist, is a gentle failure. But this simple pattern of opposition is complicated by the fact that Mazzini's daughter, at the beginning of the play, is to marry Mangan, and by the gradually revealed ambiguousness of the business relations between Mangan and Mazzini. Shotover and his daughters seem only marginally concerned with money; they need a modicum of it to maintain their hand-to-mouth existence, but their real quarry is power. Like Undershaft in *Major Barbara*, Shotover is possessor of the latent dionysiac energy symbolized by dynamite. In his cultivation of the 'seventh degree of concentration', in order to discover 'a mind ray that will explode the ammunition in the belt of [his] adversary', he is the traditional philosopher-mage, a Faustus, or a Roger Bacon, or a Prospero, seeking that mastery of the material world and physical forces that the scholar, or contemplative, apparently renounces. Ironically, and perhaps ominously, he finds the destructive aspect of his power easier to exploit than the creative; though he is hostile to negation and destruction, material greed and cruelty, he seems compelled to borrow their own means to attack them. The power that his daughters exert over men is a kind of witchcraft, the enchantment of *femmes fatales*: though Hesione suggests the benign earth-mother, she enslaves and reduces her lovers as surely as Ariadne does – *Vénus toute entière à sa proie attachée*. The climax of the play is a burglary that turns into blackmail: the ex-pirate, Billy Dunn, makes a direct attempt on Ariadne's diamond necklace only as a means of bargaining for the money, which is his real interest.

[1] In R. J. Kaufmann (ed.), *G. B. Shaw*, p. 114.

It is up to the audience to recognize the talismanic value of the necklace; having introduced it as a pretext for violent incident, Shaw is silent about it.[1]

The dream phenomenon of the doubling, fusing and splitting of characters gave Shaw a means of handling his own ambivalences of attitude – towards women and romance, money and power, art and revolution – and making them illuminate the ambiguousness of the world. Shotover and Hector, together at the end of Act I, force each other to admit the paradox of morality that good and evil coexist, must be distinguished between, yet cannot be separated. There are people like Mangan who seek first their own profit from their exploitation of others, and there are well-intentioned humanists; but the matter cannot rest there:

> CAPTAIN SHOTOVER. There is enmity between our seed and their seed. They know it and act on it, strangling our souls . . .
> HECTOR. It is the same seed. You forget that your pirate has a very nice daughter. Mangan's son may be a Plato: Randall's a Shelley . . . We are members one of another . . . Decent men are like Daniel in the lion's den: their survival is a miracle; and they do not always survive . . .
> CAPTAIN SHOTOVER. . . . We kill the better half of ourselves every day to propitiate them. The knowledge that these people are there to render all our aspirations barren prevents us having the aspirations. And when we are tempted to seek their destruction they bring forth demons to delude us, disguised as pretty daughters, and singers and poets and the like, for whose sake we spare them.

The subsequent dramatic action makes sense as a projection of conflict within the single consciousness: what seem external adversaries are shadows, or obverse aspects, of primary qualities or impulses. Apart from the antithetical pairing of Hesione and Ariadne, Shotover persists in identifying Mazzini Dunn with the rascally ex-pirate Billy Dunn, who once stole from him; the mask-personality of 'Marcus Darnley' is used by Hector Hushabye; the Nurse's manner is, at first, an exaggeration of Hesione's motherliness, but she ends as a harpy, as though personifying Ariadne's destructive malignity. Hector's amatory response towards Ellie and Ariadne, as well as Hesione, helps knit the three women into a group, as do their relations to Shotover. By engaging herself first to Mangan and then to Shotover, Ellie suggests a paradoxical association between the 'ancient mariner' and Mangan, whom he recognizes as his natural enemy. As we shall see, there is further evidence that the two

---

[1] The symbolic importance of the diamond necklace was recognized in the Chichester Festival of 1967 by the showing of its counterpart on stage, swinging from Hesione's neck – aptly enough as the necklace properly belongs to Heart-break House and the three lovely women.

were twin figures in origin, and they are immediately recognizable as alternative representations of power: the empty power of money in Mangan, who is only a shell; the undifferentiated energy of life itself morally directed, in Shotover.

Mazzini Dunn is another of Shaw's right-minded, orthodoxly virtuous characters – a successor of Praed in *Mrs Warren's Profession* – who, through their lack of scepticism and of aggressive moral vigour, connive in the deliberate wickedness of others and the evils of society. Mazzini, who cares nothing for money, has nevertheless been the tool indispensable to Mangan's success and, still purblindly, he is prepared to marry his beloved daughter to the 'hog'. Hesione's suspicion of grossly selfish motives, however well-concealed from his own eyes, is dispersed; Mazzini accommodates himself very happily to the undress of *Heartbreak House*: not failure in self-knowledge, but failure in social responsibility has been his fault. He is typically bourgeois in his addiction to liberal opinions unsupported by radical action. He has known the truth, even the economic truth, and done nothing to challenge the situation. His verdict on himself is: 'a footling person', and he knows that his type is not good enough for Ellie: 'I dont want Ellie to live on resignation.' His repudiation of his old, morally ambiguous passivity is presented allegorically in the incident of the burglary. Billy Dunn, himself a stock caricature of the Mangan type, coarsened and vulgarized, conveys the significance of what then happens:

> Have you been giving yourself out to be me? You, that nigh blew my head off! Shooting yourself, in a manner of speaking!

The destruction of Billy Dunn and Mangan together, in the pit, follows logically after this. When the Nurse runs screeching after them, it completes the purging, not of Mazzini alone, but of Heartbreak House entire; though there is still an irony, perhaps intentional, in the fact that the low-life characters, the social inferiors alone, are the ones removed.

A more directly illuminating introduction to this play than the discussion of Horseback Hall in the actual Preface can be found in 'The Perfect Wagnerite'. Shaw has, of course, often been criticized for treating Wagner's *Ring of the Nibelungs* as a socialist parable. *Heartbreak House*, which resets the economic argument in a context of myth and symbol, testifies, as *Widowers' Houses* does not, to the imaginative depth the fable had at least gradually acquired for him. The scheme revealed in his allegorical interpretation of *Rhinegold* has many features in common with the play. Hesione's view of Mangan, which is recognized even by Mazzini Dunn as 'romantic', is a portrait of the capitalist as Alberic. 'Look at the brute!' she directs, while Mangan sprawls in his hypnotic trance:

> Think of poor weak innocent Ellie in the clutches of this slavedriver, who spends his life making thousands of rough violent workmen bend to his will and sweat for him: a man accustomed to have great masses of iron beaten into shape for him by steam-hammers! to fight with women and girls over a halfpenny an hour ruthlessly! . . . Are you going to fling your delicate, sweet, helpless child into such a beast's claws . . .?

Her terms echo Shaw's earlier interpretation of the dwarf:[1]

> . . . at work wielding the power of the gold. For his gain, hordes of his fellow-creatures are thenceforth condemned to slave miserably, overground and underground, lashed to their work by the invisible whip of starvation.

> Wotan and Loki plunge into the mine where Alberic's slaves are piling up wealth for him under the invisible whip . . . This gloomy place need not be a mine: it might just as well be a match-factory . . . where human life and welfare are daily sacrificed in order that some greedy foolish creature may be able to hymn exultantly to his Plutonic idol:
> Thou mak'st me eat whilst others starve . . .

Shaw's identification of the helmet made by Mime for Alberic with the top-hat of the respectable city man reduces further the difference between Wagner's character and the unromantic image that Mangan presents on the stage.

Mangan's treatment in Shotover's house resembles Alberic's treatment by the Rhine maidens:

> He comes now with a fruitful impulse in him, in search of what he lacks in himself, beauty, lightness of heart, imagination, music. The Rhine maidens, representing all these to him, fill him with hope and longing . . . With perfect simplicity, he offers himself as a sweetheart to them . . . That the poor dwarf is repulsive to their sense of physical beauty and their romantic conception of heroism, that he is ugly and awkward, greedy and ridiculous, disposes for them of his claim to live and love. They mock him atrociously, pretending to fall in love with him at first sight, and then slipping away and making game of him, heaping ridicule and disgust on the poor wretch until he is beside himself with mortification and rage . . . It is just as if some poor, rough, vulgar, coarse fellow were to offer to take his part in aristocratic society, and be snubbed into the knowledge that only as a millionaire could he ever hope to bring that society to his feet and buy himself a beautiful and refined wife.

If we read *Heartbreak House* further in the context of *Rhinegold*, it is apparent that Ellie's role is like Freia's, bartered by the gods and offered up by the giants in return for Alberic's gold. The necklace assigned to

---

[1] The following extracts are from 'The Perfect Wagnerite', *Major Critical Essays*, pp. 172–189.

Ariadne is evocative both of the necklace of Freia and the magic ring of the Nibelungs. The scene of the burglary bears comparison with the incident of Alberic's filching of the Rhine maidens' gold:

> . . . in a moment the gold is in his grasp, and he disappears in the depths, leaving the water-fairies vainly screaming 'Stop thief!'

The equivalents are not constantly maintained, but shifting:[1] it is Billy Dunn, not Mangan, who plays Alberic's part here; but the echoing of theme and image is unmistakable. The whole range of *dramatis personae* in *Heartbreak House* can be grouped in the Wagnerian categories of dwarfs, giants and gods, as Shaw defined them:

> Really, of course, the dwarfs, giants and gods are dramatizations of the three main orders of men: to wit, the instinctive, predatory, lustful, greedy people; the patient, toiling stupid, respectful, money-worshipping people; and the intellectual, moral, talented people who devise and administer States and Churches. History shews us only one order higher than the highest of these: namely the order of Heroes.

Mazzini Dunn, 'soldier of freedom', thus had to be classified as a giant and not a god; and Ariadne, daughter of the gods, shows a remarkably dwarf-like nature. Both, however, rise to the challenge of danger and participate in the transfiguration of the final moments, which correspond to the end of *Rhinegold*, when the treasure is yielded up, Freia is restored to the gods and Valhalla is revealed in all its glory:

> At the stroke of Donner's hammer the black murk is riven in all directions by darting ribbons of lightning; and as the air clears, the castle is seen in its fullest splendor . . .

'Money is power' is not the creed of *Heartbreak House*, as it might seem to be the conclusion of *Major Barbara*. The shocking force of paradox is sacrificed for clearer distinction in the splitting of the character of Undershaft into Shotover and Mangan, the antagonists of the later play. Mangan, the millionare boss of *Heartbreak House*, has no ironic attitude to money comparable to Undershaft's: it is not for Mangan the symbol of a religion; he lacks religious sense. When he is driven by the spirit of the Shotover house to expose the unreality of his millions (and the demonstration is not merely, or even primarily, economic), the

---

[1] Cf. 'The Perfect Wagnerite', *Major Critical Essays*, p. 188: 'If you are now satisfied that The Rhine Gold is an allegory, do not forget that an allegory is never quite consistent except when it is written by someone without dramatic faculty, in which case it is unreadable. There is only one way of dramatizing an idea; and that is by putting on the stage a human being possessed by that idea, yet none the less a human being with all the human impulses which make him akin and therefore interesting to us.'

only source of his sham strength is revealed and dismissed: the superstition which confuses the symbol with the reality. Billy Dunn, his fellow victim in the ultimate explosion, caricatures Mangan's acquisitive career in his own criminal procedure: the diamonds are worthless to him except as a means towards the coin, and he leaves them behind. When Ellie Dunn argues, 'A soul is a very expensive thing to keep . . . It is just because I want to save my soul that I am marrying for money', it is Undershaft's gospel reduced to cant, a cry of meanness and cowardice, not moral audacity and spiritual courage. The force of conviction now resounds in Shotover's more traditional assertions: 'Riches will damn you ten times deeper. Riches won't save even your body.' Temporarily at least, Shaw has won free from his inclination to associate strength with money, even half-sceptically. Hesione Hushabye is not Lady Britomart, and her house is a ship, emblem of adventure rather than security. 'Keep the home fires burning', played at the end by Randall Utterword on his flute, has acquired a gleeful punning meaning from Ellie's ecstatic cry, 'Set fire to the house, Marcus.' Rejection of both money and home, almost identified in *Major Barbara*, completes the significant action of *Heartbreak House*.

The catastrophe in Act III can be seen as the fulfilment of Shotover's design: out of the profound stillness of the old man, now mystically wedded to Ellie, a vision and concentration of purpose have called to external forces – to the elements themselves – and have been answered. 'My dynamite drew him there. It is the hand of God,' he cries, on learning that Mangan had taken refuge in the cave where the bomb fell. In so far as Shotover is a projection of the artist desirous to change the actual world through the influence of his dreams upon the minds of men – as romantic an artist in this as Shelley was – the final explosion is a symbolic fulfilment of his fantasy of power. In a sense, it might be said, Shaw's aim in writing was just to reach the point at which the spell of unreality could be violently broken, giving access to a more authentic world of experience and achievement. The cumulative development of the dramatic idea leads to a release like that of sexual orgasm, felt exhilaratingly as destruction, but a destruction that is good. One thinks of the symbolic catastrophe of Ibsen's *Master Builder*, in which the renewal of the ageing artist's failing powers is brought about through his compact with a young girl – and triumph and tragic death are inseparably fused.

The noise from the outer world that penetrates the dreamer's consciousness just prior to waking is identifiable with the sound of aerial bombardment that threatened England in 1916. What is enacted in the theatre at this point is the impact of the war on the spoilt Edwardian society Shaw, on the most superficial level of his work, was depicting and its resonance in the enclosed world of his own imagination. The characters respond to the threat of destruction by bombs as an awakening and regeneration of spirit.[1] But the explosion is not certainly of a different order of reality from the rest of the dream, from which there is no clear breaking-out before the play ends. Before there can be an actual awakening, the sound is identified with the thunder of the gods and then is heard as music: 'it *is* Beethoven'; life is absorbed into art even now.

Shotover's words, 'pretty daughters, and singers and poets', indicate the place and association of sex and art in the demonology of the play. Heartbreak House itself is an enchanted palace, home of the reality within the concept of romance that Shaw had always distrusted and tried to reject. Certainly it is a palace of Sleeping Beauty, Hushabye House, where the sirens, Hesione, Ariadne and Ellie, hold men captive in their glamorous spells. But Shaw's attitude to their magic is far from dismissive: he seems to value it at least as much as Chekhov values the entranced Cherry Orchard, and it is the characters who are not in the least transfigured by glamour – Circe's hogs – who crumble to nothing at the end of the play.

The puritan philosopher's doubts about the validity of art and the active imagination which art reflects and feeds find expression through the dreamer's attempts to distinguish between his dream and waking reality. Almost immediately after the rise of the curtain: 'Sorry to wake you, miss, I'm sure,' says the Nurse to Ellie, who has apparently just fallen asleep. There is real point in the dramatist's device of *suggesting* a dream play, rather than unambiguously giving us the falling asleep, the fantasy, the waking up. The Captain's cry, 'Give me deeper darkness', which ends Act I, suggests a shift from the first sleep into the second, more profound; then, incongruously, the lights are turned up for Act II. The inert body of Mangan now occupies the centre of the stage, while other figures move round him and talk about him. His insistence on the actuality of the experience – 'Wake up! So you think Ive been asleep, do you?' – matches the audience's first assumption that it has been watching actual, waking persons in contemplation of a man immobilized by hypnotism. The dramatist is a conjuror, though, as free as he wishes to body forth dreams on stage and to baffle his audiences by a reduction of the whole of consciousness to imagination, and the phenomenal world to 'the baseless fabric of this vision', 'this insubstantial pageant'.

If Shotover is the magician in the play, he is also the most tormented by imagination. 'To be drunk means to have dreams,' he explains, recognizing the traditional association of drunkenness with dionysiac

[1] Compare the feeling communicated by Rupert Brooke's war sonnets.

ecstasy and prophetic insight. He is like the Keatsian poet, seeking 'the true, the blushful Hippocrene' of creative inspiration, but finding himself under the influence of 'some dull opiate' instead. In old age Shotover drinks to rouse himself, for:

> . . . when you are old: very, very old, like me, the dreams come by themselves. You dont know how terrible that is: you are young: you sleep at night only, and sleep soundly. But later on you will sleep in the afternoon. Later still you will sleep even in the morning; and you will awake tired, tired of life . . . the dreams will steal upon your work . . . (Act II)

He clings to rum now as a token of power, power to shatter peace, to disturb the smooth insidiousness of the dream-process and disperse 'the happiness that comes as life goes, the happiness of yielding and dreaming, instead of resisting and doing, the sweetness of the fruit that is going rotten'. Authentic and intimate emotion is something that Shavian drama only very occasionally offers – the histrionic pose, the public token of such emotion, is more usual. But the horror in Shotover's sense of old age is straight and powerful. In place of the fear of death is fear of the state of Tennyson's lotos-eaters. The house like a ship is thus an indication of Shotover's determination to retain his sense of life. He speaks – in clichés – of the exhilaration of facing the elements; yet the burlesque deflation of his line, 'Life here is stormier' (than actual life at sea in a typhoon), includes an admission that the vicarious thrill of the day-dream, or of perils staged in a theatre of gorgeous actresses and handsome actors, may offer most intensity. Instead of castigating others for their illusions, Shaw seems for once to reveal the sense of being out of touch with 'life' to the extent that he was involved in art and lost behind his public mask.

Another aspect of Shotover's consciousness is presented in Hector Hushabye, his son-in-law, equally desirous of being truly awake and heroically active, equally under the power of dreams. Hector has been lulled by the dream-come-true of his marriage to Hesione into a home-life of enacting fantasies of love and bravery in Arab costume. His *alter ego*, Marcus Darnley, is at first nothing but a romantic ideal (Ellie endorses the name, at the end, when the bombers are overhead); but in Hector himself, the hero as artist, something of a real man remains, alive and frustrated: although it looks like stage make-up, his magnificent moustache is as authentic as Hesione's magnificent black hair. And what others dismiss as his 'lies' (Hector is Loki to Shotover's Wotan, and the Wagnerite identified Loki with the power of the lie) – as literalists have always accused poets of telling lies – he defends as 'a form of invention' comparable to Shotover's.

Ignoring any connection with Wagner, Shaw described the play as

'A Fantasia on English Themes in the Russian Manner'. The fantasia mode offered him a convenient kind of short-hand (similar to the mode of composition used by Strindberg in *A Dream Play*), whereby he could evoke echoes of profound experiences, shadows of immense symbolic forms – such as reach us in dreams – without having to recreate such experiences directly and fully in his own work. It was a way of exploiting his own artistic weakness, his imaginative deficiency, in the service of what he had to say. No radical departure from his familiar burlesque technique was involved, only a more impressionistic use of it, already tried in *Misalliance*, and a denser allusiveness; for the play is multiple burlesque carried further than in any of his earlier works. However we look at it, it reflects cultural tradition: the play itself is Heartbreak House as a palace of art, fabricated out of literary echoes, the stuff of older plays. It is a claustrophobic sense of culture that it gives: art, the mirror of cultural tradition, is the embodied dream from which it is so difficult to escape.[1] The 'Russian Manner' is, of course, Chekhovian; the 'English Themes' are mostly Shakespearian.

Critical repudiation of Shaw as no Chekhov ignores the precision with which *Heartbreak House* sometimes parallels *The Cherry Orchard*, as well as the surprising general similarity between the two plays in their attitude to a decadent aristocratic way of life. Whatever the Preface to *Heartbreak House* says, the play does not contain any doctrinaire condemnation of the leisured classes of Europe before the war; they are much more sympathetically regarded than are the outsiders who lack such exotic and debonair qualities. There is nothing incontrovertibly Chekhovian about Acts I and II, except that the Nurse's clucking – 'ducky' and 'dotey' to everyone – may recall the significant nursery setting of the first and last acts of *The Cherry Orchard*. But the third act of *Heartbreak House*, the (artificial) 'moonlight' scene into which the sounds of war break, bears the mark of studious attention to the second act of Chekhov's play, the act which opens at sunset and ends in full moonlight. In both, the suspension of dramatic action reflects the arrested life of a society about to break up and from its ruin perhaps release the germ of a new order. The ensemble nature of both plays is evident in the grouping of figures in these analogous scenes: no single one dominant, as they sit, or lie, or aimlessly wander about the stage. Shaw introduces snatches of music as Chekhov does: Randall's flute-playing in place of Yepihodov's strumming of the mandoline. The 'sort of splendid drumming in the sky' which Hesione hears at the beginning of the act is variously explained by the

[1] Cf. Tennyson's poem, 'The Palace of Art', which communicates the sense of evil attaching to the cultivation of art as a substitute for life and a refuge from moral responsibility.

other characters as is the equivalent in Chekhov: the mysterious sound like a snapping string dying away. Mangan's suggestion reveals a similar practicality to Lopakhin's; Hector's fancy, that the gods are expressing their anger with men, balances old Feers's presentiment that another 'misfortune', like the Emancipation of the Serfs, is at hand. And Shaw, like Chekhov, brings the sound back at the end of his play: it may be louder, but the illusion of music is maintained. For the one overt dramatic encounter in Act II of *The Cherry Orchard*, Chekhov brings on a tramp, singing a revolutionary ballad and frightening the group from whom he begs. Shaw's equivalent of this is a send-up of melodrama, the burglary episode, which likewise ends with the proffer of a gold coin and a tip to be off. Though he signifies just such a threat as does Chekhov's tramp, the Shavian burglar is a comic terror from the Dickensian grotesque tradition, or the exaggeratedly sinister vocabulary of the nineteenth-century melodramatic stage. Shaw is not so far from the grotesque comedy of Chekhov's minor eccentrics; but the characteristic Chekhovian pathos has no analogy in *Heartbreak House*. The darker tones of the latter play belong more to fantasy and are consonant with a more popular, sensational art.

The role of Billy Dunn, the burglar, corresponds to that of old Pew, in *Admiral Guinea* (1884),[1] Captain Gaunt's villainous former bos'n, who continually calls for rum and breaks into the house at night in an attempt to steal a (non-existent) hoard of treasure. Other details of *Heartbreak House* may have been suggested by this play, but Shaw's transformation of them is complete. Captain Gaunt, 'Admiral Guinea' himself, is much more commonplace than Shotover: he is a conscience-tormented bible-reading ex-slave trader, more fearful than authoritative, and incapable of Shotover's thrilling tones. The obscurity in which Shaw has left his character's past serves him well; the explicitness of *Admiral Guinea* precludes any hint of the supernatural, as the mystery is gradually dispersed. Shaw associates his Captain with the powers of evil, an alliance with a black witch, a Faustian selling of his soul to the devil, an awe-inspiring authority over his crew, a cosmic reputation. The melodrama gives the rational equivalents and reduces evil to the plane of morality – slave-trading (the phrase 'black ivory' is potent enough) and responsiblity for the death of a slave-cargo in agony during a typhoon; a fight 'about the black woman at Lagos'. There is Captain Gaunt's evangelically phrased account of his conversion, 'Not until seven devils

---

[1] Martin Meisel, *Shaw and the Nineteenth-Century Theater*, pp. 316–17, has pointed out that this play by Stevenson and Henley is a noteworthy representative of the kind of melodrama Shaw had in mind when building the character of Shotover.

were cast out of me did I awake; each rent me as it passed'; his name, Gaunt, and nickname, 'Admiral', bear out his reputation:

> Hard as nails, they said, and true as the compass; as rough as a slaver, but as just as a judge.

Gaunt has a daughter christened Arethusa after his old ship, a fact that Shaw may have remembered when he has Shotover comment on Ariadne's choice of Hastings Utterword:

> As a child she thought the figure-head of my ship, the Dauntless, the most beautiful thing on earth. He resembled it. He had the same expression: wooden yet enterprising.

But characteristically Shaw has turned the sentimental commonplace into a joke and made it the vehicle of a serious idea; for Hastings Utterword is very significantly absent from *Heartbreak House*: he is the non-existent external authority, like a divine Providence, that Ariadne invokes.

A certain amount of folk imagination fed *Admiral Guinea*; the individual imaginative vision, which is the real substance of *Heartbreak House*, is closely associated with themes and images from Shakespeare on which Shaw must have brooded long, until they merged and blended and took on a newly active life derived from his personal obsessions. The process is a very different one from superficial imitation. Shaw's aged Captain is Lear and Prospero, apprehended as key-symbols with which humanity may explore its own darkness. The title of his play, as others have noted, recalls Lear's 'Break, heart, I prithee break'; and the group of Shotover, Hesione, Ariadne and Ellie recalls the gigantic images of the old king with his three daughters. The resemblance of Heartbreak House to a ship is more potent than a staged metaphor of the drifting ship of state likely to crash on the rocks: it embraces an identification with Noah's ark,[1] and its 'menagerie'; but more substantially it corresponds to the storm-tossed ship of the prologue-scene to *The Tempest* and is defined in a similar context of images, not least of them being the alliance of the old sage (Prospero/Shotover) and the young girl (Miranda/Ellie).

Shaw was able to draw on *The Tempest* as a repository of both sea-imagery and an imagery of intoxication. The cave of Caliban, associated with the dark power of Sycorax,[2] offered a model for the pit that holds the

---

[1] Cf. the use of this image by D. H. Lawrence in *The Rainbow* and *Women in Love*, with reference to the same historical context of 1914 and after.

[2] See A. M. Gibbs, *Shaw*, Writers and Critics series (Edinburgh: Oliver and Boyd, 1969), p. 73, on the imagery of light and darkness in *Heartbreak House*. Altogether, Professor Gibbs's discussion of the play is one of the most interesting that have appeared in print.

H

dynamite of Captain Shotover, whose awe-inspiring authority is derived
in part from some ancient intercourse with the black witch of Zanzibar.
It is also, of course, the archetypal cave familiar in Platonic tradition,
and Shotover's observatory is a version of the Platonist's tower. The
two symbols denote the poles of the supernatural power Shotover seeks,
and the metaphysical distance between them is the measure of that between Caliban (or the more commonplace ruffian, Billy Dunn) and Ariel
(who may be reflected in the flute-playing Randall Utterword). Mazzini
Dunn, answering Shotover's call, 'Bosun ahoy!' in Act I, is not only
accepting his role as the double of Billy Dunn, but acquiescing in an
identification with the comic image of villainy presented by the boatswain
of Act I, scene i of *The Tempest*, who 'bears no drowning mark upon him;
his complexion is perfect gallows'.

Of course, the tone of *The Tempest* as late Shakespearian romance is
less audibly echoed in *Heartbreak House* than are the clownish humours
of the Stephano-Trinculo plot. Marcus's tale of being found as a baby
in an antique chest in a rose garden is exceptional as a motif recalling the
Greek romance tradition Shakespeare drew on at the end of his career.
In this context, the episode in which Nurse Guinness stumbles over the
hypnotized Mangan is generally analogous to Trinculo and Stephano
stumbling upon the prostrate Caliban; but the resemblance of the discovery of Christopher Sly in the Induction of *The Taming of the Shrew*
to the Heartbreak House incident is much closer:

> LORD. What's here? One dead, or drunk? See doth he breathe? . . . O mon-
> strous beast, how like a swine he lies. Grim death, how foul and loathsome
> is thine image. Sirs, I will practise on this drunken man . . .
> SECOND HUNTSMAN. It would seem strange unto him when he waked.
> LORD. Even as a flattering dream, or worthless fancy . . .

Cf. *Heartbreak House:*

> GUINNESS. Ahoo! Oh Lord, sir! I beg your pardon, I'm sure: I didnt see you
> in the dark . . . Oh, my good Lord, I hope I havnt killed him . . .
> MRS HUSHABYE. . . . Nonsense! he is not dead: he is only asleep. I can see
> him breathing . . .
> GUINNESS. Would he be drunk, do you think, pet? . . .
> MAZZINI. . . . I really think he has been hypnotized . . .
> MRS HUSHABYE. Now, Mr Dunn, look. Just look. Look hard. Do you still
> intend to sacrifice your daughter to that thing? . . . Look at the brute . . .

and the awakening:

> MRS HUSHABYE (*sweetly*). You dreamt it all, Mr Mangan. We were only
> saying how beautifully peaceful you looked in your sleep . . .

Of course, this is reminiscent of the dream of Bottom, the enchanted ass,
too; and Ellie 'practising' on Mangan is even visually reminiscent of

Titania with her brutish love (though Titania's infatuation has been transferred to Mangan, who directs it on Hesione). Shaw, using an established convention of farce, which was a favourite with Shakespeare, appears to have worked synoptically, drawing on a number of sources, rather than following an abstract scheme.

This is evident on a larger scale in the way that reflections from *The Tempest* shift and merge into reflections of Shakespeare's earlier play of enchantment, *A Midsummer Night's Dream*. Testimony that the latter – a particular favourite of his among Shakespeare's plays – was in Shaw's mind comes in the echo of it ringing in Hesione's line, 'Fancy your grandparents, with their eyes in fine frenzy rolling!' and perhaps in Ellie's words to Mangan, 'It is a heavenly night: you can sleep on the heath. (This is *Lear* too, of course.) It is worth recalling that, when Shaw began work on *Heartbreak House*, he had for some years been writing plays specifically for Granville Barker's company, and linking them allusively with other plays in that company's repertoire; Barker, having produced *A Winter's Tale* and *Twelfth Night*, was about to put on *A Midsummer Night's Dream*. (He wanted to produce *King Lear* too, but nothing came of the ambition at that time.[1]) Shaw's reversion to the theme of love's infatuations, absurd and dangerous, is not hard to explain on biographical lines: his affair with Mrs Patrick Campbell had begun in the summer of 1912 and was continuing through 1913. In itself, this is no explanation of the significance of this element in the play. The dance of amorous illusion, a major strand in the design of *A Midsummer Night's Dream*, is conducted in *Heartbreak House* with an even more elaborate interchange of partners: Hector with Ellie, with Hesione, with Ariadne; Mangan with Ellie, with Hesione; Hesione with Hector, with Mangan, with Mazzini; Ellie with Hector, with Mangan, with Shotover; Ariadne with Randall, with Hector. Shakespeare's concern, in his earlier play, with the working of imagination in love shifted and deepened in *The Tempest*, which is more generally concerned (as, of course, the comic sub-plot of *A Midsummer Night's Dream* was, in burlesque fashion) with the role of imagination in art and life. Shaw has blended the themes of love and art in his presentation of Ellie with her devotion to Shakespeare, and Hector, who lives as an actor in plays of his own devising. Like Shakespeare, he is propounding a radical connection between love and creative imagination, rather than dismissing both as *merely* illusory.

In Prospero, Shakespeare fused the figure of the earthly ruler (Theseus

---

[1] Barker's interpretation of the storm in *King Lear* as a projection of the storm in the king's mind is comparable with the bombardment in *Heartbreak House* that is both outside and inside the dreaming mind. See H. Granville Barker, *Prefaces to Shakespeare*, 2 vols. (London: Batsford, 1958), Vol. I, pp. 266–70.

in *A Midsummer Night's Dream*) with the enchanter (or King of Fairies), as he transfigured Puck and Bottom into Ariel and Caliban, forces of the creative imagination. (*Heartbreak House* contains a short-hand reference to the Nietzschean version of these opposite poles, apollonian and dionysiac, in Billy Dunn's distinction between 'the thinking Dunns and the drinking Dunns'.) By doing so, he was able to create, in *The Tempest*, a play about right order and authority which gave imagination its due and put art in its place. The formula will serve to describe *Heartbreak House* too; and we can go further and note how the fable character of *The Tempest* – the purest example of the type in the Shakespearian canon – must have recommended the play to Shaw. The abstract themes are large and impersonal as the mind can conceive; they are not analysed out as ideas, but explored with potent images. It is the method of *Heartbreak House*, as it had been the method of some of Shaw's previous dramatic writing; it is the contrary mode to imaginative realism and distinct from the pure symbolism which seeks to establish the sacramental autonomy of art – the real presence in the tokens.

'There seems to be nothing real in the world except my father and Shakespeare' is the conclusion of the disappointed Ellie. As Miranda, she hasn't even her Ferdinand. Shaw must have been aware of how middle-aged a world he had conjured up: 'Youth! beauty! novelty! They are badly wanted in this house,' exclaims Shotover gloomily. Even Hesione's children are 'not youthful', and they do not put in an appearance during the play. As for Ellie herself, she makes perhaps a less youthful impression than Shaw intended. He is insistent on her devotion to father-figures. For Mazzini's words, 'I'm afraid Ellie is not interested in young men, Mrs Hushabye. Her taste is on the graver solider side', are borne out by the facts: she may have intended to marry Mangan for the sake of her father; but Marcus, with whom she has fallen in love, is fifty, and the marriage-in-heaven, for which she ultimately settles, is with the ancient Captain Shotover, her 'spiritual husband and second father'. Mangan protests: 'He told me *I* was too old! And him a mummy!' This could be just a trick to pass off an awkward incongruity between the *image* of regeneration Shaw offers (sexual union of age and youth) and the realistic narrative line of the plot. If so, it must represent an incompletely resolved problem in the artist's subconscious mind. But, as usual, one can guess that Shaw brought the conflict to the conscious level and deliberately presented it in the play. The pattern of Ellie's progress is anticipated in Hesione's statement in Act I:

> Girls of your age fall in love with all sorts of impossible people, especially old people.

The 'imaginary hero', who 'supplants us all in the long run', is in Ellie's case the figure of an authority that exerts its power through compelling love: the child's love for the parent of the opposite sex.

'I think my father is the best man I have ever known,' says Ellie to Shotover; but it takes Hesione very little time to come out with her verdict: 'The old brute!' When Ellie declares, 'My father taught me to love Shakespeare,' the response she gets from Mrs Hushabye is: 'Really! your father does seem to be about the limit.' Benevolent paternalism cannot go unquestioned. Potentially, there is no more tyrannical form of authority, none more difficult to judge truly, find out in its errors and rebel against. By association, Shaw has identified it with the authority of cultural tradition, which continues to determine values, the terms of men's thinking and – more than they realize – the conclusions they are able to reach. The spell of *The Cherry Orchard* is aesthetic – and nostalgic: it is a case of pure beauty, the flower of the past, calling out love and tenderness, and an image of a self-absorbed condition in which energy and free will are stifled. An over-attachment to Shakespeare is similarly binding; and the whole Shakespeare-derived fabric of the play demonstrates how the very best in tradition may be imprisoning, limiting to creative exploration and action.

The parallel with *King Lear* invites us to view Shotover himself as chief victim of 'The devil's granddaughters . . . the lovely women'. 'Daddiest' Hesione calls her father, a paradoxical superlative which is also a diminutive, a nursery term whichever way we take it.[1] Unlike Lear, Shotover is not rejected emotionally by either Hesione or Ariadne; on the contrary, it is he who at first rejects the latter, come back seeking recognition by her family. But the presence of the Nurse at the beginning of *Heartbreak House*, when she appears to be nurse to the old man's senility more than anything else, may alert us to the relevance of the charge against Lear – 'Thou mad'st thy daughters thy mothers' – to the Shavian play. There is no Nurse in *Lear* to emphasize the demotion of authority: the ancient folk-theme of dishonoured age is not subordinated by Shakespeare to the matriarchal theme as it is by Shaw. There are, in fact, two Lear-figures in *Heartbreak House*: the antagonists, Shotover and Mangan who is Lear viewed without sympathy. Martin Meisel has drawn attention to the parallel between Mangan's attempt to undress himself and Lear's ('Undo this button'). This is a tenuous connection in itself, which needs support from the more general perception that Mangan reflects one aspect of Lear. It is Mangan who is humiliated and reduced

[1] It is also, of course, imitative of the Russian use of affectionate diminutives. ('Little father' is a commoner form in English translations.)

through suffering and discovery of the truth about himself, until a real creature emerges, 'Little Alf', whimpering like a baby.

The question of Shaw's intention in so splitting the kingly image seems a crucial one. In spite of all he has passed through – and Shotover hears 'a living soul in torment' – Mangan is allowed no second chance, but is relegated to the dynamite pit along with Billy Dunn, Mazzini's villainous *alter ego*. It seems as if Shotover, slumbering in the arms of Ellie, who has been leading him about like a pet dog, had also to be purged of weakness, not on account of what he had done or not done, but because of what he represents. Cordelia is Lear's good mother, in his helplessness; Ellie is Shotover's regenerative hope – but there is a kind of dependence upon her that he cannot afford. After the explosion, the Nurse runs screeching and predatory to feed on the corpses of the two who have been destroyed, leaving the house no longer an eternal nursery and its inhabitants freed from the vicious, preying element that Shaw had always suspected in women and been terrified of. Ariadne in her hammock, like a cradle, an Ariadne who has rediscovered tenderness and been once more accepted by Shotover as his child, is a contrary image of promise. Mangan is the enemy of the whole Shotover household and has to be destroyed for its release; his special relevance to Shotover can only be conceded if the latter is seen as the author's (ironic?) self-portrait within the play, more complete than the projection of a single aspect of himself in the Don Juan figure of this play, Hector Hushabye.[1]

Heartbreak House is, indeed, open to production with Shotover either as the dominant figure, or as an important member of the ensemble. As a version of the archetypal sage he is certainly far from perfect: reduced by Ellie to the condition of her lapdog, sinking into dreams and contentment; afraid of men and women and unable to tolerate being answered; himself an image of the drunken skipper. But Shotover is a human, not an ideal character: seeking and striving and thinking, under the sense of dire necessity. The irresolution in the characterization may have been deliberately maintained as it was prepared by bringing together the figures of Lear (an image of chaos) and Prospero (image of control – however questionable). We feel uneasily, though, that the dramatist was not always sure himself of the relative profundity or silliness of Shotover's utterances: he is capable of trivially clever quips ('His half brother only', p. 65), neat epigrams ('One provides the cash: the other spends it'; 'The natural term of the affection of the human animal for its offspring is six years'), lines of more gnomic resonance ('Old men are

---

[1] Hector's outburst, 'Fool! Goat!' (Act I), may be compared to Sergius's in Act II of *Arms and the Man*: 'Mockery! mockery! . . . Coward! liar! fool! . . .'

dangerous: it doesn't matter to them what is going to happen to the world';
'I didnt say prudent. I said look ahead'), others that can carry hints of
more private emotion ('You had better see for yourself the horror of an
old man drinking', and much of what he says to Ariadne for, curiously
enough, it is in the assumed indifference of his manner to Ariadne that
Shotover's tenderness is most evident: 'She married a numskull. She
told me she would marry anyone to get away from home', which he
cannot forget; 'If you had no heart how could you want to have it broken,
child?'). Most of the passionate rhetoric in the play is Shotover's –

> We kill the better half of ourselves every day to propitiate them . . . And
> when we are tempted to seek their destruction they bring forth demons to
> delude us, disguised as pretty daughters, and singers and poets and the like,
> for whose sake we spare them . . . Who are the men that do things? The
> husbands of the shrew and of the drunkard, the men with the thorn in the
> flesh.

– and the most effective snatch of visual imagery in the play –

> The moon grows from a sickle to an arc lamp, and comes later and later until
> she is lost in the light as other things are lost in the darkness. After the
> typhoon, the flying-fish glitter in the sunshine like birds. It's amazing how
> they get along, all things considered.[1]

– and the grotesque, almost ludicrous chant, with its Swinburnian rhythm,
that ends Act I, curiously suggestive of a madness into which Hesione
and Hector are drawn. The contrived dodging on and off, for the delivery
of his oracular utterances, is suggestive of the mechanical operation of a
puppet; but Shotover can too easily step out of this role and show his
consciousness of the effect. He is not easily tied down. His author's
gleefulness breaks through in the words to Ellie that remind the audience,
too, of self-responsibility:

> What did you expect? A Savior, eh? Are you old-fashioned enough to believe
> in that?

Shotover's initial refusal to admit that he has more than one daughter –
Hesione, asleep upstairs – suggests that Ariadne is the inverse of the
seductive mistress-and-mother figure, a version of the wicked stepmother,
or scheming Regan to Hesione's more directly passionate Goneril. What
is more interesting is the selection of qualities that have gone to the
making of Ariadne: she is all for form and order; she approaches love as
a game of skill, and it is to the player in Hector that she appeals; she is
commanding and cares for power more obviously than Hesione does; she

---

[1] I owe to Glenys Stow the observation that that rarity in Shaw, the **effective**
visual image, is almost invariably elemental, connected with the sea or the air.

seems cold, though only a desire to escape from her own coldness can adequately explain her return to Heartbreak House, a desire to rediscover feeling (the diamonds are Ariadne's and diamonds are for tears). The horses, which she judges to be indispensable to balance and sanity in a household, are surely the rational horses of *Gulliver's Travels*, or Blake's 'horses of instruction'. The farcical metaphor of the ship, 'the horse of the sea', the value of which is accepted by both Hastings and her father, is thoroughly Platonic and implies reason riding the unpredictable and perilous element whose changeful power is always greater than man's mastery. The mind can never fight against it and win; but it can match itself to it and survive, borne up by the depths, however turbulent, however inaccessible. Ariadne is an idealist, and Hastings is her ideal, instead of whom she has his younger brother, 'Randall the Rotter', 'boiled in bread and milk for years', to attend her. The portrait of the effete, decaying man-about-town is vehicle for Shaw's usual scorn of the domesticated middle class and the peculiarly helpless mode of parliamentary democracy it adheres to. Yet Randall survives the bombing and discovers a faltering perkiness, the beginnings of courage in himself. The legendary Ariadne, of course, was the daughter of Minos and bride of both Theseus and Dionysus, both the wise firm ruler and the subversive force. The dramatist may have wished to denote a reunion of unconscious and conscious powers by the regeneration of Shotover's daughter, though he has not effectually gone further than to suggest a new balance of head and heart in the character.

Shotover's yearning over Ariadne supplies a quality of feeling which dissolves the harsh lines of allegory. A similar blending of abstract idea and emotion is present in the personal drama of Ellie Dunn, whose attachment to Marcus Darnley conveys the quality of any attachment to an ideal – and the pain of discovering it false and relinquishing it. There is a precise psychological truth in her reaction to Hesione's scepticism:

> MRS HUSHABYE. . . . I know too well what liars are like. Somebody has really told you all this.
> ELLIE (*flushing*). Hesione: dont say that you dont believe him. I couldnt bear that.

Ellie's immediate reaction is to become more like Ariadne, hard, calculating and pitiless. Her power of character, which Mazzini is ready to back against Mangan, now takes a more passionately negative and destructive form than the capitalist's own, similarly motivated self-assertion. Ellie, too, sees money now as salve for a broken heart: '. . . if I cant have love, thats no reason why I should have poverty.' There is a vast difference between her new practicality –

If we women were particular about men's characters, we should never get
married at all, Mr Mangan . . .

and Hesione's wisdom which it so nearly echoes:

ELLIE. . . . But how can you love a liar?
MRS HUSHABYE. I dont know. But you can, fortunately. Otherwise there
    wouldnt be much love in the world.

Love seems to be presented in this play as a faculty of recognizing truths
beyond dualistic moral distinctions. It is the emotional attitude realized
and embodied in 'this strangely happy house': the essential aesthetic
check on the destructive impulse which might otherwise, operating
simply on moral grounds, annihilate civilization. *Heartbreak House*,
completed in the middle of the war, is an anti-war play in this respect, an
act of resistance to the easy identification of evil with external enemies,
leading to the splitting of society, the splitting of humanity. Shaw is not
without a sense of evil, but he is characteristically inclined to hunt it
down in his friends. Above all, it is the insidiousness of evil that concerns
him and the difficulty of unravelling its connection with good:

HESIONE. . . . People dont have their virtues and vices in sets: they have
    them anyhow: all mixed.

HECTOR. . . . I tell you I have often thought of this killing of human
    vermin . . . We live among the Mangans and Randalls and Billy Dunns
    as they, poor devils, live among the disease germs and the doctors and the
    lawyers and the parsons . . . and all the rest of the parasites and black-
    mailers.

Shotover's view, 'We kill the better half of ourselves every day to propitiate
them', is not finally at odds with Hector's: 'We are members one of
another.' The villains of the dream-conflict are appropriately unreal
figures, material forms conjured up to suggest the devils to be driven
out of 'good' men and who draw their strength from the weakness of such
'good'.

The whole fabric and structure of the play represents an acceptance
of ambivalence which does not abandon the moral discrimination of
effects or the concept of individual responsibility. It can be seen as a
meeting place of philosophic amoralism, ultimately derived from
Nietzsche's campaign against the dualistic ethic of Christianity, with the
values of the Aesthetic movement and its Pre-Raphaelite ancestry. The
protests of Ruskin and Morris against the ugliness of nineteenth-century
philistine commercialism have been assimilated here to Oscar Wilde's
protests against the over-valuing of morality to the desperate impoverishment of life and distortion of human truth. Shaw succeeds in evoking 'the
strange fascination of the daughters of that supernatural old man', in

whom there resides 'some damnable quality . . . that destroys men's moral sense, and carries them beyond honor and dishonor.' It is his vindication of art and of quality of life (culture) preferred to the negations whereby the 'hogs' live: 'the fear of death' and 'the fear of poverty' that motivate acquisitiveness.

But the aggressive response that embraces danger and death – 'Are you immortal that you need pity him?' – is essential. Ellie has to pass beyond the disillusionment and despair that send her retreating into what is largely an infantile attachment to Shotover. Her explanation –

> When your heart is broken, your boats are burned: nothing matters any more. It is the end of happiness and the beginning of peace . . .

– conveys a senile and deathly quietude that would be more appropriate to Shotover's years. The key word which rings out from the newly '*radiant*' Ellie's last speech, which is also the last of the play, is 'hope'. It is a charmingly playful ending, a simply executed gesture whereby the actors return the audience to double awareness of theatrical convention and actual life:

> MRS HUSHABYE. But what a glorious experience! I hope theyll come again tomorrow night.
> ELLIE (*radiant at the prospect*). Oh, I h o p e so.
> *Randall at last succeeds in keeping the home fires burning on the flute.*

The audacity of inviting the German zeppelins, as well as the audience, to return moves into a festive mockery of patriotism that rescues that sentiment, too. It is only possible in the mode of fantasy which, after *Heartbreak House*, was to become the dominant form of Shaw's late drama. In *Too True to be Good* and *The Simpleton of the Unexpected Isles*, especially, fable predominates. But the scale changes, as the distance from Chekhovian realism is increased.

13

Back to Methuselah:
The Poet and the City

Back to Methuselah is the most ambitious of Shaw's plays, offered as the Bible of Creative Evolution, and even more pretentiously, if half-jest-ingly, as 'A Metabiological Pentateuch'. At the same time, none of his plays has been more generally and strongly disliked both as drama and as doctrine. On the most superficial acquaintance it invites the charges of untheatricality, verbal incontinence and monstrous proportions; and the teasing, if naïve, question of whether Shaw means what he says, when he is evidently talking nonsense, is more sharply provoked than by any of his other works.[1] Though the end of the Preface clearly invites us to see the play as a fable –

> I abandon the legend of Don Juan with its erotic associations . . . I exploit the eternal interest of the philosopher's stone which enables men to live for ever . . .

– it is hard to resist the suspicion that the fantasy of an ageing man has now supplanted the fantasy of vigorous middle age, which helped determine the theme of *Man and Superman*.[2] A great deal of *Back to*

[1] Even Shaw's most perceptive critics tend to fall foul of this play. G. K. Chesterton, *George Bernard Shaw*, 2nd ed. (London: John Lane, 1935; reissued London: Guild Books, The Bodley Head, 1949), wrote of 'those bloodless extra-vagances, which Bernard Shaw meant to make attractive', 'bloodless Struldbugs [sic] who kill people for purely sociological considerations'. Eric Bentley, *Bernard Shaw*, judges Shaw to be 'at his worst as a playwright' in the later sections of *Back to Methuselah*. Edmund Wilson, *The Triple Thinkers* (London: Lehmann, 1952), considers it a frightened play, bleak and inhuman, with 'nothing gen-uinely thrilling except the cry of the Elderly Gentleman'.

[2] Robert Brustein has seen *Back to Methuselah* as Shaw's attempt to evade his dread of death. See *The Theatre of Revolt* (Boston: Little, Brown, 1964; London: Methuen, 1965), pp. 203–4. But immortality is a common motif in Utopian literature. See (e.g.) William Godwin: 'The sum of the arguments which have been offered amounts to a presumption that the term of human life may be prolonged, and that by the immediate operation of intellect, beyond any limits

Methuselah seems to be a tug-of-war between wishful literalness and self-critical satire. The central hypothesis involves the extension of an actual tendency of the contemporary world: individual life is prolonged at the same time as population is being reduced (by decimating wars). Why should not man be able to prolong healthy individual life to a span of 300 years – or even more? The old Judaeo-Christian Bible promised men eternal life; the new Shavian Bible, formidably supported by extra-·dramatic references to scientific writings, holds out no less a hope. Darwin is confounded: religion that was lost is restored. And through the agency of the playwright whose true seriousness is vindicated in this turning of the clown out-of-doors by the philosopher and prophet. The very scale of his creation reflects a kind of megalomania in the author that has now carried him beyond the dream of secular power, the power of the ruler, contained in *Heartbreak House,* to a sustained analogy between God the Creator and the artist. Eventually the artist and the image-world he creates are put in their place; but the central tension of *Back to Methuselah* is a tension of effort – to put them there and keep them there.

Serious study of the play raises other recurrent problems of Shavian criticism. Is the glorification of mind only a cowardly flight from emotion?[1] Is the elaborate structure less useful as an objective commentary on the external world than as a means of controlling subjective conflicts? Does the puritanism in Shaw express a false understanding of human nature (including his own nature)? Does this puritanism involve an essential devaluing of art, destructive to the integrity of any work in which it is found?

Granville Barker showed himself aware of the relevance of such considerations to the last part of *Back to Methuselah* when he wrote to Shaw in 1921 upon the publication of the play:

> Part V . . . raises one question – How far can one use pure satire in the theatre? For satire scarifies humanity. The theatre uses it (*humanity*) as a

---

which we are able to assign . . . The men therefore whom we are supposing to exist, when the earth shall refuse itself to a more extended population, will probably cease to propagate. The whole will be a people of men and not of children. Generation will not succeed generation, nor truth have in a certain degree to recommence her career at the end of every thirty years . . . There will be no war, no crimes, etc.' *Political Justice,* photofacsimile of 3rd ed. (Toronto: University of Toronto Press, 1946; reprinted 1962; London: Allen and Unwin, 1949), Vol. II, Bk VIII, ch. ix, pp. 527–8. In the previous chapter Godwin quotes Franklin's prediction that 'mind will one day become omnipotent over matter' (*P.J.*, II, p. 503).

[1] T. S. Eliot wrote of Shaw's rejection of poetic values as sub-adolescent. See 'A Dialogue on Dramatic Poetry', *Selected Essays* (London: Faber, 1932), pp. 43–58.

medium and must therefore be tender to it. . . . If you degrade the token
. . . you falsify your case . . .[1]

It is doubtful if great satire is ever 'pure' in the sense that Barker gives
to the word: ever totally divorced from compassion. Gulliver is himself
a Yahoo, and the redemptive element of Yahoo-nature is at work in the
horror of his self-contemplation. The Shavian version of Gulliver among
the Houyhnhnms comes in Part IV of *Back to Methuselah*, 'The Tragedy
of an Elderly Gentleman'. Once we cease to be deluded by the fable of
longevity into seeing the whole cycle as a straggling chronicle-play, this
part emerges as the emotional centre of gravity which holds the rest in
balance. From the mouth of its hero comes Shaw's own acknowledgement
of the peril attending too complete an objectivity:

> I think that a man who is sane as long as he looks at the world through his
> own eyes is very likely to become a dangerous madman if he takes to looking
> at the world through telescopes and microscopes. Even when he is telling
> fairy stories about giants and dwarfs, the giants had better not be too big
> nor the dwarfs too small and too malicious . . .

From one part to another, and often abruptly within a single scene, the
author adjusts his dramatic technique as if he were altering the range and
focus of scientific instruments. If the reader or audience is able to receive
the impact of the five parts as a whole,[2] the play takes on the character
of a hall of mirrors directed upon human nature from many angles and
all distorting in various ways. 'Have you been sent here to make your
mind flexible?' a Guardian enquires of the Elderly Gentleman; and the
question travels on into the auditorium. But such flexibility would be
merely frivolous apart from some absolute standard of reference. This is
supplied whenever the tone of the dialogue deepens and the drama builds
up to some emotional intensity. The Elderly Gentleman, who is disclosed
weeping by the side of the ocean, and then flings himself into an absurd
butterfly-dance in top hat and frock coat, is the only heroic figure in the
entire play; for the true Shavian hero, as has occasionally been observed,[3]
is the romantic fool:

> I accept my three score and ten years. If they are filled with usefulness, with
> justice, with mercy, with goodwill: if they are the lifetime of a soul that

---

[1] A longer extract from the letter appears in C. B. Purdom, *Harley Granville
Barker*, pp. 198–9.

[2] The entire play was done at the Arts Theatre, February 1947, starting at
2.30 p.m. The National Theatre presented a cut version of the whole, 12 May
1970.

[3] This is plainly implied by K. H. Gatch, 'The Last Plays of Bernard Shaw:
Dialectic and Despair', in W. K. Wimsatt, Jr. (ed.), *English Stage Comedy*
(New York: Columbia U.P., 1955), pp. 126–47, especially in the concluding
quotation from Thomas Mann on modern tragi-comedy and the grotesque style.

never loses its honor and a brain that never loses its eagerness, they are enough for me, because these things are infinite and eternal . . .

Taking his stand on the difference between eternity and immortality (or the infinitely prolonged life of the Ancients), he exposes the pretence of the fable on which the play is based. Gulliver begs to be allowed to remain among the horses, though he can never be as they are; the elderly Joseph Barlow, O.M., otherwise Iddy Toodles, clings to the idea of truth, whatever it may cost:

> THE ELDERLY GENTLEMAN. They have gone back to lie about your answer. I cannot go with them. I cannot live among people to whom nothing is real. I have become incapable of it through my stay here. I implore to be allowed to stay.
> THE ORACLE. My friend: if you stay with us you will die of discouragement.
> THE ELDERLY GENTLEMAN. If I go back I shall die of disgust and despair. I take the nobler risk . . .
>   . . . *She looks steadily into his face. He stiffens; a little convulsion shakes him; his grasp relaxes; and he falls dead.*

Like *Heartbreak House, Back to Methuselah* was a fruit of the war. Shaw read a draft of Part II, 'The Gospel of the Brothers Barnabas', to a group of friends in 1918.[1] This part remains most nearly akin to his pre-war plays in dramatic style. The scale of character-drawing and action is as close to the naturalistic as Shaw gets in the whole play-cycle. The setting represents an ordinary middle-class Edwardian drawing-room; the passage of time on the stage matches the passage of actual time; Bill Haslam and Savvy, Conrad and Franklyn Barnabas would not be out of place among the types of conventional drawing-room comedy; even Burge and Lubin are exaggerated little enough beyond the images of themselves that men project from a political platform. First the professional statesmen and then the philosophers expound their political principles and programmes. The analogy of a political meeting, modified by the drawing-room comedy elements, is sustained in the recurring pattern of accusation and counter-accusation through which the rival candidates move, in heckling interruptions and in the way that Burge and Lubin refer every topic to the measure of electoral appeal. These two figures are animated caricatures of the rival Liberal leaders, Lloyd George and Asquith. Their responsibility for the war is brought under review. Conrad Barnabas's condemnation, 'they have managed to half

---

[1] Granville Barker was among them (see Purdom, op. cit., p. 192). The version read to them almost certainly included the section later discarded and published separately in *Short Stories, Scraps and Shavings* (see below, p. 228).

kill Europe between them', is followed up by his brother Franklyn's
comment:

> . . . you were called on to control powers so gigantic that one shudders at
> the thought of their being entrusted even to an infinitely experienced and
> benevolent God;

but the severest indictment is introduced when the statesmen and the
Brothers Barnabas have left the stage to Savvy and the young curate:

> HASLAM. Lubin and your father have both survived the war. But their
> sons were killed in it.
> SAVVY (*sobered*). Yes. Jim's death killed mother . . .
> HASLAM. . . . To me the awful thing about their political incompetence
> was that they had to kill their own sons . . .

This horror is the common ground of experience on which Shaw
approaches his audience of men, in order to turn them into an audience
of philosophers. The critical decision reached by Adam and Eve in Part I
of the cycle was to exchange eternal life for continuance through generation. From the disturbance of the natural succession of sons to fathers by
the carnage of 1914–18, the drama proceeds in strict logic to the reversal
of that fabled decision: individual life must now be prolonged, until at
last men are ready to accept the burden of eternal life that Adam found
too heavy. 'Old men are dangerous: it doesn't matter to them what is
going to happen to the world', Shotover said, in *Heartbreak House*.
Increasing their span of life might make them more responsible and less
inclined to leave the weeding of the garden to their successors.[1] In
particular Shaw is concerned with responsibility to the human race (to
the future), not just to the contemporary community, which is all that
Burge and Lubin consider in their appeal to the electorate. Part IV of
the cycle still has a contemporary focus of satire: the British Envoy has no
better question to ask of the Oracle than 'ought we to dissolve in August,
or put it off until next spring?' The presence of Napoleon of Turania in
his party is indication that the British Empire based on Baghdad has not
solved the problem of war: of how civilization can survive the channelling
of the Life Force into martial genius and dreams of glory, though the
Elderly Gentleman has a tale to tell of the collapse of nationalism and the
disappearance of the Irish and the Jews. The young Longliver, Zoo,
knows of wars that followed 'the War to end War' until the politicians
were converted to the patriotic virtue of cowardice (as Burge-Lubin was
converted at the end of Part III).

---

[1] The Voltairean motif of tending the garden is recurrent in the text, occasionally with a sinister implication, as decimation through war is a ruthless
form of weeding.

The title of the last part of the drama, 'As Far as Thought can Reach', gives a broad hint that the length of life which is Shaw's serious concern is that which the individual mind can encompass – which it is stretched to encompass, as the action proceeds. It is of major significance that Part V is to be presented with costumes and decor resembling '*Grecian of the fourth century B.C.*': the age of Plato. If its atmosphere is found a little chilling, this only corresponds to the impression that philosophic thought makes on the unreflective human being. Shaw's humanist concern is still there: in the She-Ancient's explanation of why power is not, in this Utopia, entrusted to children who would 'play with the world by tearing it to pieces', as childish men once did.

Samuel Butler reports an Erewhonian belief in a race of men whose foresight more than equalled our acquaintance with the past, but 'they died in a twelvemonth from the misery which their knowledge caused them'. He comments:

> Strange fate for man! He must perish if he get that, which he must perish if he strive not after. If he strive not after it he is no better than the brutes, if he get it he is more miserable than the devils.

This misery of the man whose vision outruns his capacity for action makes its appearance in *Back to Methuselah* as the disease of Discouragement, which threatens the Shortlivers and even the Youths of Part V. Its torments are known to Franklyn Barnabas:

> LUBIN. Why do you fix three hundred years as the exact figure? . . . I am quite prepared to face three thousand, not to say three million.
> CONRAD. Yes, because you dont believe you will be called on to make good your word.
> FRANKLYN (*gently*). Also, perhaps, because you have never been troubled much by visions of the future.

In fact, Shaw's play in its entirety derives its power from the conflict inherent in the human situation which Plato expressed for later ages in terms of the rational and appetitive faculties, being and becoming, guardian and subject. The twentieth century has come to prefer doctrines of the whole man to the theory of the divisions of the soul. Yet the older fashion of thought is fundamental to puritanism, the religion of Jonhobsnoxius (of which the Elderly Gentleman was a victim); and it is also essentially dramatic. Shaw took from the *Republic* some of the principal symbols and concepts on which *Back to Methuselah* is based. They are the more meaningful and forceful in their new context because he was able to identify them with the warring forces of his own personality: accessibility to emotion and fear of it; deprivation of family affection avenged by attacks on the family and a care 'more for the Public Thing than for any private thing';[1] revolutionist principles in conflict with authoritarian inclinations.[2]

Puritanical repugnance for physical life and shrinking from emotional intimacy are the negatives corresponding to rationality and the capacity for abstract thought. Their force is admitted in one thread running prominently through the play: it appears in Part I, in Eve's overwhelming shame (the emotion of the Fall) as she listens to the Serpent; in Part II, in the severity of the scientific rationalism of the Brothers Barnabas who themselves link it interestingly with their mother's artificial manners; in Part III, in the objectivity of the Longlivers who have outgrown human affection; in Part IV it takes alternative forms, as the tradition in which the Elderly Gentleman was brought up ('Those misguided people sacrificed the fragment of life that was granted to them to an imaginary immortality. . . . They tried to produce a condition of death in life: to mortify the flesh, as they called it'), and in the authoritarian Platonic approach to government caricatured in the strictly regimented system of Guardians; in Part V it is reflected in the adolescents' shrinking from touch and the Ancients' contempt for the body, and it is satirically embodied in Pygmalion, who brings to being a blueprint humanity that turns and destroys him. The whole evolutionary process reviewed is not only a movement out of egotism and individualism (championed by Cain) in the direction of altruism and social conscience; it is a movement towards greater abstraction, away from Adam, the type of Man, towards the dissolution of humanity in a vortex of 'life' or thought.

The antithesis between reason and the sensual soul is most clearly represented in Part V, in the relation of the Ancients and the Youths. This has appeared in variant forms in the Longlivers and Shortlivers of Parts III and IV and, in Part II, in the counterbalancing of the myopic chauvinism of Burge and Lubin with the philosophical farsightedness of the Brothers Barnabas. Shaw uses the repetition of similar elements in different parts as a device for unifying the play-cycle. He profits in this way from the theatrical necessity of reducing the cast-list by allowing for the doubling of roles. So, as in a harlequinade, Savvy Barnabas appears again as Zoo and yet again as the Newly Born; Burge and Lubin merge into Burge-Lubin of Part III and the Envoy, Badger Bluebin, of Part IV; Conrad Barnabas turns into Account-General Barnabas; Cain reappears as Napoleon, Emperor of Turania; Archbishop Haslam and Mrs Lutestring

---

[1] The observation is Chesterton's.
[2] Discussed by Edmund Wilson, op. cit.

change into the He-Ancient and She-Ancient.[1] The discarded fragment, originally intended for Part II and published in *Short Stories, Scraps and Shavings* as 'A Glimpse of the Domesticity of Franklyn Barnabas', contains the major character of Mrs Etteen, who shows recognizable affinities with Eve's portrait of Lua, Cain's wife, and with Ecrasia, the aesthete of Part V. This is one way – a visual means – whereby Shaw demonstrates his notion of the disguises in which ideas find expression. 'You are Eve, in a sense,' declares Conrad Barnabas to his niece. 'You are only a new hat and coat on Eve.'

It is Part III, 'The Thing Happens', that raises the severest doubts about the capacity of Shaw's dramatic technique to hold the stage. This section is a disquisitory play, in which action is unimportant, almost non-existent, and the situation appears to be a mere excuse for the characters to range, apparently at random, over diverse topics. The fantasy of a Britain of A.D. 2170, effectually governed by a civil service of Chinese and negresses, satirically reverses the imperialist argument of the unfitness of 'native' populations to govern themselves. Three divisions of what we must call the 'action' are discernible: a general exposition; the revelation of a precise situation in the debate of two groups over a table; and finally a conversion of the central character.

The general exposition consists of a succession of duologues between President Burge-Lubin and, first, Accountant-General Barnabas, then the Chief Secretary, Confucius, and finally the negress who is Minister of Health. Burge-Lubin is a complete figure of fun: fat clown facing thin and miserable Harlequin, when the screen is withdrawn to disclose Barnabas sitting opposite him in an identical office; stupid clown playing stooge to clever clown, when he sets up the commonplaces of English history for Confucius to overturn them.[2] Sensuality has decayed into frivolity of mind in this elected representative of the people, who flirts with the televised image of the negress and protests:

> My relations with her are purely telephonic, gramophonic, photophonic, and, may I add, platonic.

The curious dramatic flatness of these first episodes is not inappropriate, indeed. For this is Shaw's Laputa, the home of false science and false philosophy. It has its American 'projector', who has invented a method of breathing under water; like the tailors and architects of Swift's Laputa, Accountant-General Barnabas insists that actuality and human life should conform to his calculations. Abstraction reigns, 'the dupe of

---

[1] The main productions (Theatre Guild, Birmingham Repertory Company and Arts Theatre) between them exploited all these resemblances – except, surprisingly, that between Savvy and the Newly Born – and some others.

[2] This scene is Gilbertian in its repetition of the one trick of surprise.

appearances';[1] its symbol is the large television screen on the wall, a variant of the Platonic mirror that man can turn upon all things in the illusion that he is the creator of everything it reflects.[2] The shallowness of this view of life is further indicated by the attention paid to the pigmentation of the skin, the grouping of men and women according to the colour of their masks.

The duologue of Burge-Lubin and Confucius does not forward the action in any obvious way; it anticipates no change in the situation and thus lacks both suspense and urgency; an immediately evident reason for its conclusion is that it gives opportunity for a necessary scene-shift behind the curtain. In fact it is here that the dramatist makes his central statement of the link between his general theme of man and narrower theme of politics. The argument of the *Republic* is still his source: as reason should rule over appetite and passion in the soul, so should the Guardian (who is the philosopher) rule in the state. The double reference is contained in the idea of self-government:

> CONFUCIUS. . . . You could fight. You could eat. You could drink. Until the twentieth century you could produce children. You could play games. You could work when you were forced to. But you could not govern your-selves . . . you imported educated negresses and Chinese to govern you. Since then you have done very well . . . People like you . . . Nobody likes me: I am held in awe. Capable persons are never liked. I am not likeable; but I am indispensable.

The alienation of sympathy from his personifications of reason, in all sections of *Back to Methuselah*, is certainly part of Shaw's design.

The central episode of Part III is dominated by Mrs Lutestring. She is the Barnabas's parlourmaid transformed into the Domestic Minister, a silk purse made out of a sow's ear by an additional 250 years of life. She and Archbishop Haslam are god-like beside the others, and their dignity is largely a matter of deeper tones. It is possible that Shaw, in gracing her with the name of a moth (taken from Weismann?), also had her impressive style of speech in mind;[3] false etymology may have suggested to him the plangent quality of the lute:

> MRS LUTESTRING. There was one daughter who was the child of my very heart . . . She was an old woman of ninety-six, blind. She asked me to sit and talk with her because my voice was like the voice of her dead mother.

---

[1] Cf. 'A Glimpse of the Domesticity of Franklyn Barnabas', *Short Stories, Scraps and Shavings*: 'IMMENSO CHAMPERNOON. Like all men of science you are the dupe of appearances.'
[2] 'The Book of the Machines' in *Erewhon* has certainly contributed to this satire of the mechanization of life and the de-humanizing of men.
[3] Brewer's *Dictionary of Phrase and Fable* defines 'lutestring' as: 'A glossy

An unexpected grim pathos, working up to indignation, sounds in her recollections of the lives of the poor in the early twentieth century: the 'miserable pittances for worn-out old laborers to die on!' and 'the utter tiredness of forty years' unending overwork and striving to make a shilling do the work of a pound.' Burge-Lubin's conversion, in the last scene, is presented as an automatic reaction to the knowledge that he may have 300 years to live, and it takes burlesque form in his treatment of the negress (the false ideal, a coloured mask of beauty). He remains an inflated paper-bag of a character, incapable of feeling. And the *experience* of conversion is communicated to the audience only through the emotional resonance that Mrs Lutestring has given to the dry doctrine of labour and production which is under discussion.

It is in this respect that the longer and more static expository passages of Parts IV and V are artistically superior to Part III. In Part IV, Act I, in particular, Shaw is less concerned than in Part III to maintain the pretence of writing a play and not a prose dialogue in the tradition of Swift or Plato, yet his writing is more dramatic to the extent that it is a vehicle of profounder thought and strong emotion. The free development of feeling demands constant modulations in the actors' delivery. The intensity of the author's engagement with his subject gives much of the later part of the text a poetic quality beyond rhetoric. Yet it is a poetry that can pose the same kind of critical difficulty as *Paradise Lost*. How are we to judge an art that is most moving when the doctrine it expounds is most suspect? The style of Lilith's epilogue is of nineteenth-century derivation; that much said, it must be admitted that Shaw never wrote more magnificently in that style:

> . . . I stood amazed at the malice and destructiveness of the things I had made: Mars blushed as he looked down on the shame of his sister planet: cruelty and hypocrisy became so hideous that the face of the earth was pitted with the graves of little children among which living skeletons crawled in search of horrible food . . . They have redeemed themselves from their vileness, and turned away from their sins. . . after passing a million goals they press on to the goal of redemption from the flesh, to the vortex freed from matter, to the whirlpool in pure intelligence that, when the world began, was a whirlpool in pure force . . .

The savage indignation of the first sentence quoted justifies the whole play-cycle. The sound of what follows is more alluring than the She-

---

silk fabric; the French *lustrine*', and discusses the expression, 'speaking in lutestring', which is taken to refer to 'Flash, highly polished oratory'. It compares the Shakespearian 'taffeta phrases and silken terms' and the use of 'fustian', 'bombast' and 'shoddy' (which Shaw adopts as a pseudonym in *Back to Methuselah*) – 'a book or speech made up of other men's brains'.

Ancient's words which it recalls: 'The day will come when there will be no more people, only thought.' This is the voice of the dreamer who does not feel at home in the world, and it is close to despair. (Out of context, a similarity to Constantin's play in Act I of Chekhov's *The Seagull* is evident.) To the Undershafts, Barbara and Andrew, it would be heresy. In its extremity may be heard the weakness of the puritan artist who makes his art and his thought a refuge from reality. But there is another kind of artist in Shaw whose moral conscience rejects despair and takes a longer view still:

> . . . Lilith will be only a legend and a lay that has lost its meaning. Of Life only is there no end . . . the eyesight of Lilith is too short.

This is firmly one with the hope-preserving principles to which the Serpent in the Garden holds:

> I make no vows. I take my chance . . . I fear certainty as you fear uncertainty . . . If I bind the future I bind my will. If I bind my will I strangle creation.

The musical form and texture of *Back to Methuselah* (always excepting the Burge-Lubin scenes) are very notable. Part I is essentially an overture in two sections: the first, a sonata, in which the leading themes of the play to follow are sounded and lightly interwoven by Adam and Eve, then by Eve and the Serpent, and then by all three in a final development punctuated by the harsh laugh of the Serpent – the anticipatory spasm of the Comic Spirit. The second act is a noisy and vigorous operatic trio, Adam (tenor), Eve (soprano) and Cain (bass), singing against each other for all they are worth: three quarrelsome principles of human nature rocking the future of mankind.

(This is an appropriate place to recall Cain's introduction of himself:

> I am the first murderer: you are only the first man. . . . To be the first murderer one must be a man of spirit.

If we recognize in him the type of the spirited, irascible faculty, his presence in Part I, as the third figure with Adam and Eve, is philosophically justified. Certainly he is the usurper: the false superman and self-deluding idolator, who 'cannot love Lua until her face is painted'. In Cain, the theme of war, the force behind the killing of the sons, first takes its place among the characters.)

The tuning-forks, which the Guardians of Part IV carry and occasionally use, represent a new dimension in the drama: a dispersed accompaniment of sounds which have symbolic function. A pistol-shot and blasts from a police-whistle mark the scene between Napoleon and the Oracle; the entry of the Envoy's party into the temple is preluded by orchestral music through which a gong resounds; the progress of the

scene inside the temple is pointed by a series of musical motifs, beginning
with the chimes of a carillon and continuing in bursts of 'sacred' organ
music, rolling and crashing of thunder, until finally: *'trombones utter
three solemn blasts in the manner of Die Zauberflöte.'* This is all part of
the mummery with which the Guardians perfunctorily indulge the
Shortlivers and that, ironically, is likely to impress an audience in the
theatre too; for the various qualities of sound are calculated to attune the
mood of the auditorium to the dramatic movement through which Shaw
conducts his characters. He uses the drum in *Major Barbara* with like
symbolic force to increase the intensity of excitement at critical moments.
In the third act of *Man and Superman*, the Statue music from *Don
Giovanni* was a setting for the dream convention and emphasized the
extent to which the dialogue moved beyond 'mere talk' towards pure
rhetorical melody. So here Shaw is employing a device to remove his play
still further from naturalism. It is not only in the perspective of time that
Back to Methuselah is receding away from the present of the Brothers
Barnabas; the later sections are distanced in the way that a self-contained
work of art is remote from any 'slice of life'. The music of flutes, to
which the Grecian figures dance farandole and sarabande at the beginning
of Part V, is a frame to reveal the play as pure image, a moving icon of
the dance of life.

A remarkable speeding-up begins with 'The Tragedy of an Elderly
Gentleman'. The whole significant content of *Arms and the Man* is
summed up in the scene between Napoleon and the Oracle. The debate
between them is a commentary on the pantomime in which tragedy
fizzles out and the epic hero dwindles, as later the clown will grow great.
The sight of the Priestess compels Napoleon to sink to his knees; her
threat to remove her veil forces him to yield his pistol to her. The
development is repeated in yet more condensed form, as the melodramatic
climax, in which she shoots him, is promptly followed by burlesque
deflation:

> THE ORACLE. . . . die before the tide of glory turns. Allow me (*she shoots
> him*).
>> *He falls with a shriek. She throws the pistol away and goes haughtily
>> into the temple.*
> NAPOLEON (*scrambling to his feet*). Murderess! Monster! She-devil! . . .
> No sense of the sacredness of human life! No thought for my wife and
> children! Bitch! Sow! Wanton! (*He picks up the pistol.*) And missed me at
> five yards! Thats a woman all over.

As his abuse of her descends in bathos, he shrinks into a bad-tempered
small boy who, pocketing his pistol, runs out blowing furious blasts on a
whistle and glaring at Zoo as he brushes past her. So the dream of

martial glory is abandoned for the rule of law; and the Nietzschean Superman collapses gibbering at the base of a statue of Falstaff. This is the concentrated, allusive type of action that Shaw first perfected in *Misalliance* and that distinguishes *Heartbreak House* also. It may be described as symbolical farce.

In Part V, the speeding-up of time in the presentation of the Youths is even more evidently an aspect of the view of human life seen through the wrong end of a telescope. Chloe ages line by line in her dialogue with Strephon; at four, she is ready to put away childish things: 'listening to flutes ringing changes on a few tunes and a few notes . . . making jingles with words'; 'Oh, this dreadful shortness of our lives!' laments the Newly Born, an hour out of the egg. 'Nothing is great or little otherwise than by Comparison,' Swift observed, and it is in relation to the virtual immortality of the Ancients, untouched by time in their eternity of contemplation, that the childhood of the Youths is scaled down to less than a butterfly's existence,[1] human love to pastoral convention; and art is seen as play rooted in the childish needs of those who cannot yet bear much reality. This development was anticipated in Act I of 'In the Beginning':

> THE SERPENT. Love. Love. Love.
> ADAM. That is too short a word for so long a thing.
> THE SERPENT (*laughs*). . . . Love may be too long a word for so short a thing soon. But when it is short it will be very sweet.

Such is the experience of Strephon, the fool of love who suffers the pain of becoming. With him is identified the process of 'heartbreak' that transports men against their will from folly to wisdom, as it tears them from all attainable desires.[2] It is a violent experience, not the smooth process of growth without regret that is personified in Chloe. But, seen from so great a distance, the tragedy of the natural man turns inevitably to pathetic comedy and evokes a smile:

> What is the use of being born if we have to decay into unnatural, heartless, loveless, joyless monsters in four short years? What use are the artists if they cannot bring their beautiful creations to life? I have a great mind to die and have done with it all.

---

[1] Such changes in perspective recall the contemporary *Insect Play* by K. and J. Čapek, written 1921–2, first published in English in 1923. There is a striking similarity of plot idea between *Back to Methuselah* and the Čapek brothers' *Macropoulos Secret* (1922), not published in English until 1927. The New York Theatre Guild and Barry Jackson were producing Shaw and the Czech expressionist dramatists in the same period.

[2] This is a minor indication that a central theme of *Major Barbara* and *Heartbreak House* runs through *Back to Methuselah*, too, though for the most part it is submerged.

The image recedes once again, now to minimal scale, as the Youths gather round, in their theatre on the stage of a theatre, to watch a play within a play. Pygmalion's automata, Ozymandias and Cleopatra-Semiramis, recapitulate in miniature the whole argument of *Back to Methuselah*, shifting from one style of dialogue to another, as they rapidly change from the satirized puppets of modern society, through the epic pose and the glorification of deterministic science, to creatures of evil and destruction. This is the last appearance of the theme of Cain,[1] the theme of usurping passion. At this point, when the female figure has given Pygmalion a mortal bite, the Ancients transfuse into them a measure of true life, a power of altruism, which takes them back to the truth of the relation between them, as Adam and Eve recognized it in Part I:

THE MALE FIGURE. . . . Spare her; and kill me . . .
THE FEMALE FIGURE. Kill us both. How could either of us live without the other?

This is the moment of conversion, the climax of their play which is analogous to the climax of the whole play: the conversion of the Elderly Gentleman. It is Discouragement that strikes them to the ground; and out of the sense of life as 'too heavy a burden', the immediate consequence of looking reality in the face, emerges the triumph of tragic death, such a resurrection in the spirit as Strephon shrinks from:

The Musicians play.

THE FEMALE FIGURE. Ozymandias: do you hear that? (*She rises on her knees and looks raptly into space.*) Queen of queens! (*She dies.*)
THE MALE FIGURE (*crawling feebly towards her until he reaches her hand*). I knew I was really a king of kings. (*To the others.*) Illusions, farewell: we are going to our thrones. (*He dies.*)

The Music stops.[2]

The Ancients' smile of compassion is apt comment on that.

This is the culmination of the theme of the Image, which Shaw has been developing to this fully dramatized form from the moment when the Serpent teaches the word 'poem' to Eve and explains the meaning of 'conception': 'both the beginning in imagination and the end in creation'. It has been sustained in the scattered imagery of dolls and disguises, in the Guardians' rejection of metaphors and in the static symbol of the television screen. It is rendered theatrically potent in the setting, and dramatically potent in the action, of Part IV, Act III. For the temple of the Oracle is the Platonic cave, where men are prisoners watching a shadow-show that they mistake for reality.

[1] Except in the musical recapitulation of the epilogue.
[2] Note the likeness to the masque in a Jacobean play.

Major features of Plato's description are easily recognizable: the gloom and vapours of the abyss, and the violet light that flares up at intervals like the reflection of a fire; the raised gallery, brightly lit, along which move figures, some talking, including '*two men . . . holding their hats with the brims near their noses*'; the noises as of thunder that come from the void in answer to the tourists' questions. Shaw has not provided an exact reproduction of Plato's cave, but the whole scene is certainly closer to its original than the other great variant in modern drama: the cave scene which is the climax of Strindberg's *Dream Play* and where are found the figure-heads of *Justice, Friendship*, and the rest, which have sunk in the sea of becoming.[1] Zoo sits with her back to the abyss and comments on the whole business of the Oracle as the conjuring trick that she knows it to be; yet the Shortlivers remain as much impressed by the illusion as the men chained in the cave, who disbelieve the explanations of their wiser fellows. This is the point at which Shaw is able to present his indictment of the triviality of party politics with the deadliest force, as the Envoy can find no more important matter on which to question the Oracle than the most propitious date for the next General Election; in this awe-inspiring context, the petty self-importance of ambitious men shows at its most dwarfish. The Elderly Gentleman, however, has lost his shortsightedness and turns to face the Oracle in daylight, as the philosopher turns to the sun:

THE ORACLE (*with grave pity*). Come: look at me. I am my natural size now: what you saw there was only a foolish picture of me thrown on a cloud by a lantern.

Edmund Wilson has read the last part of *Back to Methuselah* as evidence of Shaw's abandonment of politics for despair. It would be truer to say that here he turns away from politics in the same sense as Socrates turns away from his theory of the perfect state to the true concern of philosophy: contemplation of the heavenly pattern of Ideas. *Major Barbara* stopped before this, at the hypothesis: 'If philosophers were kings in their cities . . .' Now the dramatist proceeds to demonstrate the relevance of the satirical art of *Back to Methuselah* to the actual political business of men – to justify it as political satire, indeed – by showing the distance between image and actuality which the political idealist ignores.

The mechanistic, deterministic creed recited by the unredeemed automata takes its form and cadence from the First Epistle to the Corinthians:

THE MALE FIGURE. . . . the king of kings and queen of queens are not accidents of the egg: they are thought-out and hand-made to receive the sacred Life Force. There is one person of the king and òne of the queen;

[1] Shaw, of course, was among the first of Strindberg's English admirers.

but the Life Force of the king and queen is all one: the glory equal, the majesty co-eternal.

Parody such as this can work both ways, and Shaw quite often employs it to an end which is the reverse of burlesque.[1] So now the tone of the passage prepares for the heightening of seriousness in the Ancients' lengthy exposition of the doctrine of Ideas. The furthest reach of consciousness to which Shaw conducts us is visionary; for the Ancients are moving beyond philosophical speculation to mysticism. Shaw has gone for its terms to the Pauline lines which bear the closest relation to the turning away of Socrates. They provide a viewpoint from which to look back on the entire design and intention of the Shavian fable:

> There are also celestial bodies, and bodies terrestrial: but the glory of the celestial is one, and the glory of the terrestrial is another. . . .
> And so it is written, The first man Adam was made a living soul; the last Adam was made a quickening spirit . . . flesh and blood cannot inherit the kingdom of God; . . . we shall all be changed. . . .

There is undoubtedly an element of what Edmund Wilson calls 'lunar horror' in Part V. The power of life and death, as represented in the delivery of the Newly Born from the egg, the making of man and woman in a laboratory, and the calcining of unfit children, corresponds to the eugenics and euthanasia of Plato's *Republic*, as well as to the potentialities of modern science; these are such things as reason would always impose upon the natural man. (The responsible use of man's powers of destruction is implicitly contrasted with the irresponsibility of war.) But the most significant figure in Part V is Pygmalion, who takes us back to Laputa, the land of the machines, where the Watchmaker is God. The scientist among the artists, he is identified with the false relation between the ideal and the actuality which the philosopher-statesman, or any dreamer infatuated with the stuff of his imagination, may labour to produce. For Pygmalion is so foolish as to do what Strephon is so foolish as to desire: bring images to life. The epilogue presents his true opposite in Lilith, who is the Serpent in another form, the creative principle opposed to the destructiveness of Cain, and free will and imagination opposed to logic and calculation.

Having based his satire on logic, Shaw recognized the need to criticize the insufficiency of logical procedures, which too easily lead from the natural dream of Eden to grotesque parodies of 'the Perfect City of God'

---

[1] A notable example is B.B.'s reaction to the death of Dubedat, where the power of the Shakespearian words and rhythms into which he falls works against the effect of the nonsense to which he reduces them. See p. 167 above.

on earth.[1] He has presented his fable as a hypothesis to be discarded when its work is done.[2] Recognition of its hypothetical quality has been deliberately nursed: like *Gulliver's Travels* or the Platonic dialogues, *Back to Methuselah* as a whole stops short of being full imaginative fiction, self-contained, and lacks the full dimensions of drama. Artistic illusion is kept subservient to argument. Dramatic action and true conflict are limited to certain areas of the cycle; what prevails throughout is the question-and-answer pattern of didactic exposition (reaching an ironic anticlimax in the episode of the Envoy and the Oracle). Logic itself is a minor form of determinism (one of the leitmotifs of the play) and, as such, tends to strangle life. Logic carried to extremes is absurd and makes all Utopias intolerable. Cain's guiding impulse, the pull away from nature, the desire to escape human limitations, is manifest in the author's idea of progress in social responsibility. But it is pushed to the stage where it degenerates into grotesque images of misshapen creatures, lapsed into non-communicating isolation, absorbed in a contemplation that seems no better than self-absorption.

The Ancients, in fact, are no less relative and partial components of the total image of man than are the Guardians of Part IV, who do not understand imagination. In maintaining the opposition between rational soul and appetitive to the very end, Shaw acknowledges that the one cannot get on without the other. The tragedy of the Elderly Gentleman lies in the fact that the philosopher cannot escape from his humanity, though he may despise it. It is counterbalanced by the comedy of Pygmalion, with its theme of the destructiveness of pure intellect in the context of human life. The artist holds the scales, as Lubin – by one of those touches of truth with which Shaw keeps his caricatures alive – was allowed to observe:

The poets and story tellers, especially the classical poets and story tellers, have been, in the main, right.

---

[1] Cf. the Elderly Gentleman's version of history: 'My Society has printed me an editio princeps of the works of the father of history, Thucyderodotus Macollybuckle. Have you read his account of what was blasphemously called the Perfect City of God, and the attempt made to reproduce it in the northern part of these islands by Jonhobsnoxius, called the Leviathan? Those misguided people sacrificed the fragment of life that was granted to them to an imaginary immortality. They crucified the prophet who told them to take no thought for the morrow, and that here and now was their Australia: Australia being a term signifying paradise, or an eternity of bliss.'

[2] Burge's misquotation of *The Tempest* ('The cloud-capped towers . . . the great globe itself: yea, all that it inherit shall dissolve, and, like this influential pageant faded, leave not a rack behind') and the irony of Shelley's 'Ozymandias', quoted by the Male Automaton, make the same point – in favour of change and decay in art and in life.

What, then, is the appropriate aesthetic judgement on *Back to Methuselah*? It is not among Shaw's finest plays, because it is only marginally a
play. Between his starting work on Part II and the writing of the later
parts, it must have become evident to Shaw that Granville Barker, who
had produced all his work since 1904, had abandoned the theatre for
good.[1] (He fulfilled his last theatrical engagement, entered into before
his second marriage in 1918, by producing Maeterlinck's *The Betrothal* in
January 1921; but his active friendship with Shaw and his interest in
directing a theatre were finished before that.) The association with Barry
Jackson was some years ahead. When it came, it encouraged a renewal of
Shaw's genius for theatre and its development in new directions. In the
interim he continued *Back to Methuselah* as another form of art not
governed by theatrical necessities, though aware of them still. *Sui generis*,
Back to Methuselah is a formidable achievement that sometimes touches
greatness. But it also has its own particular negative light to shed on the
relation between Shaw the philosopher and Shaw the dramatist: it
intimates how far the idealist-thinker could go in a form of self-indulgence when the need to communicate with an audience was not foremost
in his mind; and it also shows the whole man who is the artist rounding
on the compensatory, rationalizing tendency of the mind to check it
when the external controls fail. In fact, when the theatre had a place for
him, the practical obligations of theatrecraft happily analogized Shaw's
respect for the practical business of politics and life.

---

[1] And this was a period of abysmally low standards in the British theatre
otherwise. I have quoted elsewhere William Poel's words in *What is Wrong
with the Stage* (London: Allen and Unwin, 1920), pp. 9–10: 'The condition of
the English Theatre has moved steadily downward, and today it may be said
to have touched its lowest level on record. The reason is not far to seek. The
public has for so long seen theatrical amusements carried on as an industry,
instead of as an art, that the disadvantage of applying commercialism to creative
work escapes comment, as it were, by right of custom . . . The plays of Shaw,
Galsworthy, Barker, Masefield, with those of all men who respect themselves
and their calling, are put on one side as being impossible compositions, written
by those who do not understand the needs of the public, meaning those who are
not with the Stock Exchange financiers . . . The play-producing centre for the
British Empire is London, and the men who control the output walk the pave-
ment of Threadneedle Street.'

14

The Histories

Brecht, and later Weiss, made of the Shavian history play one of the most powerful conventions of modern drama.[1] If only on this account, it is worth going back to discover more precisely the nature of Shaw's achievement in the mode. He was certainly attracted to the historical play: *The Man of Destiny*, *The Devil's Disciple*, *Caesar and Cleopatra*, *Androcles and the Lion*, *The Dark Lady of the Sonnets*, *Saint Joan*, *In Good King Charles's Golden Days*, and the more trifling *Great Catherine* and *The Six of Calais* represent all phases of his long career and fall into the same general category, 'historical'. Even *Geneva* is subtitled, 'A Fancied Page of History', a variant on the description applied to *Good King Charles*: 'A True History that Never Happened'. Of course, all classic drama, when not performed in modern dress, takes on a certain historical colouring, and Shaw was not averse to giving some of his plays the patina of Old Masters. Traditional styles are part of the medium of artistic communication. Shaw entered the theatre at a time when the high styles of Ibsenite realism, in modern dress, and Greek ritualism were challenging the monopoly of Shakespearian tradition, the latest stronghold of which was Irving's theatre. Not even the strongest of orthodoxies was ruled out of bounds in Shaw's idiosyncratic experimentation with the range of conventions open to him, 'high' and popular. Historical drama is a principal form of costume drama, and Shaw practised it as he practised other varieties, including the Ruritanian romance. Whatever the precise dramatic content, costume is part of the pleasurable make-believe which is the strong, central appeal of theatre.

'All dress is fancy dress, is it not, except our natural skins?' says Dunois, and the Epilogue to *Saint Joan* graphically establishes a relativism whereby everything distinctive of period, even the top-hatted uniform of twentieth-century man, shows up as the equipment of human play, or dilettante experiment. Neither Shaw, nor Brecht following him, is concerned with historical perspective, with the past as distant and profoundly

[1] Before them, Pirandello had put a lesson learnt from Shaw to unique use in his *Henry IV*.

different from the present. The sense of genuine cultural otherness affecting ways of thought or even the constitution of the mind in remote periods is minimized by both dramatists. However ancient a fashion the costumes represent, the consciousness of the wearers is modern: they talk anachronistically, as with foreknowledge of modern issues. Famous names are attached to characters whose essence is the familiar, the ordinary. Such 'historical' drama is merely a special area of fantasy.

The relation between the romantic melodrama and the historical material in *The Devil's Disciple* is not close and precise.[1] The choice of setting is exploited only in a very general way: the rebellion of the American colonies provides a political analogy to Dick Dudgeon's anti-religion; and the period is also aptly chosen in that Dick's creed is a version of the challenge Blake actually issued to the religious orthodoxies of the time. More substantially the play records the dramatist's imaginative progress from the strong attraction of a romantic rebel pose (Dick Dudgeon) to an antithetical attitude of cheerful, energetic and aggressive practicality (Anthony Anderson). The shift is from a mood of doomed defiance to one intent on victory. But it involves trying out the poses on an audience: first on the naïve Effie, who registers the emotional appeal of the more Byronic figure, then on the more sophisticated Judith who, as surrogate of a sentimentally inclined public, is confounded and exposed twice over with a gratuitousness reminiscent of the treatment of Marian in *The Irrational Knot*. Judith's idealization of both men offers two versions of the hero-according-to-woman's-morality that Shaw ultimately rejects for the hero coolly acknowledged by the detached and rational male observer (General Burgoyne, himself too deficient in human warmth for heroic stature). Shaw was certainly at this stage concerned to discover a heroic image, and the conventions of historical drama kept him in countenance. The values the play asserts are the same as he put forward in non-historical drama: authentic and generous feeling, as opposed both to coldness (here the negative coldness of Mrs Dudgeon and the inhumanity of Burgoyne) and to false sentiment, is celebrated as in *You Never Can Tell*; the rejection of self-sacrifice and idealized failure for self-fulfilment and success was to be much more forcefully presented in *Major Barbara*.

A comment in the Preface to the much later *Good King Charles* represents an occasional Shavian claim that the history in his plays has a more serious, scientific value:

> The 'histories' of Shakespear are chronicles dramatized; and my own chief historical plays, Caesar and Cleopatra and St Joan, are fully documented

---

1 See previous comments on this play, above, pp. 51, 62, and on *Caesar and Cleopatra*, above, pp. 46–50.

chronicle plays of this type. Familiarity with them would get a student safely through examination papers on their periods.

Apart from the characteristic scornful aside on formal education, this indicates the rules of the game which Shaw, perhaps only subconsciously, recognized as necessary disciplines to such an imagination as his. His normal preference for fantasy has its negative aspect: it exonerates him from the precision that contemporary realism must exact if it is not to be merely unconvincing and inept. Another kind of precision is needed to give shape and weight to what otherwise might be no more than the whimsies of an idle mind. Whether the given facts were true or not, working strictly within their terms was an aid to concentration. In *Caesar and Cleopatra*, for instance, history as every schoolboy knew it in Macaulay's day is the basis of the episodes chosen for representation on stage and the matter of extra-scenic allusion. Caesar as Latin author, recalling the Gallic wars, was only too well known in the classroom and now made more congenial in an actor's impersonation that dodges the pedant to appeal directly to his pupils. The references back to the death of Pompey and forward to the assassination at the Ides of March and the story of Cleopatra and Mark Antony are among the odds-and-ends of universal education that stick in most minds. The business of Cleopatra hiding in the carpet, a picturesque anecdote that Shakespeare found in Plutarch, like the 'miracles' of Joan's identification of the Dauphin or the changing of the wind before Orleans, is typical of legendary history, an aspect of folk tradition tenaciously defiant of scientific questioning. Even in *Saint Joan*, Shaw was less inclined to verify what his authorities reported than to take over the material they offered and base his new synoptic version of the story upon it. He justified his treatment of the characters by claiming that it was not inconsistent with the available documentary evidence; but that is a late instance of the Platonic confusion over truth and fiction, over art as an imitation of life. The play stands as a self-consistent fable, simply meaningful in a way that life, and history as a record of life, cannot be.

The association with folk education is crucial. In these plays, Shaw proceeds like a village schoolmaster, inspired with a didactic purpose that outruns his expert knowledge.[1] He gets on to the stage, in *Caesar and Cleopatra*, a model of the Sphinx (little enough for the theatre), the Palace of Alexandria and its roof-garden, the Pharos and its lighthouse, a working model of an Ancient Egyptian steam-powered crane, Cleopatra's miniature shrine of the Nile and, in the 1912 Prologue,

---

[1] It is possible to see a generic likeness to the schoolmasters of Hardy's world, though Shaw's earnestness is better concealed than theirs.

the Temple of Ra at Memphis; and another Wonder of the Ancient World, the Alexandrian Library, flares just off-stage in its destruction by fire. It would all be appropriate to the painless instruction of little Ptolemy. Indeed Caesar, who proves to be a kindly and playful mentor to children, is an embodiment of the author's design upon his audiences.[1] The action of the play traces Caesar's attempt to teach the adolescent Cleopatra to be a queen and, though the lesson may be all but lost upon her, it is not lost upon us. His pupil's wayward and impatient attitude to the greater task is summarily reflected in her demand to play the harp (in one of the scenes allusively related to episodes in Shakespeare's *Antony and Cleopatra*):

CLEOPATRA. . . . you shall teach me. How long will it take?

MUSICIAN. Not very long: only four years. Your Majesty must first become proficient in the philosophy of Pythagoras.

CLEOPATRA. Has she (*indicating the slave*) become proficient in the philosophy of Pythagoras?

MUSICIAN. Oh, she is but a slave. She learns as a dog learns.

CLEOPATRA. Well, then, I will learn as a dog learns . . . You shall give me a lesson every day for a fortnight . . . After that, whenever I strike a false note you shall be flogged. . .

As we shall see, it is probable that Cleopatra's rejection of 'the philosophy of Pythagoras' was more than a joke: it is a sign of her imprisonment in a decadent civilization from which Caesar tries in vain to rescue her; he is defeated by her egocentricity, a petty manifestation of the general geocentricity of the Ptolemaic universe.

In effect, Caesar came too late. Mommsen's neglect of Caesarion, the legendary child of Caesar and Cleopatra, and his misleading reference to a sixteen-year-old[2] Cleopatra – she seems to have been twenty when Caesar was in Egypt – served Shaw's purposes well. As the inclusion of her little brother in the play shows up, Cleopatra has lost the uncorrupt innocence of the child, though she has not yet attained the self-possession – far less the wisdom – of maturity. The notions of greatness that Caesar rejects befit her adolescence. But her nubile fascination is already strong, calculated to affect audiences as it affects Caesar himself. So the dangerousness, even viciousness, of romantic pretensions in politics, and the closeness of tyranny and cruelty to notions of honour, are associated with the image of a budding *femme fatale*. At last the monstrous femininity growing in Cleopatra is fully revealed to recognition: separately embodied

[1] Even the insulting tone of the 1912 Prologue suggests a mock-ogre of the nursery.

[2] See H. Lüdeke, 'Some Remarks on Shaw's History Plays', *English Studies*, Vol. XXXVI (1955), pp. 239–46.

(a) Teatr Stary, Krakow, 1956.

18 *Saint Joan* – a puppet play?

(b) Kamerny Theatre, Moscow, 1924. (Setting shows Expressionist influence.)

19 *The Apple Cart,* Interlude. Edith Evans and Cedric Hardwick.

in the savage and dominating black slave, Ftatateeta, stupid, bloated and drunk on blood. (Only when Cleopatra has taken Ftatateeta's values to herself does the Nurse act as a true slave and not the power behind the throne that she was at the start of the play.)

The peculiar modification Shaw's attitude to women gives to his lesson-plays was not taken over by Brecht. Andrea, who is a child when Galileo first undertakes to explain to him the scientific principles at issue in terms as plain and simple as possible, aided by a demonstration that is a game in itself, remains a touchstone of virtue to the end of *Galileo Galilei*; and the Little Monk is another innocent. The simplicity of the peasan heroine Grusha, and the folk *naïveté* of the basic fable of *The Caucasu n Chalk Circle* (even Azdak is a picaresque figure familiar enough in a certain type of folk-tale) match the quality of receptivity the Singer presumes in his audience – on stage in the Prologue and in the auditorium. In this respect, at least, Shaw's relation to his audience seems more complex if not more sophisticated. And, if we look forward and compare Brecht's down-to-earth, yet radiant Grusha with Shaw's plain peasant lass from Domrémy, it is very evident that the latter is no embodiment of instinctive virtue: Grusha's maternal benevolence has to be complemented by the wiliness of Azdak for she, like Joan, has in-sufficient saving guile; but Joan represents herself as not maternal at all (her liking to play with children is a soldier's characteristic) and her virtue, far from being rooted in her female nature, is identified rather with her revolt against that nature. All told, the differences seem related to Shaw's more complete enclosure within a middle-class society and its ways of thinking and feeling.

There is a sense in which historical colouring is meaningful to both Shaw and Brecht, and not just as part of the carnival. Both had derived from Marx a sense of the value of history, of the coherent interpretation of the past as a political determinant, and they are concerned in their plays with the relation between men's views of the universe, including the retrospective view, and their behaviour in the present. Not fact, but belief, is crucial. The form Shaw's interpretation of history takes is more generally Hegelian than precisely Marxist. He presents historical process as incarnated in the career of great human beings, whose greatness is identifiable with the way in which they are forerunners of a new era and its emergent values. Thus both Caesar and Joan are drawn as Messiah figures, Caesar anticipating Christ[1] and Joan (like the non-historical Barbara) re-enacting the mission, challenge and Passion of Christ. The

---

[1] This is observed by H. Lüdeke, op. cit., and traced partly to the influence of Mommsen's portrait of Caesar, partly to the view of the naturally Christian gentleman Shaw had himself evolved and implied in *The Devil's Disciple*.

I

perspective embraces the modern world. Thus Caesar announces a New Law in opposition to the Old Law of vengeance:

> If one man in all the world can be found, now or forever, to know that you did wrong, that man will have either to conquer the world as I have, or be crucified by it . . . And so, to the end of history, murder shall breed murder, always in the name of right and honor and peace, until the gods are tired of blood and create a race that can understand.

The fallacy of the popular nineteenth-century belief in progress and the mistaken notion that humanity has learnt through experience *in* history are rejected here, as they are tacitly rejected in Shaw's general artistic annihilation of historical difference. The movement of change appears to be cyclic, the same challenge confronting men as individuals in succeeding generations.

Indeed history in Shaw's plays, as in Brecht's and Weiss's, is a moral fable for the dramatist's contemporaries, and it is not too surprising to find the issues of *Saint Joan* raised by Shaw in that earlier disquisitory play with twentieth-century characters, *Getting Married*. The Bishop, his Chaplain and the young man-about-town, Sinjon Hotchkiss, have witnessed a manifestation of Mrs George's clairvoyant powers:

> SOAMES. My lord: is this possession by the devil?
> THE BISHOP. Or the ecstasy of a saint?
> HOTCHKISS. Or the convulsion of the pythoness on the tripod?
>
> SOAMES. Shall we take you and burn you?
> THE BISHOP. Or take you and canonize you?
> HOTCHKISS (*gaily*). Or take you as a matter of course?

The questions are applicable to any highly individualized human being whose challenge to the social order is fundamentally a matter of superior personal quality. The phenomenon of 'personal gravity', with which such late plays as *The Apple Cart* and *The Millionairess* are explicitly concerned, is here seen in another aspect: the most highly evolved, most naturally gifted person becomes leader in any society – unless the mob turns on him. The conflict is always between the great man and mass-consciousness, between individual moral responsibility and undifferentiated force.

The solution Hotchkiss proposes comes in the tone of the comic dramatist whose historical 'realism' means in practice the rejection of epic glorification, nobility of sentiment and dignity of style, in favour of a drama of tantrums and sulks, domestic images and farcical incident. The Shavian Caesar is Bluntschli in a toga; his Joan has characteristics of the pantomime Principal Boy; the extreme is reached in such playlets as *Great Catherine* and *The Six of Calais*, whose Punch-and-Judy humours give opportunity for histrionic barn-storming at the opposite pole from subtle psychological realism. Shaw's reaction to conventional heroic figures is certainly ambivalent: they fascinate his imagination, yet prompt him to expose the ridiculousness of the human being and, in particular, the childishness in the man. In his version of Hegelianism, the great individual is redefined as ordinary foolish man extraordinarily endowed (viz. Napoleon), or just extraordinarily free of cant, pretentiousness and self-delusion: Charles II without his wig, or, alternatively, the distinguished company he meets:

> Here is Pastor Fox, a king in his meeting house . . . Here is Mr Newton, a king in the new Royal Society. Here is Godfrey Kneller: a king among painters. I can make you duchesses and your sons dukes; but who would be mere dukes or duchesses if they could be kings and queens?

The later plays, especially, are addicted to astronomical images of change – not gradual, but sudden and cataclysmic: the collision of stars in *The Apple Cart*; the orbit of the Earth leaping to its next quantum at the end of *Geneva*; in *Good King Charles* a backward view of the shift from a Ptolemaic to a Copernican universe and premonitions of the abandonment of Newtonian physics with the discoveries of Einstein. Galileo is Newton's hero, whom he defends against the ignorant arrogance of James, Duke of York; the period of *Saint Joan* (as of *Caesar and Cleopatra*) is too early for an anticipation of Galileo, and so the playwright there associates a new cosmology with rediscovery of neglected ancient truth:

> THE ARCHBISHOP. . . . There is a new spirit rising in men: we are at the dawning of a wider epoch. If I were a simple monk, and had not to rule men, I should seek peace for my spirit with Aristotle and Pythagoras rather than with the saints and their miracles.

And Pythagoras is then identified as 'A sage who held that the earth is round, and that it moves round the sun'.[1] Brecht's Galileo is less of a professional politician than Shaw's Archbishop, but what he sees through his telescope teaches him a political lesson that he passes on to his friend, the little Monk, and 'it's nothing to do with the planets, it's to do with the peasants in the Campagna'. The death of old piety is a signal for the release of men: 'The heavens are empty, and there is a gale of laughter over that.' The scientific nature of the cosmic imagery is not merely fortuitous: human society may demonstrate the same evolutionary principle as is at work in the rest of nature. But a total altering of the cosmic view has revolutionary implications.

[1] See above, p. 242, on the reference to Pythagoras in *Caesar and Cleopatra*.

The shift from one historical cycle to another is consistently associated by Shaw with the abandonment of an outworn faith. Caesar, who chooses to leave the great library burning in order to make for the lighthouse, is more successful than George Fox (in *Good King Charles*) in rooting out 'the sin of idolatry'. When the Romans triumph, the Egyptian priests offer their images for sale at bargain prices, and 'Apis the all-knowing' goes for five talents. Part of the strength of a Roman legion is that it is, as Bel Affris says in the original Prologue, like a man with no religion. But religion as the Egyptians understand it, and as it is demonstrated in the rites Cleopatra celebrates, is superstition wedded to barbarism; Caesar's common sense, humility and infinite readiness to forgive his enemies are premonitions of the virtues of Christ. What happens in the heavens, in Shavian drama, shows the hand of God that can shatter all orthodoxies. The 'splendid drumming in the sky', at the end of *Heartbreak House*, is as miraculous as the moments out of time when the clock of the universe stopped, or was turned back, which Newton, Fox and Charles consider together: moments of the 'sun which stood still upon Gibeon and the moon in the Valley of Ajalon' (an appropriately biblical image which Tennyson had used in 'Locksley Hall', along with the 'cycle of Cathay', to denote a rejection of the post-Darwinian ideal of progress), or when 'the shadow on the dial of Ahaz went ten degrees backward as a sign from God'. The analogy of Paley's watch ceases to be inexorably determinist when it is extended by implication in this way.

Caesar and Cleopatra is a notable early instance of Shaw's preference of a loose construction to an organically developed plot. He admitted that Act III might be dispensed with in performance to cut down playing time. Yet the act justifies its presence as a celebration of the moment of creative freedom in the midst of events.[1] It is recognizable as an upgraded harlequinade: the date-eating episode and the clowning with Britannus, the butt, usher in a version of the pantomime chase. The absurdity of Cleopatra hidden in the carpet blends with the relief from tedious thought and feeling that the acrobatics represent, with the general panache of Apollodorus, the music of the barcarole he sings and the fancy-free sentiment it conveys. The evocation of sunlit air and sea and the imagery of flight are matched by the buoyancy of Caesar's own mood as he dives into the sea after Apollodorus (there is, after all, a way out for

---

[1] Cf. Brecht's Galileo's delight in the Copernican view of the universe as an expanding, changing system, dazzling with the sense of infinite possibilities, very unlike the old system in which men felt safer perhaps, but were so shut in, with nothing but straight alternatives open to them, as in the old game of chess.

men bold enough to take it). As he swims with Cleopatra on his back, he is transformed into a dolphin; and, as Shaw filched the image from Shakespeare's Antony, one wonders if he was aware of its traditional use as a Christ-symbol, silently apt in the present context.

The physical energy of this act throws into relief the static quality of much of the play, when Caesar sits twiddling his thumbs and talking, and the audience is as disappointed as Cleopatra of decisive action. (Act II is a model of indecisive action, checked and reversed.) Indeed it is only in Act IV, when Cleopatra seizes the initiative and, by her actions, swings the play close to a tragic catastrophe, that a strong dramatic rhythm emerges. It lapses again when chance and the timing of events bring up the reinforcements to save the situation that had seemingly out-run Caesar's power of saving it. To resist tragedy appears to have been Shaw's fundamental intention and his most deliberate departure from Shakespearian example. He was willing to indulge the late nineteenth-century taste for scene-painting and exploit the glamour of stage lighting, particularly in Acts I and IV; these could be turned to good account as illusionary aids to Cleopatra's histrionic aping of an authority that is not in her character.[1] Extending the play to Rome and the Ides of March would have been to involve his hero in what he himself would judge a romantic sham. 'I do not make human sacrifices to my honor,' declares Caesar; it is exactly what Cleopatra does, and it doesn't show up as honourable. There is no moral pretentiousness about Rufio's 'natural' slaying of the savage beast, as there is about 'honour' and 'revenge' and, all but inevitably, about tragedy and tragic heroism, too.

Caesar balances not thinking too well of human nature by not thinking too badly of it either; the method is close enough to Hotchkiss's notion of taking it 'as a matter of course'. The genius of comedy stays close to Caesar in the person of Apollodorus, amateur of the aesthetic (not theatrical), who contributes to the play a gaiety like that of *You Never Can Tell*. Philip's jesting reference to Valentine as 'the man of ivory and gold', would be apt to Apollodorus, through whom the nature of Phoebus Apollo surely shines. Nothing can go finally and irrevocably wrong in a world that he inhabits. (Cleopatra, masquerading as pigeons' eggs, smothering in a carpet, is not only ludicrous, but stuffy, beside his grace.) But the play is composed largely on a principle of contrasted tones, and Lucius Septimius is a dark counterpart to Apollodorus's brightness. Gloom-ridden and sinister, the brief appearances of Lucius are ominous of the murder of Pothinus and the slaying of Ftatateeta on the

---

[1] 'Royalty, Ftatateeta, lies not in the barge but in the Queen,' says Caesar, recalling the treatment of the theme of illusion in *Antony and Cleopatra*. But his pupil fails to learn the lesson and continues to rely on her props.

altar, ominous of the treachery and cruelty of Cleopatra, at the same time as they recall the old sins and political mistakes of the historical Caesar. Lucius Septimius can be regarded as a dark shadow cast by Shakespeare's baleful Caesar, focus of the superstition which Shaw has transferred to the Egyptians. He is redeemed by the clemency of the Shavian Caesar who does not idealize evil; and so the darkness is dispersed at the end of the play, except for the knowledge that the Ides of March lie ahead: the victory of reason is not absolute.

Saint Joan invokes the concept of tragedy more decisively, but still repudiates it. It does so by virtue of being a Passion Play even more than by being – sporadically – a pantomime. The episodic structure itself recalls the pageant-drama, and the successive examinations of Joan are roughly analogous to the bringing of Christ before Annas, Caiaphas and Pilate in the orthodox Christian Passion Play. Shaw's insistence on the fairness of her judges brings them collectively close to the attitude of Pilate, and the wary collaboration of the Inquisition with English feudal power reproduces in a very general way the conditions of collaboration between Jewish orthodoxy and the Roman Imperium that led to the trial and execution of Christ. Shaw's wish to assimilate the story of Joan to that of Christ is confirmed in a series of parallels too insistent to be casual. Warwick's proposal, in Scene iv, to 'buy' Joan is followed up, just before the scene ends, by de Stogumber's echo of Caiaphas: 'It is expedient that one woman die for the people.' The symbolic figure of Judas is remembered in Joan's reproof to the Dauphin, 'Wilt be a poor little Judas, and betray me and Him that sent me?' (Scene ii), and, after her burning, in de Stogumber's verdict on himself, 'I am no better than Judas: I will hang myself.' He comments on the crowd at the execution, 'Some of the people laughed at her. They would have laughed at Christ,' and he unconsciously aligns himself with those for whom the Christian Saviour died on the Cross: 'I did not know what I was doing.' Joan's naïve vision of herself as a Messiah not only reveals the blend of simplicity and self-confident pride in her own character, it prompts fresh recognition of the breathtaking arrogance of Christ's claims by removing them from a context of pious acceptance and exposing them to a more sceptical consideration (a necessary part of the attempt to turn religion back into history). Her message to Baudricourt, in Scene i, is uncompromising:

. . . it is the will of God that you are to do what He has put into my mind.

The effect of her unconscious echoing of Christ's words, as in her challenge to the Dauphin, 'Art for or against me?', may be doubly ironic. For the device helps to establish her as a Christ-surrogate in the play, but also enables us to see the closeness of her piety to blasphemy, and the megalomaniac quality not only in *her* self-devotion but inseparable from the humanity of the Saviour. The impression given may be incidentally comic:

> I do know better than any of you seem to. And . . . I never speak unless I know I am right.

Cauchon's judgement of such self-assurance – 'She acts as if she herself were the Church' – brings out an analogy with Christ's proposal of a New Law to supersede the Old Law and makes it possible for the detached mind to see a humorous aspect in that too. The brash irreverence of Shaw's juvenile Passion Play is avoided by the indirection of his approach here; but the basic attitude of mind is not so different; he was concerned to naturalize more than the sanctity of Joan and *her* miracles. ('A miracle', explains the Archbishop, with the familiarity of professionalism, 'is an event which creates faith.')

The addition of the Epilogue most effectively debars an interpretation of the play simply as a study of Joan's self-delusion and the imaginative compulsion it exerts over others. Her final cry at the trial, 'I am His child, and you are not fit that I should live among you', sounds a mad-dened defiance without any comic overtones. The note of feeling is apt to the approach of death in torment; it also signals the translation of the human being into a world of the spirit. And, for all its extravaganza form, the Epilogue serves as Shaw's instrument to extend the story of Joan beyond the apparent finality of her death at the stake to a Resur-rection and Ascension.[1] Indeed his conformation of her legend to the central myth and ritual of Christianity is made remarkably complete, though the manner of it is condensed and allusive. The Harrowing of Hell is intimated in the liberation of the Soldier for his day's parole in the calendar of saints. The presentation of de Stogumber as a man without imagination, who needs to see with his bodily eyes before he can believe, recalls the incredulity and conversion of Thomas. The décor of the Dauphin's bed-chamber, with its candles and painted tapestries in which '*the prevailing yellow and red . . . is somewhat flamelike when the folds breathe in the wind*' is an appropriate background to a dream vision of Joan, as it suggests the *auto-da-fé* which was not actually presented on stage; taken in conjunction with the wind that now and again rushes through the chamber, it can hint an imaginative fusion of the appearance of the crucified Saviour, in the midst of his disciples gathered in an upper room, with the scene of Pentecost, the coming of the Holy Ghost in tongues of flame and a rushing mighty wind. Gospel gives way to

---

[1] Cf. the final scene at Perivale St Andrews in *Major Barbara*, which is the occasion of the heroine's resurrection after her spiritual death. See p. 144 above.

liturgy, with a formal adaptation of the *Te Deum*, addressed to the newly canonized Joan:

> The girls in the field praise thee . . .
> The dying soldiers praise thee . . .
> The cunning counsellors praise thee . . .
> The foolish old men on their deathbeds praise thee . . .
> The judges in the blindness and bondage of the law praise thee, etc.

Her response, 'Woe unto me when all men praise me!', slightly adapts an uncompleted quotation. The full text (Luke 6:26) is surely significant for an understanding of Shaw's intention, over the whole play, whether or not he expected his audiences to complete it in their minds:

> Woe unto you, when all men shall speak well of you! *for so did their fathers to the false prophets.* (My italics)

Cauchon's last words in the Epilogue, 'mortal eyes cannot distinguish the saint from the heretic', express the moral of the play. From his Archimedean point, equidistant from the historical past and the twentieth century, Shaw poses the question of whether Joan was wrong, whether her private judgement brought good or evil to the world. The difficulty has presented itself to the heroine herself at her trial in subjective terms: 'What other judgement can I judge by but my own?' Only a dialectical or dramatic mode can contain the dangerousness of that truth. It will not solve the problem to see the churchmen giving an entirely spurious authority to their private judgements by identifying them with the institution of the Church, for Joan surpasses them in identifying hers with the will of God and the messages of the saints.

She is, of course, innocent in the sense that the Inquisitor recognizes, innocent through her uncorrupted instincts: she is not self-seeking; she has a natural friendliness to all; her intentions are good. Yet de Stogumber could be speaking for her in his words, 'I did not know what I was doing.' Such childish innocence is dangerous in a world of power. The play was completed and performed in 1923 when the historical process Shaw (through Warwick and Cauchon) represents Joan as initiating had reached its evolutionary climax. Cauchon's prophecies must then have had the ring of topical comment:

> . . . the Catholic Church knows only one realm, and that is the realm of Christ's kingdom. Divide that kingdom into nations, and you dethrone Christ. Dethrone Christ, and who will stand between our throats and the sword? The world will perish in a welter of war.

This is not simply the voice of the medieval Church; the intellectual attitude which saw the high medieval period as the end of a cycle of faith and civilization giving way to the barbarism of the modern world

was currently respectable just before and after the First World War.
Yeats looked back to the beginning of the Christian cycle itself for a
parallel to the contemporary situation:

> Odour of blood when Christ was slain
> Made all Platonic tolerance vain
> And vain all Doric discipline;

and his anticipations were symbolized in the 'rough beast' of the Second
Coming. As for Joan, Shaw's new Christ of the fifteenth century, she
stands to Cauchon as a figure of similar dark prognostication:

> It will be a world of blood, of fury, of devastation, of each man striving for
> his own hand: in the end a world wrecked back into barbarism.

An interpretation of Joan as innocent fool is carried to some extent by
the pantomime conventions introduced into the play and reasserted in
the Epilogue, after lapsing in the trial scene. The theatrical unreality of
pantomime also serves to keep her in focus as an enigma challenging the
mind, never quite a tragic heroine or a victim whose boldness is finally
pathetic. The first scene, with its blustering baron and hens that won't
lay, the nicknames, Polly and Jack and Dick the Archer, which the
peasant lass impertinently applies to Baudricourt's men, the comic abuse
('The worst, most incompetent, drivelling snivelling jibbering jabbering
idiot of a steward in France'), the cool high-handedness of the girl with
her feudal lord ('I have arranged it all: you have only to give the order')
establish the relation to Christmas pantomime quite firmly, before the
final absurd 'miracle' – 'The hens are laying like mad, sir. Five dozen
eggs!' – sets its seal on the style. Appropriately, Bluebeard himself takes
the stage in the second scene, though admittedly it is Bluebeard closer
to actuality and remoter from fairy-tale than usual, in a poise that the
whole scene reflects. Joan appears here in the usual masculine garb of the
Principal Boy for the first time, and the extent to which Shaw's characterization of her is a refinement on the type of Jack or Dick (who
grows up to play Widow Twankey) is the more evident: her self-confidence, her humour, her easy friendliness with all ranks, her brave
attitudes and her bossiness are rooted in the convention; and the language she speaks ('Coom, Bluebeard! Thou canst not fool me. Where be
Dauphin?') is native to no other area. The Dauphin's clowning supplies
her with congenial company. For a moment their shared response to the
appearance and manners of the Duchess de la Trémouille can delude us
into seeing this only other female role in the play as another female
impersonation – an Ugly Sister, perhaps:

> THE DUCHESS (*coldly*). Will you allow me to pass, please?
> JOAN (*hastily rising, and standing back*). Beg pardon, maam, I am sure.

> *The Duchess passes on. Joan stares after her; then whispers to the Dauphin.*
>
> JOAN. Be that Queen?
> CHARLES. No. She thinks she is.
> JOAN (*again staring after the Duchess*). Oo-oo-ooh! (*Her awestruck amazement at the figure cut by the magnificently dressed lady is not wholly complimentary.*)

The epithet for la Trémouille himself follows pat, with no shift of style: 'Who be old Gruff-and-Grum?'

Though he never ceases to cut capers, the Dauphin merely *plays* the fool, while being as astute as any character in the drama. Even in Scene ii, his shrewdness penetrates further into the complexities of an off-stage world than pantomime can usually allow:

> I can tell you that one good treaty is worth ten good fights. These fighting fellows lose all on the treaties that they gain on the fights . . .[1]

His coolly pragmatic viewpoint undercuts Joan's ecstasies even in the Epilogue: 'You people with your heads in the sky spend all your time trying to turn the world upside down.' History played into Shaw's hands by letting the dogs of comedy, Charles and Dunois (who also views Joan soberly and never sees her other than life-size – as Hotchkiss proposes taking Mrs George for granted), survive and prosper through the period of the Epilogue. It also conveniently debarred Charles from the trial scene and the preparations for it, when the sense of make-believe had to be suspended for the intensity of crisis to be complete, and the impression of Joan as a real human being required a playing-down of the stage type. Yet these scenes substitute another clown for the Dauphin: the Chaplain to Warwick, de Stogumber, whose absurdity modulates readily into pathos.

Though politically they are on opposite sides, there is a perceptible similarity between de Stogumber and Joan. Both are innocents, country folk and patriots, out of their depth among men of subtler, more sophisticated mind. But the Chaplain is a representative of the common man, and Joan of the extraordinary, 'original' human being; the fault he exposes is lack of imaginative understanding, whereas she plays into her judges' hands through the power of her imagination, the fact that she thinks in images. Apart from this, his commonplace ignorance, prejudice and self-righteousness, the narrow bigotry of his nationalism and anti-Catholicism, caricature the attitudes of her more heroic personality at the same time as they make him a figure of the crude English philistinism which was Shaw's perpetual Aunt Sally. By balancing the two simpletons in his design, Shaw effectively throws into relief the questionableness of

[1] This had a topical edge after Versailles, of course.

the principles Joan represents. 'Sancta simplicitas!' is the blessing Cauchon confers upon de Stogumber's folly and the cruelty it embraces. Her friend, the Dauphin, is less able to contain his impatience with Joan's self-justified fanaticism, the awkward and obstinate aspect of original genius:

> It always comes back to the same thing. She is right; and everyone else is wrong.

Charles and Dunois do more than the other characters in the play to keep Joan a natural size and unfalsified by glamour. (It may be worth remarking that, in general type, Charles is a more stylized version of the Shavian Caesar and Dunois a less flamboyant, more mature Apollodorus.) Dunois, in particular, responds to her with a liking that never disturbs his judgement, or his sense of professional superiority. He has no doubt about how much of the credit is due to Joan, how much to himself, and no doubt that, when she is captured, he can do without her:

> Yes: I shall drive them out . . . I have learnt my lesson, and taken their measure . . . I have beaten them before; and I shall beat them again.[1]

His freedom from infatuation enables him to foretell her fate on reasonable grounds, and there is a Cromwellian balance that she notably lacks in his hard, practical sense, untainted by any superstition:

> I tell you as a soldier that God is no man's daily drudge, and no maid's either . . . once on your feet you must fight with all your might and all your craft.

He is as brutal as Undershaft in his verdict on mere idealism:

> . . . some day she will go ahead when she has only ten men to do the work of a hundred. And then she will find that God is on the side of the big battalions.

Under so clear and realistic a gaze, Joan's complaint that 'the world is too wicked for me' sounds less like pride of spiritual perfection than a sigh of naïve despair that the world is not simple.

In the Epilogue, the *revenante* Joan can be allowed a more sophisticated understanding of things. Her raillery of Cauchon (who is the tragic figure of the Epilogue) – 'Still dreaming of justice, Peter? See what justice came to with me!' – is not so much glibly satiric of the ways of the public world as lucidly perceptive of the truth to which this play, with its trial

---

[1] A sign of careless haste in the writing of the play is the occurrence at least three times in the text of the same rational explanation of the French failure in warfare before Joan's coming and success after: Joan herself makes the necessary criticism in the first scene; Dunois explains the matter to her in the fifth, only to have her explain it back to him a few moments later.

scene, testifies as absolutely as *The Doctor's Dilemma* did in its lighter
vein: that justice, if it is more than a game, is an ideal which it is not
desirable to have translated into actual terms. The dramatic verdict of
Saint Joan, too, goes against justice in favour of irony: the ability to
perceive and weigh all the issues and, if choice is compelled, to preserve
a knowledge of its provisional and limited validity. Such irony recognizes
what is admirable in the heroic nature, but won't follow it to hell. So
Charles adds his share to the *Te Deum*:

> The unpretending praise thee, because thou hast taken upon thyself the
> heroic burdens that are too heavy for them.

Yet it is part of the expansive ironic vision that it should know its own
weakness: its very lack of the direct simplicity, the absolute commitment,
which is the virtue of the saint and, apart from which, the cynical
Warwicks possess the world. For all Shaw's conscious ingenuity in structuring the play, *Saint Joan* has often been found less than satisfactory by
critics, mechanical, facile, or puerile in its incidental effects; yet the
central character transcends the play as an imaginative creation. Whereas
the writing of the play was not a protracted business,[1] the figure of
Joan had long been growing in the dramatist's consciousness as an image
of his profoundest dream.

Actresses who either overplay the erotic attractiveness of Joan, or sup-
press it altogether, fail in the role. For Shaw's view fluctuates and,
though it is faint and subtle and shouldn't protrude on consciousness at
all, the feminine erotic quality faintly colours the figure. (It may be
worth comparing Shakespeare's Viola who, like Joan, appears in woman's
clothing only briefly at the beginning of the play – and was, of course,
a more thoroughly androgynous figure in Shakespeare's theatre than in
the theatre of Shaw's day.) The kind of appeal this has for audiences
and readers recalls the appeal of Dick Dudgeon, in *The Devil's Disciple*,
where Shaw utilized the glamour of one type of romantic hero as a
vehicle for the serious revision of values. Joan's charm depends on her
equal rejection of the Victorian womanly ideal and the identity of
fashionable, elegant woman-of-the-world type, or *femme fatale* as it
appears to others than men-of-the-world, as Victorian popular instinct had
rejected them in its cult of the Principal Boy, more vulgar, even sexually
more vital and less insipid than the romantic heroine of pantomime.
Joan contains too much that is redolent of the popular stage and in-
dicative of the sturdy peasant[2] for the neurotic associations of the New

[1] See note 1 on p. 253.
[2] Shaw lacked Brecht's ability to draw a credibly earthy character, a Grusha;
but then he was concerned with a sophisticated social ideal, not with a personi-

Woman to corrode her image, though play and Preface accept the likelihood that the historical soldier-girl's mission was fired to some extent
by abnormal sexuality.

The relevance of the Court's questions about her male attire is endorsed
by Joan's own reference to the breach-of-promise case ('I never promised
him. I am a soldier: I do not want to be thought of as a woman. I will
not dress as a woman'), by her assertion that she has only a soldier's
responsiveness to children and, with strongest emphasis from the inventive dramatist himself, by her summing up in the Epilogue, that if she
had been a man, 'I should not have bothered you all so much then.'
Shaw was not intent on a realistic psychological study and, in fact, gives
shifting impressions even of Joan's sexual nature that tend away from
realism. If she appears sometimes asexual, still Baudricourt is able to
suspect, at the start of the play, that Bertrand de Poulengey has a sexual
interest in her and, though she is 'no beauty', she is deliberately associated with Dunois, 'the brave Dunois, the handsome Dunois, the wonder-
ful invincible Dunois, the darling of all the ladies, the beautiful bastard',
who is cut out to be the romantic lead and lends her something of his own
more conventional charm. In his company she appears unmistakably the
most feminine creature in the play's sexual spectrum, perhaps something
of a daughter-figure; though even here Shaw manages a sleight-of-hand
with the lyrical scene on the banks of the Loire: there is a slight but
definite touch of the troubadour about Dunois, as the blue flash of the
kingfisher conspires to suggest that the coming of Joan to him, despite
the disguise of her armour and bobbed hair and country bourgeois
manner, has some quality of a visitation by the Virgin to her knight.
'Mary in the blue snood, kingfisher color' is very weak poetry, and the
whole scene verges perilously on whimsy, so that only its brevity in the
playing can save it; but the conception is evident, and the kingfisher as a
traditional symbol of Christ (as it is used by G. M. Hopkins) becomes an
attribute of the androgynous Shavian saint. 'Throughout the ages',
A. J. L. Busst has remarked, 'the mystical tradition has considered
Christ an androgyne, from gnosticism through Jacob Boehme to Mme
Blavatsky.'[1] Auguste Comte recommended the worship of Joan of Arc
as an exceptional woman 'whom theologians have been afraid to recognize' for 'It was feared not without reason, that to consider Joan of Arc

---

fication of natural instinct. Brecht would hardly have failed, as Shaw does, in
the lyric scene before Orleans.
[1] See 'The Androgyne' in Ian Fletcher (ed.), *Romantic Mythologies* (London:
Routledge, 1967), p. 7. The relevant passage from Mme Blavatsky comes in
The Secret Doctrine, 2 vols, 2nd ed. (London: Theosophical Publishing Co.,
1888), Vol. II, p. 134.

as a Saint might have the effect of spreading false and dangerous ideas of feminine duty.' He argued the superiority of rational positivism over traditional religion on this basis: 'So far from her apotheosis having an injurious effect on female character, it will afford an opportunity of pointing out the anomalous nature of her career, and the rarity of the conditions which alone could justify it. It is a fresh proof of the advantages accruing to Morality from the relative character of Positivism, which enables it to appreciate exceptional cases without weakening the rules.'[1] More subtly and deeply troubling than either a simply male or female figure could be, the Shavian ideal of human nature, which breaks so shimmeringly from the possibly wrong-headed simpleton, embraces the range from Saviour to heretic. But Joan, unlike Candida, represents an intellectual or moral danger, not an emotional danger. (Youth and inexperience leave the attractiveness of a daughter-figure untouched with the sinister, threatening quality invested in the more powerful mother.) Perhaps the chief source of difference between this play and most of Shaw's is contingent on the fact that no ambivalence is built into the character of the heroine: for once, the centre of the play *is* romantic and generous in feeling, not incorporating fear and dislike in however disguised a form.

Certainly Joan is a figure of the exploring spirit, single and free, not nurse, protector and conserver of life. Shaw associates her with the air ('head in the sky'), with flight ('Are you afraid I will fly away?'), with freedom on the hills, in the light and the wind. The similarity between Joan's impulse towards such freedom and Barbara Undershaft's cry for the wings of a dove is significant: both are ideal figures, as well as idealists who need to work in partnership with practical men and in conditions of practical necessity. Joan's final cry marks her as an impossibilist, a utopian:

O God that madest this beautiful earth, when will it be ready to receive Thy saints? How long, O Lord, how long?

It is a formal, rhetorical close, the last flourish of the work of art; but it also marks the dramatist's release from the strain of maintaining throughout the play a necessary intellectual poise, committed in no direction, not even to irony.[2] His own utopian impulse, already indulged in *Back to*

[1] Trans. J. H. Bridges in Auguste Comte, *System of Positive Polity*, Vol. I, pp. 212–13.

[2] I have discussed *Saint Joan* as an example of the conversion of secular history into myth in 'Where the Action is: The History Play in the Twentieth Century', to be published in the second collection of Kathleen Robinson Drama Lectures (Sydney University Press). The same lecture includes some consideration of *In Good King Charles's Golden Days*.

Methuselah, would find new expression in the prophetic fables, the hypotheses of future history, that so largely occupied his last play-writing years.

15

Farewell to Platonism:
Too True to be Good

The curtain goes up on Act I of *Too True to be Good* to reveal a bed in the centre of the stage: the play's dominant symbol, like the dentist's chair in Act I of *You Never Can Tell*. In both instances, the stage property establishes the scene of a detachable dramatic fable, a prologue or *parade*, advertising the nature and intention of the main play to follow. *Too True* is a dream play; it is also a play of sickness and cure: the doctor appears at the bedside, like the dentist beside the chair; the metaphor of the play as medicine is clearly implied and more familiar than that of the necessary moral operation performed under cover of laughing gas. The Patient's feverish delirium passes into recuperative sleep and, though the entire subsequent action may remain within the dream world, it mirrors the discovery of health.

Whether the Nurse and her partner, the Burglar, are part of the dream from the beginning, or only after the Patient's assault on them has prepared her for a second, healthier slumber, is left doubtful, or even an irrelevant consideration. No more than in *Heartbreak House* (with which this play is linked by the common theme of the burglary of a necklace) can all that happens be accounted *only* a dream; in both plays Shaw has established an irregularity in the distinction between sleeping and waking consciousness. The Patient insists in Act III as in Act I that what happens is contained in her dream, but she herself is presented to us as one of the group, in no way different from the other characters in kind, belonging as they do to both fantasy and reality, or equally to neither. Ibsen had used the same convention to write of the artist as dreamer in *Peer Gynt*. The uncertain hovering between subjective experience and an objective view of the world involves a serious acknowledgement that consciousness is relative and 'reality' evasive. The three adventurers, whose search for 'real life' provides the main line of the action, are thus emissaries of a self-questioning imagination.

Shaw nods to Freud in *Too True to be Good* as he does in *On the Rocks*. In that play Sir Arthur Chavender has as confused a knowledge of the Oedipus complex as he has of Karl Marx. There is no equally overt allusion to psychoanalytical theory in *Too True*, but Harry Smiler, about whom the Nurse tells a remarkable anecdote, suggests the id in Freud's model of the personality:

> Harry wasnt a bad man really; but he couldnt bear dullness. He had a wonderful collection of pistols . . . and at last the temptation was too great and he went and shot the cop . . . all he could say was that it was a sort of fulfilment.

The Elder who emerges arbitrarily from a cave in the last act to deliver a diatribe, and who is identified as the Burglar's father, seems to be the voice of the superego – not of an individual alone, but of an entire society. When the Sergeant, in the neighbouring cave, speaks of the one desire stronger than the desire to kiss a girl being the desire not to be seen doing it, Shaw is presenting his old theme of hypocrisy in terms of libido and inhibition.

The whole play is an extended sketch, minimally suggestive of individual human experience. In Act I, the action develops with the swiftness and aggressive vigour of farce and a matching absence of emotional resonance. Shaw presents a domestic parable of a sick girl and her over-protective mother in the style of an animated tableau, easily translatable into abstract terms. Of the characters involved in the first scene, the Patient is unconscious, her mother, Mrs Mopply, is a type-caricature, the Doctor has no personal name at all, and the Monster (or Microbe) advertises the preposterousness of the whole affair by his presence and interposes a burlesque running-commentary which checks any possibility of the audience's direct involvement with any of the human *personae*. This last character may well have suggested itself to Shaw after Barry Jackson's presentation of *The Insect Play* at the Birmingham Repertory Theatre.[1] More typical examples of Expressionist drama, introduced to English audiences by the same company, provided a theatrical context for the grotesqueness and logical discontinuity of *Too True*, though the play's manner was a straight development out of the earlier Shavian extravaganzas (especially *Misalliance* and *Heartbreak House*). The violence of Expressionist imagery and its relation to mass emotion are unparalleled in *Too True*. Shaw has not directly imitated Expressionist techniques of dehumanization, as the concept of society

[1] See above, Chapter 13, p. 233, note 1. Barry Jackson also presented St John Hankin's *The Burglar Who Failed*, which may have suggested the burglary episode in this play to Shaw.

as a machine is hardly relevant here. Yet this play has moved considerably beyond *Heartbreak House* in the direction of abstraction and dehumanization.

Its very general significance is suggested by a dialogue heavily reliant on an abstract and public vocabulary: 'disease', 'cure', 'prescription', 'constitution' and 'change' are reiterated and call out a mental response. Another means to the same end is the send-up of melodramatic – almost Gothic – rhetoric in such lines as:

> There must be some deep-rooted cause;
> She is my only surviving child . . . Why do they all die?
> Who knows? It may have lurked here since the house was built.

It hardly needs Mrs Mopply's account of the previous doctor ('He tore aside the curtain and let the blazing sunlight into the room, though she cannot bear it without green spectacles. He opened the windows and let in all the cold morning air') to confirm a mocking resemblance to the heavily symbolic overtones of Ibsen's social plays. The punning name of the old family doctor, Newland, confirms the area of the play's relevance with a glibness characteristic of the whole dramatic mode.

The final, 'awakening' speech, delivered at the end of Act III, looks back as an epilogue on the whole play and comments on the characters:

> There is something fantastic about them, something unreal and perverse, something profoundly unsatisfactory. They are too absurd to be believed in; yet they are not fictions: the newspapers are full of them . . .

They are, in fact, images of people, counters to which meaning is arbitrarily attached, as the Burglar gives significant labels to the clothes he itemizes, at the end of Act I. They move through the play like the images which fill dreams very close to consciousness, divested of emotional colouring, unburdened with profound significance, but disposing themselves perversely, waywardly escaping the logical discipline of conscious thought. The play's violation of orthodox standards of coherence in its dramatic structure and development of themes, the succession of random occurrences it offers, and the loosely attached, meandering discussion, can be viewed as deliberate reflections of the confused contemporary world, the unsettling of traditional manners and values and general disturbance of mind in the post-World War I generation. But these features also represent the efforts of the rational mind to maintain control and impose an intelligible pattern, under pressure and close to breaking down. Shaw often applied the term 'fantastic' to his later work; the definition of it implied in that last speech – 'unreal', 'profoundly unsatisfactory', 'too absurd to be believed', 'the newspapers are full of them' – evokes the antonym 'imaginative', with its connotations of the real, the profound and convincing, the power that converts fact into vital truth. These characters in search of 'real life' lack it as characters precisely because their author has not created them imaginatively, has not made them out of material discovered by exploring his own darkness.

It is not that Shaw has inadvertently exposed his own limitations and revealed the shallowness of his enlightenment. Paradoxically, he has turned the play as a whole into an imaginative statement out of his self-critical recognition of these things. He stands outside his invention and lets its brittleness and thinness work disturbingly upon us, more disturbingly as the credibility of the surface structure fails without any accompanying breakthrough from deeper levels. *On the Rocks*, or even *Heartbreak House*, counterpoints Platonic rationalism with emotional anarchism; *Too True* stands simply, negatively, for Shaw's intellectual rejection of reason as a saving power.

The dialogue is overtly concerned with a crisis of belief – from the Doctor's association of healthy life with faith to the Elder's lament for the loss of his faith in atheism and Aubrey's final testimony to the faith he cannot find. Aubrey, the preacher without a message, has often been regarded as Shaw's satirical self-portrait and his last speech interpreted as Shaw's confession of the bankruptcy of his own thought. But it is reason's negatives that have failed, not any particular creed; and Aubrey, though he does take over from the Microbe a choric function in the play, combines it aptly with his role as a personification of reason in an allegory of the human faculties. This is first established in the partnership that breaks in upon the Patient's security: 'in our firm I am the brains: you are the hand,' 'asserts Aubrey as the Burglar to the Nurse (Sweetie). In Act II, Sweetie acknowledges that it is her office to bring a cushion for his head ('She has a conscience as a chamber-maid and none as a woman'), so that he may discourse at his ease of 'higher centres' and 'lower centres':

> Our lower centres act: they act with a terrible power that sometimes destroys us; but they don't talk. Speech belongs to the higher centres. In all the great poetry and literature of the world the higher centres speak . . .

His complacent delivery of this fragment of potted Nietzsche and the parrotted D. H. Lawrence that follows is comic in itself. Sweetie and the Patient ridicule and oppose his arrogant pretensions. The latter finds him an amusing fool but not 'real' as Sweetie is real: 'Men are not real: they're all talk, talk, talk'. He is obviously classifiable among the Shavian clowns who evade reality through words and moral attitudes, as the final curtain comes down on him ceaselessly, mechanically articulating as the mists rise and engulf him:

> I am by nature and destiny a preacher . . . I must preach and preach and preach no matter how late the hour and how short the day, no matter whether I have nothing to say . . .

Aubrey's father, the Elder, is appalled at his son's rascality. The play shows it up as the clownish rascality of intellection masquerading as the master-faculty – a species of theft. It is apt that the function of interpreting – and limiting – the play should be usurped by such a character. The dramatist's ironic detachment from Aubrey implies a wider and less dogmatic view.

The irony seems to be at work when Aubrey identifies Sweetie with the 'lower centres' and her conversation with the utterance of Balaam's Ass. Aubrey glances satirically at his memory of the tutor who told him improper stories, but it is still impropriety that shocks him, when Sweetie's vulgarity 'gives the show away'. (His own method is to 'be frank up to the point at which we should lose money by it'.) There is no true representative of the 'lower centres' within the play. The convention, with its tendency to externalize values, hardly allows of it, and Aubrey's identification of social indiscretion and the shedding of disguises to reveal the naked mind with the miraculous revelation of unconscious forces and irrational motives is a mark of the inadequacies of the dramatic form as well as of his own lack of insight. As a personification of appetite, Sweetie is unconvincing; Lawrence's phrase, 'sex in the head', can be meaningfully applied to her, and her snobbish aping of aristocracy is a measure of her general unauthenticity. Aubrey the rationalizer, who can promptly hail her sexual promiscuity as 'mobility . . . a mark of civilization', is carried away by theory into just such errors of judgement as Tanner in his defence of Violet.

The general distinction between higher centres and lower centres has a social application in the contrast between the 'vulgar' characters – the lower orders – Sweetie and the Sergeant, on the one hand, and their social 'superiors'. Aubrey's snobbery and his father's puritanical atheism are related in their need to reject certain aspects of reality as base. Neither is concerned with the devaluation of some human qualities whereby others are aggrandized, as in the sacrifice of common human feeling to the development of intellect, or of physical grace to moral virtue – or the sacrifice of truth to politeness. The grouping of the officer, Colonel Tallboys, with Private Meek offers more than another example of class distinction: here the one figure represents the aristocratic, or hierarchical, principle while the other is symbolic of human equality.

The image of Balaam's Ass is reinforced by a metaphor used by the Elder:

> Purpose and Design, the pretexts for all the vilest superstitions, have risen from the dead to cast down the mighty from their seats and put paper crowns on presumptuous fools.

The theme of the inversion of authority, the transference of power to 'the ranks', is enacted sufficiently clearly to establish the play as a ritual feast of fools,[1] of whom Aubrey is the most presumptuous. He himself, like a minor prophet, laments the state of the post-war world in which the lower centres 'speak truths that have never been spoken before – truths that the makers of our domestic institutions have tried to ignore. And now that Sweetie goes shouting them all over the place, the institutions are rocking and splitting and sundering.' Aubrey may seem to get off scot-free, but the play's farcical-symbolic climax, a blow to the head, enlightening by physical shock, is certainly a jest at his expense. It is a blow to the 'domestic institutions', too, in the person of the mother-figure, Mrs Mopply. What is achieved is no simple inversion, or exchange of roles, no simply mechanical revolution, but the liberation of the tyrant with the destruction of the hierarchical principle.

The Doctor foretells this climax:

Mark my words: someday somebody will fetch her a clout over the head. Somebody who can afford to.

The somebody is Colonel Tallboys, but the time is not ripe until he has learnt to respect Private Meek, who combines the function of 'intelligence orderly' with 'carpentering, painting, digging, pulling and hauling, fetching and carrying, helping himself and everybody else'. Meek emerges as the unchanging ideal figure of the play, omnicompetent, 'never at a loss'. Colonel Tallboys's blow is shortly followed by the statement: 'I see this man Meek doing everything that is natural to a complete man.' Wholeness, not intellectuality, or rational control of the passions, is now recognized as the desirable goal. The character Shaw singled out (in the final note) as his favourite, the Patient, comes to it by another route. Reverting from over-civilization to sham barbarism, she discovers the insufficiency of healthy animal nature and the importance of moral and social responsibility to a full and satisfying human life. The excuse she offers for her disguise, 'One has so much more control of the house as a servant than as a mistress nowadays', matches Meek's claim to have a 'freer hand' while he remains in the ranks, and the truth of Colonel Tallboys's retort, '. . . one controls a regiment much more effectively as a private than as a colonel, eh?', which Meek promptly demonstrates. In Meek, Shaw presents a human being defiant of categories, in whom intellect is no thief and labour no subordination. The alliance Sweetie

[1] Had Shaw read E. K. Chambers on the Feast of Fools, Feast of the Ass and Lord of Misrule in *The Medieval Stage*, 2 vols. (London: O.U.P., 1903; reprinted 1925)?

ultimately makes with the Sergeant and the Patient with Mrs Mopply
are alternative versions of the same ideal.

This, then, is the quality of 'real life' that all the characters have
sought and that has been identified by association with the traditional
religious concept of eternal life, or the way of salvation. Poverty and
ordinary social oppression have no place in *Too True*; the chief evils the
characters suffer are lack of purpose and lack of responsibility, which by
their absence render life 'unreal'. According to the Doctor, the Patient
is ill because she has delegated to others responsibility for her health. Her
mother's officious and intrusive care for her, excessively fearful for her,
over-protective of her, repeats the motif of Sartorius's over-indulgence
of Blanche; and it is significant that what first rouses the Patient's
energies is the threat to her property: the instinct of possession, the
passion of ownership, is the most vital force in her as in Blanche. Until
she is aware of the threat, Miss Mopply can hardly be said to enjoy the
possession of her jewels, as in the golden age the Rhine Maidens lived in
aesthetic enjoyment of their gold. Her unconscious state corresponds to the
unrealized value betokened in pearls and blue diamonds.[1] Aubrey's
description of the scene – a lake surrounded by mountains – in which he
and Sweetie conceived their plan of stealing the necklace is more like an
image of the golden age, evocative of the scene of *Rhinegold*, even while
its flippancy throws into relief the falseness of all such romantic myths:
the 'shallop' is the cheapest kind of dream-boat. Aubrey can hardly be
identified, except in name, with the Alberic *The Perfect Wagnerite*
describes as compensating for denial of love in his greed for wealth.[2] In
keeping with his role as Preacher, spokesman for the 'higher centres', he
interprets the Patient's sickness as spiritual and urges the selling of the
necklace as first condition for finding health:

> You think you are in a state of illness. Youre not: youre in a state of sin.
> Sell the necklace and buy your salvation with the proceeds.

It is to be the means to a golden age that never yet was, a 'real', rich,
exciting life – with the connotations of 'eternal life'.

The principles of law and the lie, prominent in Shaw's reading of *The
Ring*, in *The Perfect Wagnerite*, are certainly germane to *Too True*.
The evasion, or destruction, of law is necessary in a bid for freedom.

[1] There may be a reminiscence of Marx's use of the fable of pearls and diamonds in the first chapter of *Capital*, a part of the work that Shaw is generally
acknowledged to have read.
[2] In fact Aubrey is much more like Shaw's description of Loki, 'god of Intellect, Argument, Imagination, Illusion, and Reason' – 'he has no moral passion:
indignation is as absurd to him as enthusiasm . . . having a touch of the comic
spirit in him . . .'

So Aubrey and Sweetie defy law by becoming thieves, 'spoiling the Egyptians'; together with the Patient they run from Mrs Mopply, the figure of life-stifling authority, law in its decrepitude. Harry Smiler's killing of a policeman and subsequent trial for his life give Sweetie an image of the intenser existence she craves. (It is recognizably analogous to the vision of Judgement presented in *The Simpleton*, with its substitution of responsibility for intimidation.) The masquerade in fancy-dress under assumed identities is an obvious form of the lie (Shaw again draws heavily on the clothes-philosophy of *Sartor Resartus* in this play) whereby the three runaways evade capture by the forces of order and justice in the form of an imperial military expedition. Their gain is the veriest illusion of freedom, as they do in fact fall into the pattern of the greater lie: the actual social conspiracy between government and the appearances of wealth, rank and culture. Aubrey is perfectly aware of the basis of established society, its strength and unity:

> The first lesson a crook has to learn, darling, is that nothing succeeds like lying. Make any statement that is so true that it has been staring us in the face all our lives, and the whole world will rise up and passionately contradict you. If you dont withdraw and apologize, it will be the worse for you. But just tell a thundering silly lie that everyone knows is a lie, and a murmur of pleased assent will hum up from every quarter of the globe.

And it is by choosing to 'give the whole show away' that they finally do achieve liberation. The lie goes when law, in the form of hierarchical authority, is dispelled.

Medea is the mother-figure Shaw has chosen to preside over this play. 'Medea! Medea!' murmurs the Elder. Punningly, Mrs Mopply retorts, 'It isn't an idea: it's the truth.' The ambivalence of Mrs Mopply's care for her children is clear: her excessive fears on their behalf have determined their death. Aubrey's recollections of the war ('I was hardly more than a boy when I first dropped a bomb on a sleeping village . . . Later on I swooped into a street and sent machine gun bullets into a crowd of civilians: women, children, and all') provide the same topical focus for the thought as was central to *Back to Methuselah*. The cry of the nations for security, to which Aubrey refers in Act I, is naturally and inevitably counterbalanced by Harry Smiler's playing with pistols, 'for the romance of it': another of the unhealthy polarities the play presents. The horror of war itself is thus connected with the split between 'higher' and 'lower', the public attitudes of the parent-figures and the hidden will expressed in atrocious deeds.

It takes the thwack of Colonel Tallboys's umbrella to restore Mrs Mopply to the 'real self' she never has known. It destroys the mother and reveals the woman with 'sixty years of a misspent life to make up for'.

With the return of her self-interest and her rejection of the self-sacrificial role, an equality is established between her and the Patient that makes relationship possible and tolerable without driving out life. Her liberation involves discovery of the truth preached by the Burglar at the end of Act I:

> . . . what sense is there in this world of hazards, disasters, elations and vic-
> tories, except as a field for the adventures of the life everlasting? In vain
> do we disfigure our streets with scrawls of Safety First: in vain do the nations
> clamor for Security, security, security. They who cry Safety First never
> cross the street: the empires which sacrifice life to security find it in the
> grave. For me Safety Last; and Forward, Forward, always For –

Oddly, but interestingly, the tone of her invitation to the Patient ('Ive taken a fancy to you. You come with me, darling. I have lots of money . . . you will have a good time with me,') carries an echo of Kitty Warren wheedling her daughter as she has been used to wheedle the girls she recruited for her brothels. The association Mrs Mopply intends is free, not based on mutual dependence, and it matches her daughter's rejection of clinging women, women afflicted by the 'chill of poverty' (which, in the play's definition, is poverty of life), women who do not share in the common experiences of humanity. The farcical device of a physical blow links this play's climax with the two blows with a loy (the first, off stage, accidental and the second, on stage, deliberate) through which Christy Mahon, in Synge's *The Playboy of the Western World*, achieved his freedom from Oedipal bondage and his progress to independent maturity. Mrs Mopply follows her daughter from the stage, as old Mahon, lost between wonder and admiration, follows Christy; but the suggestion of a reversal of roles is fainter, in Shaw's play, than the anarchist assertion: 'I want a world without parents: there is no room for them in my dream.' The relationship of Aubrey to the Elder is, in its detail, only roughly parallel to that between Miss Mopply and her mother; not only have father and son already parted company at the start of the play (allegoric- ally suggestive of the abandonment of traditional moral authority), but the revelation is made that Aubrey's mother had already set him at odds with his father in childhood. Some reconciliation between them there is, when the latter gives his benediction to Aubrey's assumption of the mantle of the preacher and himself retires into the recesses of the cave labelled 'Sñ Pauls'. The hint of a withdrawal of external authority, leaving man self-responsible, keeper of his own conscience, is given variant expression in the Sergeant who reads Bunyan and has discovered the need for every man to be his own spiritual guide or theologian. The alliance confirmed between Sweetie and the Sergeant is in the spirit of the new Mopply 'sisterhood' as it, too, involves acceptance of human ordinariness ('Valbrioni be blowed! My name is Susan Simpkins.' – 'Well I dont mind keeping company for a while, Susan, to see how we get along together.') and the fact that humanity is not by nature functionally specialized:

> . . . men and women have a top storey as well as a ground floor; and you cant have the one without the other.

As a treatment of public themes the play fits in with Marxist tradition. It is concerned with work and leisure (Tallboys has spent his leisure profitably – until his leisure activity is recognized as valuable work) and the confusion between leisure and freedom. Empty leisure is identifiable as the *cause* of the Patient's sickness in Act I (the agent is Mrs Mopply): she is ill because she can pay others to cure her instead of curing herself, which would be hard work in recognition of self-responsibility. The doctor's own freedom and power are limited by the economic relationship which robs the Patient of wholeness. He is the first of the 'parasites' mentioned in the play: those whose work is degraded by its subordination to the commercial principle (the text explores the range of economic euphemisms – 'pay', 'earn', 'bribe', 'give', 'afford', 'buy') and whose place in society is defined by functional relationships instead of human relationships. In this context, the pearl necklace may be taken as an image of 'dead' value, the reality of human labour converted into the fetish of property.[1] In the presentation of Meek as the exemplary figure of the Complete Man, Shaw presents the positive counterpoint to Marx's – and William Morris's – view of the division of labour and the artificial separation of work from leisure,[2] as impoverishing the individual life. The class difference between Aubrey and Sweetie corresponds to the divorce of labour (the hands) from culture (the brains). The irrelevance of such a culture is exposed, and its narcissistic quality, unable to see through its own verbalization and rationalization to the truth. The Patient's nickname is meaningful: as Mops she is maid-of-all-work, finding her freedom in the combination of moral purpose in society with practicality.

But the play as a private document is at least equally consistent: in part a reaction to the speeding up of history by World War I and the consequent insecurity at the drastic change in a world gone far ahead of individual consciousness, with a power to outrage the former iconoclast, it also reveals the subjective core of the old ideals/disillusion theme in earlier Shaw plays: the dramatist's wish to escape from and through his

---

[1] See *Capital*, loc. cit.

[2] The recognition of Tallboys's achievement as a water-colourist is a minor variant of the positive view.

own fantasy to a more direct and keener apprehension of life. The apocalyptic images of Aubrey's final oration have an invocatory effect:

> The iron lightning of war has burnt great rents in these angelic veils . . . Our souls go in rags now . . .[1]

But the rhetoric is itself the most impenetrable of the veils and, despite his comparative youth, Aubrey is as vulnerable as the Elderly Gentleman of *Back to Methuselah*:

> When the old woman had the mask struck from her soul and revelled in it instead of dying of it – I shrank from the revelation as from a wind bringing from the unknown regions of the future a breath which may be a breath of life, but of a life too keen for me to bear, and therefore for me a blast of death.

He and the Elder are alike aware of the acceptance of truth and readiness for life, in the others, as an experience of falling, 'falling through the bottomless abyss', 'falling, falling, falling endlessly and hopelessly through a void in which they can find no footing'. The description corresponds, of course, to the awaking dream; the gloomy connotations of guilt and disaster cling to it – but apparently for those two characters alone, for Mrs Mopply's cheerful response is: 'you have just hit it: I don't know my head from my heels'.

Too True is a long way from the easy exuberance of *You Never Can Tell*. Not one of the characters, apart from Meek, is consistently engaging. What they all certainly demonstrate is a vigorous briskness. The aggressiveness of farcical comedy survives here, but it is rather joyless and frenetic. The one incident that stands out in contrast to this general effect is the conversion of Mrs Mopply, which leaves her with the friendliest feeling for her assailant, to whom she gives a kiss of naturally Christian forgiveness. She has in fact become a new person who discards her old personality without wasting time in regret or resentment.

For all its seeming randomness, the play is not weak in structure or dramatic rhythm. The two sections of Act I balance each other, in that the first, and more obviously fantastic, presents an expository tableau and the second a rapidly developing action in which the sense of pace is increased by the physical tussle in which the Patient '*knock*[s] *the wind out of the rascal*', as the final note on the play puts it. The dressing of the Patient gives the occasion for the first of the play's long speeches – technically, it is a soliloquy, though in effect the actor coming forward to

---

[1] The eschatological image is apt in the context of the dream of falling – which overlays the fear of death (intensified by a sense of the rapidity of change) with the puritan moralist's fear of perdition. By contrast, Mrs Mopply's 'resurrection' involves the acceptance of change and mobility as good = true, bringing in its train the aesthetic realization that it is good = beautiful.

address the audience moves half out of character to do so; and it contrasts with the Doctor's 'dialogue' with the Monster, which is nearer true soliloquy, though not so technically. It is the Monster who speaks the true epilogue for Act I:

> The play is now virtually over; but the characters will discuss it at great length for two acts more. The exit doors are all in order. Goodnight.

Nothing contributes more to the liveliness of Shaw's later work than such playful shifting in and out of illusion. It is typical of true comic drama in its representation of the dramatist as an entertainer in open communication with the audience, not hidden by the play into which the audience may be imaginatively absorbed. The statement quoted here is misleading, in that it does not prepare for the change of scene and the shift to a later stage in the story. Indeed there is no formal discussion of Act I and altogether very little disquisition in the earlier Shavian sense of the word (cf. *Getting Married*). Instead, the allegory of Act I is developed and, perhaps, as it develops the values may become clearer. Surprisingly, it opens with new characters, Meek and Tallboys, and already Meek appears in the guise of Messenger. The dialogue is straight exchange of questions and answers; gradually, as the other characters appear, the incidence of longish speeches increases, and frequently these longer speeches give the effect of self-contained units which the characters take turns to deliver; though the general pattern of a wrangle holds Aubrey, Sweetie and Mops in mutual relationship, they seem to compromise between listening and talking to each other and communicating more directly with us. Aubrey's explanation of the system based on lies is the first climax, his Balaam's Ass speech (made less formal by a mid-way interruption from Sweetie) provides the next; almost immediately the lead passes to Sweetie for her anecdote of Harry Smiler; then it is Mops's turn for a two-part declaration, with a longer interruption than in Aubrey's, before the reversal, the peroration and anticlimax:

> The truth is, I am free; I am healthy; I am happy; and I am utterly miserable. (*Turning on Aubrey*) Do you hear? Utterly miserable.

That final repetition turns the anticlimax emphatically into a full close. Shortly afterwards, the return of Tallboys ushers in a further episode of action (the battle of the maroons) and its aftermath, leading to Tallboys's self-explanation and the voice of Sweetie as Countess before the full close to the act:

> I paint pictures to make me feel sane. Dealing with men and women makes me feel mad. Humanity always fails me: Nature never.

The words recall Sempronius of *The Apple Cart* ('happy as a man in a
picture gallery looking at the dawns and sunsets, the changing seasons,
the continuous miracle of life ever renewing itself'); they also define the
nature of Shaw's later plays: catastrophes in the short run, but set in a
cosmic perspective that allows the comic poise to be preserved.

The setting of the last act emphasizes the rhetorical character of part
of the dialogue and the limited nature of the action: two rostra, side-by-
side, hold other figures new to the audience. The effect – with each
rostrum projecting from the floor of a cave – is like that of the enshrined
figures in *The Simpleton*: it is a simple way of isolating contrasted symbols
and emphasizing the association of characters with ideas while not
diminishing the substantial humanity of the actors. The contrast is between the protestantism of the Sergeant, privately searching for truth,
and the professed atheism of the Elder: like the Black Girl, the former
discovers the inadequacies of the received scriptures, particularly the Old
Testament, without losing his religious faculty or his hope, whereas the
Elder's rejection of religion entire leaves him barren and sour. When
Sweetie joins the Sergeant under the sign *Αγαπεμονε* and the Elder
still holds his solitary place in 'Sñ Pauls', the contrast between natural
balance and distortion acquires further associations of the acceptance
versus the rejection of sex-equality. The schematic tendency at work in
the visual structuring of the act is matched by the theatrical formalism
represented in the Sergeant's 'sermon' on the text of *Pilgrim's Progress*
and the Old Testament, followed by the Elder's tirade, extremely loosely
linked into the fabric of the neighbouring dialogue. After this, a duet
between father and son occupies attention until the first entrance of
Mrs Mopply. An ensemble passage leads up to the comically violent
climax, after which Meek reappears as Messenger bestowing honours
upon Tallboys, whose epigram

> Justice is none the less justice though it is always delayed, and finally done
> by mistake . . .

at once recalls Euripidean principle and invites recognition that his
knighthood is most appropriate to his paradoxically knightly bashing of
the old lady. A continuation of the ensemble gives a background for the
solo parts of Tallboys first and then the returned Mrs Mopply, before the
Messenger claims attention again with the passports that signify the
imminent departure of the characters from the stage and the return
from dream to waking consciousness. Gradually Aubrey is left alone on
the stage, lengthily orating to the auditorium until the curtain comes
down on his never-ending talk, of which – ironically – the last words
properly audible are: 'no matter whether I have nothing to say—'. This

is nothing new in the way of Shavian endings: a theatrically effective, perhaps compulsive, undercutting of the whole play at the final curtain.

Acts II and III have both been presented in beach settings. The holiday costumes of Sweetie and Aubrey turn the earlier from a scene of exotic barbarism, reminiscent of the Atlas Mountains in *Captain Brassbound's Conversion*, to an image of that barbarism within civilization, the pleasure-greedy idleness of a moneyed class with nothing responsible to do.in the world. Act III, with its rocks and caves, is more directly suggestive of the world's end. Some remnants of civilized manners and habits may cling to the characters; but the cities are gone. The expeditionary force represents civilized government in this outpost,[1] but its going is like the recall of a Roman legion when the empire is crumbling at the core. The Morality drama has played itself out in the artificial isolation of the stage. The mists from the sea that finally engulf it may reduce clarity to confusion once more, but it is in the confusion that the life outside art persists. Shaw did not forget *The Tempest* after *Heartbreak House*. *Too True to be Good* is another of the late Shavian fables that emulate the late Shakespearian relation of art to life.

[1] Shaw's use of Lawrence of Arabia as his model for Private Meek is not irrelevant, even aesthetically, as the contemporary audience's awareness of it must have helped set the play in the context of debate on Britain's imperial role. The remote locales of both *Too True* and *The Simpleton* correspond to the turning of Shaw's political concerns beyond national confines to explore the relation of Britain to the rest of the world, a change of direction that culminates in the internationalism of *Geneva*.

16

Eschatological Plays

J. B. Kaye has noted Shaw's addiction to Carlyle's metaphor of the political leader as a pilot whose business is to keep the ship off the rocks.[1] It was used prominently in *Heartbreak House* before giving its title to *On the Rocks*, which resembles that previous play in treating the rocks of destruction as the bed-rock of truth, the place of heartbreak, where an end makes a beginning possible.

The end, in the present instance, is the foundering of parliamentary democracy. The contempt earlier plays expressed for mere talkers is here turned on the whole bankrupt system traditionally revered as Britain's political legacy to the world. What Shaw represents as wrong with British democracy in 1933 was even more evidently wrong with it a generation later:

> . . . the difficulty seems to be that you cant do anything. But something's got to be done.
>
> The people of this country, and of all the European countries, and of America, are at present sick of being·told that, thanks to democracy, they are the real government of the country. They know very well that they dont govern and cant govern and know nothing about Government except that it always supports profiteering, and doesnt really respect anything else, no matter what party flag it waves.

While politicians were still conceding that parliamentary democracy might not be a universal political nostrum and a war to preserve it lay ahead, Shaw's spokesman for force states popular opinions bluntly:

> . . . the fellows who make the speeches can be depended on never to do anything else. In the first place, they dont know how. In the second, they are afraid. . . . one of the facts is that nowadays nobody outside the party cliques cares a brass button for the House of Commons.

---

[1] J. B. Kaye, *Bernard Shaw and the Nineteenth-Century Tradition* (Norman, Oklahoma: University of Oklahoma Press, 1958), p. 13.

Plain, dogmatic statement is one of Shaw's strongest rhetorical weapons, and this play uses it to maximum advantage, fantasy, irony and farce merely setting off the most exciting passages: the long speeches of political analysis and indictment. It is a style that clears the air of mental confusion and moral doubt. It clears away protective evasions so that the devil may get his due and his arguments be listened to, in the absence of other counsel.

'You cant frighten me with a word like dictator,' declares Old Hipney, the disillusioned Labour leader who is the mephistophelean tempter of this play. Shaw's later reputation has suffered, with that of numerous other artists of the day, on account of his willingness to concede virtues to fascism. His exact stance is perhaps better defined in *On the Rocks* than anywhere else in his drama. The play is remarkable for its goading attacks on the proletariat ('weve known ever since we gave them the vote that theyd submit to anything'; 'The poor silly sheep . . . didnt notice: they didnt remember: they couldnt understand: they were taken in by any nonsense they heard at the meetings or read in the morning paper . . . Adult suffrage . . . delivered us into the hands of our spoilers and oppressors, bound hand and foot by our own folly and ignorance'), combined with a generally sympathetic treatment of an aristocracy fit for little but retirement to the neighbourhood of a good golf course. It distinguishes sharply between knowledge of what ought to be done and the power to do it and, in effect, confronts its audiences with a choice between rationally approved and passionately desired alternatives. The case for benevolent tyranny is conclusively argued, then blown to bits by the emotional assault of the play's finale: a patriotic call to revolution and the rejection of official oppression. The suffering, hungry, confused and inarticulately protesting mob of unemployed that, especially at the beginning and end, seems to besiege the visible stage, a quiet area of critical thought and debate, is not just a realistic reflection of contemporary economic troubles that Shaw's theatre does not wish to obliterate; it represents the force of impulses that the play as argument deliberately holds in check.

Fascism is seen as the logical consequence of the political ignorance, indolence and fatalism of the English people. If they didn't like the prospect, they could avoid it. The political fable of *On the Rocks* is concerned with the rejection of opportunity: a Prime Minister converted to pure socialism outlines a political programme that will save the country; sectional interests at all levels of society make it impossible for him to put the proposed measures through.[1] As surely as the Epilogue to *Saint Joan*,

[1] The Depression and the economic crisis which hit the first Labour Government so hard and resulted in the formation of a National Government in 1931 was the immediate topical background to the events of the play.

this play demonstrates society's rejection of saviours; more precisely, it is a prophecy of its desertion of humanism.

The anti-realistic elements, especially the Morality-play characters of the Lady and Old Hipney (Death and Devil), make it possible to approach the play as the self-communing of an exhausted and over-wrought political leader. Hypothesis is clearly the basis of the action: suppose the country woke one morning to find the head of government converted to radical socialism; suppose he had to find a way of swiftly implementing his new principles; 'Suppose England really did arise!' ('What are you supposing now?' interjects Lady Chavender at the end of the first, privately printed version of the text.[1])

Shaw pointedly introduces the Chief Commissioner of Police, Sir Broadfoot Basham, as the first of the representative figures who confront the Prime Minister, Sir Arthur Chavender. In making his symbol of coercion articulate, the dramatist has also made him intelligent – in defiance of his name – and aware of the limitations of his power. Police action implies the maintenance of order: an external demonstration of the disciplinary powers of the mind pitting themselves against confusion and chaos. Basham's aim does not outrun Chavender's vision. In Act I he is simply concerned to keep potentially destructive elements quiet and harmlessly occupied, and he views party politics as a means to his hand: a convenient circus to distract the masses from their demand for bread. His recognition that effective police discipline depends upon consent is not voiced until Act II ('The police can do nothing unless the people are on the side of the police'). But his awareness of the possibility – and danger – of turning a police force into an army makes him present Chavender, in his first interview, with the unthinkable alternative:

> If you want these crowds settled on soldierly lines, say so; and give me half a dozen machine guns . . . All youll hear is a noise like a watchman's rattle.

In Act II, he conveys the lesson of his experience in Ireland:

> It's easy to sit here and think of exterminating your opponents. But a war of extermination is a massacre . . . and when it comes to the point you cant go through with it . . . You couldnt: you had to back down.

More recent history has confirmed the general truth of this, though we may judge it a failure of humane imagination that led Shaw to underestimate the length to which men would be capable of taking the 'extermination' policy. (Cf. successive changes in the text of *Geneva*, especially on the persecution of the Jews, as discussed by G. Pilecki.)

---

[1] 'On the Rocks: A Poli / tical Fantasy in Two / Acts, by a Fellow of / the Royal Society of Literature. / *First Rough Proof – Unpublished.* / Privately Printed 1933.' This version will later be referred to as the First Rough Proof.

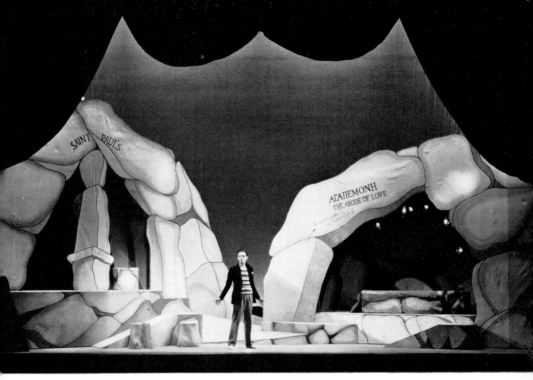

(a) Act III: Theatre Guild, New York, 1932.

20 *Too True to be Good*

(b) Dora Bryan and Kenneth Haigh as Sweetie and the Burglar. Strand Theatre, 1965.

21 *The Simpleton of the Unexpected Isles*. Malvern Festival, 1935 (see p. 293).

21 *The Simpleton of the Unexpected Isles*. Malvern Festival, 1935 (see p. 293).

22 *Geneva*. Saville Theatre, 1938. A Shavian chorus. (Note the Wagnerian helmet.)

Hitler and Stalin have come and gone without disturbing the validity of Old Hipney's conclusion:

> . . . all this country or any country has to stand between it and blue hell is the consciences of them that are capable of governing it.

It may be disappointing to be cast back upon so elementary and moralistic a truism; but Shaw's faith in the unpredictable human element, in men rather than systems, in life rather than in political machinery, deliberately abandons the advocacy of any particular political solution in order to leave the responsibility of judgement and action with his audiences. Chavender himself does add a significant observation to Hipney's:

> Until the men of action clear out the talkers we who have social consciences are at the mercy of those who have none.

(Cf. the treatment of Aubrey in *Too True to be Good*. The Fabians *par excellence* were workers, not talkers.)

The spectacle of the Labour movement hopelessly divided against itself prevents Chavender from believing in class warfare. (It may be noted that he handles the deputation from the Isle of Cats by a skilful brow-beating of the one member of his own class it contains.) What occupies him, instead, is the 'eternal war' between the profiteer and the man of good will to others.[1] In this his natural enemy is the king-pin of the coalition government, Sir Dexter Rightside, whose 'job is to prevent the world from moving' and who entertains the notion of putting the young men of his party into coloured shirts and giving them guns. It seems that strong leadership and discipline is a remedy not to be prejudged. The same doctrine has a more or less contemptuous ring in the mouths of different men:

> HIPNEY. . . . Fifty years after he founded his Red International the working classes of Europe rose up and shot one another down and blew one another to bits, and turned millions and millions of their infant children out to starve in the snow or steal and beg in the sunshine, as if Dr Marx had never been born. And theyd do it again tomorrow if they was set on to do it. Why did you set them on? All they wanted was to be given their job, and fed and made comfortable according to their notion of comfort. If youd done that for them you wouldnt be having all this trouble . . .

> SIR ARTHUR. A rope round a statesman's neck is the only constitutional safeguard that really safeguards. But never fear the rope. As long as we give the people an honest good time we can do just what seems good to us.

---

[1] Cf. (a) 'There is a gulf between Dexy's view of the world and mine. There is the eternal war between those who are in the world for what they can get out of it and those who are in the world to make it a better place for everybody to live in' (*On the Rocks*) and (b) 'There are two ways of looking at this world . . .

K

It is not the doctrine of a demagogue but a return to Platonism, a belief in the responsibility of the intellect.

The condition of unemployment, in more senses than the economic one, is the subject of the play. Chavender has been consuming time so frenziedly that, as his secretary points out, his work has been piling up unattended to, since the parliamentary session began. His wife has no respect for his 'work' anyway, reserving the term for effective action, not activity simply. The 'work' we see him at is inane and prepares us to acquiesce in the Lady's diagnosis of 'an underworked brain . . . a bad case of frivolity, possibly incurable'. The imagery of the first lines of the play (Hilda Hanway's remark that 'the streets are becoming quite impassable with the crowds of unemployed' and Sir Arthur's reply, 'What on earth good do they think they can do themselves by crowding aimlessly about Westminster and the public offices?') is applicable to the whole state of government. Admission that the puritan ethic of work (central to *The Simpleton of the Unexpected Isles*) is the basis of the political indictment made by this play comes in Basham's quotation, 'Satan may find mischief still for idle hands to do', though the aim he himself acknowledges is to keep the hands idle, not turn them to profitable deeds ('The point is to prevent the crowd doing anything, isnt it?'). Lady Chavender herself is hardly more positively occupied. The key-word in Shaw's description of her is 'bored'; she declares herself 'not born for wifing and mothering', quite unable to take any interest in politics or in love affairs; indifference is the quality with which she surprises Aloysia Brollikins, the woman of the people become Marxist borough-councillor, who wants to marry David Chavender; it is hard to credit her husband's fanciful view of her as having 'sacrificed' herself 'to keeping my house and sewing on my buttons' except as an image of conventional propriety. The Chavender children are scarcely in better case: 'Marriage seldom fulfils all our expectations' is Lady Chavender's comment on Aloysia's brash belief that David will 'work for his living'. If he and his sister, Flavia, might indeed do worse than marry Aloysia and the Earl of Barking, it is because they are giving themselves into the charge of dominating personalities:

SIR ARTHUR. May I ask how you have got over her craze for marrying a poor man?

BARKING. . . . she had a glimpse today . . . of what poor men are really like. They were awfully nice to her . . . You see, what she craved for before was their rough manners, their violence, their brutality and filthy language, their savage treatment of their women folk. That was her ideal

---

As a chaos that you fish in for your profit . . . and you can always bring something up. Then there's the world of your idea . . .' (Granville Barker, *His Majesty*, 1928.) See below, pp. 306–140

of a delightful husband. She found today that the working man doesnt realize it. I do.

It is burlesque presentation of the conditions on which a degenerate aristocracy may survive, or even be renewed.

The play is structured, still according to an Ibsen formula, in public and private areas, so as to present a domestic analogy to the political situation. The relation between the two areas is the theme of the speech Chavender rehearses in Act I for delivery at Church House. The contrast between the fantasy he eulogizes ('Not any real family,' as Hilda says, 'THE family', a combination of Holy Family, Royal Family and Swiss Family Robinson, 'foundation of the empire . . . foundation of Christianity. Of civilization. Of human society.') and his own actual family is absurd; but the parallel between his domestic situation and England's political situation is more seriously ironic. Lady Chavender's natural aristocratic authoritarianism has been frustrated by acquiescence in a popular theory of education. She irritates her children by her constant, ineffectual attempts to interfere with the freedom they claim and that she cannot respect. The nagging, the squabbles, the mutual dislike, that arise in consequence of her half-hearted compromise, seem to her the effects of an abrogation of full parental responsibility:

It serves us right, dear, for letting them bring themselves up in the post-war fashion instead of teaching them to be ladies and gentlemen.

Her feelings towards the children, that this method has produced, is matched by her contempt for the electorate and the pretence of parliamentary rule:

. . . you dont govern the country, Arthur. The country isnt governed: it just slummocks along anyhow . . .

Sir Arthur, hardened to political bickering, treats family discord in the same way, without attempting to change or ease the situation, but hoping that protest will expend itself in talk: 'They must be let talk. (*He returns placidly to his chair.*) It's just like the House of Commons, except that the speeches are shorter.' The childish and ineffectual David – both children are the victims of their parents – knows what is wrong here; if his mother's failure is in respect for the integrity and freedom of others, his father's is a failure to care:

I really think, father, you might for once in a way take some slight interest in the family.

As in his political role, Sir Arthur is indolent, vain and irresponsible in his complacency.

Yet Chavender, partly because he is the principal cause of laughter in the play, emerges as a much more sympathetic character than his wife, son or daughter. It is partly, too, because he does undergo a conversion from egotism to a more authentic view of himself and his position. There seems to be more of healthy life in him than in his wife, giving him the capacity to be cured. Certainly it is Lady Chavender who introduces the healer to him. The Lady in her grey robes of doctor of philosophy, or mage, is recognizably only 'playing at ghosts' with Sir Arthur; but it is also just 'for convenience sake [sic]' that the dramatist has them switch to accepting each other as 'real people'. The Lady as an imaginative device may represent the truth Chavender himself finds through brooding on his wife's criticisms (as Old Hipney may be described as a personification of the afterthoughts the deputation leaves). The dream-guide he conjures up for himself is free of Lady Chavender's social limitations, positive and creative where the other has only the lucidity of exhaustion:

> I am so tired of wellbred people, and party politics, and the London season, and all the rest of it . . . We were born into good society; and we are through with it: we have no illusions about it, even if we are fit for nothing better.

Bringing children up to be ladies and gentlemen gets no approval from the Lady, who elicits from Chavender an unconscious condemnation of such education:

> SIR ARTHUR. . . . We learnt to write Latin verses not because the verses are any good – after all, it's only a trick of stringing old tags together – but because it's such a splendid training for the mind.
> THE LADY. Have all the boys who made Latin verses at Harrow splendidly trained minds?
> SIR ARTHUR. Yes. I unhesitatingly say yes . . . if you go into the best society you will see that their minds are far superior to those of persons who have had no classical training.
> THE LADY. You mean that they can all be trusted to say the same thing in the same way when they discuss public affairs.
> SIR ARTHUR. Precisely. They are an educated class, you see.

If this is the aristocratic ideal, it can be dismissed as another way of institutionalizing mental idleness, perpetuating a caste system and resisting change. Authoritarian methods do not promote powers of invention and renewal.

Significantly, in an episode near the end of the play which appears in the 'First Rough Proof' but was subsequently omitted, Lady Chavender dictates the letter of resignation her husband writes to the King. It is she who formulates the proposal (though the argument has amply prepared for it):

> The only available alternative is to prorogue Parliament for some years and enable me to govern in your Majesty's name for the good of the people until the affairs of the nation are placed on a sensible footing.

This suggests that Shaw intended the advocacy of strong-arm methods to appear, finally, as biased and suspect. There still clings to the character of Lady Chavender an ambiguousness like that with which *Candida* and *Major Barbara* are riddled. Though her scepticism may have authorial endorsement, her lack of the vigour, enthusiasm and ready humour, that mark Shaw's favourite women characters from Raina to Joan and the Patient of *Too True to be Good*, leaves her unattractive. The propriety of her manners seems a particularly lifeless conventionality beside the different vulgarities of Miss Brollikins and Barking. There remain hints of something more devious about the character. One is the detail of Sir Dexter Rightside's assertion that 'anybody named Chavender can get in unopposed in his constituency because his cunning old father-in-law has every voter in the place bribed up to the neck'; it is enough to recall the relation of Candida to Burgess and of the family in Wilton Crescent to Undershaft, on the one hand, and to the Earl of Stevenage, on the other. Sir Arthur, having lost the thread of his speech, bursts out:

> One man one wife is one wife too many, if she has a lot of brothers who cant get on with the women they marry. Has it occurred to you, Miss Hanways, that the prospect of Socialism destroying the family may not be altogether unattractive?

That sounds like an allusion to the kind of situation we met in *Getting Married*. The accusation levelled by Flavia and David against their mother, 'Look at the unbearable way you treat Papa!' directs a sharper recognition of what is implied in the staged action. There remains the high-handedness with which Lady Chavender requires Hilda's presence for lunch, though it forces the secretary to cancel a private engagement. It is likely that some of these items are relics of an earlier intention on the part of the dramatist: to elaborate the family group and introduce more realistic detail in his presentation of the household. In fact, these slight and deftly placed allusions function with an economy of understatement new in Shaw's late work. The audience is trusted to pick up the hints, so that the domestic aspect of the play can be left unobtrusive, a minor element in what is essentially a play of political ideas.

The pattern faintly repeats that of *Candida*: the wife who is critical of her husband as a mere talker and does not respect his public success; the devoted secretary who arouses no comparable audience suspicions of destructive motivation. Little enough is divulged of Hilda Hanways's private attitude to the Chavenders; the children testify both to the intimacy of her knowledge of the family and to her discretion. Shaw's initial account of Hilda is borne out by the way she behaves: '*She is worried not only by an excess of business; but a sense of responsibility.*'

And her impulsive response, at the end of the play, when her sympathies drive her out to join the crowd against the police, reveal a truth in her that is fundamentally opposed to the convictions of Lady Chavender. The Prime Minister's dream Lady would seem to be an idealized composite that reflects his secretary's nature at least as much as his wife's. And when the Chavenders are finished and superannuated, the future may still lie with the young woman who escapes, as Marchbanks tried to, from the domestic setting:

> SIR ARTHUR. . . . She'll be back for tea. But what she felt just now other girls and boys may feel tomorrow. And just suppose—!
> LADY CHAVENDER. What?
> SIR ARTHUR. Suppose England really did arise!

It is the appropriate retort to the peroration of the speech he forgot to make:

> We are above all a domestic nation . . . we know that the heart of England is the English home. Not the battlefield but the fireside –

The sentence is interrupted, but endings suggest themselves. The lifelessness of Lady Chavender corresponds to the predetermined failure of Sir Arthur. (Their affectionate talk is incredibly un-Shavian in its conventionality.) Hilda is a Viking name, fit for a token figure of another way which recognizes the battlefield, not the fireside, as the place where the heart is.

Robert Brustein has suggested that an evasive fear of death saps Shaw's later work.[1] *On the Rocks* is not a very personal play (E. Strauss praised it on the grounds that Shaw 'has in this case very nearly succeeded in eliminating the personal element from the political equation',[2] and certainly the excision of the resignation passage near the end rules out the possibility of blaming the wiles of the woman for the man's defeat, as so many Shaw plays do[3]), but it certainly accepts the fact that death has a necessary and benign function in the world. The agent of healing, in the play, is precisely the messenger of death. The cure involves a cessation of futile activity, a throwing-off of the domination of time, an extra-scenic journey to a 'retreat in Wales', governed by the strange Lady. In the original text of *On the Rocks*, the willing death, or reconciliation to death,

---

[1] See Chapter 13, p. 221, note 2 above.

[2] See E. Strauss, *Bernard Shaw: Art and Socialism* (London: Gollancz, 1942), p. 110.

[3] But note that Basham judges Hipney more dangerous than Chavender because 'His heart is in the revolution . . . Your wife wouldn't like it: his would, if he has one', to which Hipney retorts: 'I'm under no woman's thumb. Shes dead.'

is consummated in the letter of resignation, like enough in its deployment to the abdication of King Henry in Granville Barker's *His Majesty*, already drawn on by Shaw as a major source of *The Apple Cart*. *His Majesty* contains echoes of the myth of the divine king who dies to be born again, or journeys to another world from which he may return in his country's need. Shaw described *On the Rocks*, in the First Rough Proof, as 'A Political Fantasy' and he has cultivated a deliberate eeriness in the appearance of Old Hipney and the Lady. The manner of Old Hipney's address, his stillness and silence while others talk, his emergence when the deputation with which he comes has taken its leave, the complete ease of his talk with Chavender and his air of intellectual mastery of the whole situation make him a figure of unaccountable authority. The way in which his appearances punctuate the two acts recalls the device of Ulric Brendel's symbolic first and last act appearances in *Rosmersholm* (as a functional device, already imitated in Doolittle's two appearances in *Pygmalion*). The Lady comes once only, like the Rat-Wife in *Little Eyolf*, though less grotesquely sinister, but the better parallel might be with Death, God's Messenger, in *Everyman*, which had impressed Shaw in William Poel's production and inspired him, as he claimed, in the writing of *Man and Superman*. It seems that he wanted to give some mystical extension to his political theme. Good Victorian as he was, he is unlikely to have christened his prime minister Sir Arthur Chavender without thought of Tennyson's use of the Morte d' Arthur theme of the necessity of total, sacrificial death of the old order for the world to change and new virtue come into being. The comparison can be sustained through the similarity of the grey-robed Lady, who takes Shaw's Arthur to Wales, and the Lady of the Lake, who conveys the traditional Arthur to Avalon.

'Sacrifice' is one of the recurrent verbal motifs of the play. The ambiguousness of the term is brought out in the first interview between Sir Arthur and Hipney:

> SIR ARTHUR. . . . Our workers must make sacrifices.
> HIPNEY. They will if you drive em to it, Srarthur. But it's you theyll sacrifice.

The superstitious performance of a rite of blood is implied in every reference to the possiblity of a popular rising. Hipney sees it as a last resource of helplessness, and the reflection is linked with his recognition of the need to find some source of power:

> They tell me the Italians are tapping their volcanoes for cheap power. We dont seem able to tap nothing . . . What can we do against labor at a penny a day and power for next to nothing out of the burning bowels of the earth?

A variation of the leitmotif of sacrifice presents itself in the deliberately alarming motif of 'extermination', which unites play and Preface. This, in turn, is caught up in the theme of the Domesday Clearances. Shaw admitted a recurrent impulse to dramatize the Day of Judgement: a puritan theme to match the rigorous self-scrutiny of an exacerbated individualism (so it is used by Ibsen, e.g. in *Rosmersholm*); a revolution-ary theme as it images the subversion of the material world. The frankly burlesque enactment of Judgement Day in *The Simpleton* is marked by the automatic vanishing of useless people. In the present play, the term 'Domesday Clearances' refers primarily to the objective historical phenomenon of forcible eviction (Aloysia swears, 'never, if we can help it, will it again be possible for one wicked rich man to say to a whole population "Get off the earth" ').[1] A new Domesday Clearance is what Basham's police force would threaten if armed with machine guns against the unemployed, or what the unemployed would make if driven to 'sacrifice' the politicians. But the image also has its subjective reflection in the voluntary decease of Chavender's retirement (and, perhaps, Lady Chavender's acceptance of supersession by Miss Brollikins), his attainment of 'the enormous freedom of having found myself out and got myself off my mind', which 'looks like despair; but . . . is really the beginning of hope, and the end of hypocrisy.' We are back at the concept of 'heartbreak', but also at the idea of responsible self-sacrifice, in recogni-tion of justification by works:

> Why dont I lead the revolt against it all? Because I'm not the man for the job . . . And I shall hate the man who will carry it through for his cruelty and the desolation he will bring on us and our like.

Very faintly, Shaw catches something like the tone of *Oedipus at Colonus* at the end of this play. His imaginative response to the theme of willing death, or voluntary sacrifice whereby natural death becomes a miraculous departure (from a grave beside a rock in Sophocles),[2] must account largely for the similarity. But an actual allusion to 'Edipus' is made by Sir Arthur late in the play, in his ignorance of the inapplicability of the Freudian 'Edipus Complex' to David's queerness in hating his mother and loving only his sister. (There may be something of Polynices in this; the inclusion of the detail is otherwise difficult to account for – except as it indicates a political preference for equality over any kind of authoritarianism.)

[1] The historical reference can be followed up in John Prebble, *The Highland Clearances* (London: Secker and Warburg, 1965; Penguin edition, 1969).

[2] The burlesque episode of the speech, in Act I, which blasphemously styles the Family 'The Church's One Foundation' and 'Rock of Ages', prepares for a rock of Sacrifice in Act II. (Cf. *John Bull's Other Island* – Larry's allusion to St Peter crucified head downward on a rock as the foundation of the Church.)

The Sophoclean play is a tragedy of peculiar serenity. Though *On the Rocks* has its burlesque elements, especially the satirical burlesque of the speech for Church House and the deputation from the Isle of Cats which is, in effect, an Aristophanic chorus dominated by the pure burlesque characters, Brollikins and Barking (to be encountered again in *Geneva* as Begonia Brown and the Betrothed), the loose comedy form, organized into a succession of episodes in contrasting modes, still accommodates a tragic action. Act II, indeed, follows quite closely the general lines of the tragedy, *Waste*, that Granville Barker had first written for the Court Theatre repertoire in Edwardian days and had rewritten completely in 1926.[1] Barker's hero, Trebell, is a political idealist of no fixed party allegiance brought into the Cabinet to design and carry through a great progressive measure. At first he skilfully wins the support he needs for his Bill; then a threatened scandal of adultery and abortion is used by his self-interested colleagues to render him politically powerless and destroy the integrity of his scheme. The destruction is the work of professionals at ease only amid compromise and the conventions of opposition on party lines; Trebell's answer is his suicide – an absolute gesture of faith in a better way. There is no equivalent to the threat of scandal in *On the Rocks*; but Chavender comes to share Trebell's preference of suicide – clearance of the talent and vision that do not match the times, or that the times cannot or will not employ – to the old futile routine. (To Lady Chavender he says: '. . . rather than go back to the old whitewashing job, I'd seize you tight round the waist and make a hole in the river with you.') And the main fabric of Act II, the assembly of big guns, leaders in the coalition government and spokesmen for pressure groups confronting Chavender, wrangling among themselves and eventually, one after another, withdrawing support from him, strikingly resembles the informal Cabinet meeting in Act III of *Waste*, at which Trebell has to defend himself and fight for the chance to go ahead with his work. Granville Barker's scene is more tautly written, more densely packed with thematic implications, than Shaw's; it is more subtly conducted and requires intenser concentration to follow the drift of the argument and the underground tactical manœuvring. *On the Rocks* has the subtlety of wit in its penetration of political tortuousness, but the characters and the movement of the scene are more broadly and simply designed, giving a more forceful and immediate impact than *Waste*. The build-up of support for Chavender has the same basis as his eventual defeat, and the two contrary stages in the debate reflect each other formally. This is a caricature of the actual politics of self-interest, in

[1] I have discussed this play in greater detail in *A Drama of Political Man* (London: Sidgwick and Jackson, 1961), pp. 109–47.

which no party looks beyond the hope of short-term sectional profits to give meaningful support to a comprehensive policy in the best interests of the whole community. The one who does *not* give any measure of approval to the least item in Chavender's proposals, Sir Dexter Rightside, his rival for the leadership, is best able to sum up the situation:

> You are trying to scuttle the ship on the chance of each of you grabbing a share of the insurance money.

The vigour and pace of the whole exchange, the orchestration of the dialogue for such a collection of voices, temperaments, manners and viewpoints, are not surpassed anywhere in Shavian drama. The effect is so exhilarating as to mask the sense of disaster that the genuine third way is closed and the future is likely to hold the alternatives of worse chaos and suffering, or a dictatorship much less principled and much less humane than Chavender offered.

The play constitutes a symbolic gesture, like the act of the 'only man that ever had a proper understanding of Parliament . . . old Guy Fawkes'. It uses the theatre to present a universal lesson of political responsibility. Hipney's view of the British working man is: 'He dont know nothing of the business that his life depends on'; Chavender sees the professional politicians as 'silly sheep who think they can govern the country without knowledge enough to run a whelkstall' (First Rough Proof). Both groups could learn, but the fact remains that 'you cant teach people anything they dont want to know', and the real trouble is the moral indolence of which Chavender is cured, the will-lessness that bows to 'the inexorable laws of political economy' and 'a merciless political machine' and excuses itself with the belief: 'I am in the grip of economic forces that are beyond human control.' The view that Shaw, in his later work, camouflaged the bankruptcy of his political thinking with his personal brand of religious mysticism needs to be balanced by a recognition that the fantastic and 'supernatural' elements in the later plays represent an answer to limited and predetermined thinking, mechanical and conventional: the human imagination is freer than society has admitted, and has resources of more original power. Like the other oriental figures in later Shavian fantasy, Sir Jafna Pandranath is a challenge by the infinite imagination to the limitations of Western intellect, as well as the challenge of the empire to the parochial vision of the 'right little, tight little island':

> I am called nigger by this dirty faced barbarian whose forefathers were naked savages worshipping acorns and mistletoe in the woods whilst my people were spreading the highest enlightenment . . . from the temples of Brahma the thousandfold who is all the gods in one . . . look at the faces of my people . . . There you see Man as he came from the hand of God, who has left on every feature the unmistakeable stamp of the great original

creative artist. There you see Woman with eyes in her head that mirror the universe instead of little peepholes filled with faded pebbles . . .

Not since *Major Barbara* had Shaw written a play as concerned with violence as *On the Rocks*: revolutionary violence and repressive violence; and it is not surprising that these are the two plays on which charges of Fascist inclinations have been mainly based. The end of *On the Rocks* can be read in the light of his denial, in the 1928 edition of *The Intelligent Woman's Guide*, that 'the inevitability of gradualness' excluded the necessity of violent insurrection altogether: as Hubert Bland had believed, it might be that England would still need to arise, at the end of is long reformist struggle, before socialism could be achieved. But the completeness of Shaw's shift from his earlier and more typically Fabian view can be overstressed. *On the Rocks* as a whole remains a rational and emotional endorsement of the fine paragraph with which he ended 'The Transition to Social Democracy' in *Fabian Essays in Socialism* (London, 1889), pp. 200–1):

> Let me, in conclusion, disavow all admiration for this inevitable, but sordid, slow, reluctant, cowardly path to justice. I venture to claim your respect for those enthusiasts who still refuse to believe that millions of their fellow creatures must be left to sweat and suffer in hopeless toil and degradation . . . The right is so clear, the wrong so intolerable, the gospel so convincing, that it seems to them that it *must* be possible to enlist the whole body of workers – soldiers, policemen, and all – under the banner of brotherhood and equality; and at one great stroke to set Justice on her rightful throne . . . But if . . . we feel relieved that the change is to be slow enough to avert personal risk to ourselves; if we feel anything less than acute disappointment and bitter humiliation at the discovery that there is yet between us and the promised land a wilderness in which many must perish miserably of want and despair: then I submit to you that our institutions have corrupted us to the most dastardly degree of selfishness. The Socialists need not be ashamed of beginning as they did by proposing militant organization of the working classes and general insurrection. The proposal proved impracticable; and it has now been abandoned – not without some outspoken regrets – by English Socialists. But it still remains as the only finally possible alternative to the Social Democratic programme which I have sketched to-day.

It is possible to argue that Shaw, like Carlyle, was one of those men of letters who compensate for their abstention from an active, practical life by an indulgence in violent imagery and inflammatory rhetoric. Melvin J. Lasky has recently made observations on a similar tendency in Utopian philosophers.[1] Certainly the deep feeling for violence, which Carlyle in *The French Revolution* declared to be religious in origin, counterbalances a powerful intellectual development, in Shaw's work as

[1] 'Revolution. The Birth of a Metaphor', *Encounter* (Feb. and March 1970).

in his own – even if it is sometimes violence in the key of farce; there is, indeed, a quality of sublimated ruthlessness in the forceful clarity of Shaw's prose in *On the Rocks* as in *Major Barbara*. Perhaps it is because the mob – which he so strongly criticizes – can still claim his sympathies that Shaw remains free of the reactionary hysteria to which the 'demonic' instinct within Carlyle was perverted. Violence in the plays is always symbolic or metaphorical, of course; but, far from being gratuitously sensational, it reflects (as in Conrad's fiction) the very real explosiveness in any political situation involving gross inequality or ideological conflict.[1]

The fertility and adroitness of Shaw's mind in this period is demonstrated by a comparison of *The Simpleton of the Unexpected Isles* of 1935 with *On the Rocks* of 1933. Not only do the two plays represent radically different conventions; the second balances a steady philosophic optimism against the realistic awareness of how wrong things were in the actual world of politics, which was expressed in *On the Rocks*. The line of thought from one play to the next is not difficult to trace. *On the Rocks* exposes the failure of one theory of government (parliamentary democracy) and the undesirability of another (fascist tyranny) and leaves with responsible minds the challenge of finding a better way. The defeat of Sir Arthur Chavender is not the defeat of G. B. Shaw, and the conclusion he comes to is not defeatism but 'the beginning of hope, and the end of hypocrisy'. Chavender's retirement amounts to the political talker's recognition of his dispensability, which is a self-judgement rather than an abandonment of the problem. Much the same note is sounded in Act II of *The Simpleton*, but the affirmation is more general, as befits the nature of the play and the very prosaic Angel from whom it comes:

> The Day of Judgment is not the end of the world, but the end of its childhood and the beginning of its responsible maturity.

It is the same psychological crisis as Shaw had earlier designated 'heartbreak', when the shock of reality penetrates and disperses illusion and makes sound judgement possible. To Chavender it represents a liberation. The recurrence of such moments in the rhythm of human experience is

---

[1] Albert J. LaValley, *Carlyle and the Idea of the Modern* (New Haven and London: Yale University Press, 1968), interestingly remarks (p. 126) apropos *The French Revolution*: '[Carlyle's] utterance of belief in the direction of modern history as inaugurated by the Revolution is unequivocally affirmative in tone and religious in intent. I would further suggest that this belief is the driving impulse behind his book . . . and the source for his conception of individual and social freedom (a statement which I think can also be made about most of the works of his Puritan successors, Ruskin and Shaw).'

an essential condition of that responsible free will which emerges, in *The Simpleton*, as the answer to the unsolved dilemma of *On the Rocks*. So the extraordinarily confident and reassuring Prola even celebrates the inevitability of failure:

> PROLA. . . . I feel like the leader of a cavalry charge whose horse has been shot through the head and dropped dead under him. Well, a dead hobby horse is not the end of the world . . . In the Unexpected Isles all plans fail. So much the better . . . We are not here to fulfil prophecies and fit ourselves into puzzles, but to wrestle with life as it comes.

This is the more persuasive because there is no rhetorical bluster about it; and the same is true of the matter-of-factness with which all the marvels of the play are presented. The images into which the words turn demonstrate the positive quality of feeling behind this attitude:

> PROLA. . . . life . . . it never comes as we expect it to come.
> PRA. It comes like a thief in the night.
> PROLA. Or like a lover . . .

We can say that Shaw, retired from the problems of the actual world, retained confidence in the poise of his own mind, and that the philosophical playfulness of *The Simpleton* is the fruit of this condition. But the play is much more than a personal testimony in dark days. In resorting to the eighteenth-century literary conventions of the oriental fable, the dramatist has aligned himself with the tradition of reason and, though it focuses on an end and a failure, his play is an indication of the philosophy of progress. For it is informed with the commonsense recognition that the life of the prosperous, educated, humane English middle class *has* been lived in a garden of man's designing from which many natural terrors have been banished and others can be. The rejection of a spectacular Apocalypse implies more than a preference for discussion plays over theatrical sensationalism: a regard for thinking as a viable alternative to suffering. The Angel makes it a matter of human choice:

> If you want a great noise, you have your cannons. If you want a fervent heat to burn up the earth you have your high explosives. If you want vials of wrath to rain down on you, they are ready in your arsenals, full of poison gases.

The Day of Judgement he announces is what can obviate the Day of Wrath. The terror is taken away; terrified men are not good at thinking. There is no serpent in the paradise of the Unexpected Isles. Shaw has been described (e.g. by Robert Brustein) as deficient in a sense of evil. More accurately, if more astoundingly in these days of confused irrationalism, we may say that he refuses to regard evil as ineradicable. If we hesitate to accept this attitude as intellectually respectable, we must be honest enough to admit that it is the same refusal in all of us that gets us up in the morning. It is also, in the face of all the odds, the final answer of Voltaire's *Candide*.

If we need yet more evidence to refute the view that Shaw's disillusion with democratic methods drove him into allegiance to totalitarian dictatorship, *The Simpleton* supplies it: 'The voice of authority gives us strength and unity. Command us always thus: it is what we need and love' is Janga's appeal, on behalf of the four Children; it gets from Prola the response: 'An excuse for leaving everything to me. Lazy, lazy, lazy! Someday Heaven will get tired of lazy people . . .' From one of Shaw's temperament, the mild-sounding rebuttal carries more weight than passionate indignation could. *On the Rocks* also confronts the difficulty of appealing to reason, when the majority of mankind is not reasonable; the kind of play it is reflects the way this is resolved in *The Simpleton*: the action takes place in a context removed from political and social actualities (which are reflected only in the most general satirical way, in news reports) and the argument is concerned only with political principles, not at all with political facts; the eponymous Simpleton, like the electorate, has little power of understanding, but great credulousness: he is the faculty of faith incarnate, and the main part of the play enacts his religious education. He pleads:

> I am weakminded and lose my head very easily. . . . I can take in anything if you will only tell it to me in a gentle hushabyebaby sort of way and call me Iddy.

So the play has the deceptive simplicity of the fable. After the pretentiousness of the 'Metabiological Pentateuch', it offers an iconography for contemplation and a sacred legend of almost childish plainness, woven about the icons and indirectly commenting on them. As a fable, it has its identifiable prototype in Voltaire's *Candide*, and the allusion to 'placid Panglossians' in the first paragraph of the Preface is one of the clues to interpretation that Shaw found, after the first production, he needed to give his critics. As ambiguous as Voltaire's narrative, the play sorts out the confusion of facts and principles, the confusion of vision and experience, and comes to the same conclusions:

> HYERING. . . . I have an uneasy feeling that we'd better get back to our work. I feel pretty sure that we shant disappear as long as we're doing something useful; but if we only sit here talking . . .

> Travaillons sans raisonner, dit Martin, c'est le seul moyen de rendre la vie supportable.[1]

---

[1] Quotations are from *Candide*, ed. A. Morize, 3rd ed. (Paris: Société des Textes Français Modernes, 1957), p. 223.

HYERING. . . . Sally: if you have given your orders for the housework today, go and cook something or sew something or tidy up the books.

Cunégonde . . . devint une excellente pâtissière; Paquetta broda; la Vieille eut soin du linge. Il n'y eut pas jusqu'à Frère Giroflée qui ne rendit service; il fut un très bon menuisier, même devint honnête homme.

SIR CHARLES (*to his wife, rising*). You might take a turn in the garden, dear: gardening is the only unquestionably useful job.

Cela bien dit, répondit Candide, mais il faut cultiver notre jardin.

Apart from these close reminiscences of the end of *Candide*, Shaw's debt to Voltaire, in this play, is of a general kind only. Out of the manifold adventures of Voltaire's hero, he has selected only the Eldorado episode and, even here, the only resemblance of detail is an exposition of the religion of the earthly paradise, and that is possibly fortuitous:

Cacambo demanda humblement quelle était la religion d'Eldorado. Le Vieillard rougit encor. 'Est-ce qu'il peut y avoir deux Religions? dit-il; nous avons, je crois, la Religion de tout le Monde; nous adorons Dieu du soir jusqu'au matin. – N'adorez-vous qu'un seul Dieu? dit Cacambo . . . Apparemment, dit le Vieillard, qu'il n'y en a ni deux, ni trois, ni quatre . . .'

(pp. 115–16)

THE LADY TOURIST. Excuse me; but can you tell me which of these figures is the principal god?
THE PRIEST (*rising courteously*). The principal one? I do not understand.
THE LADY TOURIST. I get lost among all these different gods: it is so difficult to know which is which.
THE PRIEST. They are not different gods. They are all god.
THE LADY TOURIST. But how can that be? The figures are different.
THE PRIEST. God has many aspects . . .

The many vicissitudes of Candide's pilgrimage through the world are summed up in Iddy's tale of being kidnapped by pirates, who put him ashore on the Unexpected Isles. Beside Voltaire's racy narrative, absurdly full of incident, the main part of Shaw's play is static. Precedent for introducing an angel into any essentially rationalist fable could be found in another Voltairean oriental tale, *Zadig*, and there is a similar comic matter-of-factness about the take-off of the Shavian Angel and the departure of Jesrad:

'. . . Faible mortel, cesse de disputer contre ce qu'il faut adorer. – Mais, dit Zadig . . .' Comme il disais *mais*, l'ange prenait déjà son vol vers la dixième sphère.[1]

---

[1] Quoted from *Zadig et Autres Contes* (Paris: Bibliothèque de Cluny, 1950), ch. xx, p. 156.

But not the least of the debts *The Simpleton of the Unexpected Isles* owes to the great French wit is stylistic. Shaw's writing here is astonishingly free from rhetoric. The dialogue proceeds cleanly and briskly, almost telegrammatically, in short, simple units. It is a style that corresponds happily with the Utopian fable: lucid, with a lightness of touch that can etch an absurdity neatly, but never degenerates into frivolity, and that takes a faint colouring of emotional values which never threaten judgement; its poise reflects the detachment proper to speculation, balanced by a degree of imaginative engagement. The economy of method extends to characterization: the *personae* are slightly developed types, clearly differentiated, but remaining well this side of caricature; and the action, to correspond, is quite uncomplicated by any intrigue.

The general design of a Prologue in three scenes, then an implied lapse of twenty years before Act I, and a further lapse of several years before Act II, combined with a doubt as to whether Prologue and main action are localized in the same region, suggests a deliberate avoidance of causal development. The fiction is not allowed such autonomy; these are the fancies of a mind relaxed and at ease, but alert and discriminating and deserving attention. Though there is a slight chronological thread running through the whole play, the fundamental relation between scene and scene, episode and episode, is more oblique. Iddy's remark 'We have never been able to imagine eternity properly' is pertinent to the form as well as the theme of the play. For Shaw has taken pains to place past, present and future in relation to a timeless condition, in which they are simultaneities, aspects of the complex idea his play contemplates. Superficially we follow the adventures of the Young Woman who becomes Mrs Hyering from the first scene of the Prologue right through to the end of the play (though she is excluded from the last exchange, virtually an Epilogue). But we do not begin to make sense of Shaw's design until we entertain the notion that the rest of the play is a fuller, alternative version of the content of the first scene: that it is what has happened before and will happen again, a more general version of the specific events reflected and caricatured in Scene i.

What happens in Acts I and II is highly fantastic, the stuff of cosmic fable; what happens in the Prologue is not so much fantastic in itself as fantastically presented, with the tempo and the physically violent climaxes that characterize the traditional short farce.[1] This convention is epitomized, in the first scene, by the character of the Young Woman, basically the same type as the Patient of *Too True to be Good* and Begonia Brown of *Geneva*: an incarnation of energy in general and the

---

[1] See Martin Meisel, *Shaw and the Nineteenth-Century Theater*, pp. 242–9, on this theatrical convention and Shaw's practice of it.

energy that informs a farcically comic action in particular. She represents human nature as an almost exclusively physical manifestation. (Significantly, Judgement Day prompts her to think of cultivating her mind – through crossword puzzles!) She is brisk and bracing and conceives of happiness as a matter of hygiene:

> It's not natural not to be happy . . . you dont need to be made happy. You ought to be happy from the inside . . . you can make your inside all right if you eat properly and stop drinking . . .

Her expectancy, which initiates the play in the fullest sense, is not only a vital readiness for anything, it is the receptivity of the object in which energy is latent, awaiting the force which will activate it:

> WILKS. She says she's waiting to see what will happen to her.

But Shaw, as usual, suggests allegorical identities, without drawing the life out of his play by working out a consistent allegory.[1] There is nothing passive about the Young Woman's behaviour on stage. Her will drags the Emigration Officer away from his desk as a first, burlesque instance of the process of election (in the theological sense) proclaimed by the coming of the Angel in Act II. Indeed, the Judgement Day theme, central to the main part of the play, is announced at this point in the Prologue, when the Emigration Officer lets himself be led away and his Clerk, Wilks, insists on remaining:

> THE Y.W. . . . Dispensables and indispensables: there you have the whole world. I wonder am I a dispensable or an indispensable.

The remainder of the first scene is given up to Wilks's soliloquy, which is a burlesque of tragic heroism. The long speech, which surprisingly telescopes an entire action, the drama in the life-history of a character and a parable of the rise and fall of imperialism, counterbalances the form of the earlier part of the scene, with its (token) interest in plot-movement and the interaction of characters; this, in equally token form, takes us inside character and looks back instead of forward. But the climax of the sketch, the focal dramatic gesture, certainly comes here: when Wilks puts his pistol to his head and shoots himself. This, of course, links again proleptically and by implication with the dramatic image of Judgement Day: Wilks here judges and does execution upon himself. In effect, he convicts himself of superstitious belief in election rather than free will, in fate rather than in himself:

> Why am I a clerk . . . ? Because life never came to me like it came to Rhodes. Found his backyard full of diamonds, he did . . . What did I find

---

[1] What he observed in 'The Perfect Wagnerite' remained always a principle of his own art. See passage quoted in Chapter 12, p. 205, note 1.

in my backyard? Next door's dead cat . . . And when I threw it back over the wall my mother said 'You have thrown away your luck, my boy' she says 'you shouldnt have thrown it back: you should have passed it on, like a chain letter. Now you will never have no more luck in this world.' And no more I have.

The 'back-yard' image is an index to the narrowness of the imperial vision in its most grandiose form, still as narrow and shallow as the pedantry of elementary education:

I had Rhodes's idea all right. Let the whole earth be England, I said to the school teacher; and let Englishmen govern it.

Appropriately, Wilks shoots himself before he has got far with his singing of 'Rule Britannia': 'Britannia rules the wa—'. This first bathos sets the pattern for the disturbances and 'disappearances' to be recorded in Act II:

The Premier's last words were lost through the misconduct of a cherub who butted him violently in the solar plexus . . .

Sir Ruthless Bonehead . . . disappeared as he opened his mouth to speak.

No tears need be shed for such ludicrous pretensions, and the style of Wilks's soliloquy is enough to repel them, anyway: it suggests the vernacular of a music hall skit, and its narrative of cat and mother has the sham simplicity of pantomime fairy story. It neatly conveys the mixture of the squalidly vulgar and naïvely idealistic in the imperial idea itself, and the whole scene stands clear, at the end, as the burlesque of a particular historical moment: the end of an era. Even the setting, the soullessness of an emigration office, a place of transition to an unidentified somewhere, with a deserted, ends-of-the-earth atmosphere about it, has contributed to the effect. But there is a somewhere, into which the Young Woman and the Emigration Officer have ventured. It doesn't, at this point, sound very inviting ('This climate is hell'); yet the Emigration Office establishes itself as the ante-room to the unknown that is to come.

The suicide is the first of the sensational incidents in this play which exonerate it from the conventional charge that 'nothing happens'. Shaw has, in fact, made the structure of his Prologue out of a series of sketches, technically self-contained, and the form of each has room only for the build-up to a single climactic incident, on which the curtain immediately, or almost immediately, falls. The comparable climax of Scene ii is marked by the propulsion of the Emigration Officer over the cliff into the sea – theatrically reminiscent of the diving in *Caesar and Cleopatra*, but also related (as a burlesque with serious undertones) to the Edgar and Gloucester cliff-scene in *King Lear*. Scene iii presents a variant repetition of this, when the regenerated Officer passes on the treatment he has received to the Young Woman herself. In relation to Scene i, the two following scenes depict a new beginning: a resurrection of the idea of empire after its bankrupt death. With the appearance of the two oriental figures, Pra and Prola, we are confronted with what may be interpreted as a ludicrously utopian image of what the British Empire actually was, in its linking of white and coloured peoples – the dream which failed, or the illusion that occupied men's imaginations while the practical business instincts were rather differently at work; alternatively it may be taken for a new and better attempt. A similar ambiguousness settles over the whole play: it is both a satire on the decline of the British Imperium and a fable about civilization in the abstract: it looks back as historical comment, round scathingly at the contemporary scene, and forward as a prophetic warning – and encouragement.

As the setting has changed to the exotic[1] from the off-key realism of the Customs Building, the imagery is similarly transformed, in Scenes ii and iii. The 'backyard' now becomes recognizable as the first version of the garden/paradise motif derived from *Candide*:

THE Y.W. Why, it's an earthly paradise.
THE E.O. Tell them so; and see what theyll say to you.

This sets another pattern: of advance and recoil, vision and disillusion· It will emerge most prominently in the Simpleton's arrival at the Unexpected Isles and his departure without regret. The fantastic logic of idea, whereby we proceed from the death of Wilks to the spiritual rebirth of the Officer and Young Woman, is also at work in the way that the purgation and baptism of these two characters in the sea leads straight on to the entrance of the Simpleton, the completely innocent and child-like imagination, when the curtain goes up on Act I. Meanwhile, the regeneration symbolism is reinforced by a paradisial marriage symbolism, in the banquet of fruit the Westerners share with Pra and Prola. The Young Woman's reference to the locale as 'this abode of love' (cf. the grotto, with the chalked inscription, 'THE ABODE OF LOVE' and the carved 'Agapemone' in Greek characters, in Act III of *Too True*) helps extend the significance of the love feast and make it the initiatory sacramental meal (the Eucharist without the crudeness of human sacrifice – they do not eat the dismembered Wilks) of a new holy community.

(This aspect of the play seems whimsically related to the more recent career of Shaw's old friend, Annie Besant, who had gone to India to

---

[1] In nineteenth-century theatrical style. See H.M. Winter, *The Theatre of Marvels* (New York: Blom, 1964), two colour plates of 'Jocko the Brazilian Ape', before p. 83.

reconcile East and West in the new religion of Theosophy and whose entourage, including Krishnamurti – the intended messiah – and his brother, might well have suggested the mixed family and its beautiful children in *The Simpleton*. The gentle C. W. Leadbeater, in other ways very different from Iddy, had left an English curacy to join this close circle. Krishnamurti visited Shaw on board ship in Bombay, in January 1933, not long before Mrs Besant's death.[1])

The paraphernalia of religion, with which so much of the play is to be occupied, is more literally introduced in Pra's Scene ii directions to the temples of Life, the mother-goddess, and Death, 'the weeder of the garden, the sacred scavenger', etc. These are the first principles of a Natural Religion which accepts the created universe as good and worshipful. Not superstition but reason informs the attitude of Priest and Priestess to the sacred images: 'they are personifications of the forces of nature by which we all live. But of course to an idolator they are idols.' The explanation prepares us to understand the roles of the Children in Acts I and II; and there is room for scepticism as to whether these do represent 'the forces of nature' by which alone we can live, or some aberration. Shaw keeps romance and satire in double harness: the 'barbarian' priest sets England in perspective as 'a strange mad country' (Scene ii of the Prologue); but Prola's jibes at Pra ('He inspires a doglike devotion in women. He once did in me; so I know.' / 'Don't be vindictive, Prola. I don't do it on purpose', etc.) are enough to prevent the playing of either character simply as an ideal figure. We can't settle down into certainty that the author's attitude to any of his characters will continue unchanging, or that symbolic values will not shift as the fable develops.

For the most part, Pra and Prola suggest a quality of Wisdom in which Western civilization is poor. The creative element which transforms the English characters and makes possible the founding of a new culture is supplied by the dark-skinned figures, the woman proving, ultimately, the more powerful of them. In contrast to the Young Woman, they represent a non-physical, informing power of imagination and spirit. Within the allegory of the play, they represent the Young Woman and the Officer on another level of being: the impersonal potencies in maleness and femaleness. The two names are sufficiently alike to suggest male and female representations of the same force. Shaw probably intended Pra to sound like an authentic variant of *Pater* ('He has many names; but he answers to Pra when you call him'); etymologically, Prola is identifiable with the root of the late Latin verb 'to produce', 'to bring forth', familiar in 'prolific', 'proletarian' and Orwell's 'prole'. In the Epilogue, Prola

---

[1] See A. Nethercot, *The Last Four Lives of Annie Besant* (London: Rupert Hart-Davis, 1963).

is strongly reminiscent of Lilith, in the Epilogue of *Back to Methuselah*; and Pra appears to be a supplementary and balancing power; but only, perhaps, as human life is sexual in its manifestation; for at the start Pra and Prola are certainly the alternative personifications of God chosen by patriarchal or matriarchal societies. Such societies are ill balanced in this very respect; and Shaw's ideal society needs the two figures as a token of balance. (The lesson of *The Philanderer* has not been left behind.)

There is direct continuity in the fable from the end of the Prologue to the beginning of the play proper: twenty years have elapsed, and here is the paradise established in the Unexpected Isles, with the guidance of Pra and Prola, by those Empire-building types: the pioneering young woman, the seedy civil servant, the colonial governor and the missionary lady. As no true Utopia has any pretence to reality, but is merely an image of what the mind considers desirable, so this contains hardly any of the material of the actual world. (There is much less circumstantial detail concerning the Unexpected Isles than goes to the evocation of most literary Utopias.) Shaw's effectual limitation of his play to what is merely a key episode in *Candide* is curious enough to be worth pondering. The sense of how much evil is in the world, which is responsible for so much of the force of *Candide*, is played down in *The Simpleton*. The fact is recognized in Iddy's account of the pirates, classifiable as figures of the capitalist world, spiritual brothers of Black Paquito's gang and Mendoza's brigands:

They were crooks, racketeers, smugglers, pirates, anything that paid them.

They took the young clergyman as their chaplain, with all that world's readiness to turn religion to its own practical account:

They used me to make people believe that they were respectable. They were often so bored that they made me hold a service and preach . . . Some of them were such dear nice fellows: they assured me it did them no end of good.

Iddy, it seems, is lineal descendant, in Shaw's work, of what Broadbent would have made of Keegan. But the world has changed since the beginning of the twentieth century: 'they got tired of me and put me ashore here.' The absurd and irresponsible goings-on of British democracy, the destructive follies of war and the actual divergencies of opinion and values and levels of civilization camouflaged by the same flag, or the same language, are all reflected in the play; but the pain and suffering they cause, or fail to alleviate, are never vividly evoked even in burlesque. World War I

is turned to an apocalyptic spectacle, which the creative powers of nature
can put to shame:

> . . . the spring came and created life faster than you could destroy it. The
> birds sang over your trenches; and their promise of summer was fulfilled.
> The sun that shone undisturbed on your pitiful Day of Wrath shines today
> over Heaven's Day of Judgment. It will continue to light us and warm us;
> and there will be no noise nor wrath nor fire nor thunder nor destruction
> nor plagues nor terrors of any sort.

Of course, Shaw's imagination is in some ways very different from
Voltaire's, and his medium does not permit of the narrative of calamities
that turns absurd through excess and the incredible survival power of
the victims; but his concern here is different, too, from the main concern
of *Candide*. The weighing of the case for optimism against the case for
pessimism, or despair, is less overt in *The Simpleton*. In the play, the idea
of time as making for good, though not for security, takes precedence over
this debate. The antithesis of time and change is Eldorado, the earthly
paradise. Ironically, the Angel's assurance echoes the promise of a New
Jerusalem; to 'there will be no noise', etc., one is tempted to add, 'no
more sea'. The threat of dullness, the one imperfection from which
heaven is not exempt, hangs over all.

The main part of the play is myth, legend and iconography. The
Garden into which Iddy wanders, as the curtain goes up on Act I, is as
much Xanadu as Eden or Eldorado. There is no serpent in it, only the
unfallen morning star ('my Christian name is Phosphor,' explains Iddy
to Pra, 'Phosphorus, you know? The stuff they make matches with'), like
all innocents a fool, born and bred ('I was not a natural baby. I was a
nitrogen baby'). This son of a biological chemist, nicknamed the Idiot
and fed on air, is hailed by Vashti and Maya as the enchanted poet-dreamer:

THE DARK ONE. 'For he on honey dew hath fed' –
THE FAIR ONE. – 'and drunk the milk of paradise.'

He is the only sort of being who *can* live in an unreal world: he is simple
faith itself, but also representative of that vast, credulous majority
without original ideas that is so troublesome a problem to the political
philosopher who is also a humanist. 'The albatrocity' is the insulting
jibe Kanchin throws at him, keeping us still in mind of Coleridge, while
emphasizing specifically that air is the element in which this phenomenon
comes happily into his own. The maker of Iddy changed his own name,
we gather, from Hummingtop (with connotations of the *perpetuum
mobile*, a mechanistic process?)[1] to Hammingtap (suggestive of the

---

[1] I am reminded of Carlyle's Teufelsdröckh: in his eyes 'stillness in the *sleep*
of a spinning top'.

designer and god of the forge). He is one of many creator-figures acknowledged in the play. The Parents, Pra, Prola and their disciples, sum up
their own error in peopling the Unexpected Isles with four Children
deficient in moral responsibility:

> PRA. We have taught them everything except common sense.
> LADY FARWATERS. We have taught them everything except how to work
> for their daily bread instead of praying for it.
> PROLA. It is dangerous to educate fools.
> PRA. It is still more dangerous to leave them uneducated.
> MRS HYERING. There just shouldnt be any fools. They werent born fools:
> we made fools of them.
> PRA. We must stop making fools.

This is not the last word: the motif of the fool sounds again in the
Epilogue, when Prola describes Pra as 'an extraordinarily clever fool'.
It seems that fools who are not improperly educated may be capable of
imaginative experiment:

> . . . nobody but a fool would be frivolous enough to join me in doing all the
> mad things I wanted to do.

Judgement Day releases Iddy from the spell of Xanadu. Before this, he has
learnt something from his paradisial experience and formulates it as a
scheme for sermons: change is desirable, and love is not enough. His
final discovery, which shocks him into choosing to leave the garden, is
that the apparitions that have enthralled him, and which he mistook at
the start for statues of gods and goddesses, are and always have been
illusions:

> Heaven and earth shall pass away; but I shall not pass away. That is what
> she said . . . And there was nothing.
> . . . Dont you understand? Where she had just been there was nothing.
> There never had been anything.
> . . . I have searched for the others; but she and they were one: I found
> nothing.

At the moment of his first sight of the Children, Iddy fell in love with
Maya and, in kissing her, enacted Pygmalion's kissing of the statue which
Aphrodite, in pity, possessed and brought to life. Like the automata made
by Pygmalion in *Back to Methuselah*, the Children in this play are presented in two versions: with and without a magical life in them. At
first, they are decorative figures in a *tableau vivant*, having taken the
place of the inanimate statues of Scenes ii and iii of the Prologue. With
the kiss, they are transformed into a chorus, whose chanting weaves
the spell that holds Iddy and the audience enrapt. But this is a satire,
as well as a fantasy, and the sublimity of the ideal figures sometimes

deserts them and leaves them capping each other's quips, or shouting
slogans:

JANGA. . . . No more of this endless talk! talk! talk!
VASHTI. Yes, action! daring! Let us rob.
MAYA. Let us shoot.[1]
KANCHIN. Let us die for something.
JANGA. For our flag and for our Empress.
VASHTI. For our country, right or wrong . . .

These figures have come in for critical condemnation as boringly
allegorical – but without much appreciation of the kind of play Shaw was
writing and the extent to which the device of such a chorus serves the
economy and colourful fantasy at which he was aiming.

Only one of the names he gave to the figures, Maya, is indubitably
and authentically mythological in origin, and Shaw seems deliberately to
have fused associations of the Greco-Roman Maia, Earth-Mother and
Spring goddess, with the Mâyâ of Buddhism, whose name (as *Thus Spake
Zarathustra*, itself an oriental fable, records) means 'illusions'. As
personification of Spring and Illusion, in the Shavian sense, Maya is
closely allied to Aphrodite and Venus; and the reference, in the Preface,
to Roman worship of Jupiter, Diana, Venus and Apollo may be taken to
suggest the range of powers he wished his quartet to denote. Not that
either of the youths is a Jupiter figure, though such a figure would be
appropriate to the fourth of the allegorical values Iddy ultimately reads in
the personifications: 'Love, Pride, Heroism and Empire'. The names,
Vashti and Janga, have an Indian ring (though Shaw may have fused
an Indian name with Ashtaroth to make Vashti); Kanchin is more
suggestive of lands farther east – even the earthly paradise of Kubla Khan.
The pairing of dark and fair, gentle with stern, male with female, is
typical of the mythopoetic process. Weapons are the emblems of Janga
and Kanchin: 'Their eyebrows are drawn bows' / 'Their arrows . . . are
deadly'; 'They will break thy spear' / 'They will pierce thy shield'. At
first they appear to be simply projections of the Simpleton's alarm, a
defensive reflex accompanying the attraction that draws him to the
female figures. But there is a quality of Blakean myth about them too.
The decision to limit the number of figures to four coincides happily, in
the apocalyptic context, with the frequency of quaternions in the Book of
Revelations. Prola 'taught them a game called the heavenly parliament';
but traditionally it is the Cardinal Virtues that constitute the heavenly
parliament, and Justice, Fortitude, Temperance and Mercy are recalled in
the demands the Children make of their chosen Empress: 'Thought',
'Knowledge', 'Righteousness', 'Justice' and 'Mercy'. If Love, Pride,

[1] Cf. the reaction of Harry Smiler in *Too True*.

Heroism and Empire have outlived their usefulness and turned into
vices, it is still possible that other values can be found in the four images
that promise satisfaction of Iddy's faith in 'everything that is good and
lovely and kind and holy'. Shaw's Caesar and Androcles, in effect, share
the same faith, but have little enough to do with – and take small pains
to cultivate – love, pride, heroism and domination, the virtues of Byronism;
pride and heroism, indeed, involve enlargements of egoism foreign to
both those earlier anti-heroes and to Iddy himself (though all three are
vulnerable to complacency); ideal love and domination are equally
ambitious of rising above the ordinary human level. All four are at odds
with the good-humoured humility which is the principal virtue of the true
Shavian child. So Iddy discovers that he can love and delight in them, but
needs to keeps his human distance from them:

> I cannot bear being loved, because I know that I am a worm . . . But I can
> love and delight in loving . . . I have the joy of loving you all without
> the burden of being loved in return, or the falsehood of being idolized.

(The error of the Children as objects of satire is explained by this: they
have flattered themselves and played gods and goddesses until they had
forgotten they were human and lost the power of distinguishing between
what they desired and what they had, did and were. A further significance
of Iddy's baptismal name – Phosphor – is brought out in the development
of this theme to the point at which the aim of the 'most splendid' of
England's wars is proclaimed by Janga: 'To plant the flag of England on
the ramparts of Heaven itself!' There may be no serpent in the play,
but the rebellion of Lucifer is envisaged in Shaw's Edenic myth.)

But essentially Act II balances Act I as a demonstration of the phrase
that echoes through Revelations: 'I am Alpha and Omega, the Beginning
and the End.' Though the set used for Act II may be the same as for Act I,
the imagery transforms it from the Garden of Creation to the landscape of
Apocalypse. The fleets of the nations are gathered in the harbour;
ultimatums have been issued. Vashti and Maya impersonate the Wrath
to come in their imprecations on Iddy:

> VASHTI. Rather than endure him I will empty the heavens of their rain
> and dew.
> MAYA. Silence him, O ye stars.

The Simpleton, in response, takes his text from St John of Patmos and
disserts on the theme of the New Jerusalem. From the actual world of
time comes the news, 'Dissolution of the British Empire'. The Children's
proposals for the enthronement of Prola suggests a reign of Antichrist –
until the trumpet sounds and the Angel descends among them. Though
the biblical imagery in the dialogue comes largely in negative form, it

does evoke the preternatural clarity and tremendousness of the vision of St John:

VASHTI. The stars are fixed in their courses. They have not fallen to the earth.

MAYA. The heavens are silent. Where are the seven thunders?

VASHTI. The seven vials full of the wrath of God?

JANGA. The four horses?

KANCHIN. The two witnesses?

The visitation and judgement are very prosaic after the expectation: the climax to the play proves to be a grand anticlimax, the last of a series in Act II. The vanishing of the fleets, the withdrawal of England from the Empire, the disappearances of the noisy and the powerful into silence are not instances of the emotional 'let-down', however, so much as a turning away of calamity that is in keeping both with the comic mode and the doctrines of optimism. The recurrent device is comparable to the survival or restoration of Voltaire's characters in spite of their subjection to the worst of fates: not even hanging, drawing and quartering can kill Pangloss. The fable, in each case, remains altogether a moral one, and its physical incidents have no stable reality at all.

That is the myth of the Natural Religion the play presents. The four Children are only part of its sacred iconography. They themselves recognize the Superfamily, over which Prola truly presides, but the members of which share a unity of being. In place of the orthodox Holy Family Shaw gives us the Superfamily and in place of the familiar Trinity both the Quaternion ('They hit out for themselves the idea that they were not to love one another, but that they were to be one another') and a new Trinity, in which 'Vashti is Maya; and Maya is Vashti' and their worshipper is united with them:

VASHTI. Your lives and ours are one life.

MAYA (*sitting down beside him*). And this is the Kingdom of love.
  The three embrace with interlaced arms and vanish in black darkness.

The blackout conveys Shaw's scepticism. Such eternal unity is not enough, as Iddy himself discovers. For the human being needs to recognize that the aspects of God his images incarnate do not define the whole or exclude other possibilities:

. . . they all love me so wonderfully that their three loves are only one love. But it is my belief that someday we'll have to try something else. If we dont we'll come to hate one another.[1]

---

[1] Cf. Blake's 'Spectre and Emanation': 'Let us agree to give up love / And root up the infernal grove; / Then shall we return & see / The worlds of happy · eternity.'

In the Unexpected Isles as elsewhere, there is an observable relation between social organization and the accepted myth. At the end of the Preface to the play, Shaw exonerates himself from the charge of specific advocacy of group marriage; but the fact remains that his Superfamily deserves its name not only because it is itself more of the order of myth than a blueprint for society, but because it is an enlargement of the bounds of the narrow unit of kinship recognized by the nineteenth century as the family: the British Empire embodied, in however distorted a form, a superior concept of community to the British home. The retreat of Britain announced in Act II ('Downing Street declares for a right little tight little island') corresponds to the shrivelling of the island paradise itself into the futile dream of a finally undesirable security which Prola repudiates:

> . . . the future is to those who prefer surprise and wonder to security.

The Shavian choice is made once more at the end of this play – the world instead of the womb:

> There is no Country of the Expected. The Unexpected Isles are the whole world.

In the theatrical context Pra and Prola speak the epilogue to the audience. A humorous reminder of the context is given, just before, by Hyering, as the group of Westerners disperses:

> . . . if we only sit here talking, either we shall disappear or the people who are listening to us will.

The theatrical epilogue formula can be recognized in certain phrases:

> We are awaiting judgment here quite simply as a union of a madwoman with a fool.
> . . . now brought to judgment . . .
> We have only repeated the story of Helen and Faust . . .

When Prola 'is interrupted by a roll of thunder', she acknowledges the fiction even while asserting the moral superiority of the human individual over all undifferentiated force:

> Be silent: you cannot frighten Prola with stage thunder. The fountain of life is within me.[1]

As the images grow transparent, the 'union of a madwoman with a fool' reveals itself as that of artist-man, the comedian, and the inspiring frenzy of his muse, or the union of the two masks: of Don Juan and the Woman, with whom the conflict informing all Shaw's drama has been

[1] The *fons vitae* is set traditionally in the earthly paradise, where Chronos sleeps.

continually fought out, over and over. They take leave of their public as they occupy the stage together, more real than the work of art they have conceived and played with:

> Helen was a dream. You are not a dream . . . Euphorion also vanished in his highest flight.

The end of the play could be dramatically disastrous and it may certainly be held responsible for the cursory dismissal that the piece has received from most critics. (Martin Meisel rates it quite high, but has not discussed it very closely or fully.) From the final exit of Iddy (to fly, or walk on the water, back to the neighbourhood of Malvern where the play was first performed), dramatic development ceases. The brief recapitulation in the Epilogue is not too much for the actors to get across; the real strain comes in the lengthy reports from the outer world, which are set-pieces in the satirical genre, entertaining enough to read, but surely resistant to stage presentation. In spite of the blemish – and Shaw was never an impeccable dramatist – *The Simpleton of the Unexpected Isles* does not deserve the neglect it has received. Its appeal may be less broadly popular than some of the other plays can boast; but it stands on its own in the delicacy of its wit and the neatness with which it calls in the eighteenth century to put the values of the Romantic movement in their place.

17

Late Burlesques

With *The Apple Cart* and *Geneva*, Shaw moved away from the domestic play or fantasy with political implications to a political cartoonist's version of public life. If it is public life behind the scenes, it is still at some distance even from the private experience of Sir Arthur Chavender, the Prime Minister of *On the Rocks*. The location of *The Apple Cart* in some vaguely future century and of *Geneva* in the never-never of a 'fancied page of history' is a formal indication of the attempt to translate contemporary actualities into less realistic, more abstract terms.

The chief dramatic matter of *The Apple Cart* is a trial of strength between King Magnus and his Ministers over the royal prerogatives. This involves a discussion of democracy and a demonstration of its workings. The conflict is suspended, first for a duologue between King Magnus and his acknowledged mistress, Orinthia the Beloved, and then by the arrival of news of an American project to return to the British Empire (in effect, to annex it). This crisis is left unresolved to hang over the rest of the play, which returns to domestic affairs: to the distribution of powers in the internal political system, and so, before the curtain falls, to the homely intimacy of Queen Jemima. The looming international situation, too big for any of the characters to handle or to be contained within the play, is an indication that the dramatist could not now be satisfied to examine merely national politics as an isolated problem: the complacency of Magnus's kingdom, drawing its tribute from underprivileged parts of the earth and manufacturing chocolate-creams and Christmas crackers in its leading industries, is contemptuously sketched; Breakages Limited, the enemy of men of goodwill, is an international organization. Even the Empire, that favourite concept of the nineteenth-century imagination, is too limited a theme now. The journey of Shavian drama from St Dominic's Parsonage does not stop at Downing Street or Buckingham Palace; it goes on to Geneva and the Court at The Hague to focus on the most urgent preoccupation of mid-twentieth-century politics: the necessity for a rule of law over the nations.

A sentence in the Preface to *The Apple Cart* – 'It is never safe to take my plays at their suburban face value: it ends in your finding in them only what you bring to them, and so getting nothing for your money' – operates more as a warning than an encouragement to critical interpretation. The particular view of the play Shaw is there anxious to reject sees it as 'a struggle between a hero and a roomful of guys'. Yet it must be admitted that his technique of presentation is responsible for such an impression. The Cabinet is handled as a chorus which at intervals breaks into song, with broadly comic effect; the members wear fancy-dress uniforms; there are two female soloists to introduce variety, one a soubrette and mimic, the other an operatic contralto; the Prime Minister is an adept at the histrionic striking of political attitudes; the newest recruit, Boanerges, is the principal clown of the act whose *naïveté* is distinctly attractive. The subordination of the individuals to the discipline of the group is neatly defined by the management of their entrance and exits in Act II: they process in, climbing up the steps one after another, and they place their hats in a line on the balustrade before they sit down; they take their leave one at a time, but the common ritual of picking up the hat and descending the steps ensures the triumph of pattern in a rhythmic sequence, though there is no visual simultaneity.[1] (Obviously the line of hats is intended to diminish from one end to the other, not by a casual picking of one from here, then another from there: the inanimate objects thus seem to regulate the human actions.) On the other hand, King Magnus is presented with more consistent respect, as a quiet, wise, naturalistic hero, than any other central figure in the Shavian canon. The nearest earlier approximation, the portrait of Caesar, was humorously underplayed for its anti-heroic value. Magnus is no more addicted to romantic pretensions than Caesar, but he has no occasion to catch himself out, and his self-deprecatory remarks operate as suavely prepared traps for others, the butts and the caricatures whose folly provokes the audience to laughter. There is more to be said for these others, but Shaw has refrained from saying it above a whisper. Amanda and Lysistrata are less vulnerable than the male Cabinet Ministers; but it is very clear that they are personified abstractions with little of human reality about them except for what the actors impart.

Shaw has carefully nurtured the impression of Magnus's superiority to the rest and the true authority that is in him. Satire or irony which might disturb the audience's respectful reception of this kingly figure

---

[1] It is by no means an original stage trick, of course; but the setting of the royal palace helps bring to mind especially the wit of Haydn's Farewell Symphony when the players depart, each in turn with his instrument, till the Prince is left alone.

has been carefully excluded; even being dragged to the floor by Orinthia emphasizes his humanity without injuring his essential dignity. The role is much the fullest in the play; and standing alone, as he does, is a function of his human individuality. What is more, the real equivalent of a Shakespearian heroic oration is given to him in Act I, and the interest of its content distracts attention from the artifice of its manner: this is the play's chief statement, the wise and passionate exposition of the political situation. It draws a less emotionally controlled sequel from Lysistrata: the force of her cry is a further climax, but the whole performance is a lesser, as well as a briefer, thing, and it breaks down in an admission of the failure of her heroic resolve. Lysistrata remains in the shadow of Magnus.

These speeches, not the Interlude, supply the high point of passionate intensity in the play. For the most part, a high degree of emotional and imaginative disengagement is characteristic of the play. The political cartoonist's work is a form of journalism that defeats its own end if the imaginative force informing it obliterates the starting-point of actuality, the topical situation. It is interesting, in the present instance, to see the connection between this disengagement and the history of the play's composition.

One germ of *The Apple Cart* may be found embedded in Chapter XV of *An Unsocial Socialist*, where Trefusis argues: 'A king nowadays is only a dummy put up to draw your fire off the real oppressors of society . . . Finally, having taken everything else that men prize from him, we fall upon his character, and that of every person to whom he ventures to show favour . . .' A picture of his dead wife, the romantically beautiful Henrietta, gazes upon him from an elaborately jewelled frame: a remote anticipation of Orinthia the Beloved.

Further contributions to the development of Shaw's idea seem to have been made by Laurence Housman's political satire, *King John of Jingalo*.[1] At the climax of this novel, King John asserts his constitutional power when he counters his Prime Minister's tactical threats of resignation by himself abdicating. The prospect facing the Cabinet is made worse by the republican views of the heir to the throne, Prince Max, who anticipates that a monarchy which dares to be democratic, that is, 'human and natural', will in time provide the country with its first popularly elected President. King John's disputes with his Ministers in Council offered Shaw source material for the kind of debate he was well able to make amusing on the stage; and Housman had varied these with more domestic episodes, as *The Apple Cart* was to do.

[1] My attention was drawn to the similarities of the two works by the late Sir Lewis Casson, who was told by Housman himself that his novel had been used by Shaw as a source for *The Apple Cart*.

King Magnus's family, like King John's, contains a young and charming
Princess Royal, as well as a Queen and Crown Prince. (Housman's Queen
is called Alicia; Alice is the name of Shaw's Princess Royal.) There is no
true equivalent of Orinthia in Housman's satire, and Queen Alicia is no
comfortable Jemima. King John is a very ordinary fellow under his
crown, with none of the personal distinction and political acumen that
belong to Magnus. John's trial of strength with his Cabinet is an aberration: the effect of a temporary dislocation of a bone in his skull through a
fall. Though the jolt sets his brains ticking, his political insight does not
penetrate beyond his own constitutional power. Shaw's theme is more
considerable.

King John of Jingalo was published in 1912, and it was the best part of
seventeen years before Shaw set to work on the material it offered. It
is probable that it was the publication in 1928 of Granville Barker's last
play, *His Majesty*, that brought the novel back into his mind. *Prunella*
(first produced and published in 1904) is the best-known product of a
period of extensive collaboration between Laurence Housman and Granville Barker.[1] In particular, there are striking similarities between the
first episode of *King John* and the end of *His Majesty*. The closeness of
the group of dramatists involved together in the Court Theatre experiment and its successors, and particularly the artistic and personal intimacy
between Shaw and Barker that had already linked Barker's *Voysey
Inheritance* and the contemporary *Major Barbara*, *The Madras House*
and *Misalliance*, was still bearing fruit in 1929, when something like a
process of thought shared with his old friend could still provide the background to the particular originality of Shaw's first Malvern Festival
play.

The composition of *His Majesty* took Barker from 1923 to 1928,
whereas *The Apple Cart* was written for Barry Jackson in six weeks.
His Majesty is much the more ambitious in scale and conception. It
has never been performed on the professional stage (Barker told Harcourt
Williams that he had deliberately held it back from every 'rut of chance').
When it was broadcast in 1950, a brief note by Stephen Williams in the
Radio Times (17 November 1950, p. 10) commented on the similarity
between Barker's King Henry, a master at the political game, and King
Magnus. Other resemblances are quickly discoverable: the romantic
absurdity of Orinthia corresponds to the dominant quality of Barker's
Queen Rosamund; the King's first interview, in either play, is with a

---

[1] Housman once informed me that he and Barker had collaborated on six or
seven plays, though *Prunella* was the only one published under both their
names. For further details, see Laurence Housman, *The Unexpected Years*
(London: Cape, 1937).

spokesman for democratic equality, and the new opponent introduced in the last act is the ambassador of a foreign power; the domestic relations of Henry, like those of Magnus and John of Jingalo, provide scenes of relief from the main business of political bargaining; and abdication is the weapon with which Barker's hero, too, wins the struggle. The topsy-turvydom which characterizes the encounter between Boanerges and the Secretaries recalls the subtler exposition of double-think given by Count Zapolya in Act I of *His Majesty*.

The identities are obscured by great differences of method and style. Shaw's play is *opéra bouffe*, with a deliberately dislocated structure. *His Majesty* is a tragi-comedy on the grand scale, symphonic in design and impact, and employing a fine psychological realism as the basic mode of character-drawing. It is much the more complex play, too complex to be easily summarized. *The Apple Cart* looks shallow and facile satire beside it, with a theatrical adroitness obvious enough to deserve Shaw's own comment: 'The whole affair is a frightful bag of stage tricks as old as Sophocles. I blushed when I saw it.'[1] Shaw was able to work as quickly as he did because of the extent to which he could bypass the profounder processes normally involved in the dramatic working-out of a complex theme. Granville Barker had done this kind of imaginative thinking for him and now supplied him with the tokens of it ready-minted for his own use. Shaw's further contributions was a clearer, more forceful communication of the central ideas.

Barker had taken the convention of Ruritanian romance and made it at once more realistic and more symbolical. The King and Queen of Carpathia are in exile after defeat in World War I. Their country is now an uneasy liberal republic on the verge of bankruptcy. A band of royalists, under the command of Stephen Czernyak, is advancing on the capital. Their prospects of success are slight but the threat they imply is enough to bring down the moderate government before its enemies, foreign and domestic. Most formidable is Bruckner, a convert from socialism to fascist *realpolitik*:

> THE KING. What did you go to prison for?
> BRUCKNER. Optimism. Belief in the millennium . . . in the brotherhood of man and the rest of it. I'm quite cured.

King Henry secretly returns to Carpathia, hoping to check the folly of his supporters and save the country from political disaster and further bloodshed. He succeeds in helping the Prime Minister, Madrassy, to maintain the *status quo*, an unspectacular achievement; but his fight for human values in the teeth of necessity is no matter of empty debate.

---

[1] From letter to Alfred Sutro, quoted further p. 309.

L

Henry is the anti-hero to the conventional epic hero represented by
Czernyak, whose simpler view of the world is reflected in Queen Rosamund's romantic imagination. (The Bluntschli–Saranoff–Raina pattern
of *Arms and the Man* is discernible here.) The climax is reached when
she and Czernyak flout the King's authority, misled by their loyalist
ideals into a double act of treachery; and, usurping control of the play
of diplomacy, they drag it towards the melodrama of bloody civil war.
Before equilibrium is restored, King Henry has to prove, in personal
encounter with Bruckner, the truth of the latter's dictum:

> There's one way to govern a country . . . just one. Find where its real
> power is . . . and give that play.

This reflection is the basis of Shaw's critique of large-scale democracy.
It is echoed in Magnus's comment that a capital 'will stay at a real
centre of gravity only' and demonstrated in his triumph over the united
opposition of the Cabinet. Lysistrata extends the relevance of the point:

> It is not the most ignorant national crowd that will come out on top, but the
> best power station; for you cant do without power stations, and you cant
> run them on patriotic songs and hatred of the foreigner, and guff and
> bugaboo . . .

But this is precisely the kind of performance the Cabinet, led by Proteus,
puts on stage. *The Apple Cart* exposes an actual divorce between power
and the functions of government and supports the exposure with an
attack on the (Marxist) belief that political effectiveness can inhere in
the masses. While the elected representatives of the people make speeches
in parliament and squabble over constitutional issues, the country is
dominated by Breakages Limited, the big business in which 'public
losses are . . . private gains'.[1] Boanerges's explanation of his position
has not lost its topicality:

> No king on earth is as safe in his job as a Trade Union official . . . I talk
> democracy to these men and women. I tell them that they have the vote,
> and that theirs is the kingdom and the power and the glory. I say to them
> 'You are supreme: exercise your power'. They say, 'Thats right: tell us
> what to do'; and I tell them. I say 'Exercise your vote intelligently by
> voting for me.' And they do. That's democracy . . .

Before the argument that a 'democratic' politician can only be a demagogue is dismissed as fascist, the lesson of *On the Rocks* is worth recalling.
Shaw's attack on blind faith in the parliamentary system was proceeding
logically, developing criticisms that had never been adequately answered

---

[1] Cf. *His Majesty*: ' . . . the men that fool their fellow-men and call it government and the fellows behind that they let fool them . . . that stir the mud and
fish their dirty profit from it.'

since they were launched by Carlyle and by Dickens.[1] Magnus's tempering
of idealism with pragmatism is thoroughly Fabian; and the balance he
represents, which is also the author's, is visually declared when he enters
to meet the Cabinet with Lysistrata, Powermistress-General, to one side
of him, and Amanda, Postmistress-General, to the other. For the first is
spokeswoman for the play's earnest concerns and didactic intentions; the
second is a personification of satirical entertainment, the gay theatrical
mode corresponding to an irreverence certain of its own survival power
whatsoever kings may reign or empires come to ruin.

Shaw referred to the evolution of his play in a letter to Alfred Sutro:

> Sempronius père was a false start. I began with a notion of two great parties:
> the Ritualists and the Quakers, with the King balancing them one against
> the other and finally defeating a combination of them. But I discarded this,
> as there wasnt room for it. However, I thought the opening would make a
> very good Mozartian overture to get the audience settled down and in the
> right attentive mood before the real play began . . .[2]

The 'Mozartian overture' is in fact based on many of the same leitmotifs as
His Majesty.[3] The original design seems to have remained in Shaw's
mind until its contribution to the later play, *In Good King Charles's
Golden Days*, where something like a confrontation of Quakers and
Ritualists takes place in the house of Isaac Newton, and the greatest
poise and wisdom belong to the King. (A form of leitmotif structure is
detectable in Acts I and II of that play, but it seems to be abandoned in
the final scene.) A sorting-out of themes in the first dialogue of *The
Apple Cart* illuminates some obscurities in the play and draws attention
to the thematic resonance of certain elements in the main dramatic
design.

Sempronius portrays his father as the complete ritualist (a new name

---

[1] See especially Carlyle's *Shooting Niagara – And After?* written in reaction
against the 1867 Reform Act. It is less easy to choose a single text to exemplify
Dickens's criticisms of democracy: the account of the election of Veneering in
Our Mutual Friend is, perhaps, the culminating point. His distrust of the
machinery of Trade Unionism and the opportunity it gave to unscrupulous
demagogues is expressed in *Hard Times* and anticipates the satire Shaw centres
on Boanerges.

[2] Quoted in Hesketh Pearson, *Bernard Shaw. His Life and Personality*
(London: Collins, 1942; Methuen, 1961), p. 390. American ed. entitled *G.B.S.
A Full Length Portrait* (New York: Harper, 1942).

[3] Leitmotif structure plays a considerable part in other plays of both dramatists,
apart from the two at present under discussion. An article on the track of it in
Candida is W. N. King, 'The Rhetoric of *Candida*', *Modern Drama*, Vol. II
(1959), pp. 71–83. See also M. M. Morgan, *A Drama of Political Man*, esp.
pp. 252–300 on *His Majesty*.

for Shaw's bogey Idealist). The relevance of the designation to the theatre
in general and the symbol of royalty in particular is quickly apparent:

> He was a sort of spectacular artist. He got up pageants and Lord Mayor's
> Shows . . . He arranged the last two coronations . . . All our royal people
> knew him quite well: he was behind the scenes with them.

So far, Sempronius père may be identified as a figure of the dramatist
as a dealer in symbols. Here is a clear warning that the King, in the play
to follow, is to be regarded at least in part as a metaphysical image.
Indeed, Magnus recognizes better than anyone that this is true of kings
in life as in art:

> A real man would never do as a king. I am only an idol, my love; and all I
> can do is to draw the line at being a cruel idol.

But the account of old Sempronius narrows and grows more satirical:

> He didnt know what thought meant . . . and he had an oddly limited sort
> of imagination. What I mean is that he couldnt imagine anything he
> didnt see; but he could imagine that what he did see was divine and holy
> and . . . everything that is impossible if only it looked splendid enough . . .

It is the Panglossian error again and may serve as a warning not to
take even King Magnus at his face value as an ideal symbol of authority;
certainly any superstitious reverence for democracy itself is being undermined. The old ritualist's only social resource was playing cards: it
conjures up an *Alice in Wonderland* image of two-dimensional kings,
queens, knaves, filling dramatic roles with an illusion of animation.
How far and how little this can represent the characters of *The Apple.
Cart* can only be discerned by sensitive observation. The metaphor of the
game of cards (among other games) is continued in the main body of the
play:

> PROTEUS. Now, King Magnus. Our cards are on the table.
>
> LYSISTRATA. . . . In this Cabinet there is no such thing as a policy. Every
> man plays for his own hand.
>
> NICOBAR. It's like a game of cards.
>
> MAGNUS. . . . before you play your last card and destroy me . . .
>
> PROTEUS. . . . You stole your ace of trumps from the hand I played this
> morning.

The expressions are hardly more than dead metaphors, common idioms;
yet there they are, and they have their effect in characterizing the main
action of the play as merely ceremonial manœuvring that does not touch
reality of power. Robert, Prince of Wales, reported by his father,
obviously has the right of it:

He asks me why I waste my time with you here pretending to govern the country when it is really governed by Breakages Limited.

Even the desertion of the enemy agents within the ranks points up the growing irrelevance of such conflicts as this between Magnus and his Cabinet: Nicobar and Crassus will go out of politics – 'If Breakages will let me. They shoved me into it; and I daresay theyll find another job for me,' declares the latter; 'Politics is a mug's game,' sums up Nicobar.

Shaw's overture interweaves the motif of faith with that of the image:

> Do you suppose a baker cannot believe sincerely in the sacrifice of the Mass or in holy communion because he has baked the consecrated wafer himself?

The tautological awkwardness of expression suggests an intended but undramatic pun on 'Mass', whereby 'the sacrifice of the Mass' might convey a sly reference to its possible conversion to 'holy communion' (a metaphor for the ideal society used prominently in Barker's *Madras House*).[1] The difference between a merely formal and a meaningful symbolism is a theme that *His Majesty* works out in character and action as well as in dialogue, as it plays off against each other the dominant images of the body politic and the mystical body of Christ. A contrast is maintained between the natural man (which both Henry and Magnus strive to realize in themselves) and the lifeless puppet, or sham, featured among Barker's characters as Captain Papp, son of the General's tailor. Queen Rosamund's imagination is filled with significant images of the King on his horse at the head of his troops, or at the altar, crowned, with sword stretched out, swearing 'to save Carpathia in her need'; Bruckner travesties them:

> If you do as I tell you I'll have you in Karlsburg within the week. . . . On your white horse . . . with your crown on. . . .

As Henry refuses to be turned into 'the dumb sign of a faith made tame and ridiculous', so Magnus rejects Proteus's proposal to make him 'a dumb king'. The failure of old Sempronius to know reality from illusion is described in terms that recall Queen Rosamund's imagery:

> Nature to him meant nakedness; and nakedness only disgusted him. He wouldnt look at a horse grazing in a field; but put splendid trappings on it and stick it into a procession and he just loved it.[2] The same with men and women: they were nothing to him until they were dressed up in fancy costumes and painted and wigged and titled . . .

---

[1] See ibid., pp. 178–9 and above, Chapter 11 on *Misalliance*.

[2] Snowjacket, the state charger, might be numbered among the characters of *His Majesty*.

The antithesis to this frame of mind comes in King Henry's words to
Count Czernyak:

> . . . when next I open Parliament I shall walk down the hill from the
> Castle . . . frock coat, top hat, with an umbrella if it's raining. . . . It would
> be the natural thing to do. You dont believe in my divine right, Stephen.
> But the fact is . . . if I havent that, Ive no other. Nor has any man.

Magnus's indictment of 'the india rubber stamp theory', 'because there is
a divine spark in us all; and the stupidest or worst monarch or minister
. . . is a bit of a god' sounds flat in comparison: an echoing of the thought
that has simply been intellectually received.

Little is made of the theme of faith in the rest of Acts I and II of *The
Apple Cart*; or, rather, Shaw transforms it into the idea that the individual
is the only repository of true political power. This is Magnus's chief
concern, when America threatens virtually to annex England:

> We may survive only as another star on your flag. Still, we cling to the little
> scrap of individuality you have left us.

The 'star' provides a mechanical link with the Interlude, where the
same metaphor carries an anticipation of the catastrophe that Act II
has in store:

> Every star has its orbit; and between it and its nearest neighbour there is
> not only a powerful attraction but an infinite distance. When the attraction
> becomes stronger than the distance the two do not embrace: they crash to-
> gether in ruin.

The spectacle of the King dragged to the floor in Orinthia's embrace
follows as a burlesque illustration of his meaning. But with Orinthia,
who 'reign[s] . . . in beauty like the stars' the theme of faith comes into
its own; she is, like Queen Rosamund, both an idealist and an ideal. She
tempts Magnus: 'Give me a goddess's work to do; and I will do it. I
will even stoop to a queen's work if you will share the throne with me.'
Her images carry the recognition that she belongs to heaven rather than
to earth. (The King's relations with her are, explicably, 'strangely
innocent'.)

There is an obvious theatrical motive to account for the interlude in
The Apple Cart, in that it supplies a role for a star actress in a play that
might have failed to enthuse audiences because of its lack of erotic
interest or appeal to the egotistic emotions; and something further was
needed to make a full-length play, for the business with the Cabinet
might easily have grown tedious if it was protracted. The duologue of
Magnus and Orinthia offers a pleasing contrast to the rest of the play.
But its apparently detachable quality is flaunted, whereas merely prag-

matic technical considerations would more probably have prompted
efforts to tie it in functionally with the rest. The separateness, in fact,
lends it emphasis, as a striking asymmetry gives similar emphasis to the
comparable duologue between the King and Catherine of Braganza,
in her boudoir, which ends *Good King Charles*, after the long first act
crowded with characters. Catherine and Orinthia alike appear nowhere
else in their respective plays.[1] Of course, *The Apple Cart* ends with
Magnus and Queen Jemima, alone together for a brief moment. If we
see Act II of *King Charles* as corresponding to *The Apple Cart* Interlude,
the difference of placing can be related to the fusion in Catherine of the
two aspects of Woman that Orinthia and Jemima separately represent.
Like Jemima, Catherine is the dowdy wife who holds first place in her
husband's affections despite his philanderings; but her dreams and ambitions are more akin to Orinthia's grandiose imagination. Catherine does
not illustrate in the same way as Jemima the anti-feminist gibe spoken
by the Secretary of the League in *Geneva*:

A domestic paragon: a political idiot. In short, an ideal wife.

Catherine has had a political education and is ambitious for a political
role; but it is an education that has unfitted her to survive in what is
essentially a Protestant democracy, as Charles understands better than
anyone. She is the female counterpart to James, Duke of York, in her
hankering after autocracy.

The departure from Barker's embodiment of the domestic everywoman
and the romantic ideal in the single figure of the Queen can be linked
with Shaw's double image of himself as Don Juan and husband of
Charlotte. There is a hint of self-justification about the unorthodoxly
favourable portrait of Charles II he gives, especially when the play is
read together with its Preface; and the biographers record that he connected the flooring of Magnus by Orinthia with incidents involving himself with Mrs Jenny Patterson and, later, with Mrs Patrick Campbell.[2]
But he was too much of a public artist to introduce personal allusions into
his work without transforming them into images of general significance.
So the Shavian – and typical nineteenth-century – predilection for playing
with danger (or eroticism) and settling for domestic security (with its
taboo on the erotic) is used as an instrument in the analysis of the
democratic situation. Orinthia, in effect, represents the temptation of
autocracy, as well as the dream of ideal government by which Magnus

---

[1] It must also be remarked that it takes this brief second act to confirm that
Charles, not Newton, is the central character of the play.
[2] See (e.g.) St John Ervine, *Bernard Shaw*, pp. 83–4.

steers. Jemima, surely, stands for political irresponsibility and negligence, however virtuous a wife she may be:

THE QUEEN. Now Magnus: it's time to dress for dinner.
MAGNUS (*much disturbed*). Oh, not now. I have something very big to think about. I dont want any dinner . . .
THE QUEEN (*going to him and taking his arm*). Now, now, now! dont be naughty. It mustnt be late for dinner. Come on, like a good little boy.

It is an unpleasantly ironic close[1] and may prompt reconsideration of Magnus's part throughout the play. And here we may come upon an element not simply derived from *His Majesty* and that does give some depth to the play: the emotions of chagrin and even bitterness that it has to yield in counterpoint to its superficial gaiety. From the public point of view, all that Magnus has achieved is the preservation of the *status quo*. Certainly he has struggled successfully against the complete negation of his personal qualities by the system: a limitedly responsible king with a royal veto – or any other man involved in public affairs who acts with such freedom of will as he has within the machinery of the system – may put a brake on madness and folly, as long as he is both wise and public-spirited. Both preserving this built-in check on the haphazard crudities of parliamentary democracy makes no easier ex-peditious and effective action for the public good – and against Breakages. Magnus knows this himself:

I am too old-fashioned. This is a farce that younger men must finish.

It is a statement in line with Sir Arthur Chavender's judgement of himself in *On the Rocks*: that he is not the man to deal with a situation that has outrun the best remedial efforts of parliamentary socialists and calls for stronger measures.

The unchanged perilousness of the situation is obscured, but not totally, by concentration on Magnus's diplomatic skill and limited success. And the sympathetic presentation of this nearly ideal human being among the puppets distracts attention from his feet of clay. The character is built to carry off, quite as well as Orinthia does, an absolutist claim:

I stand for the great abstractions: for conscience and virtue; for the eternal against the expedient; for the evolutionary appetite against the day's gluttony; for intellectual integrity, for humanity, for the rescue of industry from commercialism and of science from professionalism . . .

Yet he resists the dreams Orinthia lures him with, and voluntarily submits to Jemima with '*hopeless tenderness*'. The compromise is both philosophical and artistic, and necessary in either case. Magnus as a

[1] Formally, it corresponds to the final passage of *His Majesty*, though the tone is different.

symbolic norm had also to be kept naturalistically individual. For Shaw
stopped short of Carlylean hero-worship.

Breakages Limited is the villain of the piece:

> But for them we should have unbreakable glass, unbreakable steel, im-
> perishable material of all sorts.

This ranges wider than Capitalism to embrace the destructive dionysiac
element inherent in a world of change and the imperfections of human
nature that separate even one who is 'less of a fool and less of a moral
coward than any man I have known' from that great abstraction, the
symbolic king. Though the Preface suggests that there may be more hope
in Boanerges, this is hardly substantiated by the play. There he is the
able novice being broken in, and for whom the whole crisis is an object
lesson; that is all. This is another play in which Shaw refrains from
triumphantly resolving a difficult situation on stage, through the medium
of a heroic character, because his principal object is to make his audience
realize that freedom, power and responsibility are its own inalienable
privileges, whatever circumstances are given.

A word may be added here on the closely related *In Good King Charles's
Golden Days,* though chronologically it comes after the more important
Geneva. The burlesque identity of *Good King Charles* emerges most
strongly with the introduction of the King's mistresses, a chorus whose
various colourful personalities provide a contrast with the 'figures' that
concern Newton and the political philosophy that primarily occupies
Charles – just as their spectacular dresses contrast with the sober leather
suit of George Fox.[1] The minimal action of the play may be symptomatic
of Shaw's dwindling dramatic vitality: capable still of plotting the elements
of his drama quite tightly and carefully to illustrate a theme, he may
have been unable to release the energy that would carry it on its own
momentum. Yet it needs to be recognized that the inaction has its own
serious significance. The moment of history chosen represents a pause
between old absolutism (effectually killed with Charles I but reflected still
in the ambitions of the Duke of York and Queen Catherine) and the
demagoguery of which Titus Oates is a portent. Furthermore the temporal
pause has an extra-historical, philosophical aspect as the point of balance
which Charles maintains between the two extremes, the alternative
evils still recognizable in the twentieth-century choice between Fascist
tyranny and mob rule. In this view, Charles's attempt to preserve a
stability equal to the Vicar of Bray's (the familiar song is the source of the

---

[1] Carlyle's 'man in leather breeches' of *Sartor Resartus*, III, ch. 1.

play's title of course) is comparable to the sitting-still policy of the Shavian Caesar. To compensate for the lack of true dramatic action Shaw again provided the stage 'turns' that diversify burlesque or vaudeville – including the symbolic farce of the wrestling-match between Newton and James, Duke of York, and the recitations from Dryden. In this last instance, he perhaps intended a theatrical demonstration of the idea of relativity that is at the play's core, reflected now in the distance between his own prose and Dryden's verse, between the style of the actors playing their Restoration parts in the Shavian comedy and these same actors playing actors in a heroic tragedy – a recognizable Pirandellian device.

Thematically, *In Good King Charles's Golden Days* confirms *The Apple Cart* in stressing individual responsibility (as Carlyle had stressed it), but not proceeding to demand a leader, a hero to be worshipped. For Magnus and Charles are not heroes in that sense: they are simply responsible men: symbolic figures of what every man might be. The plays in which they are found develop Shaw's exposition of the alternative to the tyrant that Arthur Chavender, in *On the Rocks*, feared to be necessary; they are followed by the negative demonstration, in *Geneva*, of what such leaders are like – the end to which Carlyle's thought became perverted in Fascism. The group of plays, taken together, indicates that Shaw steered more carefully than he has often been given credit for.

Geneva is as close to Aristophanic comedy as any Shaw play gets. The fact may be connected with the publication in 1933 of Gilbert Murray's *Aristophanes*, dedicated to G.B.S. Introducing his book, Murray had written:

> In times like these one often longs for the return to earth of one of the great laughing philosophers . . . for many years I have wished quite particularly for Aristophanes and wondered whether . . . he could bring us later generations some help. Could he fight against our European war-fevers and nationalisms . . . ? He might do it, if only the Fascisti and Nazis and Ogpus could refrain from killing him, and the British authorities from forbidding him to land in England. The world badly needs a man of genius who could make whole nations listen to him . . .[1]

Here is the general programme for the play which was running in Warsaw when Hitler invaded Poland. Its style is satirical farce and its

[1] Quoted from the second edition (Oxford: O.U.P., 1965), pp. vii–viii. The connection between this book and *Geneva* has already been remarked by G. Pilecki in *Shaw's Geneva*, Studies in English Literature VIII (The Hague: Mouton, 1965), which includes a full and very useful account of Shaw's textual revisions of the play and a history of his political thought.

action carries even less emotional resonance than *The Apple Cart* possesses, yet the author's gravity underlies the whole and emerges in the argument. Just as he had done in *John Bull's Other Island*, Shaw was again using the theatre as public platform from which to address an audience of citizens – the populations of Europe this time – on urgent political questions. His concern with topical politics involved him in more textual revision than usual simply to keep up with events. Like Aristophanes, he brought caricatures of actual personages on to the stage and, in the setting of the play and the machinery of the plot, he was concerned with actual public institutions: the League of Nations, the World Court, the Committee for Intellectual Co-operation (Murray had attempted to make Shaw active in this Committee).

The presentation of Mussolini, Hitler, and Franco in caricature as Bombardone, Battler, and Flanco was chiefly responsible for the popular success of *Geneva* when it was new. (The London production of 1938–9 had a run exceeded in length by only three other Shaw plays.) Primitive magic is not quite dead in an art that makes images of the actual tyrants who terrorize over their generation and by its manipulation of these reduces the contemporary nightmare to thinkable and manageable proportions. The persecution and massacre of the Jews, the physical enslaving of minorities, the omnipresent fear of secret police throughout totalitarian Europe, the brutality of officially encouraged thugs, the general corruption and dissolution of civilized life, finally the terror and devastation caused by modern war, and all the psychic tensions behind these manifestations, were inescapable facts of existence in 1939, hardly amenable to direct treatment in comedy. The Hitlers and Mussolinis, Napoleons and Genghis Khans acquire their monstrous stature by becoming the focus of the emotions aroused by the whole range of such widespread experiences. The human faculty that produces melodrama or Grand Guignol art is at work here. With a lowering of the emotional temperature, the absurdity of the fantastic and oversimplified images becomes apparent, and melodrama reveals its special vulnerability to burlesque.

Shaw works the trick by showing up the unreality of the figures he has yet made so lifelike. Bergson's theory of the comic stands him in good stead: the characters are conceived and presented as very like mechanical dolls, inflated beyond human life-size and with no more naturalistic psychology than the ogres of pantomime, or mumming-plays, out-Heroding Herod. The arrogance requisite to any actual tyrant is caricatured in their acceptance of the roles assigned to them. 'God has ordained that when men are childish enough to fancy that they are gods they become what you call funny. We cannot help laughing at them,' says the Deaconess in the final act of *Geneva*. Critical complaints that the characterization of the dictators is unconvincing is testimony to the success Shaw achieved in evoking some sense of his living models. A clear indication of the artistic convention he was working in is provided in Act I in the simpler, less ambiguous figure of the Bishop, who three times collapses from shock like a puppet when the strings are no longer held taut; twice he is hoisted up again, the third time left lying for dead, when the Commissar's words endorse what any audience will certainly have felt: 'Was he ever alive? To me he was incredible.' It is as great idolatry to regard a human being as incarnate evil as to accept him as the epitome of virtue. The dramatic method implicitly assaults the idolatrous tendency. The puppet-master uses his dolls to quieten his audiences' alarm, so that they become more capable of thinking and acting responsibly, as the swamping, subconscious turmoil dies down.

The writing of an additional act, in 1945, to follow the original Act II and so turn *Geneva* into a four-act play[1] still does not obscure the essential structure of the work as a dramatic prologue followed by a long court scene. Act I is set in the under-occupied office of the Committee for Intellectual Co-operation at Geneva, where a series of visitors arrive and present their demands: the first is a Jew who complains of German anti-Semitism; the second, called simply the Newcomer, reports a case of the supersession of elective parliamentary government by totalitarian 'business efficiency' (Old Hipney's remedy applied); the third is the Widow of a South American President, a figure from romantic extravaganza, who brandishes a pistol and breathes the fiery ethic of the blood-feud; she is followed by an elderly English Bishop of extreme mental debility, whose bogey is Communism, and then, lastly, by a Russian Commissar. There to receive them all is the secretary from Peckham, Miss Begonia Brown, who has been flirting with her American journalist friend. These comic representatives of the most secure Western democracies are audience-surrogates on stage, required not only to listen to the issues presented but to do something about them.

At first, with the entry of the Jew, it seems that Shaw is concerned directly with actual international situations. But it becomes less easy to identify the wrongs the others plead with particular incidents or movements. The identity of the Newcomer is slippery: his native language is English, but his exact place of origin is left in doubt. He speaks '*like a shop-keeper from the provinces, or perhaps, by emigration, the dominions*'. In the course of the play, he varies between insistence on his status as a Britisher

---

[1] This is the form it takes in the standard edition, first published in 1946. The play is available in its earlier three-act form in the editions published in 1939 and 1940, illustrated by Feliks Topolski. On the variations presented by the published texts, see Pilecki, op. cit., pp. 41–73.

and talk of his own country of Jacksonland, where the new Prime Minister, having dispensed with parliament, brought in his organized body of Clean Shirts 'to help the police'. What we are told about Jacksonland will not fit any particular British dominion. Shaw may have had in mind the suspension of parliamentary self-government in Newfoundland as a result of the economic crisis of the early 1930s; but the more sinister elements in the situation described suggest the threat the Mosleyites offered in Britain itself, as well as events that had actually taken place in Europe, especially Germany, when the dictators came to power. With the entrance of the Widow from the Republic of the Earthly Paradise, it becomes obvious that topical allusions are less important than ideas in the scheme of the play. The Earthly Paradise is ironically named, but it also suggests the first primitive state of human society, before public responsibility for law and justice was instituted. The Widow has come in search of some authority that will relieve her of the burdens of private justice, the wild justice of revenge for honour. The other characters in the play are not troubled because an internal legal system has failed to develop in their respective homelands (though it may in some instances have been flouted by politicians). The central relevance of the Widow in the play is rather to the field of international politics where the supreme authority of law is still unknown. Looking back, it is possible to recognize the earlier visitors as typical of universal problems that supra-national law would have to deal with. The Jew stands for the rights of minorities in the face of a universal human tendency to turn the alien into a scapegoat; it is a problem of power, and racism in its various forms is one possible manifestation of it, nationalism another. Jacksonland defines itself, in equally general terms, as the modern Utopia of democratic man, the homeland of the elective self-government of peoples, now universally at risk. The English Bishop and the Commissar confront each other as figures of old and new religions. The former is the least sympathetic representative of Christianity Shaw ever put on the stage. (The Commissar has met a very different sort of English Bishop, more like Hewlett Johnson in the revolutionary vigour of his youth.) Indeed there is nothing left of Christianity in the character but prejudice, the closed mind, and a blind and horrified opposition to Communism. The life goes out of it before the prologue ends. It was a false attitude of British public opinion that Shaw had to dispose of before proceeding further.

His main business is philosophic inquiry, but under the pressure of a frightening contemporary situation never forgotten in the form the play takes. The court scene presents a disciplined argument which owes a great deal to Shaw's reading of the Platonic dialogues, in particular the

early books of the *Republic*, to which *Geneva* shows similarities in
thought and form. The relationship is only slightly disguised by the more
exaggeratedly burlesque elements in the play. The technique of pursuing
an abstract argument through the apparently meandering and digressive
discussion of a varied group of persons – with the names and characters
of actual people, in an actual setting – relieving the tension of logical
enquiry with bursts of humour and incidental action of a minor kind,
which may be used as grounds for raising further questions or proceeding
to further definitions: all this is familiar in the *Republic*. Shaw's court
scene is not a trial of the dictators so much as an investigation of the
thoroughly Platonic themes of law and justice and moral responsibility
in public affairs, in the presence of effigies of the dictators. The Judge,
who has no private identity beyond his Dutch origin and training,
fulfils the Socratic function and clearly communicates the author's
purpose:

> . . . do you understand that the judgments of this court are followed by no
> executions? They are moral judgments only.

This is the answer to the critical objection that the interest of *Geneva*
was limited by its topical occasion. (Plato, Machiavelli and Hobbes wrote
within the framework of actual historical situations, with reference to
actual governments, and in concern for the political future; even now,
what they wrote has more than a mild historical interest.)

The occasion is indeed a Judgement Day in the same sense as is
understood in *The Simpleton of the Unexpected Isles* and, appropriately
enough, an apocalyptic announcement brings its proceedings to an end:

> Astronomers report that the orbit of the earth is jumping to its next quantum
> . . . Humanity is doomed.

It is, of course, a device Shaw had used in previous plays and here, again,
it is only a warning: the report is false. It is not an insignificant trick
ending either, but takes up a theme sounded in Act I, in Commissar
Posky's account of his housekeeper's conversion by the Society for the
Propagation of the Gospel in Foreign Parts:

> She refused to do any work . . . on the ground that the end of the world is
> at hand.

Indeed, that would be the reasonable conclusion for humanity if the play
really did express Shaw's final abandonment of hope for man as a
political animal in favour of a long-distance faith in some new, more
highly evolved form of life. But this is clearly not how he intends *Geneva*

to be taken. He is unlikely to have abandoned his view, in *The Simpleton*, that work has a moral value; and 'personal gravitation', as Bombardone calls the principle King Magnus illustrated, will always count:

> Some of the greatest men have disliked the human race. But for Noah, its Creator would have drowned it.

These words, spoken by the Jew in his first interview with Begonia Brown, signal Shaw's concern to call out the Noahs in his audience.

The demand for justice is what brings all the callers to the office in Act I: not simply redress for the wrongs they have suffered, but a universal law and an incorruptible authority to which they can appeal. The Judge, in the court scene, knows better than to deny the British Foreign Minister's charge:

> SIR ORPHEUS. I am afraid you are a bit of an idealist.
> THE JUDGE. Necessarily. Justice is an ideal; and I am a judge.

The self-description the Widow supplies to the court indicates the sinister ground in human nature that makes some objective higher authority so necessary:

> My name is Reveng e. My name is Jealousy. My name is the unwritten law that is no law. Until y ou have dealt with me you have done nothing.

In the World Court, all private matters turn into public issues. (This seems to be the point of the hidden radio and television equipment that Begonia and the rest do not know about, when the act opens.) Settling responsibility for the random destruction caused by modern war calls for a special apparatus, but searching out the sins of the heart remains essentially its concern:

> THE JUDGE. . . . Why are the persons who give such atrocious orders not brought to trial?
> SIR O. But before what court?
> JUDGE.[1] Before this court if necessary. There was a time when I might have answered 'Before the judgment seat of God'. But since people no longer believe that there is any such judgment seat, must we not create one before we are destroyed by the impunity and glorification of murder?

The sham villains have, as usual in Shaw's plays, their own fragments of insight to contribute. Battler is aware of the nature of the leader's

---

[1] The proof-reading of the standard edition was not impeccable. The text shows variations in the form of speakers' names and the retention of abbreviations that Shaw would probably have corrected in earlier years.

authority and its relation to the moral faith of his followers, or to the
vacuum created by the lack of any faith:

> BATTLER. Your authority goes as far as you dare push it and as far as it is
> obeyed . . . What authority has any leader? We command and are obeyed:
> that is all.

The Secretary of the League recognizes that: 'We need something higher
than nationalism: a genuine political and social catholicism.' In theory, at
least, Europe used to recognize the spiritual authority of the Christian
Church, to which its secular laws bore some relation. The death of the
Bishop, in Act I, has served as a token that the old spiritual authority is
defunct, if indeed it ever was more than a sham. But the Deaconess who
wanders into the Court, when all the rest are assembled, brings back
into consideration basic Christian principle, divorced from historical
institutions. The Judge acknowledges the relevance of her interruption:
'I rule that Jesus is a party in this case.' The discussion in fact turns from
the Old Law of Revenge and the self-responsibility and self-judgement of
the 'Roman soul' to consider the claims of the Law of Love as a basis for
international justice and order.

It would seem to have been rejected in advance, in the Judge's definition
of the practical difficulty:

> Dame Begonia is making a most valuable contribution to our proceedings.
> She is shewing us what we really have to deal with. Peace between the
> Powers of Europe on a basis of irreconcilable hostility between Camberwell
> and Peckham: that is our problem.

The Deaconess's eventual answer to this comes in Platonic terms that
have an interesting bearing on the stage guying of the dictators:

> DEACONESS. . . . I was a perfect fiend, jealous, quarrelsome, full of imaginary
> ailments, as touchy as Mr Battler, as bumptious as Signor Bombardone –
> . . . Look within, look within, and you will understand. I brought it all to
> Jesus; and now I am happy . . . It is so simple.
> BBDE. It is made much simpler by the fact that you are protected by an
> efficient body of policemen with bludgeons in their pockets, madam. You
> have never had to govern.
> DEACONESS. I have had to govern myself, sir. And now I am governed by
> Jesus.

The argument, as well as the Salvation Army effusiveness of the lady's
manner, recalls *Major Barbara*. Bombardone's Machiavellian claim that
physical force is needed to ensure order is not revoked; it balances and
supplements the Deaconess's more complex statement of the subjective
origins of xenophobic nationalism and the need to put the personal life
in order and govern it according to moral principle. What is outside –

international chaos and totalitarian monsters of irresponsibility – is a projection of what is inside. Battler's subsequent comment – 'the real obstacle to human progress is the sort of mind that has been formed in its infancy by the Jewish Scriptures' – has a partial validity in the context, both as it may refer to Old Testament nationalism and glorification of vengeance (not the intended reference on Battler's part, of course) and as it rejects, in Nietzschean fashion, the submissive and masochistic spirit of 'Crosstianity'. Behind his elaborately amateur manner, this is something that Sir Orpheus Midlander[1] comprehends thoroughly and, as a practical statesmen, explained to the Judge in Act II:

> You see, my young friend – if you will allow me to call you so – justice, as you say, is an ideal, and a very fine ideal, too; but what I have to deal with is Power, and Power is often a devilishly ugly thing.

That power – the same power – is both physical and spiritual is insinuated in their quibbling discussion of the term 'sanctions'. No more than in *Major Barbara* is Shaw inclined to see the solution of political problems only in terms of spiritual authority and a change of heart. The situation of the play has its literal value: morality needs to be codified as law and implemented by political machinery. A truly effective World Court is desirable.

There was, of course, widespread disillusion with the League of Nations at the time when Shaw was composing his play. Allusions in the dialogue (especially in the additional Act III) make it clear that what goes on in the meetings of the League itself is something different from the proceedings of the World Court. Yet it is relevant and links up thematically with the business of Begonia Brown's parliamentary candidature, which Pilecki considers to be out of place in *Geneva*. The Secretary knows better than anyone that it is not a work of international co-operation and reconciliation that the League really performs:

> The organization of nations is the organization of world war . . . the League hangs over Europe like a perpetual warcloud.

---

[1] The Judge's persistent solecism in addressing him as 'Sir Midlander' is slightly out of character. In performance, it would have aided the identification of Sir Orpheus as a cartoon of Sir Austen Chamberlain (possibly incorporating certain features of Lord Grey). To have presented the British Foreign Secretary as a distortion of Anthony Eden or Neville Chamberlain would certainly have been inhibiting to the writing of the play for English theatres where the Lord Chamberlain's writ still ran. As it is, the character has a documentary quality without the same close relation to a recognizable contemporary leader as Bombardone, Battler and Flanco show./It is an artistically fortunate difference, for no contemporary English statesman was an ogre of the popular imagination to be exorcized in the play.

The charge is laid that the Powers simply use the League for the further-ance of their national ends. Like the Court itself, it is a stage that attracts histrionic personalities for the parade of public attitudes. The curtain line of the new act of 1945, 'Where the spotlight is, there will the despots be gathered', voices the perception of an inherent human need to have justice be seen to be done, and to engage public opinion in sympathy, admiration or fear. Enigmatically Battler declares at the outset that he has come to the Court to find out why he has come. An obscure impulse towards some objective standard, some principle of both power and right, deified by public response, is the answer the play implies.

The League is a stage for the enactment of national rivalries, the prosecution of national feuds, in debate. In this respect it is the Parliament of Europe, with the faults of lesser democratic parliaments. Begonia Brown, in whose jingoist British patriotism and local sentiment ('Up Camberwell') all nationalisms are lampooned, is adjudged a very fit representative of her constituency. 'If you want to know what real English public opinion is, keep your eye on me', she says. (This is a play of clear directives.) She is well-meaning, energetic, vulgar, pre-judiced and ignorant – 'she hasnt a political idea in her head'; but she will be elected because she can rightly claim 'there are lots of people in Camberwell who think as I do'; 'the House of Commons is just like Camberwell in that respect', Sir Orpheus adds.

As an indictment of democratic elections (which it is the particular concern of the Newcomer to defend), this goes quite as far as *The Apple Cart*, if not further. But Shaw has another quarry in view now, and the democratic ideal reveals itself ultimately as an ideal of the personal moral responsibility of individuals in the political world. Begonia's adoption as a parliamentary candidate and elevation to the rank of Dame of the British Empire mark stages in her growth as a responsible being, until she responds to the threat of cosmic disaster with a dignity befitting her official roles. Bombardone's self-conceit images the distance in human quality between the ordinary man and the political man of destiny in terms that ironically anticipate the astronomers' message:

> I am what I am: you are what you are; and in virtue of these two facts I am where I am and you are where you are. Try to change places with me: you may as well try to change the path of the sun through the heavens.

The Commissar, in the additional act, speaks more realistically:

> . . . infinite space is too much for us to manage. Be reasonable.

But from civilization's actual achievements in law and government to the establishment of a world order is only such a step as Begonia takes from Camberwell to the British Empire. That men as they are are intelligent enough to take it is the chief point the new act seems designed to argue. The League of Nations may have failed but it was a necessary first attempt:

> Not a farce . . . They came, these fellows. They blustered: they defied us. But they came. They came.

But 'farce' is a theatrical term for an art that presents the appearances of irrational behaviour without the emotional content that is its motive force; and these same lines make as audacious a claim as ever was made for the theatre's power over the actual world. The analogy implied is to be taken seriously as a true perception: that the power enjoyed by leaders of men is like an actor's power, equally dependent on a public stage and the imaginative investment of massed humanity in the figures that perform on it. This is not only the culmination of Shaw's long concern with idealism; it is the furthest reach of his understanding of the relation of his own identity as dramatist to his political mission: that he had come to understand political realities as themselves forms of theatre; and to see the fate of democracy, and humanity's control of its own destiny, as dependent on men's understanding of the determining part that the audience plays in the theatrical event.

18

The Shavian Muse –
In Conclusion

Shaw has been more underestimated since his death than he was overestimated in his lifetime. His long-continuing artistic fertility and the
variety and inventiveness still evident in the plays of his last period are
impressive in themselves and contribute to the character of his eminence
in the European theatre. If we are looking for signs of decline in his last
plays, it may be granted that they are more simply and directly conceived
and constructed, that the powerful control is less impressive as the vision
is less complex, and fewer interrelated conflicts are held suspended in the
artistic pattern than in some of the plays of twenty years before. Yet *The
Millionairess* is enough to challenge any generalization that dynamism has
been lost, as clarity and poise prevail. And none of his plays is stronger
testimony to his penetration of the nature of his own genius. The bright
light it sheds retrospectively on his whole career as a political dramatist
may serve in guiding the present study to its conclusions. Epifania
Ognisanti di Parerga is the Shavian muse unveiled and magnificently
named.[1] The power in Eppy has burnt up the ambiguousness that clung
to Ann Whitefield, or to Candida, as a vessel of the Life Force. In the
line of Shaw's women characters, she is the ultimate successor to Julia
Craven of *The Philanderer*, not now condemned and rejected, but
purified and apotheosized. The unhappy passion of Mrs Jenny Patterson
was not wasted after all: the young man she seduced and pursued grew to
be an old man whose art acknowledged the glamour and potency of the
life he had feared and fled. An essentially poetic manifestation took place
in a context of economic thinking.

Epifania is magnificently histrionic, an undisputed star role. Her
magnetism draws the other characters to the stage for the performance of

[1] Her names are translatable after a fashion: 'Manifestation' – 'All Saints';
and the dictionary meanings of Parerga are 'subordinate or accessory matter',
'ornamental embellishments', 'by-work'.

her play. She herself calls on her solicitor at his office. Challenged at the
end of Act I, her husband, Alastair Fitzfassenden, and her lover, Adrian
Blenderbland, do not know why they are there; the overwhelmingness
of Eppy has driven any purpose of their own out of their heads. The old
couple whose business she high-handedly takes over, in Act III, are left
dazed: 'It seems to me like a sort of dream,' says the Man, and the words
serve as comment on their pale unreality beside her vividness. The
Egyptian Doctor comes more directly to her call in Act IV:

> EPIFANIA. . . . I will live in utter loneliness and keep myself sacred until
> I find the right man – the man who can stand with me on the utmost
> heights and not lose his head – the mate created for me in heaven. He
> must be somewhere.
> THE DOCTOR (*appearing at the door*). The manager says I am wanted here.
> Who wants me?
> EPIFANIA. *I* want you . . .

It is true that Alastair brings with him his young woman, Patricia Smith,
alias Polly Seedystockings, who declares her independence: 'I have my
little bit of genius too; and she cant paralyze me.' The inclusion of her
placid ordinariness supplies a norm to set off Epifania's magnificence:
Alastair's 'Sunday wife', Patricia calls her, and the description supplies
a link between the Millionairess, Orinthia of *The Apple Cart* and Mrs
George Collins of *Getting Married*. Patricia knows the direction of her
own genius; it is 'For making people happy. Unhappy people come to me
just as money comes to her.' But she is only a token figure in the play.
Shaw acknowledges that her quality has a proper and necessary place
in life; it is not a quality that has any deep personal interest for him.

He is certainly intimately concerned with Epifania, who seems to
unite what fascinated him in capitalism, the perpetual object of his
attack, with the abounding energy that informs and characterizes his
own creative work. Epifania is not merely a millionairess; she has
inherited a gospel of money from her father, along with her fortune;
' "Stick to your money" he said "and all the other things shall be added
unto you." ' She is as certain as Undershaft that the possession of money
is necessary to a free, secure and powerful life: 'It's the difference between
living on the slope of a volcano and being safe in the garden of the
Hesperides.' The pleasure of making it is a fulfilment to her; yet neither
she nor her father, it seems, ever made anything else. Others regard her
love of money as meanness; but the avarice which determines her
unfailing and perfectly calculated economy is combined with the drive
of the born boss that organizes the productive capacities of others to
multiply her wealth. She never carries money, but lives by borrowing
from others. For her business enterprises she commandeers the finances

that others have deposited in banks, the profit of their labour. Her solicitor, Julius Sagamore, identifies her as 'An acquisitive woman. Precisely. How splendid!' and her family history is the history of capitalism, the acquisitive society:

> My ancestors were moneylenders to all Europe five hundred years ago: we are now bankers to all the world.

They have not been infallible. Epifania has arrived at Sagamore's office in despair and is administered the usual Shavian cure: die of it, or get over it. The cause of her distress is two-fold: that she has married the wrong man and that her income is much less than it should be. Her attachment to the hereditary principle – 'father-fixation' in terms of individual psychology – is insufficient to conceal that the great loss was her father's: 'the greatest man in the world. And he died a pauper . . . I have barely seven hundred thousand a year.' Adrian gets thrown downstairs for revealing in casually critical complaint that the revered parent backed the wrong side:

> I have not the slightest notion of how he contrived to get a legal claim on so much of what other people made; but I do know that he lost four fifths of it by being far enough behind the times to buy up the properties of the Russian nobility in the belief that England would squash the Soviet revolution in three weeks or so.

So far, it seems that the patronymic di Parerga is a sign that Epifania can be set alongside Mr Superflew, the middleman she cuts out in her reorganization of the old people's business: these people are all superfluous in the sense of being dispensable in a properly ordered society; they are parasitic.[1] Yet there is clearly more to Epifania than that: her restless energy and decisive force are the dynamism that transforms the 'natural ways' of the peasant into the processes of an efficient, highly industrialized society. Alastair and Adrian, Shaw's latest varieties of the young man-about-town, are very different creatures. Adrian is the mere consumer of luxuries and Eppy knows the truth about him: 'He is on fifteen boards of directors on the strength of his father's reputation, and has never, as

[1] Both names suggest Marx's doctrine of surplus value which Shaw had come to accept as practically identical with the theory of rent he had derived from Henry George, the surplus being 'the product of social labour which is appropriated by a propertied class by virtue, not of any economic function they perform, but of their special position in a society divided into propertied and propertyless.' Maurice Dobb, 'Bernard Shaw and Economics', in S. Winsten (ed.), *G.B.S. 90* (London: Hutchinson, 1946), pp. 131–9. See also A. M. McBriar, *Fabian Socialism and English Politics 1884–1918* (Cambridge: C.U.P., 1966), pp. 32–7, esp. p. 37, note 3.

far as I know, contributed an idea to any of them.' As for Alastair, he
made the money which won him Epifania as a wife in much the same
way as Wells's Kipps managed to cash in on the system – essentially
the same mode of gambling as Frank Gardner was content to live by. His
three ventures into capitalist business were all within the peripheral
area of entertainment and indeed proved to be the swings and roundabouts
of his fortunes. After the failure of an attempt to get the cash value of
his untrained natural endowments ('a startlingly loud singing voice of
almost supernatural range'), he reaped enormous profits from backing a
show, in collaboration with a quick-witted American, by a systematic
process of kiting cheques. The anecdote, as Alastair tells it to the assembled
company, provides a satire in miniature on normal big business methods
and the tenuousness of the distinction between capitalism and criminality.
Before he lost all his money in three weeks, after investing it in a circus,
he had married Epifania and so exposed the weakness of her father's test,
which the latter should himself have recognized – that it could be passed
by a lucky fluke without any sustaining ability:

> . . . ninety per cent of our selfmade millionaires are criminals who have
> taken a five hundred to one chance and got away with it by pure luck.

(The generic similarity to the test administered by Portia, in *The
Merchant of Venice*, after her father's death, is greater than is involved in
the choice of a successor to the Undershaft empire, which merely
excludes incompetents who might otherwise inherit through birth alone.)

Shaw has insinuated a distinction between irresponsible and inefficient
capitalism on the one hand, and well-managed and efficient big business
– like the firm of Undershaft and Lazarus. He demonstrates the better
alternative, in the present play, through Epifania's response to the test
proposed by her Egyptian doctor's mother, which is a variant on the
Judgement Day test of *The Simpleton*: one that will in fact prove that she
is not redundant, that she can justify her existence by earning her own
living.[1] This fable shows no hankering after a return to a pre-industrial
economy. It does make, in new terms, the *Major Barbara* distinction
between the brute power, meaningless and irresponsible, that lies in
money and the moral power that an individual, who is highly developed
in mind and spirit, can wield through it. Alastair's chief virtue in Eppy's
eyes is his solar plexus punch that has held her in control; the Doctor,
who is to replace him, is a wiser and a nobler being.

[1] The profits due to her efforts can be classified as differential 'rent of ability',
as the Fabians, following in the wake of F. A. Walker, understood it: ' differential
return going to the better entrepreneur because of his superior ability. It was
rooted in human nature; it sprang from natural differences in ability and so
would arise even in a perfect system.' (McBriar, op. cit., p. 40.)

Like Raina Petkoff, Epifania has had her aspirations after glory and has suffered the let-down of disillusionment:

> Listen to me, Mr Sagamore. I married this man. I admitted him to my world, the world which my imagination had peopled with heroes and saints. Never before had a real man been permitted to enter it. I took him to be hero, saint, lover all in one;

> I, Epifania Ognisanti di Parerga, saw myself as the most wonderful woman in England marrying the most wonderful man. And I was only a goose marrying a buck rabbit.

The hiatus between her splendid ideas and what she is and has achieved gives comedy its opportunity, at the same time as it humanizes the personification without obscuring its allegorical values. As we shall see, the presentation of Eppy as a romantic, living in imagination, is important. Sagamore, the audience before whom she chooses to perform, has a sense of humour to which her operatic temperament appeals. His laughter underlines the extent to which her histrionic egotism misses the effects she imagines. This is the area of burlesque; but it is also the area of powerful subjective emotions that external reality is inadequate to match or contain. That 'di Parerga' is appropriate to this excess, which at least conceives greatness and even tragedy, as well as other forms of the prolific abundance of nature and the money that an ineradicable human faculty tends to accumulate. For Epifania is sympathetically drawn: capitalism has its genius and, however vicious the effects of the system may be, it is a magnificent natural genius. Epifania's claim, 'I think Allah loves those who make money', is not the last word of the play, but it carries some considerable weight.[1] And it is the tremendous pulse of life in her – 'the heartbeat of Allah' – that wins the Doctor.

Sagamore's intuitive alertness to the need for life to keep in touch with reality is shown in the cure for heartbreak he offers. His prescription for an instantaneously killing poison brings the victim up against the absolute division between life and death with a jerk that shakes her emotions into perspective:

> . . . when a woman's life is wrecked she needs a little sympathy and not a bottle of poison.

(This, of course, is a variation on the suicidal leap, in *The Simpleton*, which cleanses and renews the soul for a fresh start.) Yet they are real emotions and the basic stuff from which the character is made. Epifania is not identical with Raina at play, or with Orinthia, the actress perfectly fitted with her role; and her aggressiveness is unmarred by the

[1] It is capped by the Doctor: 'I do not see it so. I see that riches are a curse; only in the service of Allah is there justice, righteousness, and happiness.' This is a larger view, but need not be read as cancelling out the other.

cruelty of Cleopatra. Her tantrums and rages belong to a genuinely proud and passionate nature that imposes suffering upon itself: the nature of a Julia Craven raised to a divine power. Her sense of guilt is masochistic:

> I want to get rid of myself. I want to punish myself for making a mess of my life . . .

It is 'the humiliation' of her reduced income that pains her, and the reaction into which she lashes out will avenge her on Alastair by heaping coals of fire on his head; she will die and leave him her whole fortune, not out of magnanimity but 'To ruin him. To destroy him. To make him a beggar on horseback so that he may ride to the devil.' She is quite beyond reason, but is checked when her natural energy and force catch her out and demonstrate that she is the sort of person who happens to things, not a predestined victim. She still tries to play it as tragedy and blame her stars:

> I cannot even sit down in a chair without wrecking it. There is a curse on me.

But Sagamore's mirth at so conventional a trick of farce is now uncontrollable, and the auditorium is at one with him. There is something intimately familiar to most of us in the ego's childish struggle to cling to its serious view of itself. Epifania manages to reconcile herself to objective reality with more dignity than is usual, as she admits and unmaliciously accepts her hostile emotions:

> The breaking of that chair has calmed and relieved me, somehow. I feel as if I had broken your neck, as I wanted to;

and puts her lawyer in his place: 'Sit down on what is left of your sham Chippendale.' Although she does not yet know it, she is ready now to throw Adrian Blenderbland downstairs.

The moral revolution accomplished in the play makes its impact, if the allegory is left uninterpreted or even unrecognized. Epifania's distress has an emotional authenticity that is not dispersed by any association of it with capitalism in decline. It is a romantic sickness which Shaw's enlightenment values predispose him to purge rather than to glamourize. Indeed, Eppy's gloomy, self-destructive emotion, built up through the internalizing of her aggression, corresponds to a common mood of political radicalism: the tendency to identify with the weaker side, the oppressed and victimized, the lost cause, which has yet to be transformed into a will to win, a fervour for change capable of overturning systems and assuming power itself.

Nothing divides Shaw more completely from such latter-day romantics as D. H. Lawrence than his relation to modern industrialism. He is divided even from Carlyle, Ruskin and Morris by his unconcern for the myth of an organic medieval society. For his temperament matched the mood of nineteenth-century commercial imperialism at its zenith: vigorous, self-confident, optimistic, productive. Epifania, positive and restored, is the embodiment of a public mood, no merely personal symbol. In accordance with the principles of 'a truly scientific natural history' which he had proclaimed in the Preface to *Plays Pleasant*, Shaw respected power and success as testimony to fitness in the evolutionary struggle. Our inability to condemn such characters as Broadbent or Undershaft as villains is conditioned by their creator's recognition of the natural morality whereby might is right. Yet his Fabianism is distinguishable from a movement towards a more efficient capitalism, even a more bureaucratic form, by values in which historical capitalism was defective. In his later plays Shaw drew his token of these values from outside the Western tradition: Pra and Prola in *The Simpleton* follow on from the Babylonian Lilith of *Back to Methuselah*. Epifania's positive motivation for change is supplied by her first encounter with the Egyptian Doctor, 'servant of Allah'. When she knows what she wants and starts employing her aggression to get it, she becomes thoroughly efficient, able to think and act straight and fast, unconfused by any emotional turmoil. But the health she now enjoys is like the perfect functioning of a machine, a negative thing – absence of illness, a health without bloom. The new Epifania is impressive and commands the obedience of others, but she is hardly a likeable character.[1] She lacks even the human warmth of Shaw's self-complacent villains, and she still has no happiness to communicate. So she seeks from the Doctor, 'the healer, the helper, the guardian of life and the counsellor of health', what she lacks in herself: the spirit of service in human community, the power to spend freely which is the antithesis of acquisitiveness. Her decision to marry him is an act of responsible judgement which proceeds (as Undershaft did) to overrule the merely mechanical conditions of the test. (Yet the Doctor is so undeveloped a figure that this 'marriage' of power and moral responsibility seems almost as formulaic as the happy ending of non-metaphorical marriage in popular theatre.)

The quality of Shavian comedy testifies that there is more than energy in plenitude of life. It does more than recognize and respect the aggressive instincts of mankind; it celebrates them in an atmosphere to which joy is added. The laughter it evokes is characteristically benign as well as high-spirited. Ellie Dunn's phrase, 'Life with a blessing', brings much the same balance of values surprisingly into line with Arnold's 'sweetness

[1] Cf. Brecht's Shui Ta in *The Good Woman of Setzuan*.

and light' (or even the anti-rhetoric of E. M. Forster) within the humanist tradition; but nothing which so underplays force can adequately represent Shaw's affirmations. The Doctor can only be ineffectual without Eppy.

It needs an effort to recall that a distinction as customary as that drawn between an individual and his society denotes aspects of a properly indivisible whole. Shaw's consciousness was, of course, moulded as part of the generalized consciousness of his time. He was also – to borrow his own image – one of the nineteenth century's most effective contrivances for transcending its limitations and growing into a new world of values. The broad lines of his development are very clear. The nineteenth-century European sense of crisis in the conflict between traditional piety, with its notion of an eternal, God-given order, and new science, with its evolutionary interpretations of phenomena, has many reflections in Shavian drama. The youthful Shaw's embrace of science (imaged in the fiction of Edward Connolly, engineer of *The Irrational Knot*) supplied the criterion of reality in the early plays. The idealism, which was his constant and declared object of attack, was rejected as unscientific. The Preface to *Plays Pleasant* explained:

> To me the tragedy and comedy of life lie in the consequences, sometimes terrible, sometimes ludicrous, of our persistent attempts to found our institutions on the ideals suggested to our imaginations by our half-satisfied passions, instead of on a genuinely scientific natural history.

Comedy and tragedy as aesthetic forms are thus media in which men can see their errors. The didactic function of art and its character as a distortion of reality are both implied. For Shaw's generation, Ibsen had demonstrated in the last scene of *A Doll's House* what it meant to get free of emotionally sustained illusions and see and respond to life with an altogether new clarity. The key realization to break through was of the world and human personality as in flux, in a condition of becoming, the future unknown and unpredictable; while human institutions, standing as bulwarks against change, falsified continuity into a fiction of permanence. Evolution as a principle of human society was precisely the issue.

Shaw rejected the pure milk of Darwin's theory of Evolution for the pseudo-Lamarckian revisionism of Creative Evolution. But the grounds of the rejection were essentially those of moral philosophy rather than straight biology. He accepted the emphasis on growth and change, on fitness to survive and on adaptability as a form of fitness – qualities of natural health – as positive moral values to be asserted against the romanticism of frustration and despair; and he asserted them in the fable of *The Millionairess* more uncompromisingly than in *Major Barbara*. The mechanistic determinism of Darwin's system and his acceptance of cut-throat competitiveness as the ruling economic principle in nature were morally repugnant to Shaw if once they were extended to bind human society (being indeed purblind interpretations derived at least as much from Darwin's social and political prejudice as from his observation of facts).[1] His drama is traditionalist in its concern with man as the responsible agent through whom moral principles enter and operate in the universe. He has just such powers of control over his environment as God gave to Adam in the story of *Genesis*. So bringing man into the evolutionary picture allowed the re-injection of purpose into process. Free will and imagination may be numbered among human faculties, and it is for the exercising and strengthening of these in his actual and potential audiences that Shaw's plays are designed. They aid the emotional adaptation of men to the increasingly precipitate metabolic rate of industrial and technological society.

In his later work, he was able to invoke Einsteinian physics as scientific backing for his rejection of absolute values (hindrances to survival, as they limit adaptability) and his insistence on the infinite potentialities of life. The perspectives of an expanding universe allowed him to accept the inevitable incidence of human error and failure in the spirit of Prola of *The Simpleton*, without regarding any disaster as ultimate. The enormous time-span implied in some of the last plays – and even the mathematical leap from millions to buoyant billions – is the element of a more clearly understood freedom of human action and orientation, set over against the desperateness of the immediate crisis.

To represent this late work as in any way turning from rationalism to mysticism travesties the facts – unless metaphysical longsightedness is regarded as a form of mysticism. Yet the obsession with religion (another nineteenth-century obsession with what was slipping from its grasp) evident from the juvenile Passion Play through to *Good King Charles* cannot be dismissed as merely negative. *Major Barbara* and *Saint Joan* are Passion plays, too, and offer liturgies to match their messianic narratives. *Back to Methuselah* demands to be read as its author had come to read the Christian Bible: as a poetic fiction tracing an authentic religious quest. Though his rational temper led Shaw to give natural explanations of 'supernatural' manifestations, he respected imaginative vision and intuition as means of penetrating the area of darkness beyond scientific knowledge. Religion, on these terms, became a necessary working hypothesis. It presented a central system of values by which

[1] See J. D. Bernal, 'Shaw the Scientist', in S. Winsten (ed.), op. cit., pp. 93–105.

to act, but still the values had to be rationally tested and endorsed. 'If your old religion broke down yesterday,' says Undershaft, 'get a newer and a better one for tomorrow.' Joan's gospel of nationalism, however apt to the feudal situation, reveals its questionableness when brought to the test of the modern world. The Black Girl's search for God discovers most plainly that evolutionary continuity, not permanence, governs religion as everything else. So the red-headed Irishman (Shaw's self-parody) joins Voltaire in digging for God as something growing and cultivable, unfinished and never to be finished, like life itself.

Creative Evolution proves, after all, to be the Religion of Humanity: positivist, relative, acknowledging no god outside man, the determiner of his own destiny – but by the light of emotionally powered images, the saints of Comte's own pantheon.[1] *Saint Joan* exemplifies the phenomenon of secular history transformed into myth: the Catholic Church's elevation of the historical personage into a religious symbol analogizes the artist's procedure in taking material from historical documents and building from it a symbolic character whose androgynous nature has a magical relation to his own psyche.

The petit bourgeois, traditionally Protestant family of Shaws in Dublin had been dominated by a woman who incarnated her society's official values, its notions of propriety in manners and conduct, self-control and narrow materialism. 'My mother . . . had been as carefully brought up as Queen Victoria'; 'My mother . . . had no comedic impulses.' So the Preface to *Immaturity* devastatingly remarks. The repressed personality is a bulwark of public order, a guarantee of the maintenance of an established social and political system. Such a condition in the petit bourgeoisie was a support to nineteenth-century capitalism, through the premium it set on thrift, industry and abstinence. How ambiguous Shaw's own relation to this negative faith remained can be judged from *Back to Methuselah*, which contains as bitter a condemnation of 'the religion of Jonhobsnoxious' as his temperament ever allowed him to write:

> Those misguided people sacrificed the fragment of life that was granted to them to an imaginary immortality. They crucified the prophet who told them to take no thought for the morrow, and that here and now was their Australia: Australia being a term signifying paradise, or an eternity of bliss.

---

[1] Caesar and Napoleon (as well as Joan) can be seen in this way. On these two, see Auguste Comte, *System of Positive Polity*, Vol. III, pp. 327–8, and Vol. II, pp. 367–9, respectively. J. S. Mill criticized what he judged to be Comte's over-evaluation of Caesar and the softening of his 'honourable' condemnation of Napoleon ('whose career he deemed one of the greatest calamities in modern history') in his later writings. See Mill, *Auguste Comte and Positivism* (Ann Arbor: University of Michigan Press, 1961), p. 190. Carlyle's view of historical figures is similar to Comte's in its tendency to symbolic interpretation, of course.

They tried to produce a condition of death in life: to mortify the flesh as they called it.

The fable of the play is a metaphor of the puritan dream, and the plight of nineteenth-century man is presented through the Elderly Gentleman, born into a world that allowed a faint possibility of living for three hundred years:

> We impose on ourselves abstinences and disciplines and studies that are meant to prepare us for living three centuries. And we seldom live one . . . I have been cheated out of the joys and freedoms of my life by this dream [of] . . . eternal life.

Here is the anti-puritan reaction rationally expressed.[1] But the puritan tendencies within the author are objectified with something short of total irony in the ultimate Utopian image of a human society where generation has given way to the virtually eternal individual and the variety of creation is moving towards 'the goal of redemption from the flesh', 'the vortex freed from matter', 'the whirlpool in pure force': 'there will be no people only thought.' The folly of the dream, the fact that its logicality is a determinist prison, may be indicated by Pygmalion's play-within-a-play. But Shaw dreams it to the end before setting it, with Lilith, where it belongs, among legends and lays, while the free potentialities of life remain.

Within the fable, freedom from matter as an ultimate human goal is first foreshadowed in the revulsion and shame with which Eve reacts to the secret of procreation whispered by the Serpent. Elizabeth Gurly Shaw's temperamental coldness was not rare in a society that had de-sexed its 'respectable' women. (The type is common in Dickens.) When such women, in turn, impressed their view of life on men, the fabric of social hypocrisy was complete and all the more baffling because genuine ignorance and self-delusion contributed more largely to it than deliberate lying and posing. Conformity without repression might have recourse to what Oscar Wilde immortalized as the bunbury. (Raina Petkoff can be classified as a female bunburyist, delighting in the deceiving of others which leaves her natural instincts free of their control.) But Voltaire fostered Shaw's discovery that the most difficult form of hypocrisy to penetrate is not consciously practised like Ann Whitefield's, but the self-complacent opacity of a Candida or a Broadbent, with all their virtues.

Aubrey, in *Too True*, sees human society as a conspiracy protective of open secrets:

> Make any statement that is so true that it has been staring us in the face all our lives, and the whole world will rise up and passionately contradict you.

---

[1] Expressed in a form strongly reminiscent of the experience of J. S. Mill.

This was the basis of the social criticism in the plays of Ibsen and his followers. Shaw's own experiences of having been taken in 'by the force of unanimous, strenuous, eloquent, trumpet-tongued lying' can be connected with that sense of let-down which Eric Bentley has identified as perhaps the most frequently recurrent emotion in Shavian drama. The moment of enlightenment when the scales fall from the eyes is often farcical, as the hero – Sergius, it may be, or Tanner – is suddenly confronted by the clownish image of his own folly. Or it may come as heartbreak, a profound emotional disturbance as necessary accompaniment to the new power of distinguishing authentic truth from conventional belief: 'It's only life educating you,' says Hesione Hushabye.

The adult Shaw had departed most obviously from the standards of *l'homme moyen sensuel* (the bourgeois) in the atrophy, or sublimation, of his sexuality.[1] It is probable enough that, in his own class and generation, his fate was most extraordinary in the publicity given to it: the long virginity and the companionate marriage hardly being cancelled out by the seduction, followed by a career of flirtation, and the brief, trumpeted episode with Mrs Patrick Campbell. In the light of his own valuation of human possibilities, it could be said that an unconsciously designed experiment produced an interesting cultural variation which it will not do to dismiss as defective or deformed. Shaw's intellectuality, his energy, his articulateness, his public spirit and his artistic genius may all have been heightened in compensation for what was repressed. Sexual aggressiveness was diverted into the combativeness and iconoclasm of the debater; it feeds the vigour of dramatic conflict and the force of theatrical impact. Diversion of the sexual drive may have increased the power drive in his work: its sense of mission to a nation, or even to mankind at large; its vital concern with the business of the governor, king, or minister, or captain of industry, or Faustian mage. As a child Shaw had believed, in his ignorance, that women were men in skirts. The day came when, as an artist, he could pluck a metaphysical truth from that falsehood.

If his puritan conditioning had been complete, no such turning of negative characteristics to positive effect could have been achieved. But it was most manifestly incomplete: puritans have never been noted for their love of the theatre.[2] The Brothers Barnabas, in *Back to Methuselah*, represent the puritanism Shaw saw in nineteenth-century science, joyless, earnest, anxiety-dominated, emotionally arid and imaginatively moronic.

---

[1] The plainest statement, and quite probably the least lubricious, is his own: 'To Frank Harris on Sex in Biography', *Sixteen Self Sketches*, pp. 113–15.

[2] This may also have been what kept him apart from 'the morally mighty Society of Friends, vulgarly called the Quakers' (Preface to *Good King Charles*), to whose position he was otherwise so close.

He may not have understood fully Blake's prescription of an increase in sensual enjoyment as a means of releasing men from their self-limitation. (It is an element in the doctrine of *The Marriage of Heaven and Hell* which is not reflected in *Major Barbara*.) But he had before him the example of Ruskin's and William Morris's attempts to give back wholeness to men and to society by restoring the truly seeing eye and the craftsman's hand. Though Shaw wrote art criticism, his own sense of visual beauty may have been defective, as has often been claimed. One form of sensuality was sanctioned for him, however, by his mother's cultivation of music: the source of her own self-fulfilment.

The music George Bernard Shaw heard at home was mainly vocal and operatic; the same human being was executant and instrument, as in the art of acting. The little positive encouragement the boy seems to have had to learn the art and join in the musical activities of his mother and sisters may have influenced the different use he ultimately made of his voice: bringing together oral sensuality and cerebral excitement in a full-tongued rhetoric.

The intuition of displaced sexuality behind such forms of self-expression is conveyed by his association of men of words and ideas with the mask of Don Juan.[1] From Morell and Tanner to Hector Hushabye and Aubrey there is something of the charlatan about this type in his plays. Their clever tongues are symptomatic of their public ineffectuality. Shotover's image of Hector, 'married right up to the hilt', speaks boldly of the yielding of virility into the power of a woman and equates it with the loss of active, heroic power in the world. The fear of woman, the fear of castration by woman, is thus distanced, objectified and made more generally significant;[2] but recognition of its private origin is maintained. It is from this that Shaw's central political insight is derived: that parliamentary democracy is doomed unless it can generate, instead of dissipating, the power of effective action; that reform by constitutional means is only possible under the impulse of a revolutionary determination. The urgency and sharp definition with which the realization is conveyed, in such plays as *Major Barbara*, *Heartbreak House*, *On the Rocks*, are the fruits of a subjectively known necessity and a subjective awareness that life is naturally dangerous and requires to be courageously lived. 'Never make a hero of a philanderer' points forward from an Unpleasant Play to these and to *Geneva* with their proposal that, when the game of

[1] See C. G. Jung on Don Juanism in 'Psychological Aspects of the Mother Archetype', *The Archetypes and the Collective Unconscious* in *Collected Works*, ed. H. Read, M. Fordham and G. Adler, trans. R. F. C. Hull (London: Routledge, 1959), Vol. 9, pp. 75–110, esp. pp. 85 and 87.

[2] Precedents – especially in Strindberg – made the shift to a psychopathology of modern culture easier.

war has ceased to work as a surrogate for the total embroilment of populations, the trivial game of politics should be transformed into a continuation of war by other means, as purposeful and as heroic: 'the ballot paper that really governs is the paper that has a bullet wrapped up in it'.[1]

The negative side of Shaw's early work is easily detectable. His art is under pressure from a personality unsure of itself, self-consciously posing and rejecting the poses in a search for authenticity that is subjective as well as objective. Tone and accent express a need for self-assertion in defying society and demonstrating personal superiority before an audience. The sense of an obsessed mind struggling against bafflement is strong in both *Candida* and *Man and Superman*, and perhaps again in *Back to Methuselah*. But the rational exposition these plays restlessly present is ironically qualified by elements in their imaginative structure, viewed across the distance between drama and audience. In particular, the nineteenth century's understanding of myth, as an iconography in which private experience and the forms, ideas and modes of feeling dominant in a culture are unified, enabled Shaw to escape the predicament of rationality. The Socratic proviso of self-knowledge applies to the artist: if he is unaware of his own profound relationship to his material, he is likely to build an essentially false construct, an elaborate evasion of reality. Writing (as even a critic knows) is not a simple, rationally determined process, but a matter of delicate psychic adjustments. It may be necessary to employ rituals and tricks of self-deceit in order to outwit the involuntary censor whose activities keep blocking the channels of articulate thinking and expression. *Heartbreak House* bears the most ample witness to Shaw's understanding of imaginative thinking as an alternative mode where reason is impotent. Shotover's commerce with dark spirits, Ellie's hypnotic powers, the 'fascination' exerted by Hesione and Ariadne, Hector's histrionic poses and ceremonial robes, with the carefully deployed symbols of observatory and pit, rum and dynamite and the tools of the old man's inventive activities, all contribute to a view of artistic practices as magical, in a way that need not be understood superstitiously.

A comment Shaw wrote on the art of puppetry may guard his own characters from ill-considered criticism:

> I always hold up the wooden actors as instructive object lessons to our flesh-and-blood players. The wooden ones, though stiff and continually glaring at

[1] This is a more positive interpretation of Shaw's stance than Professor McBriar's ('Shaw as a Critic of Democracy', *Fabian Socialism*, pp. 82–92) and rejects the charge of frivolity vividly expressed by Benedict Nightingale (*New Statesman* (30 October 1970), p. 573): 'Revolution emerges as entertainment; and Shaw himself as a bloodthirsty jester, a sort of Edwardian Abbie Hoffman, to be treated with extreme caution by all sensible democrats.'

M

you with the same overcharged expression, yet move you as only the most experienced living actors can . . . The puppet . . . its unchanging stare, petrified (or rather lignified) in a grimace expressive to the highest degree attainable by the carver's art, the mimicry by which it suggests human gesture in unearthly caricature – these give to its performances . . . an intensity which imposes on our imagination like those images in immovable hieratic attitudes on the stained glass of Chartres Cathedral, in which the gaping tourists seem . . . reduced to sawdusty insignificance by the contrast with the gigantic vitality in the windows overhead.[1]

Whereas realistic dramatists present us with characters that are imitations of people and morality dramatists personify abstractions, Shaw's characters are usually such images – looming, it seems, over life-size – as our emotional attitudes to others produce in the mind. It is so that parents appear to children, or the beloved to the lover, having the status of divinities, arbitrary, benevolent or wrathful. So the imaginative world of Shavian comedy, far from being devoid of emotion, is emotionally rich and potent as Wagner's world is, or Strindberg's. Only the tempo is often farcical or near-farcical (as in the later Strindberg), so that the authenticity of Ellie's reactions, or Epifania's, or Mrs Mopply's after the Colonel's assault on her, is rendered strange and grotesque by the speed of what would in life be a gradual, even slow, process. In fact, Shaw practised alienation effects before Brecht, checking what might easily have been empathy, so that we see, recognize and know experience in a truer social perspective. The adult mind can be aware of the absurdity of its mythic creations – the thought of Shotover dropping sticks of dynamite about the house, like a careless child, is laughable – yet it values them as means, perhaps the only means, to knowing itself profoundly. Voltaire's *Candide* has to do, *inter alia*, with the difficulty the human mind has of knowing reality. One of the most constant influences on Shaw's thinking, its title is echoed in the title of the play in which he first fully developed the strategy for handling his personal confusions – especially his unease with women and mistrust of women – by objectifying and distancing them and treating them as social or political problems. What side was Burgess's daughter on? How did respect for women and the virtues conventionally associated with them affect a man's capacity for radical social action? Auguste Comte's system had taken very seriously into account the relation between private emotions and public attitudes. Ibsen's *A Doll's House* was a theatrical exemplar exploring the correspondence between the general character of society and relationships

---

[1] From the Note on Puppets by G.B.S. published as a foreword to Max von Boehm, *Dolls and Puppets*, trans. Josephine Nicoll (New York: Cooper Square, 1966), p. 5, with a translator's note on the text and its inclusion in the original German.

within the small social unit of the family. Though the comic tone of his plays makes them very different from Ibsen's, Shaw's use of irrationally powered images as a means of orientation on the level of political philosophy is nearer late Ibsen in technique.

There is the Shavian version of the familiar Ibsen triangle: the man caught between two women of contrasted types. But the recurrent types are Shaw's own: on the one hand, the self-possessed, coolly dominant, maternal type, figure of a restrictive order, easily containing the unorthodox or rebellious tendencies of men or children, and sometimes associated with a social order of hypocritically benign aspect; on the other, the passionate *femme fatale*, obviously capable of destruction and self-destruction, a grown-up spoilt child who threatens chaos. They can be seen as symbols of contrary psychic attitudes in the author. The poise of mind in which they are reconciled may be independently symbolized in the type I have chosen to call the androgyne; which is also an image of balance, equality and disciplined creativity in society.

But finally it is the nature of his comedy, not his use of myth or rhetoric or his treatment of public and political themes, that gives Shaw's drama its uniqueness. Comedy, here, means something more than rejection of tragic form together with tragic vision, though this is an important aspect of a number of his plays from *Mrs Warren's Profession* to *On the Rocks*. The inevitability of change is a ground for optimism, not melancholy and pessimism, to his mind; and this is reflected in the open quality of his plays, even in the physical freedom of a drama that moves readily, at all periods, out of the boxed-in stage area. More strikingly, in view of the seriousness of his concerns and the substantial burden of thought that his work carries, the genius of the *farceur* enters into every play in the canon and reigns supreme in the greater part of his work. The physicality of farce may not always qualify as humorous, but it is always anti-romantic, a kind of parody of the solemn idealization that is involved in romantic notions of love or strife. The full comic range of Shavian drama further includes tricks of verbal and situational humour; grotesque and tragi-comic effects (arising from a combination of a sense of the ludicrous with a recognition of the sad, the grim or the terrible in human life); varieties of irony; high-spirited extravagance in plotting, characterization, incident, setting; even smiling sentiment (as in moments of *You Never Can Tell*, *Caesar and Cleopatra* and *Captain Brassbound's Conversion*).

But the consistent Shavian mask, the created *persona* of the author, defines the master of paradox, operative in a single phrase or in the basic concept on which an entire play is structured. (*Major Barbara* and *The*

Doctor's Dilemma, for example, can be analysed and interpreted as paradoxes in dramatic form.) Whether it is an incidental device, or a major reflection of mental attitude, it serves the general effect of liberating readers and audiences from conventional thinking. The self-contradiction at the heart of paradox confronts common sense and moderate 'reasonableness', those lowest common denominators of understanding, with the frankly nonsensical and thus joins with farce in presenting a version of the world as more fantastic than is familiarly acknowledged: fantastic, but not meaningless. An abundant use of paradox does more than shock the mind into re-examining long-accepted propositions; it encourages and gives practice in a mode of thinking which is an unorthodox constant in the Western tradition.[1] The distinction between right and wrong fades into insignificance before the growing awareness that no single rational formulation is adequate to express the many aspects of reality.

Sigmund Freud saw verbal jokes as using 'a method of linking things up which is rejected and studiously avoided by serious thought'.[2] The perception of brevity as in itself a form of wit is easily extended to a realization that compression and concentration are characteristic of most forms of wit. It flashes instantaneously. And jokes evaporate if explained. There may be a further connection with the paranormal speed of farce: its incidents and physical gestures 'speak volumes' as they hit our awareness. Wit and farce represent forms of thinking which avoid obstacles in the subconscious by proceeding irregularly, by leaps and bounds, with gathered force.[3]

Shaw uses laughter as a test of reality. Its aggressive force, spontaneously eruptive, dispels mental torpor and the languorousness of indulgence in sensation or emotion. There is a tenderness in his plays and a diffused kindliness; but a certain kind of eroticism, magnifying the isolated importance of the individual, or sentimentally attached to absolutes, cannot live in their atmosphere. Variant forms of Orinthia's catastrophic embrace of Magnus may express a private fear of erotic feeling as able to overwhelm and drown clarity of mind and threatening to individuation or what Shaw called the 'protestantism' of the authentic individual. Wit and farce, in this alignment of powers, work on the side of enlightenment, on the side of mind against undifferentiated mass. Shaw is not anti-

[1] See (e.g.) Rosalie L. Colie, 'The Rhetoric of Transcendence', *Philological Quarterly*, Vol. XLIII (1964), pp. 145–70.

[2] *Jokes and their Relation to the Unconscious*, trans. James Strachey (London: Routledge, 1960), esp. pp. 118, 140–2.

[3] See Eric Bentley's 'Psychology of Farce', printed as Introduction in *Let's Get a Divorce! and Other Plays* (Sardou, Labiche, Courteline, Prévert, Feydeau), Mermaid Dramabook (New York: Hill and Wang, 1958), pp. vii–xx.

romantic in the crude sense of rejecting passion for reason, however. Because he acknowledges the validity and importance of passion, he presents reason as adequate only when it has absorbed the intensity and concentration of passionate conviction. Mind holds a threatened position in Shavian drama, not *against* feeling, but in sustained tension with it.

On the whole, his plays became more abstract as he grew older.[1] Vivie Warren is an individual, involved in an individual's relationships with others, whose case is a paradigm revealing the predicament of most individuals in society. Though truth of feeling remains strong in the later plays, it is associated with characters that are more frankly inventions of the author's brain playing out a semi-allegorical action: the feeling is detachable from them, almost free-floating except as it clusters about Shaw's thinking of the human species, in its political and social groupings – public thinking, but always aware that intimate experience is part of the life of mankind.

The unsophisticated broadness of much of Shaw's joking is a retort to the over-refinement of puritanism. Larry Doyle's diatribe against the Irish habit of 'senseless' laughter, in *John Bull's Other Island*, is countered by the whole comic tendency of his creator's technique: as the Irish alternative to fanatical passion bred in a national context of narrowly absolute convictions. It is not simply that Shaw's pragmatism acknowledges the principles of human fallibility, so that he can – like his own Lilith or Prola – always abandon the position he has reached and start again. The charges of frivolity and irresponsibility popularly brought against him are not entirely mistaken – except as they are blind to the virtues involved – mercurial virtues apt to a world of change: a spontaneous sense of the inexhaustible resourcefulness of life and an ability to relax a little carelessly, a little playfully, in view of the infinitely extensive future lifting the burden of significance from each finite individual span. Shaw's dramaturgy is a practical discovery of the ingenious, protean qualities of the human mind and the many ways in which it may work. He showed an intuitive understanding – and it may have become conscious – that humorous thinking is an alternative to

---

[1] This can be connected with the observation Shaw made himself in his Apology for *Sixteen Self Sketches* (p. 6): 'I have had no heroic adventures. Things have not happened to me: on the contrary it is I who have happened to them; and all my happenings have taken the form of books and plays. Read them, or spectate them; and you have my whole story: the rest is only breakfast, lunch, dinner, sleeping, wakening, and washing . . .' With age, he did not even take the active part in the theatre that he had in Granville Barker's days; and money in effect isolated him from common social realities and secured him the life of a villager. Until the death of Charlotte, even the crises and agonies of ordinary family experience passed him by.

logical thinking, just as mathematical thinking may be. The mind's self-delight, a natural accompaniment to its proper functioning, has its part in the play of wit and contributes largely to the mood of Shavian comedy. And the mood aids Shaw's communication, not just that thought is provisional and experimental, and that every rational construction is a hypothesis that must sooner or later be abandoned, but that thinking itself is creative play at the service of life.

Bibliographical Note
Shaw in the Sixties

Most studies of Shaw provide the reader with select bibliographies that overlap with each other to a great extent. So I have chosen to confine myself to a note on the principal texts of Shaw's writings and on outstanding Shavian studies of (approximately) the last decade, from which readers who so wish can find their way back to publications of earlier date. References to some earlier works that I have found valuable (e.g. J. B. Kaye's, E. Strauss's and Alick West's) are scattered through the footnotes to this book.

A WRITINGS BY G. B. SHAW

The Works of Bernard Shaw. 36 vols. Standard Edition. London: Constable, 1931–50. This is the principal source of quotations in the present study, and it remains the fullest collection.

New single-volume editions of the *Complete Plays* and *Complete Prefaces* have been issued. London: Paul Hamlyn, 1965.

The first volumes of a new collection, under the editorial supervision of Dan H. Laurence, have appeared. *The Bodley Head Shaw.* Vol. I. London: Max Reinhardt, 1970. Vol. II 1971

Numerous editions of single plays or more limited collections are recorded in the *P.M.L.A.* and *Modern Drama* bibliographies issued periodically and in the continuing Checklist of Shaviana in the Shaw Society of America's *Shaw Review*. But special mention must be made of the following:

'Why She Would Not'. Playlet published in the *London Magazine*, Vol. III, No. 8, August 1956, pp. 11–20.

The Theatre of Bernard Shaw. Ten plays chosen and discussed by Alan S. Downer. New York: Dodd, Mead, 1961.

Useful collections of miscellaneous writings by Shaw are:

G.B.S. on Music. Foreword by Alec Robertson. Harmondsworth: Penguin, 1962.

How to Become a Musical Critic. Ed. Dan H. Laurence. London: Rupert Hart-Davis; New York: Hill and Wang, 1960.

The Matter with Ireland. Ed. David Greene and Dan H. Laurence. London: Rupert Hart-Davies; New York: Hill and Wang, 1962.

Platform and Pulpit. Ed. Dan H. Laurence. London: Rupert Hart-Davies; New York: Hill and Wang, 1962.

The Rationalization of Russia. Ed. H. M. Geduld. Bloomington: Indiana University Press, 1964.

The Religious Speeches of Bernard Shaw. Ed. Warren Sylvester Smith. University Park, Pa.: Pennsylvania State University Press, 1963. Paperback reprint New York: McGraw-Hill; London: Constable, 1965.

Selected Non-Dramatic Writings of Bernard Shaw. Ed. Dan H. Laurence. Boston: Houghton Mifflin, 1965. Essays and reviews from the late nineteenth century, together with *An Unsocial Socialist* and *The Quintessence of Ibsenism.*

Shaw. An Autobiography 1856–1898. Selected from his writings by Stanley Weintraub. London: Max Reinhardt, 1969.

Shaw on Language. Ed. A. Tauber. London: Peter Owen, 1965.

Shaw on Shakespeare. Ed. Edwin Wilson. New York: Dutton, 1961; London: Cassel, 1962.

Shaw on Theatre. Ed. E. J. West. London: Macgibbon and Kee; New York: Hill and Wang, 1958.

The sixth edition of *Fabian Essays* by Shaw (and others), with a new introduction by Asa Briggs, was published London: Allen and Unwin, 1962.

The Intelligent Woman's Guide to Socialism, Capitalism, Sovietism and Fascism appeared in a second edition. Harmondsworth: Penguin, 1965.

Letters

Separate collections of Shaw's letters to Alma Murray, Florence Farr, Ellen Terry, Mrs Patrick Campbell, Granville Barker and Golding Bright are most of them referred to in the notes to this book. To these have been added:

To a Young Actress. The Letters of Bernard Shaw to Molly Tompkins. Ed. Peter Tompkins. New York: Potter, 1960; London: Constable, 1961.

Bernard Shaw: Collected Letters. Vol. I, 1874–1897. Ed. Dan H. Laurence. London: Max Reinhardt; New York: Dodd, Mead, 1965. Vol. II in press.

B WORKS ON SHAW: A SELECT LIST FOR THE PAST DECADE

1 *Bibliographical*

ADELMAN, IRVING, and DWORKIN, RITA. *Modern Drama. A Checklist of Critical Literature on Twentieth Century Plays.* Metuchen, N.J.: Scarecrow Press, 1967. Shaw section pp. 264–89.

FARLEY, EARL, and CARLSON, MARVIN. 'George Bernard Shaw: A Selected Bibliography'. In 2 parts. Part I: Books. Part 2: Periodicals. *Modern Drama*, Vol. II, Nos. 2 and 3, September and December 1959. For 1945–55.

2 *Biographical*

O'DONOVAN, JOHN. *Shaw and the Charlatan Genius.* Dublin: Dolmen Press, 1965.

ROSSET, B. C. *Shaw of Dublin: The Formative Years.* University Park, Pa.: Pennsylvania State University Press, 1964.

SMITH, J. PERCY. *The Unrepentant Pilgrim.* London: Gollancz; New York: Houghton Mifflin, 1966.

See also WILSON, COLIN below.

The third edition of Hesketh Pearson's *Bernard Shaw: His Life and Personality* was published London: Methuen, 1961; and in this company limitation by date is no excuse for ignoring Archibald Henderson's formidably detailed *George Bernard Shaw: Man of the Century*, New York: Appleton, 1956.

DUNBAR, JANET. *Mrs G. B. S.* London: Harrap; New York: Harper and Row, 1963. This has obvious relevance.

The following illuminate particular aspects of Shaw's life and career:

COLE, MARGARET. *The Story of Fabian Socialism.* London: Heinemann 1961.

COSTELLO, DONALD. *The Serpent's Eye.* Notre Dame, Ind., and London: University of Notre Dame Press, 1965. On Shaw and the cinema.

LANGNER, LAWRENCE. *G. B. S. and the Lunatic.* New York: Atheneum Press; London: Hutchinson, 1964. On dealings with the Theatre Guild.

WEINTRAUB, STANLEY. *Private Shaw and Public Shaw.* London: Cape, 1963. On G. B. Shaw and Lawrence of Arabia.

5 *Critical*

CARPENTER, CHARLES A. *Bernard Shaw and the Art of Destroying Ideals*. Madison and Milwaukee: University of Wisconsin Press, 1969.

CROMPTON, LOUIS. *Shaw the Dramatist*. Lincoln, Neb.: University of Nebraska Press, 1969.

DIETRICH, R. F. *Portrait of the Artist as a Young Superman*. Gainesville: University of Florida Press, 1969. On the novels, but not superseding Robert Hogan's long article, 'The Novels of Bernard Shaw', *English Literature in Transition*, Vol. VIII, pp. 63–114.

FROMM, HAROLD. *Bernard Shaw and the Theatre in the Nineties*. Lawrence: University of Kansas, 1967.

GIBBS, A. M. *Shaw*. Writers and Critics series. Edinburgh: Oliver and Boyd, 1969.

HUGO, LEON. *Bernard Shaw: Playwright and Preacher*. London: Methuen, 1971.

KAUFMANN, R. J. (ed.). *G. B. Shaw. A Collection of Critical Essays*. Twentieth Century Views series. Englewood Cliffs, N.J.: Prentice-Hall, 1965.

MAYNE, FRED. *The Wit and Satire of Bernard Shaw*. London: Edward Arnold, 1967.

MEISEL, MARTIN. *Shaw and the Nineteenth-Century Theater*. Princeton, N.J.: Princeton University Press; London: Oxford University Press, 1963.

MILLS, JOHN A. *Language and Laughter*. Tucson, Ariz.: University of Arizona Press, 1969. (Not seen until this book was in the press.)

OHMANN, RICHARD. *Shaw, the Style and the Man*. Middleton, Conn.: Wesleyan University Press, 1962.

PILECKI, G. E. *Shaw's Geneva*. The Hague: Mouton, 1965. A study of the evolution of the play's text through successive versions and the significance of the changes.

ROSENBLOOD, NORMAN (ed.). *Shaw: Seven Critical Essays*. Toronto: University of Toronto Press, 1971.

STANTON, STEPHEN S. (ed.). *A Casebook on 'Candida'*. New York: Crowell, 1962.

WATSON, BARBARA BELLOW. *A Shavian Guide to the Intelligent Woman*. London: Chatto and Windus, 1964.

WILSON, COLIN. *Bernard Shaw. A Reassessment.* London: Hutchinson, 1969.

WOODBRIDGE, HOMER E. *Bernard Shaw, Creative Artist.* Carbondale, Ill.: S. Illinois University Press, 1963.

New editions of three valuable older books have appeared:

BENTLEY, ERIC. *Bernard Shaw* 1856–1950. London: Methuen, 1967. First published New York: New Directions, 1947; amended edition, 1957.

CHESTERTON, G. K. *George Bernard Shaw.* London: Max Reinhardt, 1961. New York: Hill and Wang, 1956; reprinted 1966; first edition London: John Lane, 1909; enlarged edition 1935.

NETHERCOT, A. H. *Men and Supermen: The Shavian Portrait Gallery.* New York: Blom, 1966; first published 1954.

Periodicals devoted to Shaw are:

The Shavian. Shaw Society, London.

The Shaw Review. Shaw Society of America.

The California Shavian.

The Independent Shavian. New York.

These all give bibliographical information.

Index

Ghosts, see Ibsen, H.
Gibbs, A. M.: *Shaw*, 211, 348
Gilbert, (Sir) William Schwenck, 2, 55, 228
Gladstone, W. E., 121
'Glimpse of the Domesticity of Franklyn Barnabas', *see* Shaw, G. B.
Godwin, William: *Political Justice*, 221–2
Goethe, Johann Wolfgang von, 83, 106
  Faust, 108, 128
Golden Bough, The, see Frazer, (Sir) James
Goldoni, Carlo, 103
Good King Charles, see In Good King Charles's Golden Days
Grand Guignol, 86, 317
Granville Barker, H., *see* Barker, H. G.
Great Catherine, see Shaw, G. B.
Greco, El (Domenikos Theotokopoulos), 3
Greene, David (ed.), with Laurence, Dan H.: *The Matter with Ireland*, 346
Grein, J. T., 9, 23
  Dramatic Criticism, 37
Greville, Eden, 24
Grey, Sir Edward (Viscount Grey of Fallodon), 323
Gulliver's Travels, see Swift, J.
Gwenn, Edmund, 119

Haigh, Kenneth, fig. 20(b)
Hamlet (mask), 13, 160; *see also* Shakespeare
Hamon, A.: *The Twentieth Century Molière: Bernard Shaw*, 158
Hankin, St John
  Burglar Who Failed, The, 259
  Return of the Prodigal, The, 161–2
Hardwick, (Sir) Cedric, fig. 19
Hardy, Thomas, 129, 241
Harlequin, 2, 86, 88, 90–1, 97, 98, 103, 104, 111, 113, 164, 166, 228
harlequinade, 10, 104, 227–8
Harris, Frank, 337
Harrison, Frederic, 76, 184
Harrison, Jane
  Prolegomena to the Study of Greek Religion, 80, 81
  Themis, 95, 152
Haussmann, W. A., 138

Haydn, Franz: 'Farewell Symphony', 304
Haymarket Theatre, 85, 95, 176, fig. 13, fig. 14
Headlam, (Rev.) Stewart, 81
heartbreak, 220, 233, 272, 282, 286, 330, 337
Heartbreak House, see Shaw, G. B.
Hedda Gabler, see Ibsen, H.
Hegel, G. W. F., 243, 245
Henderson, Archibald
  George Bernard Shaw: His Life and Works, 190
  George Bernard Shaw: Man of the Century, 167, 347
  George Bernard Shaw: Playboy and Prophet, 81
Henley, W. E., with Stevenson, R. L.
  Admiral Guinea, 210–11
  Robert Macaire, 2
Henry Esmond, see Thackeray, W. M.
His Majesty, see Barker, H. G.
Hitler, Adolf, 275, 316, 317
Hobbes, Thomas, 195, 320
Hoffman, Abbie, 339
Hogan, Robert: 'The Novels of Bernard Shaw', 348
Holberg, Stanley Marquis: 'The Economic Rogue in the Plays of Bernard Shaw', 25
Holt, Charles Loyd, 4
  'Music and the Young Shaw', 4
  ' "Candida" and the Music of Ideas', 4
Hopkins, G. M., 255
Horseback Hall, 203, 218
Housman, Laurence
  King John of Jingalo, 305–7
  Unexpected Years, The, 306
  see also Barker, H. G.
How to Become a Musical Critic, see Shaw, G. B.
Howard, Ebenezer, 137
Howe, P. P.: *The Repertory Theatre*, 7
Humanity, Religion of, 76–7, 183–4, 335; *see also* Comte, A.
Huneker, James, 72
  Iconoclasts, 73
Hyndman, H. M., 102
hypocrisy, 19, 27–8, 32, 38, 40, 42–3, 51, 55, 68, 93, 112, 126, 132, 162, 196, 230, 259, 265, 282, 286, 336–7, 341